101 TOP PICKS

FOR Homeschool Curriculum

· · · · · · · · · ·

Choosing the Right Curriculum and Approach
for Each Child's Learning Style

by Cathy Duffy

GROVE
Publishing

978-0-929320-15-1

Published by Grove Publishing
Westminster, California
www.GrovePublishing.com

Dewey Decimal Classification: 371.042
Subject Heading: HOME SCHOOLING—CURRICULA

Note: Contact information and prices listed for resources in the following chapters are the most current information available from publishers at the time this book is written. You will need to confirm current price information when you make your purchases.

Dedication

To the thousands of dedicated homeschoolers who have resisted the impulse to imitate "real schools" and chosen instead to figure out what is best for each of their children, even if it meant writing their own curriculum. You have made the world of homeschool curriculum far richer than the most well-funded schools in the world.

~ Cathy Duffy

Table of Contents

How on earth do I figure out what curriculum to use?

One of the saddest sights I've ever seen was opening day of a three-day homeshool convention. Day one had been designated for only new homeschoolers. Five hundred or more raw homeschooling recruits streamed into an exhibit hall featuring well over one hundred different vendors. Where to even start? Each vendor, naturally, claimed that his or her products were absolutely essential and the best thing on the market. If they had come with unlimited resources, newcomers could easily have dropped a few thousand dollars at the first few displays they visited. I'm certain many felt overwhelming guilt when they did not buy what they were told they needed. That's probably why so many were in tears after the first few hours of the convention.

They knew they needed to buy curriculum, but how on earth could they figure out which one to buy when they didn't even know what they needed to teach? The escape route for many beginners is to simply go to the larger companies that have complete packages for each grade level. Whatever grade the child would have been enrolled in next year at the local school becomes the grade level of the curriculum purchased.

Sometimes, but not often enough, representatives of these major publishers will take time to explain to inquirers that even if they sell a "fourth grade" package, such a package might not be the best choice for this particular child. Your nine-year-old might need fifth grade level math and third grade reading material because math comes easily to him and reading does not.

That doesn't make him a poor student or a "problem." It does mean that he's a fairly normal child, whatever "normal" means. After all, our children are not standardized products. None of them look alike (at least not much) on the outside, so why should we expect them to be alike on the inside—the way they learn, their interests, their abilities, and their temperaments?

One of the beauties of homeschooling is that it allows us to recognize and nurture each one of our very special individual children. We have the glorious opportunity to help them figure out who they are, what they want to be, and how they might get there.

In homeschooling, we can take detours unimaginable in the traditional classroom. If a nine-year-old boy is interested in rocket science, homeschooling parents can nurture that interest by allowing him to move ahead of grade level science topics into this more specialized area. They can help him search the library for biographies and other books related to the subject. They can supervise and assist him while he builds his own rockets, fiddles with fuel cells, designs recovery parachutes, estimates trajectories, and learns safety precautions.

That fourteen-year-old girl who wants to be a veterinarian can arrange her "school" schedule so that she works two days a week with the local vet, getting hands-on experience in her potential career. She'll know for certain by the end of high school whether or not she really wants to spend all those years (and all that money) in college to achieve her goal. Her other schooling can also be designed to support her budding career. She can research and write about animals, physiology, and related topics. She might study uses of and attitudes toward different animals within different cultures. Math and economics studies might include cost comparisons for animal care in traditional zoos versus "natural" parks.

I think you get the idea. Asking a supplier for a standardized package of curriculum ignores the individuality and special needs and interests of your child.

You can see this more easily if you compare feeding your child's body to feeding his mind. You don't expect all children to eat exactly the same amounts and types of food. Some have particular food allergies. All have preferences and dislikes. And some burn up twice as many calories as others.

Likewise, mental nourishment should take into consideration the strengths and weaknesses of each child—teaching to their strengths and helping to overcome weak areas. It should have extra "nourishment" for those special areas of interest. It should be provided at a pace a child can handle—not too slow, not too fast.

If you are a new homeschooling parent, and you expected to just purchase a packaged curriculum and be done with it, this sounds like bad news. Where on earth do you begin? There are far too many choices. How do you know what your child needs? How can you figure this out?

That's the purpose of this book. First, in chapter two we will cover some basic approaches you might wish to use: traditional textbooks, Charlotte Mason/real books education, classical education, unit study, unschooling, independent study, working under an umbrella program, or an eclectic mixture of approaches.

I'll walk you through some questions that will help you identify which approach (or mixture of approaches) is best for you. In chapter three I have created examples for you as if I were filling in the charts and answering the questions in chapter two myself. This should give you a clear idea of how to proceed.

Then, in chapter four, I help you narrow things down even further by identifying your children's learning styles and figuring out what features you should be looking for in a curriculum to achieve the best fit for each child.

Many parents wonder what should be covered at each grade level, especially if they choose "ungraded" curriculum. Are you doing enough? Too much? Might your child's frustration be due to expectations that are beyond his maturity level? In chapter five, I discuss academic goals and how to figure out what you should cover in each subject area.

My goal with these first few chapters is to help you become goal-oriented rather than "curriculum driven." Too many new homeschoolers let that grade-level package of curriculum they purchased dictate the content, methods, and even the schedule they follow. In other words, the curriculum itself drives their homeschooling.

To be goal oriented means working in almost a reverse fashion. You determine what your children need to learn. You decide what methods to use. And you set up your own schedule. Then you find curriculum that has the content and methodology that fits your agenda, and you use it on your own timetable.

After you use the first few chapters to figure out what content and methods are right for your children, you will be ready to explore my top 101 curriculum choices in chapter six to see what is likely to fit your situation. To make this easy, I have included charts that help you readily identify which resources have the features that you will be looking for, features you will have already identified in the early chapters of this book.

Each product featured as a Top Pick also has a complete review in the following chapters. The page number of the review is in the last column of the Top Picks charts. Select likely candidates from the charts, read the full reviews, then make your decisions. I have also included ordering and contact information in each review so you will know how to actually get your hands on each resource.

Obviously, there are many more products than the top 101 that I have chosen for this book. You might have a specialized need or a specialized topic that is not addressed by any of these resources. If so, you might want to consult my website at www.CathyDuffyReviews.com for more possibilities.

Please fight the temptation to jump right to the chart of Top Picks and the reviews! Take the time to work out your own philosophy of education and discover what you really should be doing with your children before exposing yourself to the temptation of what is still an overwhelming number of resources from which to choose. I think you'll enjoy the journey of personal discovery that happens along the way.

Drill and Kill, Real Books, Delight-Directed Studies… What's best?

Jane Jones has just shown up at her first homeschool support group meeting. One of the moms is sharing about the fantastic unit study they've just completed on trains. Since they live in the Sacramento area of California, they visited the marvelous train museum in Old Sacramento. A trip on the modern Amtrak train provided a contrast to the old trains her children explored at the museum. Books they read about the building of the trans-continental railroad and development of the frontier provided the historical background. The children learned a few "railroad songs" and each painted a picture of his or her favorite old train. It was great fun and a terrific way to learn history.

Listening to this, Jane feels absolutely overwhelmed. How on earth can she do that sort of study? How would she know what to do? How could she tell if her children were learning anything? What about meeting requirements? What Jane really wants to know right now is what phonics program works best. If she has to make up a unit study for every topic, homeschooling just isn't going to work for her family!

It is so easy to be intimidated into thinking that your homeschool should mimic those of seasoned veterans. They seem to have a handle on things. Their kids are impressive. They're obviously doing something right. But the question you really need to consider is whether or not what they are doing is right for you.

It doesn't take long to figure out that veteran homeschoolers are, overall, very independent and strong-minded. Chances are you could poll half a dozen such parents and discover they have half a dozen different ways they homeschool. There is no single RIGHT way to homeschool that everyone figures out after a few years.

In fact, the diversity of resources and methods is one of the beauties of homeschooling. Need an audio CD to teach parts of the body to your child who just loves to sing all the time? Need a math program that uses colorful blocks to teach multiplication for that child who just has to

SEE how math works and not just memorize rules? Need a science program that lets you teach all your children the same topic at the same time? You name it, and there's likely something in the homeschool marketplace to meet your requirements.

But how do you figure out what you need? You can try to find a professional curriculum counselor to work through this with you. That's great if there's one available in your area and you can afford it. However, if that's not practical for you, the material in chapters four and five will help you sort this out by addressing curriculum selection from the two most important perspectives: what fits with your family's philosophy of education, and what works for each of your children's learning styles.

We'll start at the family level to sort out some "big picture" ideas about education. What we come up with is actually a philosophy of education. Don't let the word "philosophy" turn you off because figuring out a philosophy of education is not as difficult as it sounds. Someone once remarked that philosophy is nothing more than common sense dressed up in fancy dress clothes.

So we start with some common sense questions. I want you to really think this through as you read. There are lines on which you can write down your thoughts as you consider these questions. Let's begin with a question about the big picture—about what the overall content of "school" should be.

What do you think is most important for your children to learn?

You are not likely to come up with just one answer to this question. Instead you will come up with a number of things you consider important. Before you start writing, here are a few more questions that might help you think about content:

If there were no laws requiring you to educate your child, what would you want them to learn anyway?

Would that list include strong academics, work skills, study habits, a love for reading, familiarity with scripture, physical fitness, artistic expression, practical life skills, computer knowledge, ethical attitudes? What else might you add?

At this point, you should be writing down only broad categories rather than specifics like "I want my child to learn to write poetry in fifth grade." Your list might include words, phrases or sentences. For example, you might write out a list with such items as:

- college prep academics
- strong independent study habits
- extensive reading from many genres
- scripture study and memorization
- art appreciation and expression
- familiarity with computer programs such as Microsoft Word and Excel

Or you might write your ideas more expansively:

I want my children to grow up to be self-directed learners who know how to teach themselves.
I want my children to love to learn, so I want learning to be as fun as we can make it.
I want my children to have high aspirations for both college and career.
I want my children to have virtuous character and a strong ethical foundation.
I want my children to develop habits of physical fitness that will stick with them all their lives.
I want my children to take challenging academic courses for high school so they will have opportunities to win scholarships to prestigious colleges.

Now it's time to write down your own thoughts. But make an extra copy of the blank chart

Drill and Kill, Real Books, Delight-Directed Studies…What's best?

7

before you begin!

Once you have made your list, go back through and prioritize the ideas. Go through first and mark each idea with a "1," "2," or "3" with "1" identifying a top level priority, "2" a mid-level priority, and "3" a lower level priority. You might find yourself only writing down items that you would give a level "1" or "2" priority, and that's okay. Once you've made your list, if it is helpful, use the second copy of the chart to rewrite the list with level "1" items at the top of the list. You might automatically write these down with top priorities first. In this case, there's no need to rewrite them.

If you need to see what this might look like, you can jump ahead to the next chapter for a sample, but make sure to come back here and create your own list.

Priorities

I want my children to:	Priority Level

How do you think learning should happen?

We need to next consider ideas about methods of education. Keep in mind that answers to this question are heavily influenced by your own children and your own experiences. If you have very compliant children who love to play school just for fun, you might naturally think learning should always happen in traditional school fashion. But that's not your only choice. If you have a rowdy group of very active children, you might already be thinking they need lots of activity, movement, and freedom in their schooling. At this point, the question might be difficult to answer because you simply haven't thought about or investigated possible options. If so, try jotting down just a few notes and come back tothis topic later after you've read the rest of this chapter about some possible approaches you might want to use.

_____

_____

_____

_____

_____

How do you want to teach or operate your school?

As you consider this question, you will probably start to see that what you believe about content and methods shapes your thinking about how you will actually do things. For example, if you consider it a high priority that your children learn structure and discipline you are more likely to follow a predictable schedule and use tests on a regular basis. On the other hand, if you put a higher value on developing creativity and delight in learning, you might keep the schedule very flexible so your child can concentrate on that project she started without stopping to complete her language workbook exercise.

Here are more questions to help you think through how you might operate. Make some notes as you consider each question. You might also need to revisit this section after you've worked through the next few sections that help you figure out which approaches to education are likely to work best for you.

Do you want to try to teach most or all of your children together, at least for some subjects?

_____

_____

How much of the time do you want (or are you able) to work directly with your children?

2 ½ hrs.
_____

_____

How much of the time do you expect your children to work independently? (Caution: Don't expect children below about age 8 to do a lot of independent work.)

30 min.
_____

_____

Do you want to use real books (biographies, historical novels, books written about particular science topics, etc.) as part of your curriculum?

Yes
_____

_____

Do you want to include field trips? What type of field trips?

Drill and Kill, Real Books, Delight-Directed Studies...What's best?

9

Yes, related to topics of study - social opportunities, time outdoors

Do you like to "make up" curriculum as you go, adapting to the needs and interests of your children, or do you prefer things well planned out in advance?

Planned while adding some things of high interest & sometimes creative

Do you need a set schedule to get things done or would you prefer more flexibility?

schedule

Do you prefer a curriculum that is thoroughly laid out in advance by someone else and that tells you what to do when?

? Yes & no

Any additional thoughts about how you want to operate?

Writing down your thoughts about the above questions should have helped you clarify some of your goals and preferences. Now you can use the "Approaches to Education" chart to begin to identify which of the possible approaches to homeschooling are most likely to work for you.

The first column on the chart on the next two pages lists possible features and methods you might be looking for. When you read one that reflects your own ideas, move over to the boxes to the right of the statement, and circle every number in that row. The number means that the targeted feature or method is present to some extent in the approach in the top heading. If the box is gray, that means that this feature or method is not characteristic of that approach. For example, "predictable structure" is not something you usually find in a unit study approach. Unit studies tend to use a variety of books and activities, often emphasizing different subject areas from day to day. So the box under Unit Study across from "predictable structure" is grayed out. Some features or methods are found in resources for a particular approach some of the time, but not always. Those boxes have a "1" rather than a "2." For example, the Charlotte Mason approach does not always translate into a predictable structure. Some Charlotte Mason resources have predictable structure and some don't. In such cases the "1" gives this feature "half credit" when you add up your columns.

After you've gone through the entire chart, add up the total of the circled numbers in each column. The number in the denominator of the fraction at the bottom of each column is the number of total points possible in the column for each approach to education. The total of your points in each column will be the numerator (top number) of the fraction—what you write in. Divide the numerator by the denominator for each column total. You will than have percentage numbers for each column that you can easily compare.

Keep in mind that the column with the highest number doesn't win. If you look only at your total in each box, the "eclectic" approach is likely to come out on top every time since there are so many boxes (a possible total of 36). That could be very misleading. Instead, you need to look at the fraction or percentage. Any approach with almost all of the numbers circled (the highest percentage) is likely to be in line with your philosophy of education, and there might be more than one approach that qualifies!

Approaches to Education

I prefer:	Traditional	Charlotte Mason	Classical	Unit Study	Unschooling	Independent Study	Eclectic	Umbrella Program
predictable structure.	2	1	2			2	2	2
that children have many real life experiences for learning—nature studies in the woods, building projects, etc.		2	1	2	2	2	2	
children read historical novels and biographies rather than textbooks.		2	2	2	2		2	
a program that is thoroughly laid out for the teacher and provides a feeling of security.	2					2		2
a grammar program that emphasizes rules and memorization.	2		2			2	1	2
workbooks, teacher manuals, and answer keys for most or all subjects.	2					2	1	2
children to work independently as much as possible.	1				2	2	1	1
mental training and mental discipline be placed as higher goals than stimulating curiosity and interest.	2		1			2	1	1
curriculum that ensures that my children cover the same things other school children might be learning.	2					2	1	2
informal evaluation of my children by talking over what they've read and looking at their work rather than by testing.		2	2	2	2		1	
that younger children do a significant amount of memorization, repetition, and recitation.	1		1			1	1	1
that teens gets a strong background in the Great Books of western civilization.		1	2	1	1	1	1	1
to emphasize developing a love for learning more than the ability to work in a structured, methodical way.		2		2	2		1	
that teens develop a "life of the mind" more than vocational skills.	1	2	2	2	1	1	1	1
presenting children with facts and information to learn rather than allowing them to choose their own topics to investigate.	2	1	2	1		2	1	2
highly structured resources that "script" what teacher and child are supposed to say and do.	1		1			1	1	1
lots of discussion and interaction in the learning process.		2	2	2	1		2	1
Total points for each column on THIS page	6	11	9	10	9	8	11	7

Drill and Kill, Real Books, Delight-Directed Studies…What's best?

11

	Traditional	Charlotte Mason	Classical	Unit Study	Unschooling	Independent Study	Eclectic	Umbrella Program
covering subjects (e.g., history, science, religion) at the same time with the same material with as many of my children as possible.		2	2	2			2	
making connections between different subject areas, showing how pieces of information relate to one another, and viewing that as a high priority in learning.		2	2	2	2		1	
project-based learning.		1		2	2		1	
to teach children one-on-one as much as possible.	2	1	1		1		2	2
that children learn grammar in a casual manner—e.g., some instruction, use of a grammar handbook, then working on mastery in their own writing rather than working primarily through a grammar text.		1		2	2		1	
to keep structure to a minimum so that interesting learning ideas can be pursued as they arise.		1		1	2		1	
to make field trips an essential part of schooling.	1	2	1	1	2		1	
to give children freedom to determine what they will study and when and how they will do so.				1	2		1	
an "investigative" approach that stimulates children to pursue information and research on their own.		1		2	2	1	1	
flexible curriculum and schedules so I can capitalize on "teachable moments."		1	1	2	2		1	
a mixture of structured learning and experiential/discovery learning.		2		2			2	
to set my own goals and schedule rather than adopting someone else's.		1	1	1	2		1	
to select curriculum and methods that suit my child's learning style rather than curriculum and methods widely recognized and accepted by authorities.		1	1	2	2		1	
that computer-based learning be a significant part of the curriculum.	1					1		1
Total points for each column on THIS page	1	8	5	9	8		6	
Total points for each column on PREVIOUS page	6	11	9	10	9	8	11	7
Total for each column: add the above two lines and enter total as the numerator (top number) of the fraction	7/22	19/31	14/29	19/34	17/34	8/24	17/36	7/22
Percentage for each column: divide numerator by denominator	32	61	48	56	50	33	47	32

The goal of this chart is to help you identify the approach or approaches that are most likely to appeal to you. If you see that you have many circled numbers under both traditional and classical education, and few under unschooling or unit studies, you've already narrowed your likely curriculum choices dramatically. It is important to repeat that you need not select only one approach to use. Many experienced homeschoolers blend more than one approach. Some blend approaches so much that we call them "eclectic" homeschoolers.

More About Each Approach

Next, read the descriptions for the different education approaches to verify your conclusions from the chart. As you read through these descriptions, you will be refining your own educational philosophy.

Traditional

A traditionalist might use either textbooks or worktexts (worktexts contain within a single book both textbook-style instruction and workpages to be completed by students), but there are distinct books for each subject area: math, language arts (often broken down further into separate spelling, grammar, composition, literature, and vocabulary books), history, science, etc. These books are almost always written for use in regular school classrooms, although the publisher might have taken homeschool use into consideration.

When used as the publisher intends, such curricula generally help a homeschool function much like a regular day school. Children will be studying what many other students at their grade level are studying.

In most cases, teacher manuals, answer keys, and other teaching aids are available. These sometimes are so classroom oriented that they are of little use to the homeschooling parent, but other times they are essential to the program. For example, BJU Press's language courses are designed to be taught from the teacher's manuals. Some course instruction appears only in the teacher's manual. Student books are adjuncts that support the lesson in the teacher's manual with practice exercises or activities.

Traditional programs generally give parents a sense of security while helping establish routines and teaching methods. They sometimes make homeschooling a less frightening venture because the curriculum seems somewhat like what parents themselves used in school.

Many parents begin with a traditional approach, gradually shifting to other approaches as they gain experience and better understanding of what works for their children. Others stick with a traditional approach, finding it easier for record keeping, scheduling, and accountability.

Some parents choose traditional approaches that allow their children to work independently because of time constraints or learning styles. Some students (especially those beginning homeschool past the primary grades) actually prefer this type of approach because it feels familiar and comfortable for them.

However, traditional curricula sometimes take more time to use since they often include activities, presentations, practice, and review that are needed when teaching an entire classroom of children. Even self-paced programs such as Alpha Omega *LIFEPACs*—not designed for an entire class to use together—target the amount of practice and review to the average classroom situation. For example, traditional grammar programs frequently reteach and review the same

Drill and Kill, Real Books, Delight-Directed Studies…What's best?

13

grammar concepts year after year.

Sometimes traditionalists are chided for recreating "school at home" because the experience varies little from that of regular day school settings. The concern is that traditionalists sometimes miss out on those special moments when a child comes up with a question that begs for immediate exploration. Many parents manage to find a good balance using traditional curricula while still retaining enough flexibility to respond to teachable moments when they arise.

Some parents are just "trying out" the idea of homeschooling. They figure that if it doesn't work out, they'll put their children back in school next year. These parents often want to use a traditional curriculum, frequently coupled with a fairly consistent schedule similar to that of day schools, so their children can easily integrate into a regular day school classroom in the future if need be. The big caution here is that the traditional methods might make the homeschool experience boring and unappealing, creating a self-defeating experience from the beginning.

The choice is rarely all or nothing when it comes to traditional curriculum. While some homeschoolers enroll in programs that prescribe only traditional curriculum, most homeschoolers are free to choose one or more traditional resources along with resources that might reflect other approaches as I describe under the "Eclectic" approach later in this section.

Examples of traditional curriculum publishers would include A Beka Book, BJU Press, Modern Curriculum Press, Scott Foresman, Macmillan/McGraw Hill, Houghton Mifflin, Alpha Omega (*LIFEPAC* Curriculum), and Rod and Staff.

Charlotte Mason

Charlotte Mason was a turn-of-the-century educator who frequently used the term "twaddle" to describe much of what passed for curriculum content in traditional texts as a useless waste of a child's time and energy. For example, she warned against children's history textbooks saying, "… for this intelligent teaching of history, eschew, in the first place, nearly all history books written expressly for children…. and as for what are called children's books, the children of educated parents are able to understand history written with literary power, and are not attracted by the twaddle of reading-made-easy little history books." [1]

Through her many years of teaching, she determined that there were better ways to teach children that stimulated a love for learning and helped children retain knowledge more effectively than traditional methods, all while respecting the nature of the child. She believed in a child's innate ability and desire to learn and the need for teachers to restrain themselves from controlling all learning. Mason says: "The children might echo Wordsworth's complaint of 'the world,' and say, the teacher is too much with us, late and soon. Everything is directed, expected, suggested. No other personality out of book, picture, or song, no, not even that of Nature herself, can get at the children without the mediation of the teacher. No room is left for spontaneity or personal initiation on their part." [2]

Mason wrote about the importance of nature walks and outdoor learning: "[T]he knowledge most valuable to the child is that which he gets with his own eyes and ears and fingers (under direction) in the open air…. the claims of the schoolroom should not be allowed to encroach on the child's right to long hours daily for exercise and investigation." [3]

Even so, Mason was not an advocate of unschooling. (Unschooling will be defined later in this chapter.) She believed in directed learning as well as teaching a child self-discipline and good habits. She says, "Even the child who has gained the habit of attention to *things*, finds *words* a weariness. This is a turning-point in the child's life, and the moment for the mother's tact and vigilance…. never let the child *dawdle* over copybook or sum, sit dreaming with his book before him. When a child grows stupid over a lesson, it is time to put it away. Let him do another lesson as unlike the last as possible, and then go back with freshened wits to his unfinished task."[4]

Mason is well known for her use of narration rather than workbooks. She outlines the idea: "When the child is six…let him narrate the fairytale which has been read to him episode by episode, upon one hearing of each; the Bible tale read to him in the words of the Bible; the well-written animal story; or all about other lands from some such volumes as *The World at Home*. The seven-years-old boy will have begun to read for himself, but must get most of his intellectual nutriment, by ear, certainly, but read to him out of books. Geography, sketches from ancient history, *Robinson Crusoe*, *The Pilgrim's Progress*, *Tanglewood Tales*, *Heroes of Asgard*, and much of the same calibre, will occupy him until he is eight…. He should have no book which is not a child's classic; and… it must not be diluted with talk or broken up with questions, but given to the boy in fit portions as wholesome meat for his mind, in the full trust that a child's mind is able to deal with its proper food." She goes on to explain that the teacher should read "two or three pages, enough to include an episode; after that, let her call upon the children to narrate…."[5] The child then retells what has been read in his or her own words.

Mason also emphasized the importance of developing the imagination and the value of making connections between topics studied to enhance memory. She says, "If the business of teaching be to furnish the child with ideas, any teaching which does not leave him possessed of a new mental image has, by so far, missed its mark. Now, just think of the listless way in which the children too often drag through reading and tables, geography and sums, and you will see that it is a rare thing for any part of any lesson to flash upon them with the vividness which leaves a mental picture behind. It is not too much to say that a morning in which a child receives no new idea is a morning wasted, however closely the little student has been kept at his books."[6]

Charlotte Mason's ideas are generally implemented in the elementary grade levels. Hallmarks of a Charlotte Mason approach to education are the use of real books rather than textbooks for reading, history, geography, and science; the narration technique; nature learning; hands-on learning; making connections between various topics; inclusion of study of the fine arts; and a focus upon both development of good habits and a love for learning in children.

Charlotte Mason's ideas about education are incorporated into many unit studies to varying degrees, and that would be the easiest way to get started in this methodology. However, if you don't want to use a unit study, you can still learn how to easily implement Mason's ideas by reading one or more of the following books on her methodology.

A Charlotte Mason Education and *More Charlotte Mason Education* by Catherine Levison (Champion Press, Ltd., 262-692-3897, e-mail: info@championpress.com, www.championpress.com.) These are very practical, to-the-point books that will quickly help you understand Mason's methods.

A Charlotte Mason Companion by Karen Andreola (Charlotte Mason Research and Supply, PO Box 758, Union, Maine 04862, www.charlottemason.com.) Andreola presents an in-depth journey through Mason's philosophy of education.

SimplyCharlotteMason.com (www.simplycharlottemason.com). At this website you will find print books, ebooks, audio and video recordings, and many resources for understanding and

Drill and Kill, Real Books, Delight-Directed Studies…What's best?

15

implementing this approach.

Classical

Classical education is based on models of learning that go back to the Middle Ages, although its earliest roots lie in the Greek and Roman civilizations. Dorothy Sayers was one of a number of scholars who re-popularized this method of learning in the twentieth century. Two current proponents of classical education, Gene Veith, Jr. and Andrew Kern tell us in the introduction to their book on the subject: "Classical education provides a conceptual framework for mastering the entire range of objective knowledge. It also offers a theory of human character development, and it contains a teaching methodology that is demonstrably effective and eminently practical."[7] They go on to tell us, "Classical education cultivates wisdom and virtue by nourishing the soul on truth, goodness and beauty."[8]

Personally, I think the greatest value of classical education is that it engages learners with the most important ideas—ideas about God, about life, about purpose. Classical education challenges the vocational orientation of most modern education by instead concentrating on learning which forms the inner person. At the same time, classical students learn to how to think, how to learn independently, and how to present their own ideas—all of which ultimately prepares them for a wide range of vocations.

Veith and Kern also tell us, "The substance of classical education is the liberal arts curriculum."[9] Among those "arts" are three stages or categories grouped as the trivium. The trivium's three stages are labeled grammar, logic or dialectic, and rhetoric. They provide a sequential focus for education in the elementary through high school years. You start with the grammar stage and work up through the rhetoric stage.

The word "grammar" as used within classical education means much more than the nuts and bolts of a language. Rather it is the basic structure, skills, and knowledge of any subject. Thus, in the elementary grades, a child learns the grammar of math, language arts, social studies, and science, and maybe also the grammar of religion and other electives.

In the logic or dialectic stage, students analyze information and make connections. Then rhetoric describes the stage where the young person has assimilated knowledge, thought creatively about what he or she has learned, and now expresses his or her own ideas through speech and writing at what would likely be considered adult levels.

Some classical education proponents follow the progression of the trivium, making significant changes in methods and materials as they move through the stages. Others tend to mix the stages, for example, by having children in elementary grades participate in Socratic discussions (dialectic type activity) alongside studies of basic English grammar.

A major component of classical education for dialectic purposes is the reading and discussion of real books. Consequently, "Good Books" and "Great Books" programs have been developed that use classic fiction and non-fiction titles both for knowledge and as springboards into the world of ideas and questions. Socratic dialogues are used to stimulate students to think about what they have read, to work through important questions, to move to higher levels of thinking.

Below are websites with actual lists of (or links to) the Good Books and the Great Books. Generally, the Good Books lists include modern literature and identify books appropriate for younger children through adults while Great Books lists include older literature that has acquired "classic" status and is likely most appropriate for teens and adults. Some classical programs, particularly at high school level, work with books from these lists, while others apply the methods to their own selection of books.

Good Books lists:
www.classical-homeschooling.org/celoop/1000.html
www.angelicum.net/html/the_good_books_in_print_list.html—for K-8
www.ccel.org/index/classics.html - links to books in electronic format

Great Books lists:
http://books.mirror.org/
www.interleaves.org/~rteeter/greatbks.html
www.home.comcast.net/~antaylor1/greatbooksstjohns.htm

Other classical education programs, especially for the elementary grades, focus on other learning strategies more than on using Good Books or Great Books. For example, many such programs follow Dorothy Sayers' beliefs about children's ability to memorize in the grammar stage, so they build much of their curriculum around memorization as a means of obtaining knowledge.

Personally, I believe that the goal of acquiring knowledge and skills at the grammar level does not necessarily dictate a particular methodology, so variations of classical education methodology that use methods other than memorization and drill at the grammar stage might be equally appropriate for building a foundation to move on to dialectic and rhetoric stages.

An even larger question is the role of classical languages in classical education. Historically, study of Latin and Greek was always at the foundation of classical education. More recently, emphasis on the structure of the trivium and reading the Great Books seems to have displaced the study of Greek.

As you can see, there is quite a bit of discussion (and even disagreement) about the nature of classical education. It will be up to you to decide which elements of a classical education are most important. One thing to keep in mind is that classical education generally requires more direct instruction and interaction that do some other approaches. It is often more teacher directed than other approaches. To read more about classical education:

The Well-Trained Mind (2009) by Susan Wise Bauer and Jessie Wise (W.W. Norton & Co., order through bookstores or distributors) $39.95. This is a secular book that lays out comprehensive, detailed classical education programs for all grade levels with a strong college-prep emphasis. Even if you don't do everything the way they suggest, this is a treasure trove for anyone considering classical education.

Teaching the Trivium: Christian Homeschooling in a Classical Style by Harvey and Laurie Bluedorn (Trivium Pursuit, 309-537-3641, www.triviumpursuit.com) $34. The Bluedorns, pioneers in classical Christian education, temper their enthusiasm with cautions about "pagan" content. Rather than buying into the "Great Books" model of classical education, the Bluedorns apply the methodology while carefully selecting resources that support a biblical Christian worldview. They suggest numerous ideas for content, presentation, and timing but leave it to parents to decide what makes sense for their own children. They approach their subject from a Reformed Protestant perspective. Even those Christians who might not share the Bluedorn's theological perspective should find this book helpful if their goal is to use the classical model of education

Drill and Kill, Real Books, Delight-Directed Studies...What's best?

17

by drawing from it that which is worthy, while staying true to biblical principles.

Classical Christian Education Made Approachable (Classical Conversations, www.classical-conversationsbooks.com) $10. The folks at Classical Conversations wrote this very readable, 110-page book that both argues for the classical approach and explains what it is. It outlines each subject area in relation to the classical model, stressing the importance of learning Latin. It also outlines the trivium, the basic principles and approach underlying a classical education.

Natural Structure: A Montessori Approach to Classical Education at Home by Edward and Nancy Walsh. This book is now available free at the Natural Structure website. (www.hstrial-nwalsh.homestead.com/index.html). "Natural Structure" is the name given to this form of education which combines Montessori and classical education. Edward and Nancy Walsh have brought them together by adopting the framework of the trivium and quadrivium as outlined by Dorothy Sayers, then using Montessori's detailed teaching methodology to present the content. The program as presented in this book is Montessori-style education, but with resources selected to ensure content coverage reflective of the various stages of classical education. As children move past the preparatory and grammar stages of the trivium, Montessori materials are used less frequently and methodology becomes more similar to other forms of classical education. The Walshes rely on Montessori's original ideas, including her foundational Catholic perspective. While *Natural Structure* can be adapted by those with other religious beliefs, it does not readily fit non-religious situations. (Learn more about Montessori education at: http://en.wikipedia.org/wiki/Montessori_education.)

Classical Education: The Movement Sweeping America, by Gene Edward Veith, Jr. and Andrew Kern (Capital Research Center, www.capitalresearch.org; order through Amazon or other booksellers using ISBN 189293406X). This book covers the broad range of classical education, the different approaches and different settings as well as key organization and resources. This is one of the most objective resources if you are trying to sort out what approach within the classical education models you might use.

Unit Study

Unit study, sometimes called delight-directed study, appears under different names and formats but can be recognized by the presence of a unifying theme. Rather than approaching each subject and topic as isolated things to be learned, information is integrated across subject areas, helping children better understand what they are studying. According to the theory behind the unit study approach, when children really understand what they are learning because of the integration of subjects, they remember it better.

A unit study might focus on one primary subject area or many subjects. The major published unit studies generally encompass social studies, science, and the fine arts, with varying amounts of coverage of language arts and religion. Generally little to no math is included.

Examples of comprehensive unit studies are *Tapestry of Grace*, KONOS, and *Five in a Row*. Examples of limited unit studies are Amanda Bennett unit studies (www.amandabennett.com), *Further Up and Further In* (www.cadroncreek.com), and Media Angels science units. (those without web addresses are reviewed in this book.)

Here's my paraphrased example of a typical unit study that comes from the first chapter in

KONOS Volume 1 on the character trait attentiveness.

First, we choose an aspect of attentiveness we wish to study such as listening and sound. We study related scriptures, then study about the human ear (science), listen to music (music), make musical instruments (crafts), study about musical composers (music history), practice listening games (character development), study about and apply the speeds of sound and light to thunder and lightning (math and science), and write a headache commercial describing irritating noises (creative writing). These ideas are only a fraction of what is offered within a typical *KONOS* unit!

However, there are also limited unit studies that focus more narrowly on a single subject. For example, a study of horses might include the history of horses and the different breeds around the world, a study of their anatomy and physiology, and a written research paper on a horse-related topic. Thus, history, science and language arts are taught around a single theme selected primarily as a science topic.

You might also create your own limited unit study from resources on hand. For instance, if you are studying about the California Gold Rush, you could study those sections in a California history textbook along with sections about mining and minerals from a science textbook. You might also integrate a language arts activity by assigning a creative writing task related to the Gold Rush.

Unit studies typically use real books rather than textbooks for learning material. Many unit studies incorporate Charlotte Mason's ideas on the use of real books, nature study, and narration.

Unit study is often, but not always, multi-sensory, using hands-on experiences or activities for more effective learning.

Most unit studies are constructed so they can be used across a wide age span, with adaptations suggested for various levels. Unit studies for high school level tend to be more book-based than activity-oriented. While unit studies at elementary levels require heavy parental involvement, those for older students frequently require a good deal of independent work.

Unit studies work best for families with more flexible schedules since activities might take more or less time on any given day. Most also require preparation and presentation time. You will need to gather materials and resources for the study and figure out how to use them; the different published unit studies vary in how much of such work is already done for you.

The parent or teacher generally spends more time working directly with students in most unit studies—reading aloud, discussing, or leading an activity. The trade-off for extra time invested is that children retain the information presented in such interesting ways, and parents are then relieved from reviewing and reteaching the same material again. An added bonus of this type learning is that it tends to get children excited about the process—a real motivational boost.

Some parents are overwhelmed by the idea of unit studies, but some of them (e.g., *KONOS In-A-Box*) are so thoroughly developed that they provide all the resources you need and tell you exactly what to do when.

Unschooling or Relaxed Homeschooling

The idea of letting children follow their own inclinations in their education has been called unschooling. The philosophic ideas behind this approach are most often associated with John Holt, author of numerous books such as *How Children Learn, How Children Fail, Instead of Education*, and *Teach Your Own*. Holt's books are available from libraries and bookstores, especially from Holt Associates/Growing Without Schooling at www.holtgws.com.

A true unschooler would allow a child to determine what, when, how, and even "if" a child learns anything. But few people go to that extreme. What seems closer to reality in most

Drill and Kill, Real Books, Delight-Directed Studies…What's best?

19

unschooling situations is a much greater consideration for each child's interests and the timing of when they tackle various topics and skills. Also, unschooling parents often ask for their children's opinions about resources and learning methods. This approach is also sometimes called "relaxed" homeschooling.

Hallmarks of an unschooling approach are likely to be a very loose schedule, emphasis on developing a love for learning, rare use of traditional textbooks unless selected by the child, more hands-on projects and/or field trips.

To learn more about unschooling, read one of John Holt's books listed above or:

The Unschooling Handbook by Mary Griffiths (Three Rivers Press, www.primapublishing.com; order through bookstores or distributors) $14.99. Mary Griffiths helps explain what unschooling might look like with anecdotes and examples from many different families. She also includes specific ideas about how to help your children become educated without the normal structure and curriculum.

The Relaxed Home School by Mary Hood, Ph.D. (Ambleside Educational Press, www. archersforthelord.org, email: maryhood@archersforthelord.org) $10.95. This is a practical book that seems to reflect what many families are actually doing. Mary Hood stresses the need for goals coupled with an openness to many ways of attaining them. She suggests letting children have significant input into goal and strategy decisions, taking into consideration their talents and interests.

Independent study

I include independent study as a distinct approach even though it often uses resources listed under other approaches. They key idea here is that parents are looking for resources that allow a student to operate with little direct teaching or interaction regarding lessons. This means there has to be a preset curriculum that is self-instructional.

School of Tomorrow, Alpha Omega (*LIFEPAC* curriculum), and Christian Light all have courses very similar in structure that work this way although these are not your only choices for independent study.

In the aforementioned curricula, a number of booklets (typically 10-12 for a year-long course) comprise a course. Each booklet contains information students read (much like that found in textbooks). However, short sections of text are followed by questions. Students answer the questions referring back to what they have read. If they get most answers correct, they move on to the next section. If not, they review the material and answer questions again. Periodic tests operate the same way. So a student, theoretically, masters the material before moving on from each section. No direct teaching is required other than checking answers.

Alpha Omega took their *LIFEPAC* curriculum a step further by creating a computer-based version called *Switched-On Schoolhouse* (*SOS*) as well as a web-based version called *Monarch*. See the review of both programs in chapter thirteen.

While the above-mentioned resources are designed for independent study, many textbooks may also be used this way. Some of A Beka's textbooks work well this way. *Saxon Math* from *Math 54* and up are primarily used for independent study.

Independent study works best for self-directed learners who are responsible about their use of time. Most young learners do not do well with independent study, but many high schoolers thrive on it.

Parents faced with difficult time constraints often see independent study resources as the only way they might manage to home school. However, it is important to keep in mind that when you choose independent study resources, you forsake most of your opportunities to adapt to meet learning style needs of your child.

In addition the format of independent study means that most learning is at the lower levels of thinking—knowledge and comprehension—rather than higher levels of synthesis and analysis. Answers for lower level questions can be simple, factual answers, while those for higher level questions tend to be complex and subjective—the type of answers that requires sentences, paragraphs or discussion rather than multiple choice or fill-in-the-blanks.

While the previous paragraph describes resources designed particularly for independent study, there are many others that homeschoolers use for independent study that actually involve higher levels of thinking. Examples are *Wordly Wise* vocabulary series, almost any of The Critical Thinking Co. books, Apologia Science courses, *World Views of the Western World,* and *Rosetta Stone* language courses, all of which are reviewed in this book.

Eclectic

For want of a better name, we identify those who pick and choose from among a variety of philosophies and resources as "eclectic" homeschoolers. In reality, I suspect the large majority of homeschoolers are eclectic to some extent. Few rarely use everything in a given curriculum. Homeschoolers tend to supplement even the best resources or programs with other interesting things they find.

The goal for eclectic homeschoolers is generally to combine the best ideas that work for their family. This might even mean using philosophic opposites such as a very structured grammar program and a discovery approach to science.

Eclectic homeschooling requires more parental decision-making and responsibility, so it works best for those with some experience and/or confidence. Many homeschoolers will start their first year with a traditional program or even a unit study. Then the next year, they'll branch out, keeping what they liked from the prior year and adding new ideas and different resources each year.

While using an eclectic program generally means putting it together yourself, Sonlight Curriculum actually has put together eclectic programs for you. Each level includes a mixture of workbooks and real books that you might say represents a mixture of traditional, Charlotte Mason, and classical approaches. Sonlight is a great place to start if you really don't know which direction you would like to go. (See the complete review in chapter thirteen.)

Umbrella Program

I use the designation "Umbrella Program" to mean distance learning programs that have a preset curriculum with only a few possible options (e.g., Calvert with optional advisory teaching service at www.calvertschool.org, Christian Liberty Academy's full enrollment option at www.homeschools.org, or K12's online program at www.k12.com/courses. Enrollment in such programs provides parents with not only curriculum but guidance and evaluation assistance.

Umbrella programs can be a boon to parents who want assistance in choosing curriculum, planning schedules, and maintaining records. Generally, these programs don't require a great deal of preparation or teaching time. Some umbrella programs might even use resources for independent study such as computerized curriculum (e.g. *Switched-On Schoolhouse* or *Monarch*),

Drill and Kill, Real Books, Delight-Directed Studies...What's best?

21

although most will use a mix of resources from various publishers (unless the umbrella program is offered through a publishing company like A Beka or BJU Press).

The negative trade off when using such programs is that you loose flexibility in curriculum choices and scheduling and in your ability to adapt to each child's needs. Nevertheless, such programs help parents who lack confidence, are disorganized, or do not have time and energy to go it alone.

While many umbrella programs are very restrictive about curricula choices, there are some that allow families to choose from among a broad range of curricula, and there are some like the aforementioned Calvert and Christian Liberty Academy that offer options where you can use their curriculum without reporting and accountability requirements.

Yes, this is confusing, so check out such programs carefully before enrolling. In addition to the obvious questions—How much does it cost? What grade levels do they offer? Is it Christian, secular, etc.?—ask what curriculum they use, what options might be available, what sort of record keeping they require, if there are time limits, if there is any possibility of a refund once students have begun the program, how much help is available, and how quickly you can get it.

Finding Umbrella Programs

I've mentioned Calvert and Christian Liberty Academy since they have been around quite a while, but there are many other such programs available that meet the needs of families with various educational and religious philosophies. Following are links to two very helpful websites that have lists of such programs with brief annotations.

www.gomilpitas.com/homeschooling/methods/DLPsCorrespondence.htm
www.christianhomeschoolers.com/hs_christian_schools.html

Figuring Out What Works For You

Okay. You have added up the numbers on the chart, read through the descriptions of different approaches, but you still might not have developed a clear preference. Take heart! You can narrow this down even more as you consider some very practical issues. Your thoughts about the questions I pose next are so important that I've left space for you to jot down your responses on each one.

How much confidence and/or experience do you have regarding homeschooling?

If you have a great deal of both, then you will probably do fine with unit studies, unschooling and loosely structured approaches. If not, you might easily be overwhelmed by resources that require you to make many choices, find resources, plan projects, and create your own assessment. It is sometimes better to start out with more structure, gradually adding more and more adventurous ideas as you gain confidence.

How much time do you have available for working directly with your children and for planning and preparation?

Be realistic about this! If you've got two little ones in diapers, a beginning reader, and more work than hours in the day, choosing curriculum that requires lots of preparation, direct instruction, and your constant attention will inevitably cause you undue stress, destroy any household routines you may have had, and make the homeschooling experience an unhappy one for everyone. It doesn't matter how much you love real books, project learning, and field trips if you don't have time to do them.

Figure out where your children REALLY need you and which subjects MUST be taught this year, then find the most efficient resources you can for those. If there is time left over, add more subjects and interactive learning activities. This doesn't mean your budding reader needs to learn how to read from a computer program. While that's possible, it will be much better if you squeeze in *some* time for one-on-one work together.

Keep in mind that you can easily provide some reading instruction as you go about your daily routine. You can have magnetic letters on the refrigerator that your child identifies by sound while you're preparing a meal, or have your child find letters on signs as you drive to the grocery store. The same idea applies to math. Have your child count silverware while setting the table, maybe adding the total number of spoons and forks. Or have them count coins that made it all the way through the laundry into the clothes dryer.

If you are one of the fortunate few with plenty of time, you have much more freedom to choose time-consuming resources. However, most of us are somewhere in between the two extremes. We can usually function well if we balance some one-on-one time with some group time and some independent study time.

I strongly recommend trying to group your children together whenever you can for efficiency's sake. It's easiest to do this with religious devotions and instruction, history, science, and the arts. Math and language arts generally require more individualized work. Of course, methods like unit study and Charlotte Mason work better for grouping children than do traditional curriculum or correspondence courses which have different books for each student for each subject.

So how much time do you really have to devote to homeschooling, both for direct teaching and for planning and preparation?

How much money can you spend?

If the world were your oyster and cost were no problem, then choices would be simpler. Unfortunately, most of us have sacrificed a second income and operate on a limited budget, so we cannot buy everything we would like to own.

First, I would like to reassure you that the most expensive resources are not necessarily the best. Expensive resources sometimes provide more assistance for parents, saving you time and energy. However, sometimes they only provide you with many more things that you will feel obligated to do, but which are really not essential to your goals. If your child does not need lots of hands-on work to grasp math concepts, money spent on a program with pricey math manipulatives would have been better budgeted for a family vacation or a more comprehensive science program.

Secondly, you might not even need many resources designed primarily for educational purposes. We already have a wealth of "unintentional" learning resources if we simply open our eyes to learning opportunities that surround us in real life. Kitchens are loaded with possibilities for learning and applying math. Building projects, board games, budgets, checkbooks, allowances, family businesses, and shopping add even more opportunities. Children can practice language

Drill and Kill, Real Books, Delight-Directed Studies...What's best?

23

arts if you simply capitalize on opportunities all around you—writing thank you notes for gifts, creating shopping lists, writing directions to their friend's home, and copying and posting a "quote for the week" or memorization verse on the refrigerator are just a few examples.

You *do* need information beyond your own limited knowledge, but your local library stocks more books than you can hope to own. Make friends with your librarian and get the most out of this marvelous resource.

The easiest way to tune into learning opportunities in your environment is to ask yourself what it is, specifically, that your child needs to learn then think about how he or she might learn it with whatever is available. For example, your son needs to learn both standard and metric linear measurement. Grab a ruler or yardstick marked with both inches and centimeters and start measuring and comparing. Need to teach about adjectives? Use many, many of them as you talk to your child—get flowery, silly, alliterative, and imaginative: "Just look at this fuzzy, filthy, fungus-covered floor covering! It must need vacuuming." Then challenge your child to come up with his or her own descriptive sentence. (Be careful not to include over-used words like "very" and prepositional phrases like "under piles of junk." Explaining the difference is another lesson.)

I could continue with many more examples, but I think you get the point: learning need not happen the way it happens in schools. This means you can save some of the money you might have spent to recreate a traditional school at home. Keep this in mind as you come up with a budget amount for your homeschooling.

How do your religious beliefs impact your homeschooling?

Families have different feelings in this regard. For some families, spiritual knowledge and development is the highest priority. Some parents make academic excellence or something else like raising independent, self-motivated learners their highest priority. Religion might be a lower priority or it might have no place at all in their homeschooling. Many families haven't thought about their priorities enough to know how to answer this question. I want to suggest to you that thinking through this question is very important. Religious beliefs will play a role in your home education whether you plan for that to happen or not.

Many parents think that most secular textbooks present a "neutral" education, one that doesn't include any kind of spiritual viewpoint. In reality, all resources reflect a spiritual outlook, even though it might not be Christian. Now, I can just picture some of you shaking your heads and saying, "Come on. There's no religion in my child's spelling book." Or, "Math doesn't have anything to do with religion!"

A humorous piece which has been wending its way around the internet for a number of years illustrates the point I'd like to make. I have no idea who originated the first version, and it has been updated with additions to reflect ideological changes on a number of websites where it is posted. Here's a version I pulled from one website:

"The Loggers New Math"[10]

Teaching Math in 1950: A logger sells a truck load of lumber for $100. His cost of production is 4/5 of the price. What is his profit?

Teaching Math in 1960: A logger sells a truck load of lumber for $100. His cost of production is 4/5 of the price, or $80. What is his profit?

Teaching Math in 1970: A logger exchanges a set "L" of lumber for a set "M" of money. The cardinality of set "M" is 100. Each element is worth one dollar. Make 100 dots representing the elements of the set "M." The set "C," the cost of production, contains 20 fewer points than set "M." Represent the set "C" as a subset of set "M" and answer the following question: What is the cardinality of the set "P" for profits?

Teaching Math in 1980: A logger sells a truck load of lumber for $100. Her cost of production is $80 and her profit is $20. Your assignment: Underline the number 20.

Teaching Math in 1990: By cutting down beautiful forest trees, the logger makes $20. What do you think of this way of making a living? Topic for class participation after answering the question: How did the forest birds and squirrels feel as the logger cut down the trees? There are no wrong answers.

Teaching Math in 1996: By laying off 40% of its loggers, a company improves its stock price from $80 to $100. How much capital gain per share does the CEO make by exercising his stock options at $80? Assume capital gains are no longer taxed, because this encourages investment.

Teaching Math in 1997: A company outsources all of its loggers. The firm saves on benefits, and when demand for its product is down, the logging work force can easily be cut back. The average logger employed by the company earned $50,000, had three weeks vacation, a nice retirement plan and medical insurance. The contracted logger charges $50 an hour. Was outsourcing a good move?

Teaching Math in 1998: A laid-off logger with four kids at home and a ridiculous alimony from his first failed marriage comes into the logging company corporate offices and goes postal, mowing down 16 executives and a couple of secretaries, and gets lucky when he nails a politician on the premises collecting his kickback. Was outsourcing the loggers a good move for the company?

Teaching Math in 1999: A laid-off logger serving time in Federal Prison for blowing away several people is being trained as a COBOL programmer in order to work on Y2K [Year 2000] projects. What is the probability that the automatic cell doors will open on their own as of 00:00:01, 01/01/00?

These are mostly exaggerated examples of what folks have found in math textbooks over the years. You might have noticed that there's no mention of religion in any of them. But what does it imply when feelings take precedence over the facts of math as in the 1990 example? Or, what about the other agendas (like ecological extremism) that work their way into supposedly neutral subjects? And what do you think of presenting business ethic questions as mere mathematical calculations rather than moral challenges?

Do you doubt that some very different beliefs about God and man, man's purpose in life, and man's responsibilities in relationship to others shape many texts used in schools?

Even more subtle are the choices of what to include and what to leave out of textbooks. For

Drill and Kill, Real Books, Delight-Directed Studies...What's best?

25

example, history books that start with an evolutionary explanation of the origins of life, proceed as if the theory has been proven. They ignore the possibility of man being a special creation of God. They also ignore all historical evidence of God being a real part of history. Less subtle are science texts that teach that accident and random chance are what brought man out of a primordial stew to our present evolving state.

More blatantly, in supposedly secular literature texts and readers we often encounter folk tales of various pagan gods that show us how each of the gods "blessed" those who followed their instructions. The implication is that all "gods" are simply reflections of different cultures and are equally real. Those same texts probably include no stories about the God of Christianity and certainly none that give Him precedence. You can see how this type of content might be offensive to Christians.

Parents who try to leave *all* spirituality out of learning are either purposely or inadvertently teaching their children a materialistic philosophy. If spirituality and transcendence never enter the discussion, you are teaching children that the world consists only of what they experience with their senses and know with their minds. It might allow for the possibility that God exists, but if He does, He is so irrelevant that He has nothing to do with important things like history and science. Even though most people don't think of materialism as a religion, it serves that purpose with its own answers to the big questions of life and the reason for our existence.

If, on the other hand, you believe in God, it should be important enough to impart to your children—or else what's the point of believing in Him at all? If faith and knowledge of God are important, then they need to be incorporated into the learning process within the content as well as the methods of presentation. You teach what you believe and you demonstrate your belief by the way you act, how you speak, and how you treat people.

You must keep spiritual goals and influences in mind as you select your curriculum. A resource might be very popular with home schoolers in general, but it might not reflect your family's spiritual beliefs. Sometimes you can work around these issues with minimal effort, but sometimes it's more trouble than it's worth and you would be better off using other resources. Be especially careful when selecting resources that your children will be using independently. You might seldom look at the curriculum once they start working, and you won't have opportunity to spot content that undermines your family's beliefs.

Back to the question:

How do your religious beliefs impact your homeschooling?

_____

_____

Before you pull all this together, look at the samples in the next chapter to see how to combine the information you've gleaned to put together your own philosophy of education.

3

Putting Together Your Philosophy of Education

There was a lot to work through in chapter two, and you might be confused at this point. To help make things clear, I have created examples of how this might look as you work through each section of chapter two. I've written responses and completed charts as I would have when my sons were about ages 7, 10, and 12.

After you read through these completed questions and charts, I'll show you how it all comes together. Let's begin with the first three questions.

What do you think is most important for your children to learn?

Remember that "1" indicates highest priority, "2" the next highest, and "3" the lowest.

Priorities

I want my children to:	Priority Level
have a strong sense of God's reality in all aspects of their education.	1
love to learn, so that they will become self-educators.	1
have a broad education so they can consider lots of possibilities for their future.	2
develop excellent reading skills.	1
develop excellent thinking skills.	1
develop excellent communication skills.	2
learn how to work with other children and adults in groups.	2
develop good work habits.	2
develop excellent knowledge of scripture and religious beliefs.	1
prepare for college so that they have more life choices.	1
develop a heart for service to others.	1
cover all the normal subjects so they can pass tests when necessary.	2

figure out their special talents and gifts.	2
be computer literate.	2
have exposure to the arts and develop some "artistic" skills.	2
be physically fit.	2
develop a strong Christian worldview.	1
read widely from both classic and good books .	1

Notice that there are still some blank lines. You don't have to fill all of them in just because they're there. On the other hand, if you need more space, feel free to grab another piece of paper and make your list even longer. Also notice that there are no level "3" entries. I realized that I had so many level "1" and "2" entries that any entries that might be level "3" were too low on my priority list to even bother writing them down. However, you might write out your own list, then find on reflection that some of your entries actually rate a level "3."

How do you think learning should happen?

I have three very active boys who need to be able to move around and do lots of hands-on learning. I want lots of interaction and experiential learning. I also want them to learn how to operate independently and learn to teach themselves through their independent reading, especially as they get older. So a balance that combines these two ideas is best for us.

How do you want to teach or operate your school?

Do you want to try to teach most or all of your children together, at least for some subjects?
> *Absolutely!*

How much of the time do you want (or are you able) to work directly with your children?
> *I want to start together in the mornings for about 1½ to 2 hours, do some group classes or park days a few afternoons a week, and have them work independently or one-on-one with me the rest of the time.*

How much of the time do you expect your children to work independently?
> *My middle son works independently better than the other two—at least a few hours a day. My youngest will do a few, scattered, 15-minute to half-hour periods of independent work. My eldest will do at least two hours of independent work as long as I check up on him frequently.*

Do you want to use real books (biographies, historical novels, books written about particular science topics, etc.) as part of your curriculum?
> *Definitely.*

Do you want to include field trips? What type field trips?
> *Yes. Field trips related to unit study topics plus any good opportunities that come up.*

Do you like to "make up" curriculum as you go, adapting to the needs and interests of your children or do you prefer things well planned out in advance?
> *I like to have a general plan completed during the summer for the coming school year, then adapt as I go.*

Do you need a set schedule to get things done or would you prefer more flexibility?
> *Flexibility, although we need to start with together time first thing in the morning.*

Do you prefer a curriculum that is thoroughly laid out in advance and that tells you what to do when? *No.*

Any additional thoughts about how you want to operate?

I want my lesson plans to become my record keeping books, so I work from my spiral notebook that I use during each summer to make general plans for the year. I periodically fill in my lesson plan/ record book for the next few weeks with specific books and page numbers, activities, field trips, etc. so it is easy to make changes to my original plan.

I'm not concerned about grading in the elementary grade levels, but I will give grades once in a while so they have concrete feedback about how I think they are doing. Grading becomes more important to me in junior high.

Note: When I complete this chart I come up with high numbers (and large fractions) for unit study, Charlotte Mason, unschooling, classical education, and eclectic approaches. Traditional education, independent study, and umbrella programs are clearly not my preferences.

Which approach to education should I use?

I prefer:	Traditional	Charlotte Mason	Classical	Unit Study	Unschooling	Independent Study	Eclectic	Umbrella Program
predictable structure.	2	1	2			2	2	2
that children have many real life experiences for learning—nature studies in the woods, building projects,etc.		(2)	(1)	(2)	(2)	(2)	(2)	
children read historical novels and biographies rather than textbooks.		(2)	(2)	(2)	(2)		(2)	
a program that is thoroughly laid out for the teacher and provides a feeling of security.	2					2		2
a grammar program that emphasizes rules and memorization.	2		2			2	1	2
workbooks, teacher manuals, and answer keys for most or all subjects.	2					2	1	2
children to work independently as much as possible.	1				2	2	1	1
mental training and mental discipline be placed as higher goals than stimulating curiosity and interest.	2		1			2	1	1
curriculum that ensures that my children cover the same things other school children might be learning.	2					2	1	1
informal evaluation of my children by talking over what they've read and looking at their work rather than by testing.		(2)	(2)	(2)	(2)		(1)	
that younger children do a significant amount of memorization, repetition, and recitation.	1		1			1	1	1
that teens gets a strong background in the Great Books of western civilization.		(1)	(2)	(1)	(1)	(1)	(1)	(1)
to emphasize developing a love for learning more than the ability to work in a structured, methodical way.		(2)		(2)	(2)		(1)	
that teens develop a "life of the mind" more than vocational skills.	(1)	(2)	(2)	(2)	(1)	(1)	(1)	(1)
Total points for each column on THIS page	**1**	**11**	**9**	**11**	**10**	**4**	**8**	**2**

Statement	C1	C2	C3	C4	C5	C6	C7	C8
presenting children with facts and information to learn rather than allowing them to choose their own topics to investigate.	2	1	2	1		2	1	2
highly structured resources that "script" what teacher and child are supposed to say and do.	1		1			1	1	1
lots of discussion and interaction in the learning process.		(2)	(2)	(2)	(1)		(2)	(1)
covering subjects (e.g., history, science, religion) at the same time with the same material with as many of my children as possible.		(2)	(2)	(2)			(2)	
making connections between different subject areas, showing how pieces of information relate to one another, and viewing that as a high priority in learning.		(2)	(2)	(2)	(2)		(1)	
project-based learning.		(1)		(2)	(2)		(1)	
to teach children one-on-one as much as possible.	2	1	1		1		2	2
that children learn grammar in a casual manner—e.g., some instruction, use of a grammar handbook, then working on mastery in their own writing rather than working primarily through a grammar text.		(1)		(2)	(2)		(1)	
to keep structure to a minimum so that interesting learning ideas can be pursued as they arise.		(1)		(1)	(2)		(1)	
to make field trips an essential part of schooling.	(1)	(2)	(1)	(1)	(2)		(1)	
to give children freedom to determine what they will study and when and how they will do so.				1	2		1	
an "investigative" approach that stimulates children to pursue information and research on their own.		(1)		(2)	(2)	(1)	(1)	
flexible curriculum and schedules so I can capitalize on "teachable moments."		(1)	(1)	(2)	(2)		(1)	
a mixture of structured learning and experiential/discovery learning.		(2)		(2)			(2)	
to set my own goals and schedule rather than adopting someone else's.		(1)	(1)	(1)	(2)		(1)	
to select curriculum and methods that suit my child's learning style rather than curriculum and methods widely recognized and accepted by authorities.		(1)	(1)	(2)	(2)		(1)	
that computer-based learning be a significant part of the curriculum.	1					1		1
Total points for each column on THIS page	1	17	10	21	19	1	15	1
Total points for each column on PREVIOUS page	1	11	9	11	10	4	8	2
Total for each column: add the above two lines and enter total as the numerator (top number) of the fraction	$\frac{2}{22}$	$\frac{28}{31}$	$\frac{19}{29}$	$\frac{32}{34}$	$\frac{29}{34}$	$\frac{5}{24}$	$\frac{23}{36}$	$\frac{3}{22}$
Percentage for each column: divide numerator by denominator	9%	90%	66%	94%	85%	21%	64%	14%

Check Your Results

As I read through the actual descriptions in chapter two, I find that there are elements of unschooling that appeal to me, but not enough of the philosophy that I would really consider unschooling as my own approach.

I really like certain aspects of classical education—Great Books, discussions, higher level thinking—but I'm not enamored with some of the memorization-based programs that are also called classical education. This dilutes my strong preference for the aspects I like and makes my preference for classical education appear weaker than it actually is. (This should be a caution to others who, like me, prefer some aspects of what is labeled classical education. You need to investigate resources described as classical to ensure that they really are what you want.)

With my highest numbers appearing for unit study and Charlotte Mason approaches, it would make sense for me to see if there is a way to incorporate the classical education and Charlotte Mason ideas I like within a unit study format. (Yes, such curriculum actually exists!)

The Next Four Questions—The Reality Check

Next, I wrote down some notes on the next four questions, thinking back a few years to when I had children in elementary grades through junior high:

1.) How much confidence and/or experience do you have homeschooling?

I have lots of confidence and enough experience that I don't mind trying unusual approaches.

2.) How much time do you have available for working directly with your children?

My time is very limited because of other demands. My husband doesn't have much time to help. But I can work with other families to do some group classes, so that will help on the time question. I have about 3 hours a day available for direct teaching and interaction. I need to do a lot of planning over the summer when I have more time, then I should have about three or four hours each weekend to plan for each week.

3.) How much money can you spend?

We're on a limited budget, so I should spend less than $1000 total this year.

4.) How do your religious beliefs impact your homeschooling?

My religious beliefs are a critical part of homeschooling. They will underlie everything we do. I would like to use resources that reflect my beliefs, but I can work with others as long as they are not in direct conflict.

When I consider my answers to these four questions, I can see that my time constraints will make time-consuming planning and projects difficult. I need to compromise on my desire to do unit studies and a lot of project learning. Money will be a limitation, but I'm not set on only one way of doing this, so I can look at many different options.

Incorporating religious beliefs is easy within Charlotte Mason, unit study, and classical education approaches since they use real books and require discussion and interaction.

Putting It All Together

Now I am ready to gather what I have learned so that I can verbalize my own personal philosophy of education and what that might look like for my family. While you can do this in any order you wish, I will describe my own process.

First, I summarized my educational philosophy primarily from the first section, actually copying from some of what I wrote there. I did not need to include everything from that section.

My philosophy of education: *I believe that my children's education should help them develop a strong sense of God's reality in all aspects of their lives. I want my children to love to learn so they will become self-educators who choose to learn on their own. I also want them to have strong academic skills so they have the tools for independent learning. I want them to have a broad education since I do not know what direction God has for each of them.*

Next, I looked at the chart where I've circled numbers reflecting different educational approaches. I've already come to some conclusions about which approaches I like. In my notes following the last four questions, I already noted that one of my highest priorities, incorporating religious goals into education, is easier to do within one of the "real books" approaches.

Another priority I set in the first section—and one of my strongest—is that my children love to learn. That means I will want to be particularly attentive to methods and resources that are appealing to them and that encourage that love of learning. I know enough about learning styles to recognize that this might mean choosing different resources for each of them. However, I noted in the last section that we have a limited budget so I might not be able to purchase everything I would like to use. Time is also a precious commodity. I know I don't want to plunk my boys down with workbooks all the time if I really want them to love learning. On the other hand, they will have to do some independent work both for their sakes and mine. I do not have time to do everything with them, and I want them to eventually become independent learners, so they DO need to learn how to work independently.

I will need to come up with a balance of interesting, interactive learning activities and independent work. I realize that I can primarily use the educational approaches I prefer, but I will probably have to include some traditional workbooks just to make things manageable.

I want to incorporate worldview education, even more so at junior high and high school levels. That will narrow down my choices in some ways. I would like to use classical methods from the dialectic and rhetoric stages for a good part of worldview education.

Realistically, I can see that my time demands are going to be heavy. One of the smartest things I can do is work with all three together whenever possible. Unit studies might help me do that. Group classes with other families will be another way to help with the time issue.

All of this tells me that I should probably look to unit study ideas, especially those that have a strong Christian worldview orientation plus those based on either Charlotte Mason's ideas or classical education (the latter especially for my eldest sons). I can likely use traditional textbooks for subjects not covered by the unit study.

Now it's your turn. When you've completed this section, go on to chapter four to see how understanding both your own learning style and the learning styles of the children you'll be teaching will help fine tune your curriculum choices.

Learning Styles: How does MY child learn best?

If you are like me and most other parents I've asked, teaching your child to read is probably the scariest part of homeschooling. We have this sense that if we blow it with reading, then how can we possibly accomplish anything else?

Given that so many of us share this common insecurity, you might well be one of the thousands of parents who shelled out $200 to $300 for one of those reading programs that have been widely advertised. The glowing testimonials really convinced you that this would be money well spent.

Like thousands of parents who invested in such programs, you might have had a very discouraging experience with the program. Let's say you bought the one that teaches the alphabet and phonetic sounds to rap tunes. When you played the first CD for your child to listen to, you discovered a couple of disconcerting things: your child doesn't like rap music, and your child couldn't make any connection between what he was hearing and letters on a piece of paper. If you figured this out quickly enough, you were able to return the program within the allowable time and get your money back. If not, the program got added to your collection of white elephants.

So how do we save ourselves this sort of expensive grief? One of the best ways is tuning in to our children's learning styles.

Unfortunately, this was something I learned after making some big mistakes in my initial curriculum choices. When we first began homeschooling in 1982, my strongest conviction was that I wanted to use a Christian curriculum. The only Christian curriculum publisher I knew of was A Beka Book. This was the "dark ages" of homeschooling—a time when most publishers were not interested in selling to homeschoolers, if they even knew such a thing as homeschooling existed. Nevertheless, I went to a great deal of trouble to obtain A Beka worktexts to use with my two eldest sons, first and third graders at the time.

It took no more than two weeks to figure out that this sort of curriculum was about the worst choice for my eldest son, Chris. You'll understand why shortly when you read the description of the Wiggly Willy learning style. I had to get busy adapting and doing other things to enable Chris to learn. If it depended upon him working through A Beka lessons, reading the text and completing the activity pages, we were doomed.

So I first started using methods relating to learning modalities. You might already be familiar with learning modalities, the idea that people tend to prefer one of three types (or modes) of sensory input:

- auditory (hearing)
- visual (seeing)
- kinesthetic (feeling or experiencing with one's body)

Understanding learning modalities might have helped the parent who bought the phonics program that uses audio CD's for most of the teaching if she had known that her child was not an auditory learner. Learning by listening would not be the method of choice for such a child.

Learning modalities helped me with Chris since I knew he was a kinesthetic learner. I pulled out math manipulatives and other concrete objects to teach lessons even though A Beka made no provision for that sort of learning. But it was a lot of work to come up with such adaptations for different subjects while also sorting out what parts of the A Beka worktexts I might still be able to use.

Learning modalities help to a certain extent, but it's a bit too simplistic. For example, what do you do with a child who is a strong auditory learner but who can't sit still long enough to listen to a lesson being read to him?

That's where learning styles come in. The term learning style refers to the way (or style) a person most easily learns and processes new information or skills. Learning styles are just a bit more complex than learning modalities. Learning styles include awareness of children's preferred learning modalities, but they go further to look at other personality and learning traits such as a desire to work with other people or independently, an orientation toward either the big picture or the details, and preferences for a more or less structured environment.

Learning modalities play a partial role in understanding learning styles. For example, the kinesthetic learning modality is an obvious match with Wiggly Willy learners. However, visual and auditory modalities cross learning style boundaries, and should be taken into account no matter which style learner a child seems to be.

Which System Is Best?

Experts have come up with many different systems and labels for identifying a person's learning style. All of them are useful. The most significant differences are in their complexity. Some systems are so complex that an expert needs to administer an assessment and analyze the results.

When I first read about learning styles, hardly anyone was using them to address the needs of children. The first book I found that did so was titled *Learning Patterns and Temperament Styles* (published by Manas Systems) by Dr. Keith Golay. Dr. Golay discussed learning styles in relation to traditional, public school classroom settings. Although it was very useful, the fact that it lacked a Christian outlook and didn't address homeschooling motivated me to come up with my own approach that I use in this book.

The learning styles I use in this book fall into four categories. Yes, it could be much more complex, but our goal with learning styles is not a thorough analysis of each of our children so much as developing an awareness that each one will have ways of learning that are easier and ways that are tougher. By identifying learning styles, we are able to choose teaching methods and materials that are more likely to be successful for each child.

For example, one child's learning style might be very physical in a whole-body sense. This child learns math best when she puts two blocks plus two more blocks together, then counts to see that there are four. She needs to move her body as she counts each number. She learns prepositions best by putting her teddy bear ON the chair, UNDER the chair, OVER the chair, and BESIDE the chair. You can imagine how challenging children with this learning style might be to teach in a typical classroom setting!

Another child with a different learning style responds well to traditional classroom textbooks. He learns just fine by reading textbooks and doing workbook exercises. He doesn't need to feel or experience things to learn. But he also depends upon the predictability and security of those workbooks. He really struggles when it comes to creative writing and art projects.

Yet another child learns best when it's a social experience. She thrives on "unit study day" when you get together with a few other families to do all those creative unit study activities together. She blossoms when she gets to role play a character in an historical event. Her writing is impressive because she wants to do her very best on her writing project that she will be reading aloud to her group class.

Recognizing these differences within each of your children will help you make better choices in the methods and materials you use. But that's only part of the curriculum equation.

But Of Course My Way Is Best!

The other part of the equation is the parent's own learning style. The reality is that we parents have our own learning style preferences. And we tend to teach our children in ways that WE learn best rather than ways THEY learn best. So our preferred learning style, by default, becomes our teaching style. That's what we're most comfortable with. That's what comes naturally to us.

Structure, organization, and schedules will be important to some of us, while exploration, creativity, and flexibility will be higher priorities for another parent. Some parents love to do messy art projects while others would rather their children watch an art appreciation video. There's no right and wrong to such choices. Rather, it is a matter of recognizing your own preferences then checking to see if those methods are really what work best with your own children. I like to think that in God's graciousness and wisdom, He usually gives parents children of contrasting learning styles so we have more opportunities to stretch and grow.

Page 35 will help you identify your own learning and teaching style. Read through the description of each learning style. Don't get hung up on the names at the top (Wiggly Willy, Perfect Paula, etc.). These are the labels I use to help you remember each style, but they don't mean that those with a Wiggly Willy style are all male and that Perfect Paulas are exclusively female.

You are not likely to find that every item under any one learning style fits you while none under the other three do. More likely, you will find a number of items under one learning style that describe you and only a few under one or more of the other learning styles. Try to rank yourself in descending order from the learning style most like you down to the one least like you. If you should find that you are fairly evenly spread across one or more learning styles, that's just fine.

ADULTS

Wiggly Willy
- has trouble organizing and following through
- would rather play and have fun than work
- tends to do things impulsively
- probably did poorly in school (often due to lack of interest or boredom)
- looks for creative and efficient solutions to tasks
- dislikes paperwork and record keeping
- prefers activity over reading books
- prefers to teach the fine arts, physical education, and activity-oriented classes

Perfect Paula
- likes everything neatly planned ahead of time
- likes to follow a schedule
- is not very good at coming up with creative ideas
- is comfortable with memorization and drill
- gets upset easily when children don't cooperate
- worries about meeting requirements
- often prefers to work under an umbrella program for home educators
- prefers to teach with pre-planned curricula
- is more comfortable with "cut and dry" subjects than those which require exploration with no clear answers

Competent Carl
- likes to be in control
- thinks and acts logically
- likes to understand reasoning and logic behind ideas
- is selectively organized
- likes to work alone and be independent
- is impatient with those who are slow to grasp concepts and those who are disorganized
- is often uncomfortable in social situations and has trouble understanding others' feelings and emotions
- tends to avoid difficult social situations
- likes to make long-term plans
- prefers to teach math, science, and other logic-related subjects rather than language arts and social studies

Sociable Sue
- enjoys social interaction
- likes to belong to groups, especially for activities
- worries about what other people think
- tends to be insecure about how well he/she is doing with home education

- is idealistic about expectations and goals
- may or may not be organized, depending upon accountability
- is more interested in general concepts than details
- prefers to teach subjects related to language arts, social studies, and, possibly, the fine arts

If I create an analogy as to how adults with different learning styles might visit Disneyland (or Disney World or Universal Studios, etc.), I think it might help you sort this out even better. For Wiggly Willy, it's all about the rides. He wants to experience all of them. Forget the shops and the shows that you sit and watch.

Perfect Paula is likely to have organized the event in the first place. She'll make sure there's a meeting place in case someone gets lost. She'll know what time various events take place and try to schedule out the day to make sure she gets to all the things that are on her list.

Competent Carl won't mind going off on his own if everyone else takes too long figuring out what they want to do. He'll choose rides over shops, but particular shows might also intrigue him. His choice activities will be ones with special effects, because the fun for him is in figuring out "how they did it."

Sociable Sue will make sure all her friends have come along. She'll enjoy whatever happens as long as everyone sticks together. For her, the fun is in the company. They could spend hours standing in lines waiting for rides and that would be as much or more fun than anything else.

Pay attention to your group next time you go to a theme park and see if you can't identify some of these patterns!

If you matched up a single learning style with most of your characteristics and found very few that described you under the other three, you will have to pay more attention to learning styles than a parent who is more evenly spread across the learning styles. You might tend to be "lopsided" in the learning methods you use with your children, leaning heavily toward those favoring that especially strong learning style of yours.

On the other hand, if you recognized a number of your characteristics in two or more learning styles, you are likely to have an easier time adapting to the needs of your children since you already have a tendency to work across one or more learning styles.

Keeping in mind what you've discovered about your own learning and teaching style, it's now time to try to identify your children's learning styles. Remember that your children, just like adults, are not likely to fit neatly into only one category. They, too, are likely to have one stronger learning style, and one or two that are weaker, and maybe one that just doesn't fit them at all.

Children's Learning Styles

Wiggly Willy

Wiggly Willys are those children who learn best by doing—the hands-on learners. They like to be free to move around and act spontaneously. Do you have a little boy who just seems to fall off his chair if he has tried to stay put for more than ten minutes? That's typical for a Wiggly Willy.

They have short attention spans most of the time, although it's interesting to see how their attention span lengthens when they get into something of their own choosing! These children are usually not interested in deep thinking or analysis if it means sitting still very long.

On the other hand, they generally do very well with hands-on projects. They can be very creative and imaginative.

These are carefree children who live for the moment. However, they can be difficult to motivate. Wiggly Willys hate being bored. They'll create "interesting moments" to break the boredom.

They don't think ahead about consequences, positive or negative. You cannot usually motivate them with: "Study hard and get good grades so you can get into a good college ten years from now." Ten years from now is a non-existent concept for them, so why on earth would they sacrifice present pleasure for that? These children need short-term goals and immediate rewards.

Wiggly Willys can be disruptive in groups. Sometimes these children are labeled as having attention deficit disorder (a disorder that I do believe is real), although the actual problem is that, because of their age and temperament, they really need to be moving around more than is allowed in a typical classroom.

Perfect Paula

I call our second type of learner Perfect Paula. This is the responsible child who likes to see that everything is done correctly. She likes things to be clearly structured, planned, and organized.

Perfect Paulas have a narrow comfort zone. They feel more secure when things are orderly. Consequently, they seldom act spontaneously and are uncomfortable with creative activities that lack specific guidelines. For example, if you want them to do an art project, they will ask, "Show me what it's supposed to look like." They want to make sure they will do it correctly rather than seize an opportunity to express their own creativity.

They follow rules and respect authority, and they often feel it their duty to make sure everyone else does likewise. They like to follow a typical school curriculum and feel that they are accomplishing the same things as other children their age. They prefer to be part of groups, and they need approval and affirmation to let them know that they are doing what is proper.

Perfect Paulas can be easier to homeschool than other learners, but you might have to work at helping them develop more flexibility and creativity.

Competent Carl

Competent Carl likes to be in control of himself and his surroundings. He tends to be analytical, constantly trying to figure out what makes things tick. Problem solving is typically something he enjoys.

Their analytical and logical bent typically makes math and science their strong subjects while the more subjective humanities (i.e., language arts, literature, social studies) might be weaker subjects.

Social skills can be another weak area. Often Competent Carls have difficulty understanding and relating to their peers. Because of this, and sometimes simply by choice, they enjoy solitary activity. They expect others to operate the same way they do, and they don't find it easy to adapt to other ways of doing things.

Competent Carls tend to be self-motivated and enjoy long-term, independent projects. They have their own ideas about what they want to learn, as well as when and how they want to learn.

Some Competent Carls love to brainstorm—think out loud. These more verbal Competent Carls will probably want a more interactive learning environment or at least one that allows them to ask questions and talk through what they are learning. One-on-one teaching or small groups are likely to be better than large groups for Competent Carl.

Sociable Sue

Sociable Sues are, of course, sociable. They often have warm, responsive personalities. They are interested in people, and as they get older, that interest expands into ideas, principles, and values.

But they also tend to be big picture people; concepts are more interesting to them than details and technicalities. They don't like memorizing names and dates for history, but they want to understand how different cultures and events affect one another.

They love change and new things. They can be very excited about a new project or assignment but easily "lose steam" once the novelty has worn off. Sometimes you have to switch what you are doing or add something new with Sociable Sues to reignite their interest—a different curriculum, a new supplemental workbook, an educational game, a field trip, etc.

They are motivated by relationships and care a great deal about what others think of them. They like to be recognized and acknowledged for their achievements. Because of this they will sometimes be over-achievers, putting out extraordinary effort to impress people.

For the same reason, they are vulnerable to conflict and criticism. They often dislike and avoid competitions, preferring cooperation so that no one's feelings are hurt.

Cautions

I have to throw out a few cautions here as we talk about children's learning styles. First of all, think of a typical two-year-old child in terms of learning styles. Most two-year-olds fit into the Wiggly Willy category. They don't sit still very well. They are totally hands-on as they explore their new and expanding world. They aren't interested in deep thinking, long-range planning, or delayed gratification.

But they grow beyond their two-year-old world and, eventually, their true learning style becomes evident. This might happen at age five, eight, or ten. They might seem one learning style as they begin kindergarten then seem a very different style at age ten. So don't try to peg your preschooler's learning style. And don't think you've figured out your older child's learning style and expect it to remain forever the same.

Another caution. It's tempting to use learning styles as an excuse to ignore bad behavior or spiritual issues: "My son's a Wiggly Willy, and he just can't sit still." So you let him drive everyone crazy with his uncontrollable behavior.

Every learning style has both positive and negative character qualities. Wiggly Willys can be enthusiastic and fun-loving, but they struggle with self-discipline. Perfect Paulas can be very self-disciplined, but they might also be bossy or self-righteous. Competent Carls can be so self-sufficient that they lack charity or concern for others. Sociable Sues can be very concerned about people but absolutely hopeless when it comes to other areas of personal responsibility.

Recognizing these strengths and weaknesses in each of our children helps us identify our job as parents. We build on their strengths, but we also help them overcome their weaknesses.

Conflicting Learning Styles

Maybe you have already spotted the biggest problem with learning styles—the potential conflict between the learning styles of parents and children. For example, let's say you identify many of your own characteristics under "Competent Carl." You tend to be a very logical, analytical type person. You like independent work. And you've got little patience with drama queens. You might have an especially hard time with your Sociable Sue daughter who tries to use emotional manipulation to get out of doing what she doesn't want to do.

Or consider a very common situation in homeschooling, Perfect Paula mom and Wiggly Willy son. Mom has her lesson plans organized, her curriculum well-planned, and her daily schedule on the refrigerator for all to see. Wiggly Willy would much rather be outside doing practically anything other than school. He freaks out at the sight of the inch-thick math workbook, not to mention the pile of other books mom has purchased to make schooling easy for her to manage.

A far less common situation might be the reverse of our last scenario: Wiggly Willy mom and Perfect Paula daughter. Mom gets up in the morning and it's a beautiful day for a field trip. Besides, she has yet to get around to creating any lesson plans, so a field trip is a good excuse to put off planning for another day. Meanwhile, her daughter has compared notes with her age-mates and knows that she is way behind on math. And she worries that their real-book and field-trip approach to history might not help her know enough to get a high score on the standardized test she'll have to take at the end of the year. She would just love it if her mom would get some REAL school books and let her stay home and do school.

Most of us parents tend to think that the way we like to approach homeschooling will be equally appealing to our children. One of the most important lessons we can take from learning styles is that the opposite is more likely true. As parents, we need to stretch ourselves out of our own learning style comfort zones to try to meet our children's needs.

For parents without a single, strongly-dominant learning and teaching style, this will likely be easier. Such parents will more easily adapt to their children's needs than will the parent with a narrower range of personal learning styles.

Teaching to Their Strengths: Methods That Work Best for Different Learners

Meeting your children's needs in terms of learning styles does not mean that you have to construct your entire curriculum around these learning styles. Generally, your children will have stronger subjects and weaker subjects.

Perhaps your child is good at math and weak in language arts. If you are using a math program that doesn't really use methods best for that child's learning style, but he is still learning just fine because math comes easily for him, then don't worry about it. Stick with what you are using. But if language arts are a challenge, then you will want to look for resources and methods for composition, grammar, spelling, etc. that work best with his learning style.

Use learning styles as a tool to help you tune into your child's needs and to choose methods and materials that help in troublesome areas.

Let's look at methods that are most likely to work with different learning styles.

Wiggly Willy

Wiggly Willy is a kinesthetic learner. The more he can use his body and his senses to learn, the better. So hands-on learning works well. That might be math manipulatives, building projects, making 3-D maps, learning facts set to music, and anything else that involves both large and small-muscle movement plus as many senses as possible.

When you need to directly teach Willy, it is best if you can use a multi-sensory approach; the more he can hear, see, and touch what he's learning, the easier it will be for him to tune into and remember the lesson.

If you recall, Willy has a short attention span, so if you have something important to say to him, say it quickly. Don't use it as the final point in a five-minute lecture. He won't have heard you past the first minute unless you've done something interesting to re-engage him.

These children really need freedom to move around. Often they learn best when their bodies are moving. Some therapists have recommended that children with attention-deficit disorders do things like practice saying math facts while jumping on a trampoline. I know this isn't the way they do things in school, but it might be a very good idea to let Willy play with something in his hands while you are trying to present a grammar or history lesson.

Project learning can work well with Wiggly Willys, but you need to keep in mind that these children do not think about consequences so they need supervision. If they tackle a project, set up periodic checkpoints so you can ensure they are staying on task and making progress in the right direction.

Likewise, unit studies often are a good choice for Wiggly Willys. Many unit studies include a healthy mix of book learning (including real books) and activities that stimulate and hold his interest. Unit studies that offer a number of activity options are especially good since Willy probably will need more hands-on activities than the average learner.

If you do not want to get into a total unit study approach, you should still consider using real books rather than textbooks, especially for history and science, but also for other subjects. It can be like creating your own mini unit studies that stay within a subject area. For example, for science in the elementary grades, choose three or four topics to study during that school year. Find one or two good resource books on each topic as your sources of information—these will have far more information than a typical textbook, and will invariably be more interesting. Find ideas for hands-on activities, experiments, and field trips related to each topic. Then study those three or four topics in-depth instead of trying to cover ten to twenty topics superficially as do most textbooks. (Actually, this approach to science is good not just for Wiggly Willy, but for all types of learners.)

Willys are easily overwhelmed by what seems to them too much reading or pencil-and-paper work. A math book with one hundred practice problems on a page might look impossible. However, half that number of problems broken down into 25 per worksheet, supplemented with practice using manipulatives or a computer game, would be no problem at all, even if the total number of practice problems were higher.

Another example: an assignment for an older child to write a lengthy report should be broken down into manageable chunks due each day rather than one big project due in two months.

If math is a problem area, you should use manipulatives like Cuisenaire Rods or Base Ten Blocks to teach new concepts. You can purchase these as supplements to use alongside a more traditional math text or you can purchase a program that has manipulatives built in such as *Math-U-See* (reviewed in this book) or *Right Start Math* (www.rightstartmath.com).

Consider supplementing even these manipulative-based programs with math games (i.e., card games, board games, computer games), applications through building projects, cooking activities, etc.

For beginning readers, use a movable alphabet (rubber or magnetic letters children can arrange into words), phonics games, and interesting reading material.

For Willys who are generally reluctant writers, try first making a shape book or some other interesting art format for presentation of the writing project. Then have Willy write what goes into the book. Houghton Mifflin Publishing has a website with free shape book patterns at www.eduplace.com/rdg/hme/k_5/shapebook/toc.html. Lapbooks might be another way to accomplish this within some subject areas. (Learn about lapbooks at www.lapbooking.wordpress.com/.)

With Wiggly Willys you should probably reduce your use of traditional texts and workbooks, and try to find resources that are stimulating and interesting.

Wiggly Willys pose special challenges, but the trick is for parents to pay attention to what does and doesn't work, no matter how unusual it might seem. In summary:

Wiggly Willy Prefers:
- hands-on activity
- multi-sensory audio-visual aids
- short, dynamic presentations
- freedom to move around
- whole-body physical involvement
- project learning
- texts or workbooks that are not overwhelming
- learning games
- variety in learning methods

Prefect Paula

Many parents wish all their children were Perfect Paulas when it comes to homeschooling because they actually care about doing what's expected and pleasing you. Perfect Paula tends to work well with typical school curricula. She likes the security and predictability of knowing what's expected and how it is to be done each day. She can usually work well independently as long as instructions are clear.

However, recall that Paula has a narrow comfort zone. She's most comfortable with review, repetition, and drill because she's already familiar with most of the answers. New concepts can be challenging. So work closely with her when introducing new concepts. Give her lots of encouragement at this stage.

Paula would rather receive information than think creatively. She's not likely to do as well in a Socratic discussion (classical education method) as most other learners. If you are planning such a discussion or other activity that will take Paula out of her comfort zone, give her plenty of advance notice, reassurance, and as much encouragement as possible.

She's not likely to be enthusiastic about creative writing, dramatizations or other self-expressive learning activities. You should not eliminate these from her experience but introduce them gently, a little at a time. Unit studies might be a good tool for stretching Paula since most of them offer a variety of activities that might be used in this way.

One of the biggest problems for Paula is that she might do well memorizing and repeating information (typical for early elementary grades) but struggle when it comes time to start making connections, analyzing and synthesizing information.

For example, A Beka's math program might be working fine up through third or fourth grade. Paula loves the continual practice, clear presentation of the rules for each process, and she does well on timed drills. But by fourth or fifth grade, she might be struggling because A Beka has not explained concepts—why math processes work the way they do. She memorizes her math facts very well and knows how to do multi-digit multiplication and division, but two-step word problems throw her for a loop. You might want to use math manipulatives or supplemental books alongside A Beka that present math "brain teasers" to push her to deeper levels of thinking so she develops conceptual understanding. Or you might want to choose a program that incorporates more work with math concepts like *Math Mammoth or* Singapore's *Primary Mathematics*.

Paula probably will not need as much hands-on work as Wiggly Willy, so a manipulative-based program is generally not essential although it might be helpful.

Perfect Paula is likely to be weak in creative writing skills so you should look carefully at some of my Top Picks for developing composition skills.

Since the structure of most traditional curricula fits Perfect Paula's learning style fairly well, you should probably look for supplements to help with difficult areas and to stretch her beyond her comfort zone. In summary:

Perfect Paula Prefers:
- workbooks
- consistent structure in both schedule and curriculum
- rules and predictability
- lectures or lessons that follow an outline
- repetition and memorization
- drill and review
- time to prepare for any discussion
- gentle help to develop creativity and deeper thinking skills

Competent Carl

If you recall from looking at adult learning styles, control is a big issue for Competent Carl. He has lots of ideas of his own and little patience for listening to others. So discussions are okay only if he gets to do a lot of talking. He'll tune out of an hour-long lecture—or even a fifteen-minute lecture! Unlike Perfect Paula, however, he might love Socratic discussions if questions are meaningful and such discussions are productive.

Many Competent Carls like to think out loud or brainstorm. For example, you might find that he writes better when you first take plenty of time to talk through possible organizational strategies or ways to tackle writing assignments rather than leaving him on his own to figure it out.

Because of his logical mind, he prefers curriculum that is well-organized and purposeful rather than entertaining with lots of extra activity involved. He wants to know in advance what he is doing and why. Structured, traditional curriculum can work well for Carl as long as it doesn't have too much busy work built into it.

Carl has plenty of his own ideas to explore, so long-term independent projects can work well for him. One approach that can work well is to present the learning objective and offer two or three possible ways for Carl to achieve it. Let him choose, then write up a learning contract that details what assignments will be completed and when they will be turned in.

Competent Carls are more likely than other learners to challenge you with, "Why do I need to learn this?" It's probably wise to take time to explain why to him since it will improve his motivation if he understands the purpose for each task.

He's also likely to challenge you about repetition, practice and busy work. Sometimes Carl doesn't like to do review and practice once he's already covered something, even though he really needs the practice for proficiency. However, sometimes he is correct, so you should choose curriculum with a minimal amount of busy work and review OR have him skip such material when it is unnecessary.

For instance, once Carl knows how to read fairly well, let him read books selected from your "approved" list rather than reading anthologies (textbooks). You can use novel study guides (such as those from Total Language Plus and Progeny Press) or carefully selected supplemental activity books or workbooks if you want to work on comprehension, vocabulary and other analytical skills. He will be more engaged in the process if he is able to select what he wants to read and if he isn't bogged down with what he might consider redundant exercises in a reading text or workbook. You can focus on particular skills he needs to develop rather than that wide range of skills covered in a text.

While Competent Carls generally prefer independent work, you will probably want to involve them in some group learning situations simply to help them develop social skills. For example, you might do a family unit study where everyone is together for foundational reading or discussion. Carl would then pursue the same topic as your other children by doing more independent research, reading, and writing while you continue with group activities with the rest of your children. You might also have Carl participate in a Friday afternoon art activity with the whole family.

Probably the most important thing to keep in mind with Carl is that he wants his learning to be efficient. Don't bog him down with manipulatives and hands-on activities if they aren't helpful. They can do more harm than good. In summary:

Competent Carl Prefers:
- independent work
- logically organized lessons
- clear sense of purpose for lessons
- long-term projects
- talking rather than listening
- problem solving
- brainstorming

Sociable Sue

Sociable Sue is a perfect candidate for unit studies such as *TRISMS*, *Tapestry of Grace*, and *Five in a Row*—all reviewed in chapter thirteen. She will thrive on group projects and interactive learning. Read-aloud sessions will also be appealing to her, so using real books rather than textbooks might be a good choice.

Sue picks up on social dynamics better than other learners. She's sensitive to your attitude toward subjects, so you had better choose curriculum that you can be enthusiastic about. If she senses that you don't like the curriculum, she probably won't like it either. You will also notice a dynamic that makes things even more complicated—if her friends like or use a particular resource, she's likely to be have a positive attitude about it solely for that reason. This can play havoc when you try to purchase resources since you're not likely to know ahead of time what her friends are going to be enthusiastic about.

Because approval from others matters so much to Sue, she generally likes "public presentations" such as reading her writing assignment aloud, dramatic reading of a poem or speech, performances (e.g., music recitals), or sharing her artwork.

Creative activities usually are more appealing than repetitious review and drill. Sue gets bored with the same learning format. She thrives on variety. Choosing a resource that alters the lesson format from time to time is a good idea. Otherwise, you will need to supplement or adapt what you're using to keep her motivated. Often, hands-on resources you might choose for Wiggly Willy work well for Sue because they require social interaction.

One of the worst things you can do with Sociable Sue is to purchase a workbook-based program that is designed for independent study and expect her to spend three hours a day working in isolation through her books. She can work like this for short periods, but not all day. If you have to use independent workbooks, alternate sociable or interactive learning activities with the workbooks to keep her going.

Sue will also need help learning how to persevere even when learning isn't sociable and fun. She has to develop the self-discipline to follow through on assignments even when it gets boring. In summary:

Sociable Sue Prefers:
- real books
- unit studies
- discussions
- social interaction
- enthusiastic teaching
- variety in types of resources
- creative writing
- public presentations
- novelty and creativity in curriculum presentation
- situations where she is personally recognized and valued
- (needs but does not necessarily enjoy) repetition for detail and help with self-discipline

Keep In Mind Learning Modalities

As I mentioned earlier, your children might also have a strong learning modality—visual, auditory, or kinesthetic. They might learn best by seeing, hearing, or hands-on experiences. For example, a Sociable Sue who is kinesthetic will prefer more project-oriented learning while an auditory Sociable Sue will prefer more sedentary, read-aloud activity. Coupling what you discover about both learning styles and learning modalities gives you a great deal of information that you can use to make better curriculum choices for each child.

Teach to Their Strengths

You can see that teaching methods appropriate for one type of learner might be ineffective for another type. This does not mean that you teach each type of learner only with methods that suit his personality and temperament. For some children, it would be all fun and games, and they would learn no self-discipline.

Instead, you use methods that work best for each child when introducing new or difficult subject matter. Once they have grasped a concept, use other more-challenging methods when they are less likely to be stressful or produce failure.

You can help strengthen students' weak areas such as short attention span or lack of creativity by working on these problem areas within subjects that are especially interesting to your child or subjects in which they excel. For example, many Wiggly Willys do not like writing assignments, but reading an exciting historical adventure or biography aloud, then asking them to draw a picture about the story and write a few descriptive sentences will develop writing skills in a more enjoyable way than most workbook activity.

After initial instruction, you should review and reinforce learning through methods that will help each child stretch himself and strengthen his weak areas. For example, a very active Wiggly Willy can learn math by using objects, without paper and pencil. Once he has mastered a concept, he can get out the paper and pencil to do review and practice.

To sum it up, with both younger and older children you should teach new concepts through a child's strongest learning style then review and practice using other learning style methods that are not as comfortable.

It helps if you recognize those subjects that are easier and those that are more difficult for each child. While there are some typically strong subjects within each learning style, there are many, many exceptions. Wiggly Willys usually prefer physically-active subjects such as music, the arts, and athletics. Perfect Paulas like more structured and predictable subjects like math, spelling, history, and geography. Competent Carls often excel in math and science, exhibiting less interest in the humanities. Sociable Sues will often prefer whatever subjects are presented with the most enthusiasm and interaction, but their strong areas tend to be writing and literature, languages, social studies, and performing arts. These are very general observations that may or may not apply to your child.

You must observe which subjects consistently are handled with ease and which cause frustration. Then, for the frustrating subjects, consider using other teaching methods that better fit your child's learning style. Avoid using the difficult learning methods with a child until he understands the basic concept and has reached a review or application stage.

Matching Learning Styles To Curricula

When I put together the charts of my 101 Top Picks (in chapter six), I did not include columns headed only Wiggly Willy, etc. This is because there are rarely direct matches between resources and learning styles. Instead, there are columns for primary characteristics of curriculum that tends to suit each of the four learning styles: "Multi-sensory/hands-on (WW)," "Structure/rule-oriented (PP)," "Appeals to logical/analytical learners (CC)," and "Has social activity/interaction (SS)."

But you also need to look at other columns that might be equally important such as whether or not it works for independent study, how easy it is for the teacher to use, how much writing is required, or what methodology it reflects. Only you can decide which characteristics of a particular curriculum are most important.

Sometimes your teaching style and your child's learning style are drastically different. Suppose your child really needs a unit study approach with lots of creative activity. But your Perfect Paula style makes you shudder at the thought of trying to gather all the stuff you need plus having to choose among activities. What if you choose the wrong ones? And then how will you know if your children did enough or too much?

There are what I call "compromise solutions" for such situations. For example, KONOS publishes *KONOS In-A-Box*, a unit study that includes step-by-step instructions plus all the books and materials (even craft materials) you need. Cornerstone Curriculum publishes *Making Math Meaningful,* a math program that includes manipulatives but has scripted lessons that tell parents exactly what to say and do. While *Making Math Meaningful* did not make it into the ranks of my Top Picks, it works well in such situations. (If you need to look beyond the Top Picks, check out the many hundreds of reviews at my website: www.CathyDuffyReviews.com.)

So keep in mind that while you are looking for resources that suit your children's learning styles, you must also choose resources with which you can work.

Motivation

Motivation is often a two-part process. If you want a child to do well in math, then you motivate him first by providing a program that fits his learning style and makes it easier for him to grasp concepts. If you can make learning more enjoyable for children (not that it always will be!), you solve part of the motivation problem. By using creative approaches and relating learning to the interests of your children, you make learning more of a partnership than a struggle.

You also might try to improve motivation by using rewards or incentives. Just as different style learners are likely to be successful with different learning methods, they are also likely to respond to different types of rewards or incentives.

Wiggly Willy might respond well to prizes, special trips, play time, or food—the more immediate the reward, the more effective. Perfect Paula can be motivated with stickers, good grades, and other concrete affirmations as well as with personal praise. Competent Carl, who enjoys being independent, can be motivated by self-designed contracts, or rewards of free time or money. Sociable Sue—interested in people and relationships—is more likely to be motivated by personal affirmation (praise) and recognition or an opportunity to do something special with a friend.

Experiment with different types of motivation to figure out what works best with each of your children. Don't be afraid to use different incentives with each of your children.

Disguised Learning Disabilities

A word of caution is needed here. Sometimes you can mistake the characteristics or evidence of a learning disability for a learning style. If you have tried everything—paid attention to learning styles and methods and retaught five different ways—and your child still "doesn't get it," he or she might have a learning disability. Sometimes a child will appear to be a Wiggly Willy because a learning disability interferes with reading, writing, or thinking processes. If the work is too difficult, your child might act bored, restless, or inattentive to avoid dealing with the "impossible" task. Active learning that requires less paper and pencil work or reading will appear successful, but it is only masking the real problem. You will see this when you have already taught a concept and they seem to have grasped it. Picture teaching multiplication with manipulative blocks—when you transition from the blocks to writing down what they have done, they are unable to make the shift.

If you suspect that your child has a learning disability, you should seek professional assistance. Generally, your local homeschool support group can recommend a professional in your area who can help you determine what is going on.

Fine Tuning

The goal here is not labeling your child but becoming aware that each child will have strengths and weaknesses in the ways he or she learns. You have to recognize your own tendency to teach the way you like to learn rather than the way your children learn best. Then you need to look for resources and methods that best meet the needs of your child, while still being practical for you to use.

When you combine your philosophy of education and ideas about approaches you would like to use with what you have discovered about learning styles, you can fine tune your curriculum choices.

For example, I ended chapter three noting that unit study, Charlotte Mason, and classical education ideas should be part of the curriculum for my sons. When I add learning styles to the mix, I know that my Wiggly Willy eldest son still needs some projects and hands-on learning mixed in with the worldview and unit study type education I would like to pursue. I would still like to shift toward classical education, so when I look at the Top Picks Charts in chapter six, I find that *Tapestry of Grace* looks like it fits the situation quite well.

In addition, since math is my eldest son's most challenging subject, I need to be particularly careful about his math program to find one that still has manipulatives at junior high level. In chapter six, I look for math programs with a "4" or "5" in the first column for multi-sensory/hands-on, then go to the actual reviews in chapter eight to find those that carry on with manipulatives up into junior high and beyond. *Math-U-See* looks like a good option since it has manipulatives and continues with them up even into high school.

Now there's one more thing to take into consideration: what will you actually teach your children this year? The next chapter will help you figure that out.

CHAPTER
··•● 5 ●•··

Who should learn what and when?

Most home educators worry about whether or not their children are keeping up with what "other schools" are teaching. This sort of concern can be a helpful prod to keep us focused and making progress. However, it can also be a distraction or even a diversion from what we really need to be teaching each of our children.

On both state and national levels, there has been a push to develop common standards for each subject area that describe what all government school students should be learning. As those standards have been developed, textbooks have been rewritten to reflect them. While there are minor variations from state to state, standards are actually similar enough across the country that a handful of textbook publishers produce books that can be used in just about every state. Standards are so similar that the push is on to develop what are called Common Core State Standards for the entire country. Thus far, these have been developed for math and language arts. Here are a few examples from the Common Core State Standards so you can see what I am talking about:

From kindergarten English language arts standards:
RF.K.1. Demonstrate understanding of the organization and basic features of print.
Follow words from left to right, top to bottom, and page by page.
Recognize that spoken words are represented in written language by specific sequences of letters.
Understand that words are separated by spaces in print.
Recognize and name all upper- and lowercase letters of the alphabet.[1]

From fourth grade mathematics standards:
4.OA.4. Find all factor pairs for a whole number in the range 1–100. Recognize that a whole number is a multiple of each of its factors. Determine whether a given whole number in the

range 1–100 is a multiple of a given one-digit number. Determine whether a given whole number in the range 1–100 is prime or composite.[2]

You need to consult state standards for the other subjects. For example, here are some California state standards:

From fifth grade science standards:
"Students know that each element is made of one kind of atom and that the elements are organized in the periodic table by their chemical properties."[3]

From eighth grade history-social science standards:
8.9.3 Describe the significance of the Northwest Ordinance in education and in the banning of slavery in new states north of the Ohio River.
8.9.4 Discuss the importance of the slavery issue as raised by the annexation of Texas and California's admission to the union as a free state under the Compromise of 1850.
8.9.5 Analyze the significance of the States' Rights Doctrine, the Missouri Compromise (1820), the Wilmot Proviso (1846), the Compromise of 1850, Henry Clay's role in the Missouri Compromise and the Compromise of 1850, the Kansas-Nebraska Act (1854), the Dred Scott v. Sandford decision (1857), and the Lincoln-Douglas debates (1858).[4]

Because these standards are so detailed, the compilation of standards for each state could fill an entire book per state! So I cannot include the standards themselves within this chapter. Instead, here are websites where you can access standards for yourself:

• www.corestandards.org - This is the Common Core State Standards Initiative web site where you can find the newest national standards for math and language arts.
• www.cde.ca.gov/be/st/ss/index.asp - This is the site for "Content Standards for California Public Schools, Kindergarten through Grade Twelve." California, being one of the largest states, has some of the most well-developed and widely accepted standards.
• www.doe.virginia.gov/testing/index.shtml - Like California, Virginia has also been a leader in developing standards. This is their site where you can view the "Testing & Standards of Learning (SOL)."

You can easily search for any state standards on the internet by entering the state name and "educational standards."
It is important that you notice how detailed and prescriptive some of these standards are. In years past, schools had much more freedom to teach what they deemed most useful within the general subject areas. A class with many ESL students would spend more time on language fundamentals and oral language before tackling more sophisticated grammar and composition skills. The more general directives left much to individual schools and teachers to determine as far as teaching each classroom of children. Interestingly, the Common Core Standards use more general language than do some other standards documents. Nevertheless, state and national standards leave little room for schools or teachers to determine what to teach because coverage of so many specific topics is required.
Schools are held accountable for teaching to the standards by high-stakes standardized tests,

and this is the type of testing required under recent educational reforms. These tests ask questions based upon the content of the standards. Such tests have big consequences for students as well as for schools and teachers. Student advancement to the next grade level, summer school attendance, or even high school graduation might be based upon tests called exit exams. (They might well become gatekeepers for colleges in the future, too.) High-stakes tests might also determine whether schools (and teachers) gain or lose funding, whether principles and teachers lose their jobs, whether schools get taken over by the state, and even whether students might be given vouchers to attend private schools.

A side effect of the standards movement has been that private and homeschools have often adopted those same standards by default rather than on purpose. You might have noticed in advertisements for curricula and resources marketed to homeschoolers, that many mention that they "meet or exceed" national standards. Publishers of these resources have taken into consideration the large government school market and made sure that they are creating resources that can be sold to those within government school systems. And that means many homeschoolers end up teaching the same things as do government schools simply because that is what is in textbooks or other resources.

A Contrarian View

Most parents rarely question what their children are learning in school unless it has to do with sex or drug education. They assume that whatever the school has decided to teach must be what children need to learn. This might or might not be true.

There are two underlying assumptions within the standardized approach that need to be challenged: the uniformity of children and the authority of government to dictate education.

As to the uniformity of children, anyone who has spent any time at all around children knows that they are as different as pistachio ice cream and pepperoni pizza. The notion that they should be learning the same things as all other children who happen to be their age is silly when you think about it.

Children develop on their own personal timetables. Some are ready to read at age four and others at age six or seven. Some can easily learn their multiplication tables at age seven and others at age nine. As I discuss in chapter four on learning styles, some children can read something in a book and learn it just fine while others need to touch, handle, or manipulate things to get information into their brains.

The notion that you can put thirty children of the same age in a classroom and expect that all will learn at approximately the same rate and through the limited ways information is presented might work if children were machines to be programmed. But children are so much more complex than this.

As a Christian, I believe that God created each one as an individual with particular gifts, abilities, and interests. He has a unique plan for each one. God's creativity gradually becomes visible within each child as he or she matures, an unfolding delight that we can either appreciate or deny. We appreciate it by recognizing and working with each individual child, or we deny it by trying to force children to adapt to others' ideas about how they should grow and learn.

In light of the individuality of each child, parents should view their state's educational standards or the Common Core Standards with skepticism rather than accept them as a foundational directive for homeschooling.

The second problem with standards challenges the right of government to dictate what a child should learn. In addition to the problem of children's individuality, there's a problem regarding the purpose of education and, consequently, its content.

Government management of schools springs from a societal concern that everyone be educated as well as the government's desire to maintain peace and order—a sort of conformity—within society. It has nothing to do with religious beliefs and personal development except as it affects larger "societal" goals. At the present time, societal goals are primarily economic.

The mantra of much of the national education reform legislation over the past three decades has been "educating for the high-skill, high-wage jobs of the 21st century." Translation: children need to learn knowledge and skills that others have predetermined are necessary to prepare them for the workforce.

We see this very clearly in our present educational system at the high school level. Education is becoming primarily about vocational training rather than development of a human being with a body, mind, and soul. Part of that training might require learning enough to get into college, so they can get a degree, so they can get a job—simply a more complex form of vocational training.

While young people should be prepared to get a job when they get out of school, many parents believe that education is as much or more about personal development, learning to think, developing integrity, and spiritual development. After all, what profits a man if he has all the job skills in the world but he is a spiritual and cultural barbarian? And isn't this what we see with corporate executives who think nothing of using their "job skills" to siphon off money illegally and use their language arts skills to lie and convince others that they were just doing their jobs?

A Higher Goal for Education

Personally, I think one of the most important components of homeschooling is worldview education. This is where we address the most important life questions: Is there a God? Who is man in relation to God? What is the purpose of our life on earth? Is there life after death?

The way we answer these questions reveals our foundational philosophic and religious beliefs. Our worldview determines how we think about life as well as how we live.

Everyone operates by one worldview or another. The default worldview of our modern society is a materialistic humanist worldview. (Some might call it secular humanist.) It teaches that man is an accidental product of evolution. There is nothing more to him than his physical existence. God doesn't exist and there's nothing after death. It shouldn't be surprising if people with this worldview believe that each person should try to get the most he can from this life because this is all there is.

A Christian worldview colors everything with the belief in God's existence. Because God is real, we believe He has revealed truth to us. Part of that revelation is the reality of life after death, the fact that we have a soul, and the fact that Jesus Christ died for us so that we can have eternal life with God. This understanding means there's much more to life than the present physical reality. There is a larger purpose and meaning to almost everything. Our lives are not to be lived as if we are accidental entities. Instead, God calls us to live life "on purpose," trying our best to live out the purpose God has called us to.

These conflicting worldviews produce some conflicting educational goals. Certainly, they would share some common goals such as acquiring reading, writing, and computation skills. However, we are likely to differ in some choices of other subjects to be taught, what is to be taught each year, the amount of time and attention we spend on each subject, and details within subject areas.

For example:

- Religion or Bible study might be a major subject in your curriculum even though it is not on any standards list and no standardized test asks any religion questions. It might be important enough to you that this is the first subject covered every day of the week.
- You might be a musically-inclined family, so music education is a much higher priority for you than for most other families.
- If you are following a classical education model, you might teach your children Greek and Latin in the elementary grades as a foundation for study of primary sources in high school.
- That same preference for a classical education might mean that your high school students study philosophy, logic, and rhetoric in place of or in addition to physics or calculus.

Even if you choose to teach the same subjects taught by most schools, you might still have different ideas about what should be taught within each subject. One of the thorniest issues is evolution and creation. One of the California standards for high school biology/life sciences reads: "Evolution is the result of genetic changes that occur in constantly changing environments. As a basis for understanding this concept: a. *Students know* how natural selection determines the differential survival of groups of organisms." [emphasis in the original][5]

This science standard requires students to parrot the evolutionary teaching that different species came about by natural selection. Since evidence for evolutionary theory is shaky at best, requiring children to learn and believe this is very much a part of a worldview that denies the existence of God. The implied logic is that if man came into existence as an accident through the process of evolution, then God did not make man, and the whole story of Genesis and the Fall of man is nothing more than folklore. Logically, there is then no need for a savior as a consequence of a Fall that never happened.

Other worldview problems crop up in textbooks reflecting state goals. For example, multicultural goals translate into stories about pagan gods and goddesses who are every bit as credible as the Christian God. Students are taught they can make no value judgments regarding religion and morality because these are simply expressions of personal or cultural belief rather than reflections of any one reality or Truth that exists for everyone. Along the same line, literature is analyzed for whatever personal meaning a student might draw from it rather than to grasp an author's message or any transcendent meaning.

While purporting to be non-religious, government schools actually have an agenda that turns out to be anti-religious. Students learn what schools claim to be the essentials of education, and God is no part of any of it. This teaches them that God is irrelevant. They learn that all gods are created equal and that it is intolerant to expect others to accept your beliefs about God and His commands about how we should live. A parent who asks that her child not learn witchcraft spells in school is charged with narrow-mindedness. A parent who does not want her child to learn "safe" ways to fornicate is called "unrealistic."

I realize that much of this happens within government schools themselves and is not required by the standards, but the standards reflect the worldview that teaches and encourages the above (and even worse) classroom practices.

Beyond that, the time required to teach to those government-selected standards steals time that you might devote to other goals that are more important to you.

The point of all this is that homeschooling parents should use Common Core or state standards as well as the resources built around them with caution. Parents need to have goals for their children's education, but these should not simply be copied from government schools.

Choosing Your Own Goals

The IDEAL way to come up with your goals is to start from scratch and figure out what you think is important for each child to learn, then write it all out. The more REALISTIC way to do this is to start by looking at one or more lists of standards, then work from those to come up with your own goals.

With standards readily available on the internet, you can choose those you think appropriate in each subject area. You might look across a range of grade levels to find standards that are appropriate. Then you can change ones that you think need rewriting before adding any additional goals of your own.

For example, I might agree with most of the California goals or standards for third grade mathematics, but I do not agree that children at this age need to be learning probability and graphing. If my children have to take a standardized test, this is an item they are likely to be tested upon. So I then have to decide whether a higher test score or sticking to my conviction is more important. Since I live in a state that does not require standardized testing, I would opt to drop probability and graphing from my goals for third grade. I also believe it important that children develop a Christian understanding of math from the earliest years, so I would add a goal that my child understand that mathematics reflects God's order and consistency. (I might illustrate this concept for my child by trying to get him to come up with another sum than four when I add two items plus two items. The impossibility helps him understand that the consistency of math reflects the nature of God.) So, essentially, I copy the third grade standards and make them my own with these deletions and additions.

My situation might be a bit more complicated if my "third grader" already has mastered about one quarter of the standards or goals listed for third grade. Then I look to the fourth grade list to see which goals might be better drawn from that level.

I do this for each subject as much as is practical. When it comes to history and science, I generally find my goals are so different from the state goals that I work from scratch. Further on in this chapter, I will share some ideas about studying those subjects.

Obviously, there are no goals or standards already written for religion or study of the Bible, so you're on your own there. However, once you've worked through the other subjects, you should understand how you might do this for religion or Bible study if you choose that as a subject for your curriculum. Likewise, you will not find goals for a Latin or other foreign language class for the elementary grades, and you will have to come up with your own standards or goals.

Now some of you might be considering unit studies or a real books approach at this point and are wondering how you can match up your goals or standards with these approaches. Actually, it works well as long as you understand that all of the objectives or standards covered in a year-long unit study or real books program are unlikely to be found in a single grade level list of standards.

Unit studies and real books programs usually assume that children will be at many different grade levels. Some programs try to categorize learning activities by groups of grade levels (e.g., K-2, 3-6, 7-8, 9-12). Some are written for only grades four through eight or some other limited audience. Still others leave it to you to sort through all of the activity choices on your own to identify grade levels. You might find that the study you undertake this year and the activities you choose reflect goals from second, third, fourth, and fifth grade levels. You will not be covering all the "normal" goals for any one of those levels in a single year, but over the course of three or four years you will have done so. Consequently, unit studies require you to have a more long-range view of your goals.

In reality, if you stick with a comprehensive unit study program such as *Tapestry of Grace* or *Connecting With History*, or a real books program like My Father's World or Sonlight, the authors have thought this through so that the necessary material is covered over a span of years. Many unit studies and real books programs will also tell you what subject areas they do and do not cover so you will know what other resources you might need to purchase. More traditional curricula have their own sets of goals, and you might do well to simply adopt those goals, perhaps adding or subtracting only a few.

What Do I Do With My Goals Now?

Writing down your goals is next. You can use the reproducible chart at the end of this chapter or you can work from other lists of goals that might come from a list of standards, from a publisher, or from another resource. If you start with someone else's list, I suggest you add three columns to the right as is done on my reproducible chart. For example, in the sample below, I've adopted some goals from California's Common Core State Standards for Mathematics for second grade math[6], made slight changes, then added the columns to the right.

Sample Chart: Writing Out Your Own Goals

School Year: 2012-13   Student Name: Brandon Smith

Goals for Math	Introduction	Review/ Practice	Mastery
1. Use addition and subtraction within 100 to solve one- and two-step word problems involving situations of adding to, taking from, putting together, taking apart, and comparing, with unknowns in all positions.			
2. Fluently add and subtract within 20 using mental strategies. By end of Grade 2, know from memory all sums of two one-digit numbers.			
3. Determine whether a group of objects (up to 20) has an odd or even number of members...; write an equation to express an even number as a sum of two equal addends.			
4. Use addition to find the total number of objects arranged in rectangular arrays with up to 5 rows and up to 5 columns; write an equation to express the total as a sum of equal addends.			

	Introduction	Review/Practice	Mastery
5. Use repeated addition and counting by multiples to demonstrate multiplication.			
6. Use repeated subtraction and equal group sharing to demonstrate division.			

The three additional columns are labeled "Introduction," "Review/Practice," and "Mastery." The reason for these columns is that teaching a child about a concept one time rarely means he or she has learned it. Generally, you'll need to review and/or practice the material until they know it. By setting up the three columns, you will remind yourself to go back over these goals to make sure you work toward actual mastery rather than simple, short-term retention.

These standards or goals can now help you in three ways:
• figuring out what to teach
• checking progress through the school year
• assessing year-end accomplishments

Note that many resources state their goals clearly and have forms or charts for tracking progress that will work just as well.

Figuring Out What to Teach

Sometimes when we start homeschooling, we have no idea where to begin. It really is helpful to have a list of standards or goals at least as a reference point to know what others might be doing. Assuming you are familiar with what your child already knows (through observation, your own experience, testing, or an evaluation by someone else), you can look at these lists and determine at what grade level your child seems to be functioning. My hope is that you will consider your goals BEFORE selecting your resources so that you choose those that are accomplishing what is most necessary for your child each year.

You should set goals that are challenging but not frustrating. If there are goals listed at a lower grade level that your child hasn't yet mastered, you need to consider whether to make them a priority, put them off until later, or skip them altogether. If you choose to add them, write them down on the list with your other goals.

Your lists of goals might also help you figure out what comes next. For example, if your child has mastered construction of basic sentences, your list of goals will remind you that writing a paragraph might be the next skill to tackle. Or if you are using a real books curriculum, you can check your list of goals to ensure that the appropriate skills or concepts are being taught as you progress. For many, the curriculum you choose will set the sequence for teaching, but your list of goals might remind you of additional goals that need attention.

Checking Your Progress

Are you pushing your children too hard? Are you too lax in getting things accomplished?

Your list of goals can help answer this sort of question. As often as you need to you should refer back to these lists of goals for each subject. How many have been introduced, reviewed and practiced, and mastered? Are you making reasonable progress on checking them off? If you've checked them all off by the end of the first quarter you might be pushing your children too hard. If by the end of that same first quarter, you have checked off fewer than a third of the introduction boxes and nothing beyond that, you might need to get more focused on reinforcing your initial lessons. If you reach the end of the third quarter and half of your goals remain untouched, you need to do some serious evaluation of how you are operating—too many field trips and park days? Lack of self-discipline on the part of parents, children, or both? Overly ambitious goals? Don't panic. You still have time to make mid-course corrections.

Assessing Year-End Accomplishments

At the end of the year, instead of judging your accomplishments by completed (or incomplete) textbooks, judge by how many of your goals have reached mastery level. If you find that you have fallen far short, don't despair. If you've gone way beyond your goals, don't plan to take a year off.

Instead, spend some time evaluating. Did you set reasonable goals? Did you set too many goals? Did you include some that could have been skipped? Did you underestimate your child's ability? Did the curriculum you selected work well in helping you meet your goals? Did your child go through a period of emotional turmoil causing some of your goals to be put on temporary hold? Did you move, have a baby, experience a death in the family or some other event that accounted for lost school time? Do you have too many books for your children to get through, some of which contain material that is purposeless busywork?

If you haven't a clue why you are having trouble, it might help to find a veteran homeschooler or someone else with some educational experience who will look over what you are doing and give you some advice. Sometimes enrollment in a program to get professional advice is a wise investment.

After this, consider what you might do about what you have learned from your evaluation. Should you plan to do summer school? Should you consider following a different type school schedule, i.e., shifting from nine months on/three months off to year-round schooling with periodic week-long breaks? Do you need to get more organized or work out a different type schedule? Is your child having such difficulty accomplishing things that you ought to get him or her tested for learning disabilities? Are you all so unhappy with the way you are doing things that neither you nor your children are motivated to get things done? Do you need to rearrange things so that a particular child gets more one-on-one attention? Perhaps a different curriculum might help the situation.

I know you will be able to add more questions to these lists, but I think you get the idea. Your goals should be your touchstone to help you get focused, stay focused, and accomplish what needs to be done.

Of course, you never want to become a slave to those goals to the point where you ignore the needs of your children. Even the best of plans needs to be modified from time to time. You might even find yourself adjusting your goals on a quarterly basis rather than waiting till the end of the year. That's great! It means you've taken control of what is going on and are really tuning in to your children's needs.

As you gain experience, generally you will feel freer to create your own goals and worry less about what everyone else is doing.

School Year: _____   Student Name: _____

Goals for _____	Introduction	Review/ Practice	Mastery

Top 101 Picks

By this point you should have some insight into what philosophy of education appeals to you. You know what teaching style is most comfortable for you as well as which learning styles work best for each of your children. And you should have a fairly good idea of what subject matter and skills you actually need to teach this year.

That's a lot of information, but it doesn't do you much good unless you can match up what you've learned with the many curriculum options available to you. That's the purpose of the charts in this chapter. The charts help you easily identify key features or characteristics of resources.

The following descriptions of the meaning of each column will help you understand the information in the charts. I have generally used a scale of "1" to "5" with "5" representing the highest correlation with the feature listed in that column. A "1" usually means that it has little or none of this feature.

I'll explain the chart headings as well as other "codes" that I use below.

Column Headings

- **Multi-sensory/hands-on (WW)** - A "5" in this column means this is a particularly good choice for the kinesthetic learner, the one who needs movement and multi-sensory activity. This resource fits Wiggly Willys best, but Sociable Sues often benefit from similar curriculum since it usually involves some sort of personal interaction.
- **Structure/rule-oriented (PP)** - This is likely a more traditionally-structured resource that has a consistent format and/or a rules and memorization approach. Perfect Paulas generally prefer this sort of resource because it's predictable.
- **Appeals to logical/analytical learners (CC)** - Resources with a "4" or "5" in this column

require higher-level thinking and analysis and particulary appeal to Competent Carls.

• **Has social activity/interaction (SS)** - items with a "4" or "5" in this column require an interactive setting. Sociable Sues prefer learning in such social settings rather than independently. The interactive setting might be as minimal as a parent working directly with one child.

• **Needs parent/teacher instruction** - A "4" or "5" means you will need to read, explain, or otherwise present information to your child. It might be only a short introduction after which a child can work independently, in which case it has a mid-range number of "2" or "3." If you are short on time, don't choose many resources with a high number in this column.

• **Independent study (ind), one-on-one (1 on 1), or group (g)** - This very important column helps you plan your time as well as select resources that are best for each child. Some resources are specifically designed for one type of setting while others can be used in a number of ways. Abbreviations for each setting that should work for a resource are included. An independent study resource allows the student to do most or all of his work on his own. One-on-one means a parent works directly with a child as he or she progresses through the lesson. Group means the resource works well in a setting with two or more students. Most resources will still have independent assignments or other work to be done in addition to a required group or one-on-one presentation.

• **Amount of writing** - If you have a child who is resistant to writing, you probably want to teach new concepts with resources that do not rely on a great deal of writing. On the other hand, if you are teaching a child at a stage where he or she needs to practice writing skills, you might purposely choose a resource that requires more writing. Generally, you'll want no more than one or two resources that require a good deal of writing. A "5" indicates the resource requires a great deal of writing while a "1" means little to none. A "U" means it's "up to you"—that the parent has a great deal of discretion to decide how much writing to require.

• **Prep time** - This one is fairly obvious. It will give you some idea about how much time you will need to spend preparing lessons or learning to teach the program. "5" means it will take a great deal of time, "4" less time, and so on.

• **Grade level specific (s) or multi-level (m)** - If you want to teach children at more than one grade level using the same resource, ungraded resources obviously work better because they will generally address the needs of a span of grade levels such as grades 1-5 or maybe even 1-12. An "m" indicates one of these multi-level resources. You might also want to use an ungraded resource for a third grade child who is working below grade level in reading and who will be discouraged by a textbook that advertises that fact with a "grade 2" designation. An "s" indicates resources designed to be used only for single grade levels. Some resources, marked "s/m" might be used either way or might differ by grade level.

• **Ease of use for teacher** - A resource might be great once you can figure out how to use it, but getting past that hurdle might be impossible for one reason or another. Most resources are not that difficult to use, but some DO require more time than others to sort out. The most challenging ones are marked "1" or "2." A "5" means it's easy to figure out. You should avoid the more challenging resources if you are short on time. Also, if you are easily discouraged or confused, stick with resources labeled "4" or "5." This might apply also if you are new to homeschooling.

• **Teacher's manual: e = essential, na = not available, nu = available but not useful, u = useful, ak = answer key only** - Teacher's manuals are not created equal. Some are essential—the book or program cannot be used properly without them (e). Some are window dressing—save your money (nu). Some are useful, but if you don't mind figuring out answers yourself and skipping the extra helps they offer, you can manage without them (u). Some serve only as an answer key (ak)—usually you will want these if you are past second grade level material. And, of course, some resources do not have teacher manuals (na).

• **Supports Charlotte Mason's philosophy** (see p. 13) - A "4" or "5" indicates that this resource is very much based upon or supportive of Charlotte Mason's ideas. Mason's ideas about secondary education are a bit different from those for the elementary grades, so it is difficult or impossible to rate upper level resources in this column. Those have been marked na.

• **Supports classical education** (see p. 15) - Resources with a "4" or "5" are based on or supportive of classical education. However, keep in mind that folks have differing ideas about what classical education requires, especially in the elementary grades, so read reviews of these items carefully.

• **Religous content: Protestant (p), Catholic (c), secular (s), secular but "Christian friendly" (sc)** - This column reflects the religious or non-religious perspective presented. Some religion-based resources have such minimal religious content or it is expressed such that almost everyone is able to use the resource. Similarly, many secular resources will be inoffensive to those wanting to provide their children with a religion-based education. Check the full reviews for details or cautions. I use the "sc" designation for resources that, while written for secular or non-sectarian audiences, have content that should present no problems for Christians. "p/c" indicates resources suitable for all Christians.

• **Page # for review** - This is where you will go to find the complete review for each resource.

Working Through The Charts

Let's consider one example. You've worked through the earlier chapters and discovered the following.

~ You lean toward traditional curriculum, but you also like the idea of using real books to make learning more interesting.

~ Your ten-year-old daughter, an only child, seems to be a Perfect Paula in regard to learning style.

~ She is likely to thrive on traditional workbooks and independent study for just about every subject except composition.

~ You want Christian curriculum.

~ You like structured lessons that do most of the work for you.

~ Teacher preparation and presentation time is not an issue since you have plenty of time.

~ You don't really need hands-on or multi-sensory resources, but they might be more fun.

~ She doesn't like to write, so that area needs special work this year.

~ Your daughter will be working at fifth grade level.

Starting on the left-hand page of the first chart, read through the charts looking for resources that reflect the characteristics and needs you've identified such as those listed above.

Given your situation, you don't really need items with a high rating in the first column. The second column will be more useful as a starting place since it lets you know which resources fit your daughter's Perfect Paula need for structure and order. Then the fifth column deals with direct teaching needed. She really likes to work independently, so you want to look for resources with a low number in this column.

The sixth column will help you spot items that will work for independent study, but you might also look for one or two that you can use one-on-one since you have time for some interaction with your daughter.

Also, you should specifically focus on a composition resource appropriate for a group so you can invite another child to join your daughter for a writing class to make that subject more interesting to her.

Continuing on the right-hand page, "Amount of writing" is of concern in that she needs more writing practice than she's had. You might look for at least one or two resources that require at least some writing and one that requires a great deal.

Prep time isn't an issue, and either multi-level or specific grade level resources will suffice since you will be teaching only one child most of the time. You want resources that are easy to moderately demanding for the teacher ("5" to "3") because even though you have the time, you do not want to be bothered figuring out a complicated program. You are easily overwhelmed if you have to get very creative in putting together lessons.

You like to purchase teacher's manuals when they're available so you'll order those that are marked as essential or useful.

You want Christian material, but you're willing to use secular resources as long as they're not offensive to you. (You will need to check the individual reviews on secular items for mention of possible content problems.)

Resources that seem to fit the bill:

• *Horizons Math* - structured math program that has minimal hands-on work and works well for independent learners

• *Switched-on Schoolhouse Social Studies* - computerized course that allows independent study

• Progeny Press study guides and the associated novels for literature - allow students to read and write about real books, while providing you, the teacher, direction as to how to ask appropriate questions and teach reading skills within the context of each book

• *Wordsmith Apprentice* - for that "group" writing class you plan to organize for your daughter and a friend to provide more interaction

• *Easy Grammar* - a simple-to-use workbook approach for learning grammar independently

• *BJU Press Science* OR *Switched-on Schoolhouse Science* - since your daughter wants structure and accountability in her learning, and you like quizzes and tests to help ensure she is actually learning something, either of these might do. You might also plan to get together with another family to do science experiments, using those from the curriculum or experiments from a supplemental book.

• Your own Bible curriculum

Let's take another example. We'll say you're a harried mom for whom time is the most critical element since you've got five children, three of them school age. We'll focus primarily on your eight-year old son to keep this example manageable.

You've determined the following.

~ You lean toward an eclectic approach to education.

~ You put a high priority on making learning engaging so that your children will love to learn.

~ You don't mind using Christian resources as long as they aren't too "preachy."

~ You are not overly concerned about tests and grading in these early grade levels.

~ Wiggly Willy describes your son so you'll be looking for hands-on and multi-sensory resources.

~ You have minimal preparation and presentation time.

~ You want to teach all of your children together whenever possible to save time, energy and the hassle of dealing with three different texts for every subject. You will look for resources that allow you to teach history, science and fine arts to the whole group.

~ Your Wiggly Willy can work independently in short bursts, so using some workbooks for independent study would be helpful.

~ You son is in third grade, but he'll need a lower level math course since he's working below grade level in that subject. He can work at third grade level for other subjects.

Given this challenging situation, you might choose the following:

• Susan Wise Bauer's *Story of the World, Volume I* - You can read aloud and discuss this with all of your children together. You will appreciate the minimal preparation time required. You would also purchase the companion curriculum guide and use ideas and activities from it with all of your children.

• *Noeo Biology I* - All of your children can participate together listening to the books and doing activities. The pre-packaged experiment kits make this a practical choice. The amount of writing seems perfect.

• *Reading Detective Beginning* level on CD-ROM - He reads fine on his own now, but you will use this computer program to develop better comprehension and a larger vocabulary. He'll enjoy the game aspect. No prep or presentation time is needed; he can use this on his own.

• *Easy Grammar* - provides grammar basics in preparation for next year when you want to move into a more challenging grammar resource. Again, no prep or presentation required once you are past initial lessons on prepositions.

• *Spellwell C* - reinforces his phonics knowledge while teaching spelling rules. He can do this independently most of the time.

• *Math-U-See Beta* level - Since math is so difficult for him, the hands-on materials for this program make it easier for him to grasp math concepts. You will need to watch the videos to understand how to present concepts, but once you've been through it, you'll be able to work much more efficiently with your other children. Alternatively, you can let your son sometimes watch with you, stopping the DVD and trying out what has been shown. The *Beta* title won't alert him that this program is typically for second grade.

Why Aren't There Any Bible or Religion Top Picks?

Good question! I suspect that most of those reading this book will see Bible or religion as an essential part of their curriculum. In chapter five, I also mentioned teaching a Christian world-view as a possible goal very much related to Bible and religion. The problem here is the huge number of possible options.

Do you want to focus more on scripture memorization, doctrinal teaching, developing a relationship with Jesus, studying church history, or some other area? Are you ready to get into an intense worldview study? Each of these might be appealing at one time or another to families, but you cannot do it all at once. And the content and methodology might differ based on each family's faith tradition. Consequently, I decided to leave those choices entirely up to you rather than state my own preferences. However, if you want to investigate some of these possibilities, check out my reviews online at www.CathyDuffyReviews.com under the sections for either "Bible/Religion" or "Worldview."

One Last Note Regarding the Charts

Just because I have included an item within my Top Picks does not mean it is perfect. I have selected some items about which I have reservations. But I know they meet certain needs very well. After working through the charts, please take time to read through the reviews of items you think will meet your needs. Remember the saying, "One man's trash is another man's treasure"—things that bother me about a particular resource might be the very things that make that resource a good choice for you!

The charts begin on the following page. Please note that contact information and prices listed for resources in the following chapters are the most current information available from publishers at the time this book was written. I try to post updates for significant changes in resources reviewed in this book under "Updates for 101 Top Picks" on my website. However, you will need to confirm current price information when you make your purchases.

Chart of 101 Top Picks (1 = low, 5 = high)

	Multi-sensory/ hands-on (Wiggly Willy)	Structure/ rule-oriented (Perfect Paula)	Appeals to logical/ analytical learners (Competent Carl)	Has social activity/ interaction (Sociable Sue	Needs parent/ teacher instruction	Independent study (ind), one-on-one (1 on 1), or group (g)
Phonics, Reading, and Literature						
All About Reading	4	5	3	5	5	1 on 1
Explode the Code	print-1, online-3	5	3	2	print-1, online-3	ind
McRuffy Phonics and Reading	4	4	2	5	5	1 on 1, g
Noah Webster's Reading Handbook	2	3	3	3	5	1 on 1
Phonics Pathways	3	4	4	4	5	1 on 1, g
Spell to Write and Read	2	5	5	2	5	1 on 1, g
Teach a Child to Read with Children's Books	4	1	2	5	5	1 on 1
Drawn into the Heart of Reading	3	3	4	5	3	ind, 1 on 1, g
Progeny Press Study Guides for Literature	2	3	3	3	3	ind, 1 on 1, g
Reading Detective series	books-3, computer program-5	3	5	4	1	ind, 1 on 1, g
Total Language Plus	2	3	4	4	3	ind, 1 on 1, g
BJU Press Literature (grades 7-12)	2	3	4	3	4	ind, 1 on 1, g
Teaching the Classics	1	3	4	5	5	1 on 1, g
Language Arts: Grammar and Composition						
A Beka Book Language series	1	4	4	1	2	ind, 1 on 1, g
Analytical Grammar	2	5	4	3	4	1 on 1, g
Building Christian English series	1	5	2	2	3	ind, 1 on 1
Create-A-Story	5	2	4	5	4	group of at least 2
Easy Grammar	2	5	3	1	2	ind
Fairview's Guide to Composition and Essay Writing	2	3	5	4	4	1 on 1, g
First Language Lessons	2	5	2	4	5	1 on 1
Jump In	3	3	2	depends on interaction provided	4	1 on 1, g
Michael Clay Thompson Language Arts	2	3	4	4	4	1 on 1, g
Saxon Grammar and Writing	1	5	5	2	2	mostly ind

Chart of 101 Top Picks (1 = low, 5 = high)

Amount of Writing: 1-5 OR U=up to parent	Prep time	Grade level specific (s) or multi-level (m)	Ease of use for teacher: 1=difficult through 5=easy	Teacher's manual: e = essential, na = not available, u = useful, ak = answer key only	Supports Charlotte Mason's philosophy (na = not applicable)	Supports classical education	Religious content: Protestant=p, Catholic=c, Secular=s, Secular but "Christian-friendly"=sc	Page # for review
1	2	m	3	e	3	3	sc	73
2	1	m	5	ak	3	3	s	76
3-5, increases by level	2	s	2	e	3	3	sc	77
1	1	m	4	e	3	3	p	81
2	2	m	5	e	3	3	sc	82
5	3	m	3	e	3	3	p, but minimal Christian content	83
1	varies	m	2	e	5	3	sc	85
U	4	m	3	e	5	4	p/c	89
U	2	m	4	e	5	4	p	90
1	1	m	5	ak in back of book	4	3	s	92
U	2	m	5	e	5	4	p/c	94
U	depends on parent's familiarity with readings	s	3	e	3	3	p	96
4	5, less with experience	m	2	e	5	5	sc	99
4	1	s	5	ak	2	5	p	104
3	1	m	4	na	2	4	sc	107
4	1	s	4	u, e for upper grades	1	3	p	109
4	2	m	3	na	4	3	s	111
3	1	s/m	5	e	2	2	sc	113
5	2	m	4	e	5	5	sc	116
2	1	s	5	e	2	5	sc	117
4	2	m	4	e	2	2	p	119
4-5	3	m	3	e	5	5	s	120
4	1	s	5	e	3	4	sc	124

Chart of 101 Top Picks (1 = low, 5 = high)

	Multi-sensory/ hands-on (Wiggly Willy)	Structure/ rule-oriented (Perfect Paula)	Appeals to logical/ analytical learners (Competent Carl)	Has social activity/ interaction (Sociable Sue)	Needs parent/ teacher instruction	Independent study (ind), one-on-one (1 on 1), or group (g)
Teaching Writing Structure and Style Seminar	3	4	4	4	5	1 on 1, g
Winston Grammar	4	4	3	4	4	1 on 1, g
Wordsmith series	3	3	4	depends on interaction provided	3	ind, 1 on 1, g
WriteShop	4	4	3	4	5	1 on 1, g
Writing for 100 Days	2	3	3	3	5	1 on 1, g
Language Arts: Spelling, Vocabulary, and Handwriting						
All About Spelling	4	5	3	5	5	1 on 1
Building Spelling Skills	1	5	4	2	2	ind
English from the Roots Up	2	4	4	3	5	1 on 1, g
Spelling Power	3	4	4	3	4	ind, 1 on 1, g
Spellwell Series	3	4	3	5	3	ind, 1 on 1, g
Vocabulary from Classical Roots	2	5	5	2	3	ind, 1 on 1, g
Vocabu-Lit	3	3	4	2	3	1 on 1, g
Wordly Wise	2	3	4	3	3	ind, 1 on 1, g
Handwriting Without Tears	3-5, depending on optional items	3	3	3	5	1 on 1, g
Peterson Directed Handwriting	2	4	3	3	5	1 on 1, g
A Reason for Handwriting	2	4	3	4	3	ind, 1 on 1, g
Getty-Dubay Italic Handwriting Series	3	4	3	4	4	1 on 1, g
Mathematics						
Horizons Math	3	5	4	3	4	ind, 1 on 1
Mathematical Reasoning	4	1	4	5	4	1 on 1, g
Math Mammoth	3	4	4	4	4	1 on 1, g
Math-U-See	5	4	5	5	4	1 on 1, g
Singapore Math (Primary Mathematics)	2	4	5	3	4	ind, 1 on 1, g
Teaching Textbooks	3	3	4	1	1	ind
Saxon Math Intermediate 3 and up	1	4	4	2	2	ind, 1 on 1, g
Horizons Pre-Algebra	4	4	4	3	3	ind, 1 on 1, g
Kinetic Books	3	4	4	2	1	ind
YourTeacher	3	4	4	2	1	ind
Elementary Algebra (Jacobs)	3	4	5	2	2	ind, 1 on 1, g
Geometry: Seeing, Doing, Understanding (Jacobs)	2	4	5	2	2	ind, 1 on 1, g

Chart of 101 Top Picks (1 = low, 5 = high)

Amount of Writing: 1-5 OR U=up to parent	Prep time	Grade level specific (s) or multi-level (m)	Ease of use for teacher: 1=difficult through 5=easy	Teacher's manual: e = essential, na = not available, u = useful, ak = answer key only	Supports Charlotte Mason's philosophy (na = not applicable)	Supports classical education	Religious content: Protestant=p, Catholic=c, Secular=s, Secular but "Christian-friendly"=sc	Page # for review
4	3-depends on how the course is used	m	3	e	5	5	sc	126
2	2	m	3	e	3	3	sc	128
4	2	m	4	e	4	3	sc	129
4	2	m	4	e	5	4	p	131
5	1	m	4	e	4	4	sc	133
1	2	m	3	e	3	3	sc	135
3	1	s	5	ak	2	5	p	138
U	5	m	2	e	4	5	s	140
4	2	m	3	e	3	4	sc	141
2	1	s	4	ak	2	2	s	143
2	1	m	4	e	3	5	s	144
3	1	s	4	ak	3	2	s	144
3	1	s/m	4	ak	2	5	s	145
3	2	m	4	e	3	3	s	147
4	1	m	4	e	3	3	s	149
4	1	s/m	5	u	3	3	p	149
4	1	s/m	3	e	4	3	s	150
5	2	s	4	e	3	4	p	154
2	1	s	2	na	4	2	s	157
3	2	s	3	ak	4	3	sc	160
3	3	s	3	e	4	3	sc	162
3	2	s	3	e	4	4	s	166
2	1	s	5	na	3	3	sc	168
3	1	s	5	ak	1	3	s	173
4	3	m	3	e	4	4	p	180
1-2	1	m	5	na	na	3	s	182
2	1	m	5	na	na	3	s	184
3	2	m	4	ak	na	3	s	185
3	1	m	4	ak	na	5	s	186

Chart of 101 Top Picks (1 = low, 5 = high)

	Multi-sensory/ hands-on (Wiggly Willy)	Structure/ rule-oriented (Perfect Paula)	Appeals to logical/ analytical learners (Competent Carl)	Has social activity/ interaction (Sociable Sue)	Needs parent/ teacher instruction	Independent study (ind), one-on-one (1 on 1), or group (g)
Discovering Geometry	4	3	5	4	4	1 on 1, g
History/Social Studies						
All American History	3	4	5	4	3	ind (high school only), 1 on 1, g
A Child's History of the World	2, higher with full course	2	3	5	4	ind, 1 on 1, g
Genevieve Foster books	2	2	4	4	2	ind, 1 on 1, g
Guerber History Series	2	3	3	4	2	ind, 1 on 1, g
History of the World (MFW edition of DK Book)	4	3	5	3	3	ind, 1 on 1
The Mystery of History	4	3	3	5	5	ind, 1 on 1, g
The Old World's Gifts to the New	3	3	3	3	3	ind, 1 on 1, g
The Story of the World (with study guides)	4	3	4	5	5	1 on 1, g
Take A Stand!	2	2	5	4	5	1 on 1, g
TruthQuest History	3	3	4	4	4	1 on 1, g
Ultimate Geography & Timeline Guide	5	3	5	5	5	ind, 1 on 1, g
Science						
Apologia Science for Jr. & Sr. High	3	3	4	2	1	ind, g
Behold and See Science Series	3	3	3	3	3	1 on 1, g
BJU Press Science, grades 1-6	3	4	3	3	4	1 on 1, g
Christian Kids Explore Science Series	4	2	4	5	5	1 on 1, g
Exploring Creation Young Explorer Science (Apologia for grades 1-6)	4, but might have too much writing	4	4	4	5	1 on 1, g
God's Design Science Series	4	4	4	4	4	1 on 1, g
A History of Science	3	2	3	5	4	1 on 1, g
Living Learning Books	4	2	4	5	5	1 on 1, g
Media Angels Science	4	4	3	4	5	1 on 1, g
Noeo Science	5	3	4	4	5	1 on 1, g
The Rainbow	4	4	4	4	4	ind, 1 on 1, g
Supercharged Science	5	2	5	3	depends on program	ind, 1 on 1, g
The World of Science (MFW/Master Books edition)	5	1	3	3	depends how it is used	ind, 1 on 1, g

Chart of 101 Top Picks (1 = low, 5 = high)

Amount of Writing: 1-5 OR U=up to parent	Prep time	Grade level specific (s) or multi-level (m)	Ease of use for teacher: 1=difficult through 5=easy	Teacher's manual: e = essential, na = not available, u = useful, ak = answer key only	Supports Charlotte Mason's philosophy (na = not applicable)	Supports classical education	Religious content: Protestant=p, Catholic=c, Secular=s, Secular but "Christian-friendly"=sc	Page # for review
3	3	m	1	e	n/a	4	s	187
varies	2	m	4	e	3	3	mildly Christian	199
1, more with full course	1, more with full course	m	5, 4 with course	u	5	5	s	201
1	1	m	5	see review	4	3	s	202
1	1	m	5	na	3	4	p/c	203
1	1	m	5	na	4	2	sc	204
U	4	m	4	e	5	2	p	205
U	1	m	4	na	3	4	c	208
U	3	m	3	e	5	5	sc except Vol. 2 (see review)	209
5	4	m	2	e	4	5	sc	211
U	3	m	2	e	4	4	p	215
3	4	m	2	e	5	4	sc	218
3	2, labs require more	m	4	ak	4	4	p/c	223
varies	varies	s	3	na	2	2	c	227
U	4	s	4	e	3	3	p	230
U	5	m	3	e	5	3	p/c	231
4	3	m	3	na	3	3	p	234
3	3	m	3	e	3	3	p	236
U	2	m	3	e	5	5	s	239
U	4	m	3	e	5	4	sc	239
3	2	s	3	e	3	3	p/c	242
3	2	m	4	e	4	3	p/c	243
3	2	s	4	e	3	3	p/c	246
varies	varies	m	3	na	3	3	sc	247
1	1	m	4	na	4	3	sc	249

Chart of 101 Top Picks (1 = low, 5 = high)

	Multi-sensory/ hands-on (Wiggly Willy)	Structure/ rule-oriented (Perfect Paula)	Appeals to logical/ analytical learners (Competent Carl)	Has social activity/ interaction (Sociable Sue)	Needs parent/ teacher instruction	Independent study (ind), one-on-one (1 on 1), or group (g)
Unit Studies/All-in-One Programs						
Connecting with History	4	3	4	5	3-5, varies by age	ind (older students), 1 on 1, g
Five in a Row	3	3	1	5	5	1 on 1, g
Heart of Dakota	5	4	3	5	varies by age	ind (older students), 1 on 1, g
History Links	5	3	3	5	5	ind, 1 on 1, g
KONOS Character Curriculum	5	see review	3	5	5	g
My Father's World	3	3	4	4	2-5, varies by level	ind (older students), 1 on 1, g
Sonlight	3	3	3	3	4, lots of reading together	ind, 1 on 1, g
Tapestry of Grace	4	3	3	5	5	g
Trail Guide to Learning	4	3	4	4	varies by level	1 on 1, small group
TRISMS	2	4	5	3	varies by student	ind, 1 on 1, g
World Views of the Western World	1	1	4	depends on interaction provided	2	ind, 1 on 1, g
Complete Curriculum	2	5	4	2	3	ind, 1 on 1
Switched-On Schoolhouse OR Monarch	2	5	2	1	1	ind
Foreign Language						
The Learnables	4	1	3	2	1	ind
Rosetta Stone	4	2	4	3	1	ind
Greek Alphabet Code Cracker	4	4	4	3	2	ind, 1 on 1, g
Henle Latin	1	5	4	2	3	ind, 1 on 1, g
Memoria Press Latin	2	5	4	3	4	ind, 1 on 1, g
Lively Latin	2	4	4	2	2	ind, 1 on 1
Critical Thinking & Art						
The Critical Thinking Co.	3	3	5	3	3	ind, 1 on 1, g
The Fallacy Detective	1	3	5	2	2	ind
The Art of Argument	1	4	5	2	3	primarily ind
Artistic Pursuits	3	3	3	3	varies	1 on 1, g
Feed My Sheep	5	2	4	4	4	ind, 1 on 1, g

Chart of 101 Top Picks (1 = low, 5 = high)

Amount of Writing: 1-5 OR U=up to parent	Prep time	Grade level specific (s) or multi-level (m)	Ease of use for teacher: 1=difficult through 5=easy	Teacher's manual: e = essential, na = not available, u = useful, ak = answer key only	Supports Charlotte Mason's philosophy (na = not applicable)	Supports classical education	Religious content: Protestant=p, Catholic=c, Secular=s, Secular but "Christian-friendly"=sc	Page # for review
U	4	m	1	e	4	5	c	252
U	2	m	4	e	5	1	s, p with supplement	255
U	2	m	4	e	5	3	p	256
U	4	m	2	e	5	3	c	261
U	5, unless using "Box" or "Bag"	m	1, "Box" or "Bag" = 4	e	4	3	p	263
varies	2	m/s	3	e	5	3	p	265
3	2	m/s	4	e	5	3	p	272
U	5	m	1	e	5	5	p	274
U	4	m	3	e	4	3	s, p with supplement	276
5	3	m	3	e	3	4	s/p/c - adaptable	280
5	2	m	3, depending upon student initiative	na	4	4	p	284
varies	2	s	3	e	1	1	s	289
3, much is on the computer	1	s	5	na, except for specific courses	1	1	p	291
1	1	m	5	na	3	2	s	296
1	1	m	5	na	2	1	s	299
3	1	m	5	na	4	5	sc	300
3	1	m	4	u	3	5	c	301
3	1	m	4	e	3	5	p/c	302
3	1	m	4	e	3	4	sc	306
2	1	m	4	e	3	5	s	310
1	1	m	5	na	5	5	p/c	312
3	varies	m	4	ak	3	4	p/c	313
2	3	m	3	na	4	3	sc	314
1	3	m	4	e	5	4	p	315

CHAPTER 7

Phonics, Reading, and Literature

While I believe that phonics is a critical component of a good reading program, not all children learn best from programs that use an intensive phonics approach. One child seems to figure out the phonetic elements in words on his own with little direct instruction while another needs explicit instruction with plenty of practice and reinforcement. One child is content to learn to read with syllables and lists of disconnected words while another prefers the context of meaningful sentences.

Whatever you decide works best for each of your children, please make sure that they do not learn to read only by memorizing individual words. Sight-reading without any decoding skills (identifying phonetic elements) makes it practically impossible for children to sound out unfamiliar words.

You might choose to work with any one of the excellent reading/phonics programs available. These programs are generally similar in their goals, but they vary greatly when it comes to methods and presentation. Some programs offer leeway for a less formal presentation while others are more rigid and detailed. Some begin teaching phonics with the "consonant-vowel" approach (e.g., ba, be, bi, bo, bu) while others reverse this, beginning with vowel-consonant combinations (e.g., at, am, ad). Some programs include readers, while others don't. Some have games or hands-on activities, while others rely only on oral and written activity.

I have selected programs that are easily accessible, appropriate for homeschool use, and that approach reading from a variety of educational philosophies. There is certainly something for everyone amidst all the choices.

I have to mention that there are many other excellent phonics and reading programs that I could have included. Please forgive me if I've left out your favorite! Also, don't forget that some comprehensive programs such as Sonlight and My Father's World (for kindergarten and first grade levels) incorporate reading and phonics programs.

I would be remiss if I didn't also mention one of the most valuable resources for teaching beginning reading even though it isn't a program. Ruth Beechick's *The Three R's* (Mott Media, www.mottmedia.com) is a compilation of three smaller booklets that were previously published separately. Two of the booklets are on math and language arts, while the third, titled *A Home Start in Reading*, addresses phonics and reading. *A Home Start in Reading* demystifies the process of teaching a child to read and gives you enough instructional material that you could actually teach your child to read from those 32 pages. I know that this approach is too "barebones" for most parents, but even if you choose to use a more complete resource, this book will help you know what's important and what's not so you are in control of your program rather than the reverse.

Following the reviews of phonics programs, I've listed some beginning readers that you might want to use alongside your program.

Once past the beginning reading/phonics stage, children need to shift their primary focus to comprehension and understanding as well as the study of worthwhile literature. While some reading programs build these aspects into their courses, some do not. So I have included some resources that address those needs following the list of readers. Then at the end of this chapter are reviews of resources for teaching literature specifically for junior and senior high school, along with a list of recommended literature (real books) titles.

• • • • • • • • •

Phonics and Beginning Reading

All About Reading

by Marie Rippel
All About Learning Press, Inc.
615 Commerce Loop
Eagle River, WI 54521
715-477-1976
www.allaboutlearningpress.com

Marie Rippel's *All About Spelling* (also reviewed in this book) has become one of the most popular spelling programs among home

educators, so I was naturally curious about her *All About Reading (AAR)* program. This is a relatively new curriculum with the *Pre-reading Program, Level 1*, and *Level 2* currently available. *Level 3* should be available in 2013 and *Level 4* in 2014.

AAR consists of two main parts: the *Pre-reading* program (teaching essential pre-reading skills) and the *Reading* program (consisting of *Levels 1-4*).

AAR is an intensive phonics program that uses Orton-Gillingham methodology. With this method, 97% of English words can be learned according to phonetic rules, leaving only 3% to be learned as sight words.

AAR is a highly interactive multisensory program that needs to be taught by the parent or teacher. However, the open-and-go lesson plans are scripted and illustrated, making it simple for the inexperienced parent or teacher to present the lessons with little or no prep time. Even though it is scripted, *AAR* is easy to adapt to each child's needs by selecting among the suggested hands-on activities, choosing their favorite books for read-aloud time, and adjusting the pace and amount of interaction.

The phonetic readers are beautifully illustrated hardcover books that could stand on their own. They feature finely detailed black-and-white drawings that are a delight in themselves.

All About Reading Pre-reading Program

basic package: $79.95,
deluxe package: $119.95

The *All About Reading Pre-reading Program* teaches essential pre-reading skills. The primary focus is on what Rippel calls the Big Five Skills™, five components that she explains are foundational to a child's future reading and spelling abilities:

- print awareness
- phonological awareness
- letter knowledge
- listening comprehension
- motivation to read

The *AAR Pre-reading Program* components are a teacher's manual, a student packet, two read-aloud books, the *Letter Sounds A to Z* CD-ROM, a Ziggy the Zebra hand puppet used to help teach many of the lessons, a card filing box, reading divider cards, and a tote bag.

Lesson plans include pictures and illustrations so you can quickly see which components of the program you'll need for each lesson. It should take no more than fifteen minutes to read the introduction and start teaching.

The student packet includes the *My Book of Letters* student activity book, a progress chart, picture cards, letter sound cards, uppercase and lowercase alphabet charts, and a certificate of completion.

My Book of Letters contains one or two activity sheets for each lesson in its 192 pages. Some activity pages function more as teaching tools while others focus on arts and crafts, but all activity sheets contribute toward teaching the Big Five Skills. The activities can be simplified for children who don't need as much of the cut-and-paste craft work. You will need some

additional resources for the activity pages: scissors, glue, crayons, markers, scraps of fabric and yarn, paint, toothpicks, cotton swabs, construction paper, colored pencils, a hole punch, star stickers, pipe cleaners, glitter, and twigs.

The cards in the student packet are printed and perforated on card stock, ready for you to separate and store in the special card filing box that comes with the complete set. The alphabet charts are used as teaching tools. Uppercase letters are taught first, then lowercase.

The read-aloud books are titled *The Zigzag Zebra* and *Lizard Lou*. *The Zigzag Zebra* introduces letters and their sounds in the context of rhymed text that often is a bit silly—just what children love. Alligators, kangaroos, frogs, snails, yaks, and other "critters" are the subject matter. *Lizard Lou* continues in the same vein but with lengthier poems, some from famous authors. These read-aloud books are used to develop listening comprehension and recognition of sounds in relation to illustrations. Poems contain sentence structure and vocabulary likely a little beyond what is already familiar to most preschoolers, so you might have discussions about some of the words and sentences. The nature topics themselves are also likely to engender discussion. I see this as a positive feature in the way that reading great books to older children exposes them to the beauty of language and the nuances of vocabulary and usage.

The *Letter Sounds A to Z* CD-ROM plays in a computer. This is a simple program that displays the letters of the alphabet. Children click on a letter to hear the sound. Only short vowels are included. Parents already familiar with the phonetic sounds might not need this.

All of the components and activities in the *Pre-reading Program* work together nicely to contribute to the development of other readiness skills as children work with following directions, cutting, and coloring as well as listening, comprehending, identifying syllables auditorially, making inferences, developing vocabulary, and otherwise acquiring the Big Five Skills.

Although you can purchase individual components, you will probably want to purchase one of the packages. The deluxe package includes all eight components, while the basic package includes all items except the puppet, the tote bag, and the card filing box.

All About Reading Level 1

Level 1 Materials: $99.95, Basic Interactive Kit - $28.95, Deluxe Interactive Kit - $48.95

Beginning in *All About Reading Level 1*, five key components of reading are taught: phonological awareness, phonics/decoding, fluency, vocabulary, and comprehension. Before starting *Level 1*, students should already know the alphabet and be able to identify both uppercase and lowercase letters. They might have completed the *All About Reading Pre-reading Program*, but that is not required if you have introduced the alphabet in some other fashion.

All About Reading Level 1 materials include a teacher's manual, a student packet, and three hardcover readers. The student packet contains the *Blast Off to Reading!* student activity book, phonogram cards, word cards, and a viewfinder bookmark. The perforated phonogram and word cards need to be separated and stored in a 3" x 5" index card box or the Reading Review Box offered by the publisher.

You will also need an Interactive Kit, which is used in all levels of the reading program. There are two Interactive Kit options: Basic or Deluxe. Both kits include a set of letter tiles, magnets, *The Basic Phonograms* CD-ROM, and reading divider cards to organize the phonogram and word cards in your index card box. The Deluxe Kit adds a customized storage box for the cards, star stickers for use on the progress chart, and a custom tote bag for storing all the components. (Note: the *All About Spelling* program uses the same letter tiles and *The Basic Phonograms* CD-ROM, so if you are using both the reading and spelling programs, you can avoid duplicates by purchasing individual items instead of a complete Interactive Kit.)

In addition to the essential items for *AAR*, you should also have a 2' x 3' magnetic white board for both storing and working with the letter tiles. Once you have set up your letter tiles and separated the phonogram and word cards, the program is easy to use. The scripted lesson plans guide you step by step. If you are not familiar with the sounds of the phonograms being taught in a lesson, you can pop *The Basic Phonograms* CD-ROM into a computer and click on any phonogram to hear the pronunciation.

The program is incremental. The first lesson uses phonogram cards and letter tiles to teach the four sounds: /m/, /s/, /p/, and /ă/. Tiles are also used to introduce blending for three-letter words and to demonstrate how switching the first letter (e.g., using the words *sam* and *pam*) changes only the initial sound. Students also learn to identify vowels and consonants, which are color-coded on the tiles. Activity sheets in the student workbook add additional practice and, sometimes, additional instruction. For example, the first worksheet has four words that students are to cut out and match with four pictures: *Pam, Sam, map,* and *sap*. The first lesson concludes with students practicing reading three word cards and then listening to 20 minutes of read-aloud. Students can then put a sticker on their progress chart.

Lessons continue in this fashion, sometimes alerting teachers to strategies for overcoming common problems they might encounter. The introduction of letters follows a progression similar to that of other intensive phonics programs, gradually introducing vowels with consonants in a way that allows students to begin reading immediately.

AAR provides fluency practice through the word cards, fluency sheets in the activity book, and readers. The teacher's manual includes tips on using the fluency sheets to prevent overwhelming some beginning readers.

The *Blast Off to Reading!* student activity book is a major component that adds much variety to the lessons through short reading games and activities that motivate young learners. For example, in Lesson 3 students play "Feed the Monster" by reading words and then "feeding" them to the monster, and in several lessons they work with a phonogram manipulative that helps them create new words containing a particular pattern.

The three hardcover readers for *Level 1* are just as topnotch as those for the *Pre-reading Program*, with lovely illustrations and relatively interesting content for vocabulary-controlled reading material.

Lessons in *Level 1* cover both short and long vowels, as well as some consonant digraphs, sight words, and even compound words.

AAR can be used independently or together with the *All About Spelling* program. Handwriting is not included as part of this reading program.

All About Reading Level 2

Level 2 Materials: $99.95

All About Reading Level 2 continues to teach additional phonograms and rules. The *Level 2* materials include a teacher's manual, a student packet, and two hardcover readers. You will continue to use the letter tiles from the previous level. Fluency worksheets are separated into "Easier Vocabulary" and "Harder Vocabulary" sections; you can work with both sections or just one, depending on your student's needs. They also include phrases and sentences to provide practice that is closer to reality than simply reading word lists. Students also use letter tiles to learn how to divide words into syllables as a decoding strategy.

In summary, *All About Reading* is a very reasonably priced option for an interactive, multisensory reading program that is scripted and easy to use. All components except the student workbooks and star stickers are reusable, so the value is even greater when you use it with more than one student.

Explode The Code

by Nancy M. Hall
EPS/School Specialty
PO Box 9031
Cambridge, MA
02139-9031
800-225-5750
www.eps.
schoolspecialty.com
student books - $9
each , teacher's
guides - $8.95
each, 12-month subscription to *Explode The Code Online* for one student - $65

There are fourteen separate workbooks in this series, although you may not want to use them all. You might want to use these for phonics reinforcement alongside something like *Noah Webster's Reading Handbook* (reviewed later in this chapter) that doesn't have a writing or workbook component, but many families use *Explode the Code* as their primary phonics teaching resource. Some families also use it with older children who have a weak phonics foundation.

These workbooks each teach selected phonetic concepts rather than covering most of all of them in each book. Students learn all phonetic concepts by completing *Books 1-8*. While phonic decoding skills are the primary focus, reading comprehension and vocabulary also get some attention.

Books are printed in black and white. They feature large print and less of it per page than some other phonics workbooks, making them a good choice for children who can do only limited amounts of writing or have trouble focusing.

Students should be able to do most work independently once someone has read the instructions for that page to them. After a while, students will become familiar with the types of exercises and will seldom need even that assistance.

Books 1 through 8 are the most important. Content of each is as follows: *Book 1*—short vowels; *Book 2*—initial and final consonant blends; Book 3—open syllables, silent-e rule, digraphs, and simple diphthongs; *Book 4*—syllable division rules; *Book 5*—word families, three-letter blends, "qu, -ey," and the three sounds of "-ed;" *Book 6*—more difficult diphthongs and r-controlled vowels; *Book 7*—soft "c" and "g," silent letters, sounds of "ear, ei, eigh," and the digraph "ph;" *Book 8*—suffixes and irregular endings. *Books 1½, 2½, 3½, 4½, 5½,* and *6½* offer more practice on topics covered within *Books 1, 2, 3,* etc. respectively. Post-tests are included within each book.

If you use *Explode The Code* as your primary teaching tool, you will need to provide reading practice with other books.

Teacher's guides each cover a number of books. For example, the teacher's guide for *Books 1-2* covers *Books 1, 2, 1½,* and *2½.* Guides include the program description, answers, and dictations for the post-tests. Other teacher's guides are for *Books 3-4, 5-6,* and *7-8.*

Those with preschoolers or kindergartners might want to use the "primer" series of three books that teach letter formation, phonemic awareness, sound-letter correspondence, tracking, and other pre-reading skills. The three books are titled *Get Ready for the Code, Get Set for the Code,* and *Go for the Code*—also known as *Books A, B,* and *C.* A single teacher's guide covers all three books.

Explode The Code Online

Explode The Code Online provides web-based instruction using lessons adapted from the entire series of *Explode The Code* books. Lessons are presented in full-color with audio instructions so that children may work independently. Student responses are recorded and their progress assessed. The program then makes adjustments for students to move ahead or review so that they are working only on skills they need to learn. The program might even skip lessons that review a concept if the student has demonstrated mastery. As a helpful extra feature, students are rewarded with various colored "buttons." The parent or teacher can quickly glance at the buttons and see how well a student is doing by the color of the buttons instead of analyzing results.

You access the program by purchasing a one-year subscription. Students may access all levels during that subscription period. You can renew for subsequent years as needed. The program will track one student per subscription, and you can purchase additional subscriptions. This program can serve as your core program for teaching reading.

I think the online option might be even more appealing than the books since it tailors assignments for students. This keeps students from getting bored and frees the parent from having to decide which books or lessons a student needs to complete.

· · · · · · · ·

McRuffy Language Arts Programs

by Brian Davis, M.A. Ed.
McRuffy Press
PO Box 212
Raymore, MO 64083
816-331-7831
email: sales@mcruffy.com
www.mcruffy.com
Kindergarten, First Grade, or Second Grade Complete Special Edition

Curriculum - $109.95 per level

McRuffy Language Arts programs for kindergarten through fourth grade cover phonics, reading, spelling, grammar, and composition. Optional handwriting workbooks easily integrate with the other components of each course. While the complete programs for all levels are very good, I particularly like the kindergarten, first, and second-grade programs, especially their coverage of reading and phonics. This is a very teacher-intensive program. Most phonics programs require direct instruction for the beginning levels, but some reduce the amount of direct teaching around third grade. However, McRuffy continues with a teacher-intensive program all the way through. While this might be helpful for struggling readers, I think some parents might want to use a program that does not require so much direct instruction once students are able to read independently.

This program made my *101 Top Picks* list for a number of reasons. It has an appealing appearance with full-color workbooks and readers. The program is comprehensive and uses sound teaching methods. Teacher's manuals are easy to use. It incorporates multi-sensory learning, and it is surprisingly low priced. Even better, if you have more than one student or reuse the program another year, you need only purchase a second set of workbooks.

Both teacher and student books have lay-flat spiral bindings, jelly-proof covers, and sturdy pages, so they should hold up well. Teacher's manuals have step-by-step lesson plans and include reduced, color reproductions of student pages. Lessons are scripted, making it easy for the inexperienced teacher to know exactly what to do and say. Even so, there are frequent open-ended questions that might lead you off the script for a short time. This is not a predictable question-response type program.

There are two teacher's manuals for each level for first grade and above. At the beginning of each teacher's manual (only in the first volume of two-volume sets) are an overview of the program and its components, a scope and sequence, spelling lists, game ideas, suggestions for helping students with creative writing, and other helps. There are also two student workbooks for each level.

I reviewed the Special Edition (SE) which is the latest edition and the one most readily available to home educators. The most noticeable difference is that these are printed in color while earlier editions were not. However, the SE editions also have more material than the earlier editions.

Kindergarten Level

McRuffy teaches phonics in a fairly traditional fashion. Students should have some exposure to the alphabet before beginning the kindergarten program. The first lesson begins by having children identify the letters "a" through "e." They learn that there are capital and small letters as well as how to distinguish between them. They learn the /ă/ sound and they write both capital and small "a's"—all within the first lesson. Students begin blending the letters "b" and "a" together in lesson three. This is a rapid pace for students who do not already have fairly good phonemic awareness and who do not already recognize the letters of the alphabet by name. The program quickly moves students into reading sentences with lesson 23 presenting "Pat has a cat" for students to read. The kindergarten level introduces all of the letters, both long and short vowels, some digraphs, a few sight words, and the names of colors. Spelling is taught as reinforcement for phonics.

There are two sets of readers for kindergarten. These are printed in full color on matte-finish card stock. While they are attractive, they are not likely to become a child's favorite bedtime storybook collection. In the first set of ten readers, each book has only four pages. In the second set of twenty readers, each book has from 12 to 15 pages. Illustrations do provide visual clues, but as sentences get longer and especially when there is more than one sentence on a page to read, students will not be able to rely on visual clues to decode the words. The words used in each reader are printed in a large font on the back of each reader for easy review and reference. The teacher's manual directs conversation about each story that expands beyond simple comprehension into critical and creative thinking. Students practice "story creating" orally, in writing, and with cut-out puppets.

The program does include some drill. As part of a daily routine, children are drilled on the alphabet, sounds of the letters, short vowels, long vowels, capital and small-letter identification, color names, and other words they have been learning. Flashcards and laminated charts for drill and review are in the resource pack for this level.

A typical lesson might begin with some drill and review. Then following the script in the teacher's manual, you introduce a new concept. Students complete a workbook activity related to the new concept. These activities might be matching columns, circling the correct answer, reading and writing phonograms or words, puzzles, fill-in-the blanks, word searches, or cut-and-paste activities.

In some lessons students will use "sliders." Sliders are sleeves constructed from heavy card stock into which you insert strips of letters or phonograms that will appear in the window. Corresponding phonograms that will allow students to create words are already printed on each slider. Preprinted forms with sliders and instructions as well as preprinted strips for the sliders are in the resource pack.

Games add another hands-on, interactive dimension to this program. Games use laminated game boards and playing pieces that come in the resource pack. You will cut out some other game cards and pieces from card stock in the resource pack. Many games can be played solo, but most are more fun with at least one other player, even if it's a parent.

The Kindergarten Resource Pack also includes cardstock pages with figures from each storybook. These can be cut out, colored, and mounted on ice cream sticks for use as puppets. Students use these to retell the stories or do creative story telling.

Students can also use the coloring sheet for each story that has lines for writing at the bottom for them to add a caption or write a sentence. Students who prefer to draw might use the formatted pages in the resource pack that have space for drawing their own pictures and writing their own captions or sentences.

McRuffy Press Flip & Draw™: Ruff's Pre-Writing is an extra bonus included in the Kindergarten Resource Pack. This resource for developing eye-hand coordination helps children learn basic handwriting strokes and skills such as controlled lines, curves, and slant. This ingenious book has a clear overlay that can flip to cover either the front or back of any page in this book. Students should use fine line wipe-off markers as they practice tracing the various lines and shapes as well as printing their own names. The 30 pages in the book are also reproducible. The *Flip & Draw* is not incorporated into the lesson plans. Use it as you wish.

The teacher's manual includes models for handwriting in both traditional and modern manuscript forms with arrows showing directions for letter formation. At the front of the teacher's manual you will find suggestions for tactile learning for students who might benefit. Also, there are "Assessment Item Analysis" grids for the weekly assessments that will help you identify likely problem areas.

The kindergarten program also teaches language fundamentals: sentences, periods, question marks, capitalization of the first word in sentences, rhyming words, antonyms, and vocabulary. Adding handwriting instruction with McRuffy's books (choose from traditional or modern manuscript or cursive workbooks) or those from another publisher rounds this out into a total language arts program.

First Grade

At the first grade level of the McRuffy program, students have a *Spelling and Phonics* workbook *(SAP)* and a *Language and Reading* workbook *(LAR)*. Instructions in the two-volume teacher's manual direct you to teach from both workbooks and one of the storybooks in most lessons.

The first unit of *LAR* is largely review of concepts taught in kindergarten. From there it progresses to more challenges phonograms, prefixes and suffixes, contractions, and two-syllable words. By the end of first grade, most of the phonograms will have been introduced.

LAR workbook activities include writing words or sentences, sorting, circling, matching, alphabetizing, unscrambling words, proofreading and making corrections, puzzles, fill-in-the-blanks, and multiple-choice questions. The amount of writing increases significantly from the kindergarten level. The *LAR* workbook also includes a few original poems that students will read with the teacher. Phonics activities that follow relate to each poem. Every fifth workbook page is an assessment of phonics, language, and reading skills.

The teacher's manual instructs you to direct students in writing their own stories, often developing their ideas based on discussion of one of the storybooks. You can use the reproducible forms from the resource pack for this level (either single pages or forms to create books) or any other paper you choose for story writing. Instructions for creative writing, the writing process, and how to make a book are at the front of the first volume of the teacher's manual. Creative writing is one area where the instructions are general rather than prescriptively detailed. Students determine what they want to write about from your discussion time, then it is up to you to direct and assist them with ideas from the manual.

The *SAP* workbook is somewhat similar to other spelling programs, although the lessons relate directly to *LAR*. The first five weeks review concepts taught in kindergarten. After that the lessons work with a new list of spelling words each week. Words with common phonetic elements are introduced on Monday, and students complete workbook activities Monday through Thursday. Friday is for the weekly spelling test. Four weeks out of the year, the lessons review phonetic concepts previously covered in spelling lessons, but they do so with new words covering a number of phonetic elements—sort of a comprehensive review and reinforcement. Activities vary from lesson to lesson, sometimes overlapping with broader language arts skills such as adding suffixes and identifying rhyming words.

First grade level includes 34 storybooks that each have about 16 pages. The resource pack for first grade is very similar to that for kindergarten minus the flash cards. While it also has games, there was no packet with dice and pawns as there was for kindergarten. (You can use those from the kindergarten set or from any other game.)

Second Grade

The second grade program is constructed like the first grade program with a two-volume teacher's manual and two student workbooks: *Language and Reading (LAR)* and *Spelling and Phonics (SAP)*. It quickly reviews previously taught phonics skills then adds more challenging phonograms such as "ou, ough, augh," and "ph." Common phonetic elements continue to serve as the basis for spelling lists. The grammar component is much stronger as the program introduces nouns, verbs, adjectives, adverbs, pronouns, types of sentences, tenses, quotation marks, syllables, homophones, contractions, root words, prefixes, suffixes, and other topics. It teaches then reviews each topic a number of times.

The second grade course is very strong in developing reading skills. Some lessons use graphic organizers to analyze story elements, but much reading skill development occurs through the interactive dialogue led by the teacher. The 28 readers for this level generally have 16 pages each. Stories are quite complex with lengthy dialogues and many paragraphs per page. However, they still retain full-color illustrations on every other page. In addition, the *LAR* workbook includes non-fiction reading activities.

Composition work continues to challenge students with creative writing activities, but it also teaches book report writing, letter writing, recipe writing, and a few other forms of expository writing.

Instead of a resource pack there is a Test and Assessment Packet. While there are assessments in the earlier levels, those for second grade include four-page quarterly tests along with phonics and language tests for every fifth lesson.

McRuffy's optional handwriting workbooks include either printing or cursive options or a transitional book that covers both, with your choice of either traditional or slant-print style printing. Handwriting lessons correlate with phonics and spelling instruction. These worktexts are bound at the top and lie flat which makes them easy for either right- or left-handed students to use them.

Of course you can continue with this excellent program beyond second grade level, but it provides a very solid and easy-to-use foundation in reading and language arts for the early grades when it is so crucial.

· · · · · · · ·

Noah Webster's Reading Handbook

Christian Liberty Press
502 W. Euclid Ave.
Arlington Heights, IL 60004
800-348-0899
email: custserv@homeschools.org
www.christianlibertypress.com
$8.99

This has got to be just about the cheapest resource for teaching phonics and beginning

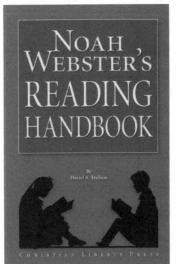

reading! It does a very adequate job, which should not be surprising since it's an updated version of Webster's original *Blue-Backed Speller* that was used to teach thousands (at least!) of children in past centuries.

It follows a fairly standard progression, introducing short vowels first then using consonant-vowel practice to help beginning readers learn to blend. (This is the same method used by A Beka's reading program and *Sing, Spell, Read, and Write*.) Practice words and sentences are included on each page as soon as is appropriate. Lengthier reading selections (Bible-based) are at the back of the book. Rules are presented in boxes at the bottom of pages, but this program does not teach very many rules compared to programs such as those based on *The Writing Road to Reading*. A few pages of technical information are at the back of the book for parents who want to better understand the functions of the alphabet and sounds.

No frills, no confusion, straight-to-the-point phonics, and there seems to be little missing other than more work on sight words, complete treatment of the "ough" sounds, and the extra practice and review students need to really master reading skills.

Add this to your list of possibilities if you're looking for a simple, uncluttered approach. This book also suits remedial learners of all ages. If using it with readers beginning in kindergarten or first grade, consider using Christian Liberty Press's *Adventures in Phonics* series for written practice and reinforcement.

· · · · · · · ·

Phonics Pathways

by Dolores G. Hiskes
Jossey-Bass/an imprint of John Wiley & Sons
800-956-7739
www.josseybass.com
Also available through the author at
Dorbooks, Inc.
800-852-4890
www.dorbooks.com
Phonics Pathways - $32.95, *Boosters* -
$24.95, *Reading Pathways* - $24.95

Phonics Pathways is one my Top Picks because it does a great job of teaching phonics, it is very reasonably priced for such a comprehensive program, it is easy for parents to use, and it has options that can make it more multi-sensory.

This is a complete phonics program, self-contained within one large book so you do not need a separate teacher's manual. There are extras that you can use alongside *Phonics Pathways*, but they are not essential.

The program will work for all ages as well as for remedial readers. Sounds of the letters are taught, beginning with short vowels. As each consonant is taught, it is immediately used to begin making blends with the short vowels. Beginning blends are taught "consonant-vowel", i.e., "ba, bi, bo," etc. Because of the quick movement into blending practice, children are reading three-letter words very soon.

Multi-sensory learning methods (hearing, saying, tracing, writing) are used with each letter. Dorbooks' supplemental card games add more hands-on activity for those who want it.

Upper and lower case letters are shown from the beginning, although children work primarily with lower case letters. You might need to take some extra time to work specifically on recognition and writing of upper case letters, although this could be done late in the program.

Each new concept taught is followed by words, phrases, or sentences for practice, so no extra reading material is necessary. Reading practice is designed to improve tracking skills from left to right, which is especially important for preventing dyslexic problems. Some of the phrases and sentences are purposely nonsensical or humorous to keep it entertaining. The "Dewey the Bookworm" character and positive-thinking type proverbs are also used throughout the book for the same reason.

The program covers all phonetic sounds, diacritical markings, suffixes and prefixes, plurals and possessives, contractions, and compound words. Teaching instruction is on each page. It is brief enough that no significant preparation time is needed.

One oddity worth noting pops up frequently in the instructions. Sometimes they are written directly to students even though students of this program cannot yet read sentences this complex. But this is no big deal. Parents or teachers just need to read through the instructions and present whatever is necessary to students.

An index to spelling rules, spelling and pronunciation charts, plural and suffix spelling charts, and two pages of "Vision and Motor Coordination Training Exercises" are found at the back of the book. Try some of these exercises if you have a child who seems to have minor learning disabilities.

Phonics Pathways introduces "pyramids" as another reading strategy within its lessons. However, there is also an entirely separate book using the pyramid concept titled *Reading Pathways*. The subtitle, *Simple Exercises to Improve Reading Fluency*, reflects the content. Reading exercises expand in pyramid fashion from a single word to complex sentences. Within each pyramid, the single word is repeated in each subsequent line, but each time one or more additional words are added to create and then expand a sentence.

You might also want to supplement with *Phonics Pathways Boosters!: Fun Games & Teaching Aids to Jump-Start Reading. Boosters!* is a collection of five items: Sound-Spelling Flash Cards, Blendit!, The Train Game, WordWorks, and *Speaking Pathways.*

Sound-Spelling Flash Cards is a set of 46, double-sided, illustrated flash cards. These flash cards are unusual since they have all possible spelling variations for the letter or phonogram on the reverse side. *The Train Game* functions as a movable alphabet to be used as a learning activity rather than as a game. Blendit! has two Bingo type games, one that focuses on two-letter blends, and one that focuses on short-vowel words. WordWorks has three sets of cards (36 per set) that are used in games played like Old Maid or Go Fish to reinforce phonics. All pages are printed on heavy cardstock, and the cards for these first four resources need to be cut apart before use. You might consider laminating them. *Speaking Pathways* is a 35-minute audio CD packaged at the back of the book. *Speaking Pathways* features Dolores Hiskes explaining and pronouncing phonics sounds as taught in *Phonics Pathways* plus spelling rules and patterns. This might be very helpful for the parent without a phonics background or for the student who would benefit from the auditory presentation.

All of these supplements are useful but not essential. However, both *Reading Pathways* and *Boosters!* should also work well with other phonics programs that use the consonant-vowel approach.

One problem that crops up in this and other programs that begin with consonant-vowel combinations is that children are guessing at vowel sounds since actual vowel sounds are generally determined by what comes after the vowel—and in the early stages of the program there's nothing "coming after" to give them a

clue. When children start reading long vowel words they need to be taught to scan ahead for signals such as silent "e" that determine the vowel sound. *Phonics Pathways* as well as *Reading Pathways* have tried to address this problem in their newest editions by adding diacritical markings to vowels when children might run into problems determining the vowel sound.

· · · · · · · · · ·

Spell to Write and Read

by Wanda Sanseri
Back Home
Industries
PO Box 22495
Milwaukie, OR
97269
www.BHIbooks.net
Core Kit - $105;
SWR - $35; *WISE
Guide* - $35

Wanda Sanseri wrote this guide for teaching the first four years of language arts—phonics, penmanship, spelling, reading, composition, logic, and introductory grammar—using methods originally presented by Romalda Spalding in *The Writing Road to Reading. The Writing Road to Reading* has a challenging organizational structure that makes it difficult for parents to use without assistance, so Wanda came up with her own easier-to-follow presentation.

The heart of *Spell to Write and Read* (SWR) is the phonograms which children practice saying, writing, seeing, and reading. Phonetically-taught spelling is the primary tool used for teaching writing and reading rather than a skill to be picked up later through reading.

The program uses its own system for marking the phonograms and highlighting rules in spelling words. Students internalize spelling in a way that naturally blends into reading.

This program has more rules and fewer sight words than most others. The result is that

99% of the 1000 most-frequently-used English words have rules that apply to them in *SWR*. In most other programs, students memorize more sight words but learn fewer rules, so there's a trade off here.

Students build their own spelling textbook, so there is quite a bit more writing than in other programs. At first glance, this program seems designed more for Perfect Paula and Competent Carl learners who might like the detailed analysis of words more than Wiggly Willys and Sociable Sues who might be frustrated with the detail and notebook work. However, many teachers who have followed the program's suggestions for using multi-sensory activities and for keeping the pace moving have been able to use it successfully with such children. (Wiggly Willy parents might still have trouble *teaching* the program.)

In addition, some learning disabled children who need much repetition and very complete, specific instruction have benefited greatly from this method. Much depends upon the parent or teacher's ability to make the program enjoyable and adapt lessons to meet the needs of each child.

SWR is to be used with Wanda's *WISE Guide for Spelling. WISE Guide* covers 2000 basic words (plus hundreds of derivatives) to teach the foundational principles of English spelling. While *SWR* provides the methodology, *WISE Guide* provides much of the content.

Wise Guide lesson plans each cover a set of twenty words in *SWR*. Recommended preliminary activities include warm-up drills and motivational comments for introducing the lesson. Sentences are provided to illustrate each word. Selections come from literature, quotes of famous people, or instructive comments. Each word is divided into syllables and highlighted to amplify phonograms and spelling rules. Information to explain the spelling is provided.

Creative ways to reinforce the spelling words are suggested. Rather than uninspiring activities like copying a word five times, students actively use spelling words in a variety of ways. The teacher is given simple instructions and the student works from the words dictated for him to write into his spelling notebook. No worksheets are needed. Spelling lists actually cover up through twelfth grade level, so you can use this program as a spelling resource for older students.

WISE Guide is much more than a spelling resource. Enrichment activities involve a wide variety of topics: literature, grammar, antonyms, synonyms, derivatives, etymology, contractions, compound words, alphabetizing, keyboard instruction, punctuation, alliteration, homonyms, analogies, words of comparison, oxymorons, figures of speech, verb conjugation, poetry, plurals, subject and verb agreement, Greek and Latin roots, possessives, and appositives. Assignments utilize art, pantomime, refrigerator magnets, deaf signing, and games. Numerous approaches are used to improve composition skills including: creative writing, letter writing, diary work, vivid word selections, descriptive writing, feature writing, and dictation.

Supplements available from Back Home Industries include 70 Basic Phonogram Cards, *Phonogram CD, Primary Learning Logs, SWR Charts, Alpha List, New England Primer,* some beginning readers, and *McCall-Crabbs Test Lessons in Reading.* When purchased from the publisher, *SWR, WISE Guide,* Phonogram Cards, Spelling Rule Cards, and *Phonogram CD* are sold as the Core Kit at a discounted price.

Sanseri and 22 other teachers she has trained and endorsed offer seminars for groups across the country and in Canada. I have received positive reports from those who have attended Sanseri's seminars and used her materials. They tell me that she gives them practical instruction that really works for homeschoolers while clearly explaining the basics so they have confidence in their knowledge and ability to teach their children. If you cannot attend a seminar, you might be interested in a four-hour instructional DVD by Sanseri titled *Hidden Secrets to Language Success*. This teacher training DVD features clips of Sanseri teaching students of various ages plus scenes from a teacher training seminar.

· · · · · · · · ·

Teach a Child to Read with Children's Books, fourth edition

by Mark Thogmartin and Mary Gallagher
New Learning Concepts, Inc.
PO Box 338
Bloomington, IN 47402
800-925-7853
www.teachachildtoread.net
$24.95

I have reviewed more phonics and reading programs than I can recall over the years. I have written up reviews of many that I liked and found useful and ignored many others. However, when I actually taught my own children to read, I never used a complete phonics program. I used bits and pieces and ideas from some programs, but we primarily used real books, magnetic letters, and encounters with the real world for developing reading skills. This might sound totally disorganized to you, but there was an underlying progression as my children first learned some of the letters and their sounds, then started recognizing some words, then mastered more letters and sounds, gradually building up a reading vocabulary from simple words to more complex. While I had a few simple beginning practice readers on hand, the most successful "learn to read" books were my sons' own favorite books like *Green Eggs and Ham*.

As I read through *Teach a Child to Read with Children's Books*, I felt like I was reading a description of my own experience. One of the most important recommendations in this book is that we read lots and lots of books to our children from the time they are little. Children develop a love of books, and they learn what reading is all about and how it works by watching and interacting with someone who reads to them. This is so foundational that the authors point to a study that tells us that, "Children who entered school with a large bank of vocabulary words they had heard and used consistently scored higher on vocabulary and comprehension tests at ages 9 and 10 than those whose vocabulary was limited" (p. 14). But it's not just about good test scores. Rather it's about developing a love for reading.

The authors, Mark Thogmartin and Mary Gallagher, discuss the conflicts between the intensive phonics and whole language camps over how to teach reading, showing that the best approach uses both methods. The authors identify problems at both extremes. Children taught with pure whole language approaches do not usually learn how to decode; everything is learned through sight and context. On the other hand, children taught with some intensive phonics programs, get so bogged down in the rules and minutiae of phonics that they associate the drills and workbooks very negatively with the whole idea of reading.

Instead of either extreme, they propose a combination of both, but one that starts with and continually works from good children's literature with phonics used when and as is appropriate. The phonics instruction grows from the child's own curiosity and interaction with words.

Recognizing that word formation and writing reinforce reading skills, the authors present an integrated use of magnetic alphabets, all sorts of beginning writing formats, dictation, copying, story writing, writing letters, and much more.

This is not a step-by-step program, but

rather a guide for parents to create their own program. Lest that sound overwhelming, they present very concrete suggestions and steps that you might follow, including a lengthy journal from one homeschooling mother who taught her daughter this way. But the methodology cannot be presented as scheduled lesson plans, because the essence of it requires that we respond to our children's own developmental timetable and select books that appeal to them. One parent might find herself working through Dr. Seuss's *Green Eggs and Ham* over and over with her child as I did while another might be focused on Eric Carle's *Do You Want to Be My Friend?* Parents will likely have a shelf full of favorite books that a child requests to hear every day, but each child is likely to have his or her own personal favorites that make great jumping off points for beginning reading.

At the back of the book are lengthy lists of children's literature that might be good choices for different levels. One list recommends read-aloud books that are predictable and use rhymes and patterns—elements that are particularly appealing to preschoolers. Some books on this list, such as Shel Silverstein's *Where the Sidewalk Ends*, might appeal to older children. The read-aloud recommendations also have a separate list for chapter books and short novels that you can continue to read aloud to older children. Other lists are recommendations for books that children might tackle themselves at each of five levels from emergent readers (pre-K) through second grade.

Lest you still think this is a totally disorganized method, record keeping forms are included. Among these are a checklist for tracking "Basic Concepts about Books and Print," a "Letter Identification Checklist," "Letter Identification Check Sheet," "Lesson Plan/Journal," "Books Read," and "Known Words." While you might use other methods of accountability such as writing "known words" on a large sheet of paper covering the back of a door, these forms might provide parents the

security and accountability they need.

I think that Mark Thogmartin and Mary Gallagher's research and recommendations are so important that I would love to see every parent of preschoolers read this before making a decision about purchasing any other program.

Beginning Phonics Readers

When children are learning phonics they need lots of practice with simple reading material. Beginning readers are sometimes included in phonics programs, but other times you need to find your own. Those listed below are not included in my 101 Top Picks since they are only representative of what is available.

A Beka Book
Box 18000
Pensacola, FL 32532
877-223-5226
www.abeka.org
$14 for all 12, teacher edition - $17.25

These are 12 small, colorful readers, divided into three sets of four books each. The sets progress in difficulty, reflected in the set titles: "I Learn to Read," "I Do Read," and "I Can Read Well." They begin with short-vowel words, shift into long vowels by the fourth book, and continue up through words like "south," "ground," and "bright." You can purchase the individual books or you might purchase the teacher edition that includes all of the readers in one comb-bound book.

Bob Books
Scholastic, Inc.
800-325-6149
www.scholastic.com
$19.99 - $21.99 per set

These sets of beginning readers are phonetically organized with controlled vocabulary, yet the stories are a bit more interesting than many other such readers. There are 12 small books in each set. The sets begin with *My First Bob Books: Pre-Reading Skills* and *My First Bob Books: Alphabet* to prepare a child for reading.

The next five sets are the actual readers that will correlate with many phonics programs. *Set 1: Beginning Readers* concentrates on short-vowel words. *Set 2: Advancing Beginners*, with 12 slightly longer books, continues with short-vowel, consistent words, adding double consonants, blends, endings, some sight words, and longer stories. *Set 3: Word Families* adds longer words and suffixes. *Set 4: Compound Words* adds sight words and compound words. *Set 5: Long Vowels* adds long vowel words.

In addition, there are two sets of *Sight Words* readers, one for kindergarten and one for first grade. Each set has ten readers. Both sets support a phonics approach while introducing sight words.

Illustrations are simple black-and-white line drawings that children can color, and both the stories and drawings have an appealing child-like character. Teaching instructions are short and simple.

Reading for Fun Enrichment Library

A Beka Book
877-223-5226
www.abeka.com
$44

Fifty-five small readers come in this boxed set. While they do not follow as strict a phonetic progression as the *Phonics Practice Readers* (reviewed next), they do begin with short vowels and gradually increase the phonetic complexity. For most children, you will still need additional practice with short vowel words beyond these readers. While there are a few Bible stories and some character-building stories, most are about children, fairy tales, nature, and other common subjects. Books are illustrated in full color. The price is very reasonable for so much good quality reading material.

Phonics Practice Readers

Modern Curriculum Press/Pearson Learning
800-848-9500
www.pearsonlearning.com
$26.97 per set

For variety's sake, Modern Curriculum Press (MCP) offers three different series (A, B, and C) of these secular readers from which you can choose. You need not purchase them all. Within each series are four sets: short vowels, long vowels, blends, and digraphs. Each set consists of ten, eight-page books. You might need only short and long vowels before your children are ready for many beginning reading books. These are inexpensive and colorfully illustrated. Each set comes with a teacher's guide.

Beyond Phonics

Once children have begun to read, the natural inclination is to get a reading program with readers and workbooks. However, this is another place where focusing on your goals can save you time, money, and effort, and possibly produce better results with your children. Here are four things to think about before deciding what to do next:

1.) If one of your goals is to improve decoding proficiency—which means being able to figure out how to say or read words—just about any reading material that is not too difficult can be used as fodder for practice. Those early reading books by Dr. Seuss and others can be much more fun than readers while providing essentially the same type decoding practice.

2.) Other goals should have to do with children understanding what they are reading. You begin at lower levels of thinking, asking children to narrate back simple data or events from what they have read. As they progress, you move on to more challenging levels of thinking. Children begin to interpret what they read, draw parallels to their own experience, or make connections to other things they know.

Later, they begin to compare and contrast, analyze, and otherwise focus more on the content than on the mechanics of reading. Reading programs can help with this, but simply applying Charlotte Mason's narration techniques with real books can accomplish the same thing.

3.) Readers and workbooks were created to help teachers with classroom management rather than because they are the best way for children to develop reading skills. With groups of children, it is much easier to manage them if everyone is reading the same book and completing the same workbook pages. However, in our homeschools, our children are generally all at different levels with reading, so we are not trying to keep all our children on the same page at the same time. In fact, I wish you luck if you even try to do such a thing!

4.) A reading program might help you stay on track and focus on some of the necessary skills if you are working with a child individually. They might be more useful for the parent than for the child! But the downside is that your child has to read someone else's collected anthology of readings, many of which might have little appeal for your child. Your child also has to work through the exercises created to go with that particular anthology whether or not those exercises really target skills your child needs at the time.

All of this doesn't mean that reading programs are necessarily bad. But I have found that selecting real books for my children to read and using supplemental resources to focus on particular skills has been far more fun and effective for all concerned. There are so many supplemental resources for reading that are useful that I want to warn you that the selections I have made for my Top Picks are very arbitrary and limited. Please explore other options too. You can easily find them at teacher supply stores, in catalogs, and online. Some will be broad in their skills coverage, while others might focus narrowly on comprehension, work with analogies, or other particular aspects.

Here I have gravitated toward some that I believe work well when you skip traditional reading programs with children past the beginning reading stage. Since reading real books is part of my recommended strategy, many of my recommendations here include guides for doing this. (Note: some resources for vocabulary are reviewed in chapter nine, and they might also be part of your reading skills development strategy.)

For those who might be leery of abandoning traditional reading programs, I suggest you pay particular attention to *Drawn into the Heart of Reading* since this "program" provides structure for a real-books approach that might give you the confidence to give it a try.

Those who still want traditional readers or reading programs might check out one of the following series.

A Beka Books has a number of readers with teacher guides for each grade level. Many readers have a single theme such as nature, heroes, or fables; some are anthologies; and some are novels. (www.abeka.com)

Christian Liberty Press Readers are an assortment of readers with different themes for different levels. (www.christianlibertypress.com)

Little Angel Readers (Stone Tablet Press) are a set of beginning readers for Catholic children. (www.stonetabletpress.com)

Nature Readers (Christian Liberty Press) feature science topics as the content. They are a bit more like "real books" than other readers. (www.christianlibertypress.com)

Pathway Readers (Pathway Books) are an excellent Amish series that reflect the rural, agricultural Amish community. Content is God-honoring and wholesome. These readers also have companion workbooks. (www.anabaptists.org/bookstore.html)

BJU Press reading courses combine anthologies and novels in complete reading programs that include workbooks. (www.bjup.com)

Rod and Staff's Bible Nurture and Reader series has been very popular with homeschoolers looking for Biblical content and no fantasy or modern sagas of cultural decadence. This series also includes workbooks. (606-522-4348, www.rodandstaffbooks.com or www. rodstaff.com)

Resources for Developing Reading Skills

Drawn into the Heart of Reading

by Carrie Austin
Heart of Dakota Publishing, Inc.
1004 Westview Dr.
Dell Rapids, SD 57022
605-428-4068
www.heartofdakota.com
packages: *Level 2/3 - $78.12, Level 4/5 - $84.55, Level 6/7/8 - $88.98, superset - $134.29;* individual student books: *Level 2/3 - $21.95, Level 4/5 - $28.95, Level 6/7/8 - $33.95*

Subtitled, "A Multi-Level Reading Program to Use with Any Books You Choose," this guide can be used along with your choice of real books for children in grades two through eight. It consists of a teacher's guide that covers all levels plus student workbooks, available at three levels: grades 2-3, grades 4-5, and grades 6-8. Workbooks can be reproduced for use with all students within your family. You will also want to purchase the appropriate level of *Book Projects To Send Home*, small activity books published by McGraw-Hill and available through Heart of Dakota Publishing for $9.95 each.

You should start with one of the packages that each include the teacher's guide plus one student book and a Sample Book Ideas list. The Superset includes the teacher's guide plus all three student books and the Sample Book Ideas list. You may also purchase additional student books individually.

You can use *Drawn into the Heart of Reading* as a core reading program (assuming young students are already able to read independently) or as a supplement. It is arranged into nine sections, each focused upon a different genre: biography, adventure, historical fiction, fantasy, mystery, folk tales, nonfiction, humor, and realistic fiction. You or your students select books representative of each genre. Because the program is structured for different levels of difficulty you can reuse it for a number of years, even reusing the same level but having your student read different books from each genre.

The program is written for use with groups or individual students; groups can be either your own children working at various levels or same-level groups. *Drawn into the Heart of Reading* is also a Christian character-building program that incorporates scripture and Biblical standards. For most families this means that your entire family will be reading books from the same genre, discussing and comparing similar story elements, and learning about the same character traits.

Some broader language arts skills are covered, and students do a good deal of writing, increasingly so as you move up each level. The guide suggests that young students may dictate some of their lengthier responses rather than writing them themselves. It also suggests writing responses on a whiteboard for students to copy.

The writing assignments themselves actually bring up one point of concern I have with the student workbooks. Workbook pages are formatted for students to fill in boxes, blanks, and circles in response to questions and instructions. However, once in a while the space allowed seems inadequate, especially in the *Level 2/3* workbook.

In addition to writing activities, the program incorporates a good deal of discussion, a little drawing, and lots of project ideas. This can be a strong multi-sensory program depending upon which elements you choose to use.

The large, softbound teacher's guide (with lay flat binding) features daily lesson plans with specific instructions for work to be done together with students as well as for independent work for each of the three levels. I really appreciate an extra feature found in each student book called "emergency options." On days when there is no time for the "together" activities, you can turn to emergency options that will fill in with independent-work assignments.

Overall, I really like the flexibility of this sort of reading program that allows parents and children to select their own reading material. The drawback to this approach is that children might be reading books with which parents are unfamiliar. Unless parents have time to also read the books, they might have trouble determining whether or not their children are identifying characters, actions, motives, plot, etc. correctly. Children might narrate to a parent about what they are reading, but a parent's ability to ask probing questions is limited. The teacher's guide *does* direct students in the first two levels to read some portions of their books aloud to parents, which helps somewhat to overcome this potential problem. Another possible strategy is for parents to provide a list of books as options—books with which parents are already familiar. In response to my concern, Carrie Austin told me that "having the parent skim the chapter as the child answers the questions provides accountability and helps give the parent a good idea of whether the child's answers to the questions are going in the right direction."

Suggested questions range from simple comprehension through higher-level thinking skills. Thus, children learn to read more thoughtfully and analytically as they work through the "lessons."

I suspect that after parents and students have worked through a number of books using this program, parents will feel more comfortable allowing children to use unfamiliar books since children will have become accustomed to noticing key information and thinking beyond the surface of the story.

· · · · · · · · ·

Progeny Press Study Guides for Literature

Progeny Press
PO Box 100
Fall Creek, WI 54743
877-776-4369
email: progeny@progenypress.com
www.ProgenyPress.com
guides for: lower elementary - $11.99 each, upper elementary - $16.99 each, middle school - $18.99, guides for high school level - $21.99 each; CD-ROM or download versions are from $1 to $3 less per guide

Progeny Press novel study guides are tools for parents who want to use real books rather than literature anthologies with their children or for supplementing study of an anthology. Available for all grade levels, they focus more on critical analysis and reading comprehension than on writing and spelling skills (as in *Total Language Plus* which is also reviewed in this chapter). Four guides are recommended per year for one full literature credit.

Although written by different authors, all come from a Christian perspective. Thus, we find questions that refer to scripture such as "Read Proverbs 17:17. 'A friend loves at all times, and a brother is born for adversity.' Tall John was Sarah's friend. At the end of Chapter 7, how did he comfort her?" (from *The Courage of Sarah Noble* study guide). Or another example from *The Hiding Place Study Guide*: "Read through I Corinthians 12:12-27. How does this passage reflect the importance of each individual within a church or family?"

The study guides deal with both literature as art and literature as a reflection or source of ideas. However, at the primary level children study vocabulary and meaning with little attention to literary constructions or style. At older levels there are studies of vocabulary, literary terms, plot, and so forth, as well as studies about the characters, events, and ideas presented.

The format varies from one study guide to another but with many common characteristics. A synopsis and some background are presented first. Ideas for pre-reading (and sometimes mid- and post-reading) activities are next. Then studies are divided up to cover groups of chapters at a time. Questions go well beyond the recall level, asking students to infer meanings, identify symbolism, draw analogies, and apply principles to their own lives. Each study section has vocabulary activities along with comprehension, analysis, personal application, and thought questions. At older levels, a lengthier writing assignment completes each section. A variety of vocabulary activities are used within each guide, so the studies maintain a higher level of interest than those that use the same format for every lesson. Particularly at younger levels, guides include extra activity suggestions; for example, *The Courage of Sarah Noble* study guide includes some art, craft, game, and cooking suggestions.

Students might be able to work through the study guides independently if their reading skills are adequate, although discussion enhances any literature study. Answer keys are found at the back of each book, so each study guide is self-contained aside from the novel itself. All study guides are reproducible for your family.

Within the Progeny Press series are a number of study guides geared for the primary grades. They are for books such as *The Courage of Sarah Noble; The Josefina Story Quilt; Keep the Lights Burning, Abbie; The Long Way to a New Land; Ox-Cart Man; Sam the Minuteman;* and *Wagon Wheels.*

Study guides geared for the upper elementary grades include such titles as *The Best Christmas Pageant Ever; The Cricket in Times Square; The Door in the Wall; Little House in the Big Woods; Sarah, Plain and Tall;* and *Charlotte's Web.*

Middle school titles stretch sometimes as low as fifth grade and up through eighth grade. Among them are *Amos Fortune, Free Man; Bridge to Terabithia; The Bronze Bow; Carry On Mr Bowditch; The Hiding Place; The Giver; Island of the Blue Dolphins; Johnny Tremain; The Magician's Nephew; Maniac Magee; Roll of Thunder, Hear My Cry; The Secret Garden;* and *The Lion, The Witch and the Wardrobe.*

For high school level, there are a number of study guides for both novels and plays such as *The Red Badge of Courage, The Yearling, Heart of Darkness, Jane Eyre, The Merchant of Venice, Hamlet, Out of the Silent Planet, To Kill a Mockingbird, A Day No Pigs Would Die, The Great Gatsby, The Adventures of Huckleberry Finn, A Tale of Two Cities,* and *Perelandra.*

Guides for 106 books (with more being added each year) are available as printed books, on CD-ROM, or via downloadable PDF files. The CD and downloadable versions are fully interactive. The digital versions include weblinks, but even more useful is the fact that students can answer multiple-choice questions and complete their written work entirely on the computer. However, you will probably still want to have students participate in discussions and complete some of the other optional activities that will not be done on the computer. The digital answer keys are in a separate file so you can keep the key on a separate computer if need be. The novels themselves are also available from Progeny Press if you need a source.

• • • • • • • • •

Reading Detective series: Using Higher-Order Thinking to Improve Reading Comprehension

by Carrie Beckwith, Cheryl Block, Christine Broz, Margaret Hockett, and David White
The Critical Thinking Co.™
800-458-4849
www.CriticalThinking.com
$24.99 each for print editions; $29.99 each for a computer home license

The Reading Detective® series is available in book or software versions with some distinct differences between the two.

The Reading Detective® series print editions

differ from most other reading comprehension workbooks that allow students to work totally independently. While students can complete much of their work independently in this series, one or more questions in most lessons ask students to explain their answers. This will require either extensive writing or discussion.

The variety of material in the reading passages surpasses that of most other reading comprehension books. For example, in book *A1* there are excerpts from *The Jungle Book* and *Where the Red Fern Grows*, a fictional letter from a gold-rush miner, a retelling of *Little Red Riding Hood* from the wolf's perspective, a skateboarding story, a mystery about a missing diamond, a biography of Cesar Chavez, instructions on how to make dough ornaments, an explanation of air pressure and the creation of wind, an article on ancient Egyptian hieroglyphs, and much more.

Students read and respond to fiction and non-fiction passages throughout these workbooks. They answer simple comprehension questions as well as more challenging questions that require them to analyze or make an inference. However, even on the simple questions, students are asked to provide evidence by indicating the number (or numbers) of the sentence(s) in the reading passage that best support the student's answer. This forces students to read closely, which might be especially helpful with children who tend to skim a reading passage and guess at the multiple-choice answers. While many questions are multiple-choice, some require students to come up with their own responses.

There are four books in the series:

Beginning (Grades 3-4) is divided into lessons addressing eight areas: inference, vocabulary (from context), story parts, main idea, theme, cause and effect, prediction, and mixed skills. Instructions and examples are at the beginning of each section so that students understand how to tackle each type of lesson. Most reading passages are written by the authors of this workbook, but some are excerpted from well-known literature.

A1 (Grades 5-6) has only three sections although students work on a variety of reading skills within each section. The ten lessons in the first section use excerpts from well-known literature. At the front of the book are ten optional literature essay questions that relate to each of these lessons. The second section uses brief fictional pieces while the third section works with non-fiction. All reading passages in the second and third sections are written by the authors of this workbook.

B1 (Grades 7-8) is arranged in the same fashion as book *A1* with three sections: fiction passages from well-known literature, other fictional short stories, and non-fiction articles. A few of the lessons include work with data analysis.

Rx is written for remedial students in grades 6 through 12. This workbook is written at a fourth to sixth grade reading level, but the content is for older students. Like the *Beginning* book, it has 11 units with instructions at the beginning of each unit. Unit topics are: main idea and supporting details, conclusions and inferences, story elements, literary devices, theme, vocabulary (from context), figurative language, cause and effect, prediction, fact and opinion, and mixed skills.

Permission is given to photocopy the lessons for use in one family or one classroom. Pre-tests and post-tests are included in each book as well as complete answer keys with suggested explanations for pertinent questions. Aside from instruction, pre-tests, and post-tests, there are about 50 lessons per book, and each lesson should be completed in one day. If you use the optional essay assignments that appear only in book *A1,* those will take additional time.

The software version of each book varies in some very significant ways. The CD-ROM for each program needs to be installed on a computer (either Windows or Mac systems). Each level has all of the same reading content and questions as the books, including instruction, pre-tests, and post-tests. However, with the program it is not always as obvious to the student what type of assignment he or she is doing; for example, a pre-test looks just like a regular lesson and accumulates points toward games just as a lesson does. The arcade games and points is another major difference from print editions. As students complete activities correctly they accumulate points to play simple arcade games included in the program.

In addition, the discussion or writing component is eliminated. Students are asked to identify the sentence, sentences, paragraph, or paragraphs that provide the best evidence for their answers instead of explaining in their own words. While this does still require close reading, it also allows guessing instead of requiring the student to compose his or her own response.

The software versions also automatically track and grade student work, allowing for totally independent work. Although you may install the program on only one computer, you may register more than one student and track their progress.

While students are able to jump around in the program, they really should work in sequence to ensure that they get the proper instruction before tackling the next category of lessons.

Content of *The Reading Detective* is secular and reflects mainstream ideas, so you might want to preview lessons. I spotted one mention of millions of years and one story on global warming that attributes the cause solely to human activity, but I did not spot anything else problematic enough that I would not be comfortable allowing one of my children to work through these lessons independently.

The variety of content and thought-provoking activities make this series appealing, and the choice of print or software options allows you to select the approach that is most likely to work with different types of learners.

• • • • • • • •

Total Language Plus

by Barbara Blakey
Total Language Plus, Inc.
PO Box 12622
Olympia, WA 98508
360-754-3660
email: customer@totallanguageplus.com
www.totallanguageplus.com
guides for grades 3-4 - $25.95 each,
guides for grades 5 and up - $21.95 each

Total Language Plus (TLP) novel study guides cover "...reading, comprehension, spelling, grammar, vocabulary, writing, listening, and analytical and critical thinking with a Christian perspective." Each volume is both student study guide and workbook for study of a companion novel. Study guides are written for various levels from third through twelfth grades. For example, the study of *Caddie Woodlawn* is suggested for grades five and six while *Anne of Green Gables* is suggested for grades seven through nine.

Students read sections of the novel each week and answer comprehension questions. But that's only one aspect of *TLP*. The week's study also includes vocabulary work consisting of four lessons working with words drawn from the reading. There are also four activities for a list of spelling words drawn from the reading. Grammar worksheet activities include dictation exercises and grammatical work with the dictated material.

In the guides for fifth grade and up, lessons dealing with grammar, writing, and spelling rules are for application and review rather than instruction. There are occasional exceptions in some of the high school level guides such as *To Kill a Mockingbird* and *Around the World in 80 Days* which do include some instruction in composition and literary analysis. Aside from that, a basic understanding of grammar, spelling, and composition skills is assumed in the guides for grades five and up.

The new series of *TLP* guides for third and fourth grade maintain intensive coverage of reading comprehension, spelling, and vocabulary, while they add detailed grammar and composition instruction along with some spelling rules. These levels also have students create and work with spelling and vocabulary flash cards in drills and games. Keep in mind that you might need to use other resources for grammar for these levels because grammar instruction is spotty; there is no set progression of skill or topic coverage. Because of the additional content, these guides are larger than the others.

In all of the guides, students create their own glossary toward the back of the book by entering definitions and parts of speech labels for their vocabulary words each week.

At the beginning of each unit are Enrichment/Writing suggestions. These always include writing activities, but other activities depend upon the book being studied. For example, the guide for *Around the World in Eighty Days* includes map and geography work. Some activities are not tied directly to any one chapter so you can use them when, if, and how you wish. You can select more activities to turn your study into an in-depth unit study or choose fewer and stick to the basics. You might use some of these for discussion and some for writing assignments. The activities are presented as suggestions rather than as fully developed plans, so they will require independent research and work beyond what is presented in the guide. *TLP's* effectiveness in developing broader writing skills is also dependent upon your selection of assignments from the Enrichment/Writing suggestions as well as upon your work with your students on the writing process within those assignments.

Study guides get more challenging at high school level, especially with the addition of extensive writing activities and oral readings. I am particularly impressed with the quality of the writing activities. They teach and stress organization and planning, while offering students ideas about the main points they might wish to include. This is very helpful since this seems to be a challenging area for many students, and many parents are unsure about how to develop these writing skills. *TLP's* writing assignments at upper levels should provide a significant part of your composition instruction.

In addition, the level of the vocabulary and spelling in advanced-level guides is quite challenging. The amount of both vocabulary and spelling practice is appropriate for high schoolers, although some students might need to work on additional vocabulary words that are at a less challenging level.

A "Note to Teachers and Students" in each book explains how to use each study guide. Answer keys are at the back of each book. Suggested responses are given for some questions, but parents really need to read the novels themselves to be able to fairly evaluate all student responses as well as to be prepared for discussions. Other than that, preparation time is minimal. Students will need access to a Bible, dictionary and thesaurus for some of their work.

The number of lessons in the various volumes of *TLP* ranges from five to eight, so some books are likely to take longer to study than others. Generally, a volume should take from nine to ten weeks to complete, so plan to complete about four per school year.

If impatient students want to read through the novel quickly rather than spread it out, they can do so covering the comprehension and critical thinking questions as they go and working through the remainder of each week's lessons on a slower schedule.

You need to obtain the novel for each study, so TLP sells inexpensive copies. There are more than 50 guides for novels available at this time. Novels covered for third and fourth grade are *The Courage of Sarah Noble, Charlotte's Web, Pippi Longstocking, Shiloh, Sign of the Beaver,* and *The Whipping Boy.* Among novels for which TLP has guides for fifth grades and up are *My Side of the Mountain; The Cricket in Times Square; The Light in the Forest; The Lion, the Witch, and the Wardrobe; A Wrinkle in Time; Johnny Tremain; The Bronze Bow; Caddie Woodlawn; The Giver; Wheel on the School; The Trumpeter of Krakow; Where the Red Fern Grows; The Call of the Wild; The Hiding Place; The Swiss Family Robinson; Carry on, Mr. Bowditch; Rifles for Watie; Anne of Green Gables; The Scarlet Letter; Oliver Twist; To Kill a Mockingbird;* and *Jane Eyre.*

Three additional anthology guides are also available. *American Literature: Nonfiction, American Literature: Poetry* and *American Literature: Short Stories* are intended to be used along with the guides for *To Kill a Mockingbird* and *The Scarlet Letter* to comprise a high school level American Literature course. The *American Literature* guides include examples of poetry and short stories, but you will need to find most of the readings used along with the study guides within anthologies or on the internet. These guides include planning schedules for completing the modules that might take from six to ten weeks each depending upon the academic needs of students and the time available.

TLP also has a unique anthology guide, *Christmas: Volume 1* ($15.95). It is a smaller guide covering three short stories: "A Pint of Judgment," "The Fir Tree," and "The Gift of the Magi." It is designed for multi-level use and should take about four weeks to complete. Unlike other guides, the three stories are already included in the study guide.

In all of the aforementioned guides, scripture verses are often used for dictation, and exercises have very general Christian references once in a while such as in the example sentence given for the word "approbation" which reads, "God bestows His approbation on all who seek to do His will" (TLP, *The Swiss Family Robinson,* p. 80).

TLP guides might serve as a supplement or a primary learning tool depending upon the needs of each student. It should be your primary resource for reading skills; you do not need another reading program. It complements other instruction in grammar, composition, and spelling. However, it might be your primary resource for composition at high school level.

Focus Guides ($8.50 each), a new series of much smaller guides to novels, do not include spelling or grammar and have limited work with vocabulary. Instead, they focus on reading comprehension, substantial writing assignments, scripture applications with memory verses, and either a particular writing skill or a character trait. For example, the study of *Animal Farm* works on discernment, while the study of *Crispin: The Cross of Lead* pays special attention to descriptive writing. Guides are written for students about sixth grade level and above. These guides should each take only about three weeks to complete. They might still function as the core of your language arts program when TLP develops enough of them to cover a full school year. The scripture applications give the Focus Guides more overt Christian content than the other TLP guides.

Junior/Senior High Level

Literary analysis becomes more important with older students. There are some excellent series that use high quality literature and do a good job teaching literary analysis and appreciation. Some of my personal favorites use the literature as a springboard for teaching Christian worldview.

Anthologies that contain collections of short stories, poetry, scripts, and excerpts from lengthier writings can be very helpful for exposing students to a broad range of literary types without overwhelming them with ones they find less appealing. It might also be an easier way to introduce them to more variety in literary genres than you could cover with complete books. So sometimes it makes sense to select a literature anthology for study rather than a selection of complete books. Keep this in mind when making choices for your children. If they need broader exposure or if that better fits

your educational goals, then you should use an anthology like the BJU Press Books or extra resources such as the Norton Anthologies (easily located at libraries or through online sources such as Amazon). If you would rather go in-depth with a few of the best books, then *Teaching the Classics* (reviewed in this chapter) or the novel study guides from Progeny Press or Total Language Plus might better suit your situation.

No matter which way you go, junior and senior high school students should be reading at least a few full-length books each year. Because this is so important, after the upper level reviews I have included a list of recommended reading for high school level (gathered from a number of sources) that might help you make selections. Notice that some of these books are covered by study guides in the Progeny Press and Total Language Plus series reviewed earlier in this chapter.

· · · · · · · ·

BJU Press literature courses for grades 7-12

BJU Press
Greenville, SC 29614
800-845-5731
www.bjup.com

Literature courses are not all created equal. Some seem to have selected reading material to meet multicultural or social goals rather than as examples of good literature. Others seem to focus on simple comprehension questions (e.g., identify the protagonist and the antagonist) and never get into "meaty" discussion questions that really engage students.

The BJU Press series for grades seven through twelve does a great job on both ends, especially if you are interested in developing a strong Christian worldview in your students. Courses in the series are *Explorations in Literature* (7th), *Excursions in Literature* (8th), *Fundamentals of Literature* (9th), *Elements of Literature* (10th), *American Literature* (11th), and *British Literature*

(12th).

They feature an interesting mix of reading material. Many reading selections authored by non-Christians are included both for literary value and to help students learn how to identify different perspectives authors bring to their works. However, literary analysis and enjoyment is taught from a Protestant perspective; so much so in *American Literature* and *British Literature* that those with other religious beliefs will have trouble with some of the selected readings, discussion questions, and the "Application" part of the lessons presented in the teacher editions. Application sections at all levels almost always relate the reading selection to biblical ideas or principles.

One of the main purposes of this series is helping students to progress beyond simply reading for pleasure to the point where they enjoy reading for inspiration and wisdom. Discussion questions are one of the primary tools used to make that happen.

The discussion questions are particularly good in this series, and they might be used for either oral discussion or writing assignments. At junior high level, they focus more on recall and comprehension. *Fundamentals* and *Elements* shift toward more literary analysis. *American* and *British Literature* challenge students to think much more broadly. For example, *American Literature* includes a short story "The Minister's Black Veil" by Nathaniel Hawthorne. Among discussion questions are the following: "In your opinion, does Hooper's self-imposed isolation represent self-denial for the edification of others, or is it symbolic of misdirected religious zeal? Discuss Hawthorne's theme in light of I John 1:8-10" (p. 306).

Parents and teachers need to be familiar with the readings so they can lead discussions. While students can do a certain amount of work independently, parents will need to invest some time preparing for each lesson. Teacher editions provide background, analysis, and suggested answers, so even teachers without background in literature can teach these courses. As with all literature anthologies, parents and teachers are not expected to use every selection. Choose some from each section to fit your own goals and time schedule.

Each course has a student text and spiral-bound teacher edition, with two volumes each for the teacher editions for *American* and *British Literature*. Teacher editions have reduced student pages. Below student pages and in side margins is valuable teaching information. Tests and answer keys are in separate packets. In each teacher edition, words, sentences, or paragraphs of the student text are highlighted in up to six different colors to match similarly colored margin notes to the teacher. They might indicate a point for discussion, a definition, an example of a literary element, or a cross-reference. Reproducible, supplemental activity pages and some teacher helps are at the back of each teacher edition.

Teacher editions for *Explorations*, *Excursions*, *Fundamentals*, and *Elements* include a CD-ROM with teacher support materials such as worksheets, graphic organizers for students, quizzes, writing rubrics, and standardized test practice in reading and vocabulary.

All courses have tests and answer keys that are included in the subject kits along with a student text and the teacher edition.

Explorations in Literature, *Third Edition*
subject kit $126.50

Explorations in Literature and *Excursions in Literature* are similar in format, so these first

two paragraphs describe both courses. Lessons in the teacher edition follow a format of overview, objectives, potential problems (e.g., objections to authors portraying animals as having human qualities), introductory discussion, the reading, analysis, application, and additional activities. Suggestions for journal writing are given. Vocabulary words with definitions are inserted right into the text of each piece in the student text.

There are questions at the end of each literary piece (or section of a piece for lengthier writings), and these are preceded by an insert called the "Thinking Zone." Thinking Zones are visually-separated inserts that might take up about a third of a page. Thinking Zones highlight key literary elements and show how they have been implemented in the selection students have just read. They feel more like sidebars than instructional material although they accomplish the latter's purpose. Questions that follow are thought provoking, addressing literal, critical, interpretive, and appreciative elements. (Each question is labeled as to which of these areas it addresses.) Each unit has a review in the student textbook. Reviews are tests that include multiple-choice, true/false, matching, and short-answer questions along with one or two essay questions. Space is provided within these texts for students to answer questions from both chapters and units directly in the book.

The seventh-grade-level text covers a wide range of themes while emphasizing character. Content sections are titled Courage, Nature and Man, Generosity, Our Land, Humility, and Family. While some selections are by well-known authors (e.g., Carl Sandburg, O. Henry, Charles Finney, and James Thurber), most authors are not readily recognized. Nevertheless, both literary quality and appeal for young teens are high. Selections are primarily prose, but there is also some poetry.

Excursions in Literature, Third Edition
subject kit $126.50

See the description in the first two paragraphs under *Explorations in Literature* since the format of these two texts is similar. The theme of this eighth-grade text is a Christian's

journey through life, including choices he must face. Illustrations from scripture appear at the end of each unit. The text continues the character emphasis of the seventh-grade book. Units are titled Choices, Friends, Viewpoints, Adventures, Discoveries, and Heroes and Villains. Some authors and writings (or excerpts) included are Lew Wallace (*Ben Hur*), Louisa May Alcott (*Little Women*), Charles Dickens (*A Christmas Carol*), Jack London (*The Banks of the Sacramento*), George MacDonald (*The Princess and Curdie*), and Amy Carmichael (*Make Me Thy Fuel*). A short novel *In Search of Honor*, studied in the final unit, is included within the textbook.

Fundamentals of Literature, Second Edition

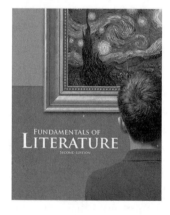

subject kit $131

Suggested for grade nine, this textbook is the foundation for the study of literature throughout high school. It teaches conflict, character, theme, structure, point of view, and moral tone through both traditional and contemporary selections. Representative authors are Sir Arthur Conan Doyle, Lord Tennyson, Shakespeare, Carl Sandburg, Sir Walter Scott, John Donne, and Saki (H.H. Munro). The drama *Cyrano De Bergerac* is also included within the text, with a DVD available for $14.95.

Elements of Literature, Second Edition
subject kit $126.50, Romeo and Juliet DVD

$14.95

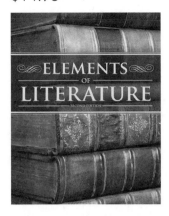

This text, suggested for tenth grade, teaches literary analysis at a more challenging level than does *Fundamentals of Literature*. It delves into topics such as themes, allusions, symbolism, and irony, as well as teaching more about the forms of literature—fiction, poetry, biography, drama, and so on. Shakespeare's *Romeo and Juliet* is included for study within the text. You might want to use the optional DVD of selected scenes from a BJU production of *Romeo and Juliet*. The DVD also has director's explanations of what has happened leading up to each scene.

American Literature, Updated Second Edition

subject kit $131.50

This text, written for eleventh grade, covers American literature from the colonial period up through the twentieth century. Representative authors are William Bradford, Benjamin Franklin, Nathaniel Hawthorne, Henry David Thoreau, Herman Melville, Samuel Clemens, Thornton Wilder, and Bruce Catton. Selections are organized by historical literary periods, while addressing some of the philosophical movements that influenced literature. There is significant discussion of the worldviews reflected by authors and their works.

British Literature, Second Edition

subject kit $131, Macbeth DVD $14.95

This twelfth grade course covers eight literary periods from Old English to Mod-ern.

Selections are often chosen to illustrate philosophical and cultural issues from various perspectives. Religious developments receive far more attention here than they do in most other British literature texts. Representative authors include John Wycliffe, Geoffrey Chaucer, Thomas More, Shakespeare, Ben Jonson, William Wordsworth, and Robert Browning. The play *Macbeth* is also included for study. An optional DVD of *Macbeth* is available.

• • • • • • • • •

Teaching the Classics: A Socratic Method for Literary Education

by Adam and Missy Andrews
The Center for Literary Education
3350 Beck Road
Rice, WA 99167
509-738-2837
www.centerforlit.com
DVDs and book - $89

Teaching the Classics: A Socratic Method for Literary Education teaches parents and teachers how to understand and analyze literature using Socratic questioning and discussion. This seminar consists of a book and a set of four DVD's.

I began my review by reading through the book. Halfway through the book, I began wondering why I would need the DVDs. The book was so well explained and provided concrete models to work with. I expected the DVDs to be redundant. To my surprise, they were not. On the DVDs, Adam Andrews presents a live seminar, covering the material in the book and much more. His goal in the seminar presentation is to ensure that parents and teachers leave feeling competent to apply the methodology themselves. I think he accomplishes this very well while also providing the sort of inspiration that makes you feel like you just can't wait to try this out.

The DVDs run about 5.5 hours. I expect you might watch through the entire course, then come back and rewatch sections as you begin to work with the different teaching strategies with your students.

In the first half hour or so of the seminar, Andrews lays the foundation. This part could possibly be a little redundant for those already very familiar with classical education, Socratic questions, and their use in conjunction with literature. But, it is absolutely essential for those unfamiliar with these things. Once past the introduction, Andrews introduces a method of tackling literature that applies to adult level fiction all the way down to children's story books. In fact, children's stories are generally easier to work with, so he recommends beginning (even with high school students) by analyzing a story written for children.

Three very useful appendices at the back of the book are referenced during the seminar. The first appendix contains "The Socratic List," an extensive, ten-page list of questions to use for discussions, arranged under broader categories of key questions. Questions are arranged from easier to more challenging levels of difficulty in each category. The teacher should select just a few of these questions to use for each discussion. Appendix B is an annotated, recommended reading list catalogued under three levels for young children through high school. Appendix C lists and defines literary devices students will learn to identify such as metaphors, alliterations, and onomatopoeias.

To help you get started, Andrews uses a number of literary works to demonstrate how to work through different aspects of analysis and discussion. Among this eclectic selection are "Paul Revere's Ride," *The Tale of Peter Rabbit*, *Rikki-Tikki-Tavi*, *The Adventures of Tom Sawyer*, *Macbeth*, *To Kill a Mockingbird*, and "Casey at the Bat."

You can teach all types of literature once you've gone through this seminar. No other student books need to be purchased other than the literature itself. You might purchase (or borrow) one or more of the *Norton Anthologies*, *Cliff's Notes*, or other resources that will provide you with context and background information for a particular piece. But the reproducible "Story Chart" (for identifying plot, theme, characters, setting, and conflict) and questions at the back of the *Teaching the Classics* book provide the rest of your "lesson plan."

You can begin to have Socratic discussions with younger children, assisting them in completing the Story Chart until they are able to do this on their own. Older students can follow up with essays or papers that further develop a particular topic. (Andrews recommends Institute for Excellence in Writing's *Structure and Style* approach for teaching composition skills. The two programs fit together very well.)

The Socratic dialogues generated by this type of learning are effective far beyond the knowledge of literature. They teach children how to think and how to express their thoughts. Within those dialogues, it will be up to the parent or teacher to introduce his or her own worldview perspective. Some of the questions naturally lead into that type of discussion, particularly with certain books. Andrews' recommended reading list includes a wide variety of books while shying away from current popular literature in favor of more classics that are likely to be great for discussion. For those who want a stronger worldview emphasis, the *Worldview Supplement* has two DVD's and a 60-page book that expand ideas for worldview analysis.

Socratic teaching requires more from the parent or teacher than most of the novel study guides that are popular among homeschoolers. The teacher must read and be familiar with the literary work to be able to lead a discussion. The Center for Literary Education does have DVD presentations, each with a companion syllabus, for some works such as *Huckleberry Finn* and *Hamlet*. These might be helpful for those parents with limited time, but they still require the parent to lead discussion.

Once a parent or teacher becomes familiar with the techniques taught by *Teaching the Classics*, those techniques are likely to become "second nature"—teaching this way will become easier and easier. And you are likely to enjoy it so much that you won't mind the extra time it might take.

Recommended Reading for High School Level Literature

The following are taken primarily from core literature recommendations for high school students, but I have added some titles I think important from a Christian perspective. Some of the listed titles are recommended by educational authorities but are not necessarily titles I personally would recommend.

- *The Adventures of Huckleberry Finn* and other works by Mark Twain
- *The Aeneid* of Virgil
- *Alice's Adventures in Wonderland* by Lewis Carroll
- *All Quiet on the Western Front* by Erich Maria Remarque
- *All the King's Men* by Robert Penn Warren
- *Anna Karenina, War and Peace,* and other works by Leo Tolstoy
- *Anne Frank: Diary of A Young Girl* by Anne Frank
- *Anne of Green Gables* and other titles by Lucy Maud Montgomery
- *Billy Budd, Moby Dick,* and other works by Herman Melville
- *Black Like Me* by John Howard Griffin
- *Brave New World* by Aldous Huxley
- *Canterbury Tales* by Geoffrey Chaucer
- "The Charge of the Light Brigade" and other works by Alfred Lord Tennyson
- *The Chosen* by Chaim Potok
- *Christy* by Catherine Marshall
- *Crime and Punishment* by Fyodor Dostoyevsky
- *Cry the Beloved Country* by Alan Paton
- *David Copperfield, Great Expectations, A Tale of Two Cities,* and other works by Charles Dickens
- *The Death of Socrates* and other works by Plato
- "The Devil and Daniel Webster" and other works by Stephen Vincent Benet
- *The Divine Comedy* by Dante
- *Don Quixote* by Miguel de Cervantes
- *Exodus* by Leon Uris
- *A Farewell to Arms* by Ernest Hemingway
- *The Good Earth* by Pearl S. Buck
- *The Grapes of Wrath, The Pearl, The Red Pony, Of Mice and Men,* and other works by John Steinbeck
- *The Great Divorce, Screwtape Letters,* and *Mere Christianity* by C.S. Lewis
- *The Great Gatsby* by F. Scott Fitzgerald
- *Gulliver's Travels* and other works by Jonathan Swift
- *The Guns of August* by Barbara W. Tuchman
- *Hamlet, Henry V, Macbeth, A Midsummer Night's Dream, Othello, The Merchant of Venice,* and other works by William Shakespeare
- "The Hollow Men" and other works by T.S. Eliot
- *The Hound of the Baskervilles* and other works by Sir Arthur Conan Doyle

- *The Iliad* and *The Odyssey* by Homer
- *In His Steps* by Charles M. Sheldon
- *The Invisible Man* by Ralph Ellison
- *Jane Eyre* by Charlotte Bronte
- "The Legend of Sleepy Hollow" and other works by Washington Irving
- *Lés Miserables* by Victor Hugo
- *The Life and Times of Frederick Douglass* by Frederick Douglass
- *The Light in the Forest* by Conrad Richter
- *Little Women* by Louisa May Alcott
- *A Man for All Seasons* by Robert Bolt
- *The Marquis' Secret* and other works by George MacDonald (in updated versions)
- *The Martian Chronicles* and other works by Ray Bradbury
- *Men of Iron* by Howard Pyle
- *The Miracle Worker* by William Gibson
- *Moby Dick* by Herman Melville
- *1984* and *Animal Farm* by George Orwell
- "Oedipus Rex," "Antigone," and other plays by Sophocles
- *Okay for Now* by Gary D. Schmidt
- *One Day in the Life of Ivan Denisovitch* by Alexandr Solzhenitsyn
- "Ozymandias" and other works by Percy Bysshe Shelley
- *Paradise Lost* by John Milton
- *Perelandra, Out of the Silent Planet*, and other works by C.S. Lewis
- *Pilgrim's Progress* by John Bunyan
- "The Pit and the Pendulum" and other works by Edgar Allen Poe
- *Pride and Prejudice* by Jane Austen
- *The Prince* by Niccolo Machiavelli
- *The Princess Bride* by William Goldman
- *Pygmalion* by George Bernard Shaw
- *A Raisin in the Sun* by Lorraine Hansberry
- "The Road Not Taken" and other works by Robert Frost
- *Robinson Crusoe* by Daniel Defoe
- *The Scarlet Letter* by Nathaniel Hawthorne
- *Silas Marner* by George Elliott
- *The Spy* and other works by James Fenimore Cooper
- *Stranger in a Strange Land* by Robert A. Heinlein
- "Tiger, Tiger" and other poems by William Blake
- *The Time Machine* by H.G. Wells
- *To Kill a Mockingbird* by Harper Lee
- *Treasure Island, Kidnapped*, and other works by Robert Louis Stevenson
- *A Tree Grows in Brooklyn* by Betty Smith
- *The Trilogy of the Ring* by J. R. Tolkein
- *Twenty Thousand Leagues Under the Sea, Around the World in Eighty Days*, and other works by Jules Verne
- *Uncle Tom's Cabin* by Harriet Beecher Stowe
- *Wuthering Heights* by Emily Bronte
- *The Yearling, Cross Creek*, and other works by Marjorie K. Rawlings

Obviously, the above list is not comprehensive. You might also want to focus more on the Great Books, only a few of which are included in the above list. Websites where you can find lists of both the Great Books and Good Books are on p. 16.

Language Arts: Grammar and Composition

"Language Arts" is a broad term that encompasses all areas of English communication. Thus, reading, phonics, grammar, composition, handwriting, spelling, and vocabulary are all part of language arts. However, in the world of curriculum each of these subjects is often isolated from the others. While focusing on a single area can be useful at times, it often makes sense to integrate the various language arts areas with each other. You might want to use resources such as *Total Language Plus* novel study guides (reviewed in chapter seven) that develop various language arts skills in relation to each novel that is read. Or maybe you will choose a unit study program (such as those reviewed in chapter thirteen) that integrates language arts with other subjects such as science and history.

Since I have already covered reading and phonics recommendations in chapter seven, in this chapter, I will present my Top Picks for composition and grammar. Then you will find my Top Picks for spelling, vocabulary, and handwriting in chapter nine. I begin with composition and grammar resources since these two subject areas are usually the primary focus of language arts once past the beginning reading stage and because these two areas are often combined within language arts courses. Reviews of my Top Picks are in alphabetical order, but notice that some resources are just for grammar, some just for composition, and some for both.

. . . .

A Beka Book Language series

A Beka Book
PO Box 19100
Pensacola, FL
32523
877-223-5226
www.abeka.com

I include A Beka's *Language* series in my Top Picks with some hesitation. I know that some home-schoolers have strong negative feelings about these books. However, I think they are very useful when used with discretion. That means parents pick and choose how much of which activities to use within each book. It also means that you should not do every book in the series or you might give your children good cause to hate grammar forevermore.

On the plus side, A Beka *Language* does a thorough job with grammar instruction. I've yet to find anything I like better, especially at upper grade levels. Over the years, as A Beka has published new editions of these worktexts, they have beefed up instruction in composition skills. However, A Beka's composition instruction remains pedestrian in comparison to other available options, so you may want to use other resources for developing composition skills.

Grammar and broader language instruction is A Beka's forté, and their approach will be especially appealing to parents who want their children to know all the ins and outs of grammar, including sentence diagramming.

As good as the grammar coverage is, it does repeat much of the same material from year to year. So you might use A Beka for alternating years. For example, use A Beka one year, then the next year focus on composition with one of the other great resources available, while using *Daily Grams* (reviewed under *Easy Grammar*), *Editor in Chief* (www.criticalthinking.com), or another such tool to review grammar skills.

While A Beka has books for first and second grade, I begin my review with the third grade book. The first and second grade books are closely integrated with the rest of A Beka's language arts curriculum for teaching phonics, reading, spelling, and handwriting as well as grammar and composition. It is possible to use only the *Language* books (especially *Language 2*) for these early grades apart from the rest of the curriculum, but there are better resources to use that stand alone. A Beka *Language* books stand on their own for third grade and above.

A Beka is well known for strong Christian and patriotic content in their books. They incorporate these topics throughout their exercises. For example, in *Language 3*, a lesson about capitalizing the first words of sentences has five practice sentences that, taken together, read as a paragraph about the American flag. In a lesson on quotation marks, one child asks his friend, "Have you accepted Jesus as your Savior?" A punctuation exercise uses the sentence "D.L. Moody was a great preacher." Bible stories are frequently used in the same manner.

All books except those for grades 11 and 12 are in worktext format; instruction and exercises are in a single, consumable student book. This makes it easy for students to complete most of their work independently.

An answer key for each book has answers overprinted on reproduced student pages. Books for grades 1 through 6 are printed in full color with appealing illustrations. Upper level books are very businesslike in appearance, printed in two colors with no illustrations.

Separate student quiz/test books and answer keys are available for every level. A Beka also has *Homeschool Language Arts Curriculum/ Lesson Plans* (or *Parent Guide and Student Daily Lessons*) for each grade level with detailed lesson plans and extra teaching ideas. Homeschool editions of these teacher books for each level coordinate spelling, vocabulary, handwriting, reading, and language lessons from A Beka books for all these subjects—not just language.

These teacher books are not essential, and I suspect most homeschoolers will be able to function well without them.

The book titles in the series are a little confusing. *Language 1, 2,* and *3* are for grades 1, 2, and 3 respectively. Then *Language A, B,* and *C* are for grades 4, 5, and 6. *Grammar and Composition I* through *IV* are for grades 7 through 10.

For grades 11 and 12, A Beka provides a single *Handbook of Grammar and Composition* and companion workbooks for each year. Instruction is in the handbook, while practice activity is done in the workbooks and separate writing assignments.

Language 3
student worktext - $15.90, answer key - $21.50, curriculum - $40, test book - $5.75, test key - $11

Language 3 reviews beginning grammar skills such as punctuation, capitalization, suffixes, and proper word usage that are typically taught in resources for this level. It also introduces parts of speech (nouns, verbs, adjectives), simple diagramming, and beginning composition skills.

The *Language Arts 3 Curriculum* book adds suggestions for developing composition skills not found in the worktext, so if you are relying on this course for composition as well as grammar coverage, you might want to purchase the *Curriculum* book. However, instruction and assignments are in the student worktext, and blank templates for creative writing and journal pages are at the end of that book, so there is some composition coverage without the *Curriculum* book.

A "Handbook of Rules and Definitions" toward the end of the student book is handy for reference. Periodic review quiz pages are in the worktext.

It is possible to work only from the student worktext, but you should probably also purchase the answer key. A separate student test booklet and answer key are also available.

God's Gift of Language A (grade 4)
student worktext - $15.65, answer key - $21.50, curriculum - $35, quiz/test book - $5.75, quiz/test key - $11

Compared to the rest of the series, *Language A, B,* and *C* do a better job on composition skills. The first third of *Language A* focuses on the writing process, although it also includes mechanics such as punctuation, abbreviation, capitalization, and possessives in this section. The second section teaches all eight parts of speech along with traditional sentence diagramming. The third section concentrates on word usage and dictionary skills. Review exercises or quizzes (depending upon how you choose to use them) are at the end of each section. One quibble: When they teach letter writing and addressing envelopes, they spell out state names in addresses which is unacceptable to the post office.

A set of *Language Charts* ($11) is also available. These are small "posters" with the steps of the writing process, state of being verbs, and other helpful items that you might post in your "classroom" area. The same charts are used for grades four through six.

God's Gift of Language B (grade 5)
student worktext - $15.65, answer key - $21.50, curriculum - $35, quiz/test book - $5.75, quiz/test key - $11

Both writing and grammar skills receive comprehensive coverage in *Language B*. Writing instruction covers topic sentences, paragraphs, and transitions. Outlining, taking notes, and preparing bibliographies are also taught in the context of report writing. Students complete a library research report, including use of note cards and creation of a bibliography.

Capitalization, punctuation, word usage, dictionary skills, and parts of speech are reviewed extensively, with more complex concepts added to those taught last year. The text also introduces complements and the use of a thesaurus.

God's Gift of Language C (grade 6)
student worktext - $15.65, answer

key - $21.50, curriculum - $35, quiz/test book - $5.75, quiz/test key - $11

Language C covers most of the same material we find in *Language B* but at more challenging levels. Grammar, composition, and mechanics are thoroughly reviewed. If your child has studied grammar in a hit-or-miss fashion up to this point, this is a good book for reviewing and making sure that everything has been covered. However, it will probably be overwhelming for a child who has studied little to no grammar. While this worktext is intended for sixth graders, the "C" designation allows you to use it for an older child if need be since the grade level is not obvious.

The writing process is taught with explanations and examples. However, instruction moves quickly from composing a paragraph to writing a research paper using note cards and including a bibliography. As with grammar instruction, there is some review, but it is likely to be too challenging for the student who has not already done a significant amount of writing. "The Student Writer's Handbook" is a helpful reference aid placed at the end of the text; it has an assortment of tools such as a key to proofreading marks, a checklist for book reports, how to use the Dewey Decimal System, and sample letter formats. Note that cursive rather than printed words are used in diagramming examples.

Grammar and Composition, Books I – IV (grades 7-10)

student books - $17 each, teacher keys - $21 each, quiz/test books - $6.75 each, answer keys - $10.75 each, curriculum books - $17 each

These worktexts offer thorough review of grammar with fairly comprehensive coverage of writing skills. A significant handbook (more than 75 pages in *Book IV*) is at the back of each book for handy reference.

Instruction is presented in a rules-and-explanation format in boxes at the beginning of each lesson. In the composition lessons, the explanation sometimes extends to a few pages. This is followed by practice and application exercises.

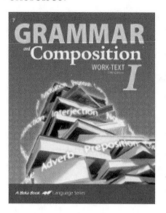

Students who have been studying grammar every year will find these books repetitious. However, those who have neglected grammar for a few years should find them comprehensive enough to catch up on missed concepts. Since these books review parts of speech, punctuation, capitalization, types of sentences, diagramming, library skills, and other concepts they need to know, students are certain to cover anything they might have missed or forgotten in regard to grammar.

Composition skills begin with paragraph structure, outlines, improving style, writing summaries, book reports, and research papers in the first two books. The series continue through writing projects such as critical book reviews, character sketches, and research papers in the fourth book. From the first book on, lessons on writing research papers include instructions for footnotes and endnotes as well as how to document digital sources. The fourth level adds an unusual but helpful section on diction.

If you purchase only the student texts and teacher editions, you might have difficulty figuring out how to use the writing instruction and assignments. If this is the case, you might want the *Homeschool Curriculum/Lesson Plans* for grades seven or eight or the *Parent Guide and Student Daily Lessons* books for grades nine or ten. The *Homeschool Curriculum/Lesson Plans* are intended for parental use but could easily be referred to by students. They list daily activities and page numbers so it is easy to see what needs to be done each day. I really like the *Parent Guide and Student Daily Lessons* books for ninth and tenth grades since they are written for students to use. These include detailed, daily lesson plan assignments for students. Students can use them to check off assignments as they complete them and to keep track of time spent each day. Parents have a line to initial when they have checked each day's assignment. Separate test and test key booklets are available.

Handbook of Grammar and Composition plus Workbooks V and VI (grades 11-12)

handbook - $18.30, workbooks - $8.50 each, answer keys - $11.75 each, test/quiz booklets - $6.75 each, answer keys to tests/quizzes - $10.75 each, *Homeschool Curriculum/Lesson Plans* OR *Parent Guide and Student Daily Lessons* - $17 each

Workbook V is for 11th grade and *Workbook VI* is for 12th, while the *Handbook* is the primary instructional resource used for both. The *Handbook* presents numbered rules with examples in a more comprehensive fashion than some other handbooks since some do not include examples. This is an excellent handbook with thorough coverage of both grammar and composition, including research papers. The fourth edition (2003) has up-to-date information on footnotes and citations. Grammar coverage, which includes sentence diagramming, is extensive. The companion *Workbooks V* and *VI* direct students to study particular sections in the *Handbook*, then apply what they have learned in exercises or writing activities.

You will want the answer keys to the student workbooks, but the test books and their answer keys are optional. The *Parent Guide and Student Daily Lessons* should be very useful. These are daily, detailed lesson plans that tell the student exactly what to do. There are lines for students to check off assignments as they complete them; lines for them to note time started, time completed, and total time; and lines for parents to initial when they have checked the student work.

Analytical Grammar

by Robin Finley
Analytical Grammar
7615 Vista Del Rey Lane
Raleigh, NC 27613
919-783-0795
www.analyticalgrammar.com
JAG OR *JAG Mechanics*: student and teacher book set - $39.95 each, student books - $19.95 each, DVDs - $19.95 each; *AG*: student and teacher book set - $94.95, student book - $49.95, DVD set - $39.95 *AG Reinforcement & Review* - $19.95; *High School Grammar Reinforcement* books - $19.95 each

Robin Finley drew upon her years of teaching experience to come up with very practical course material for covering English grammar. *Junior Analytical Grammar (JAG)* is appropriate for fourth and fifth graders, while *Analytical Grammar (AG)* should be used for students in grades six and up.

JAG might be completed in as few as eleven

weeks. It focuses on parts of speech and syntax (word functions within a sentence), introducing sentence diagramming early in the process. While it also has writing assignments at the end of each lesson, it does not cover punctuation, usage issues such as verb tenses and comparative forms of adjectives, dictionary skills, comprehensive composition skills, and other language art skills. *Junior Analytical Grammar: Mechanics* can be used to cover punctuation, capitalization, and usage when students have completed *JAG* or just the first part of *AG*. With fifteen week-long units, *JAG: Mechanics* can be used in the same year as

JAG.

AG is more comprehensive than *JAG*. It reviews and expands upon *JAG* in the first ten units. These ten units should be used during a single school year (likely sixth grade). You can continue that same year with the next section (units 11 through 17) which cover sentence structure, clauses (adjective, adverb, and verbal), and appositives. Or you might save this section for the next school year.

Units 18 through 28 of *AG* teach punctua-

tion. Of course, students will have learned some basic punctuation before this point, but Finley saves intensive punctuation instruction until this point because she says, "students must understand the grammar of the English language before they can be expected to internalize rules of punctuation." The final lessons in units 29 through 35 deal with specialized usage issues such as pronoun-antecedent agreement, who/whom, and errors regarding adverbs and adjectives. Although the book is divided into its three "seasons" to spread out over two or three years, an older student (grade nine or higher) can easily get through the entire program in less than a full school year.

Lessons follow a common format in both books, beginning with an introductory page or more of "notes" that teach the lesson. The parent/teacher should go through this material with the students, especially in *JAG*. Three exercises follow. Students should complete only one of these per day, going over each

completed exercise with you before going on to the next one. A writing assignment follows the exercise, and then each unit ends with a test. Complete grading information is provided for the teacher. Finley thought out all of the difficulties in grading sentence diagrams as well as writing assignments, and she has come up with easy ways for parents to score student work.

These courses have a combination of special features that set them apart from others:

- Students learn parts of speech and syntax at the same time.
- Diagramming is a key component.
- A sentence parsing process is used (as in *Shurley Grammar*). This is similar to a flow chart approach with questions and answers.
- Grammar is taught thoroughly so students need not repeat the same material year after year. It is taught in context so students are more likely to understand and remember it.
- "Notes" pages remain in student books while exercise pages are removed. The student ends up with a reference notebook at the end of the course.

Since Finley suggests taking a break from *AG* after the first ten units, she has created a *Reinforcement & Review (RR)* book with exercises for students to continue sharpening their grammar and writing skills. As with *AG*, *RR* is divided into sections. The first 18 worksheets use excerpts from well-known literary works and are intended for students to use, one every other week, during the break from doing *AG*. Students parse sentences, write paraphrases, then parse AND diagram sentences using all of the concepts taught in units 1 through 10. Answer keys for these worksheets are in this same book. The next section in *RR* is intended as a week-long review after the break between units 10 and 11 for those who need to do a little more intensive work before continuing on into the next section of *AG*. Students review their notes pages from *AG* then complete these worksheets in *RR*. At the end, ten more reinforcement lessons like those at the beginning of *RR* are to be used during the next scheduled break between units 17 and 18. These are higher-level reinforcements that cover everything from unit 1 through unit 17. While *RR* is not essential, I think breaking up the *AG* course with the *RR* worksheets will be more interesting for students in addition to giving them more practice.

A few additional notes on *AG*: while this book has composition activities, it isn't intended for composition instruction such as how to structure a paragraph or essay. Also note that although the *AG* course is expensive, you will be using it over at least two years. While *AG* isn't a specifically Christian curriculum, one of the literary selections is Psalm 23, and I spotted one sample sentence that mentioned Jesus and His disciples. Books are all plastic-spiral bound.

Overall, these courses do a thorough job with grammar and diagramming and are easy for both teacher and student to use. However, you might need to work through sentence analysis and diagramming together with some students more than others. Optional teaching DVDs are available for *JAG*, *JAG: Mechanics*, and *AG*; these feature the authors providing instruction for each lesson and demonstrating a few practice sentences. These can lighten the load for parents. In the end, I think most students will appreciate the efficiency of this approach even if it is challenging.

High School Grammar Reinforcements

If high school students have completed *AG* or another rigorous grammar program, parents and teachers generally want them to have some sort of review or practice on skills. Robin Finley and Erin Karl have teamed up to create four books for this purpose. Each book has activities that reinforce sentence parsing and diagramming, grammar analysis, punctuation, and usage. With 18 lessons per book, you would use approximately one lesson every two weeks for a school year. Each book also contains its own answer key. You might select a book to coordinate with literature studies. The titles are *The Great American Authors*, *The Great British Authors*, *Shakespeare's Plays*, and *The Great World Authors*. Sentences and passages with which students work all provide information about authors and their works that is readable for its own sake—something we rarely find in grammar resources.

• • • • • • • •

Building Christian English series
Rod and Staff Publishers
PO Box 3
14193 Hwy. 172
Crockett, KY 41413-0003
606-522-4348

This series is excellent for those who prefer a formal academic approach and don't need any fluff. Comprehensive coverage, clear explanations, examples, and plenty of practice provide a solid, if unexciting, foundation in the language arts. A great deal of scriptural content as well as frequent references to farm life also serve to differentiate this program's content from most others. Some of the examples and writing assignments reflect Mennonite life so strongly that non-Mennonite children might have trouble relating to them. Despite these possible drawbacks, instruction in grammar and other language arts is better than in most other programs.

Books are all hardbound, printed in black-and-white with minimal illustrations. Children do not write in the textbooks, so they can be reused. The teacher's manual includes teaching instructions plus answers to student exercises. Lessons require teacher involvement and allow for some independent work, increasing the latter as children move to higher grade levels.

Like other classroom-designed texts, these books include extra busywork for classroom purposes, so it is not necessary for children to do all exercises. Both oral and written exercises are included within each lesson. The amount of writing might be too much for some students, especially at the younger levels. If this is the case, more exercises can be done orally or skipped altogether.

Original composition work is included, but there is a minimal amount in comparison to other written exercises until students reach ninth and tenth grades. Students should complete textbook exercises in a separate notebook. Answers, oral reviews and written quizzes are in the teacher's manuals. For grades three through eight there is a set of extra worksheets ($2.95 each level). Grades two through eight have test booklets ($1.95 each). Tests are combined with editing worksheets for assessment for grades nine and ten. While worksheet sets are essential for levels nine and ten, for other levels they provide additional work rather than serve as the primary source of student exercises.

Building Christian English 2, Preparing to Build

student book - $12.90, teacher's manual - $15.25

In keeping with its subtitle, this book lays groundwork by providing substantial work in both composition and grammar. Coverage is very broad and comprehensive for a second grade text. Composition work includes basic sentence structure up through paragraph development and writing poetry. Grammar includes parts of speech (nouns, verbs, pronouns, and adjectives) and usage. Other chapters work on alphabetical order, dictionary use, synonyms, antonyms, and homonyms. Diagramming is not introduced until the third grade.

Building Christian English 3, Beginning Wisely

student book - $12,
teacher's manual - $15.25

This level introduces nouns, pronouns, verbs, adjectives, and adverbs as well as noun usage as subject or direct object. Diagramming is taught along with each part of speech. Dictionary work, capitalization, punctuation, and oral communication are also taught. At this level, the teacher's manual states that the worksheets, oral reviews, and written quizzes are not required for the course.

Building Christian English 4, Building with Diligence

student book - $14.90,
teacher's manual - $20.20

The grade four text includes all basic parts of speech except interjections, along with diagramming. Original composition writing is included, but it teaches within limited patterns reflecting Rod and Staff's educational philosophy—emphasis is on organization and clear writing rather than upon creativity. There are many student exercises in the textbook, so it is unnecessary to purchase the extra worksheets with even more exercises.

Building Christian English 5, Following the Plan

student book - $15.30,
teacher's manual - $21.90

This comprehensive text covers the eight basic parts of speech, writing skills, speaking and listening.

Building Christian English 6, Progressing with Courage

student book - $17.35,

teacher's manual - $23.95

This text reviews and expands upon previous levels. There is heavy emphasis upon grammar. It might be too detailed for some students, but Rod and Staff's comprehensive grammar coverage in elementary grades allows students to concentrate on other language skills in high school if they master grammar by the end of eighth grade. Composition, listening, reading, and speaking skills are also taught.

Building Christian English 7, Building Securely

student book - $17.45,
teacher's manual - $23.95

Rod and Staff covers grammatical concepts by eighth grade that other publishers spread out through high school, so this text is more difficult than others for seventh grade. However, this text is too detailed for some students and has extra busywork that should be used only as needed. Using the exercises selectively helps overcome any problems this presents.

Building Christian English 8, Preparing for Usefulness

student book - $18.05,
teacher's manual - $23.95

This book reflects the shift from learning grammar to applying it. Remaining elements of grammar are covered, but, more importantly, students work with many forms of written communication.

English 9 and 10, Communicating Effectively, Books One and Two

student books - $14.95 each, teacher's manuals - $18.95 each, tests and editing sheets - $2.55 each

By high school, students have thoroughly studied grammar, so the emphasis shifts toward composition and speech. For the most part grammar and mechanics are reviewed, although a few more complex grammatical concepts are taught. Chapters alternate between grammar and composition/speech. Even then, grammar chapters all have subsections on "Improving Your Writing Style," "Improving Your Editing Skills," or "Improving Your Speaking Style"—students are continually working to improve writing and speaking skills.

These two books were written with much in common so that either can be used first. The first book covers outlining, arguments, writing book reports, character sketches, letter writing, and poetry while the second covers parliamentary procedure, descriptive essays, expository essays, bibliographies and footnotes, and story writing.

I appreciate the fact that Rod and Staff is one of the rare publishers that recognizes that grammar skills can be mastered in fewer than twelve years.

· · · · · · · · ·

Create-A-Story

Create! Press
PO Box 2785
Carlsbad, CA 92018
877-CPWRITE (279-7483)
email: orders@createpress.com
www.createpress.com
Create-A-Story game - $44.95,
Stepping Stones game - $24.95,
workbooks - $21.95 each, Writing Adventures Game Pack - $24.95

The folks who came up with the Create-A-Story board game deserve high praise for incorporating some of the best story-writing strategies into a game format. The game actually has two parts: the first, moving around the game board and collecting cards that will become components of your story; and the second, putting the pieces together into an actual story, then writing and scoring the story according to how many of your game cards were incorporated into it.

Part of the difficulty for young writers is figuring out what to write about. It is sometimes difficult for them to come up with characters, plot, theme, setting, conflict, climax, and resolution, all while using elements of style like description and dialogue. This game makes the process much easier by providing a number of these elements for the writer.

There are decks of cards that have topic sentences, settings, characters, plot elements, resolutions (as in how the story turns out), lessons (the moral of the story is…), descriptions (e.g., hairy, cold and rainy, majestic), and dialogue (words like "laughed," "questioned," and "roared" that are to be used after direct quotes). Some blank cards are included so you can add story elements of your own.

Every player selects a topic sentence card before play begins, then as they move around the board they land on other story elements and draw a card each time from the dialogue deck if the space says "dialogue," from the description deck if the space says "description," etc. There are some "Free Choice" spaces so players can select a story element they are lacking.

When they reach the end of the game board path, they are ready to put their story together. They need not use all story element cards they have drawn, but they get points for those they do use. They will generally have some cards that just won't fit with the others, but they should still have plenty with which to work.

Each player takes an Outline Sheet from the pad provided with the game and begins to write down story elements he or she plans to use. Players decide which characters will be good guys or bad guys. They choose which plot to use. Then they write down the key plot elements: the conflict and four steps for what happens first, second, etc. All of this has to lead up to the resolution shown on one of the cards they have drawn.

After they've written down these story elements, they actually write their story. The length of the story should depend upon the age and ability of a child. With a younger child, I might require them to sort through all their cards and limit their selections to fewer than I would allow an older child, just to keep the story brief. Generally, I would expect stories to be anywhere from one to two pages long, but it certainly is possible for students to write much longer stories if time permits.

Once stories are complete, you use the score pad that assigns point values for the various story elements that were used in the story. As the teacher, you can also set your own standards for spelling and grammar, perhaps giving extra points in those areas. Note that references to transition words on the score sheet and in the instructions are a bit confusing since no list of transition words is actually included in the game. However, the list is available on the publisher's website at: www.createpress.com/pages/tips.htm along with free downloads for "Writing Adventures Journal Plan" (to help students learn to journal) and a supplemental teacher's manual for the Create-A-Story Game.

The game requires adult assistance unless you have older students who have become familiar with the game and who are able to select and fashion story elements together without assistance. There are pawns for up to six individuals or groups of players; children can write stories on their own or as teams in a cooperative effort. However, the game will actually work with only one child if you think of it as a tool for writing a story rather than a competition. Ultimately, story writing is the goal more than winning the game even though children might not catch on to that right away. The story elements in the game will frequently require silliness and creativity to fit them together into a cohesive story. That means that children are likely to have a lot of fun figuring out which ones to use and how to put them together.

Stepping Stones, another game from the same publisher, assists students with expository writing. Students tackle informative, persuasive, comparison/contrast, or operational essays as they move through the game board, actually writing as they move through each step. This game is more controlled in that students select cards in a particular order that fits the writing process. The game provides guidance and inspiration as students work through the writing process step-by-step. Graphic organizers and outline masters serve as additional tools. Parent or teacher guidance is required. This game is a little more complex to figure out at first, but like Create-A-Story, it makes the writing process much more interesting and manageable.

Create! Press publishes other products that you might find useful for composition and grammar. Their two workbooks, *Writing Adventures, Books 1* and *2*, teach basic grammar, punctuation, and composition skills in a format that seems most suitable for older students needing remedial work. Beginning with identification of subjects and verbs, the first book presents simplified, condensed coverage that should help a student gain a foundational grasp of grammar. All activities include writing as well as what I would consider optional drawing activities. Composition lessons move quickly from sentence building, through paragraphs to very short stories (as students might write in the Create-A-Story game). The second book adds more challenging grammar lessons and shifts into essay writing. A number of reproducible visual organizers for essay writing are included.

The Writing Adventures Game Pack reinforces lesson material in the two workbooks. A double-sided game board comes with sets of sturdy cards (that you need to cut out) and playing pieces. You can play numerous variations depending upon which side of the board

and which cards you choose to use: identifying parts of speech, punctuation corrections, subject/verb agreement, editing sentences with errors, identifying phrases, constructing sentences from sentence parts collected as they move around the board, constructing compound sentences, and identifying similes. Although designed as a companion for the workbooks, these games also work well on their own.

• • • • • • • • •

Easy Grammar series
by Wanda Phillips
Easy Grammar Systems™
PO Box 25970
Scottsdale, AZ 85255
480-502-9454
800-641-6015
www.easygrammar.com

There are essentially two strands in the *Easy Grammar* series for the elementary grades: teaching books and review books. I will use the term *Easy Grammar* to refer to the teaching books and *Daily Grams* for the review books. To make things interesting, *Easy Grammar: Grade 2* is actually a teaching and review book! You can use either teaching or review books or both for all other levels.

Easy Grammar

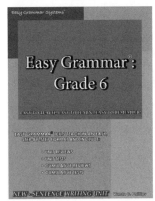

Easy Grammar 2 - $24.95 *Easy Grammar* teacher editions: *Grades 3 & 4* - $27.95 each, *Grades 5, 6,* and *Plus* - $32.95 each student workbooks for *Grades 3-6* and *Plus* - $13.95 each *Easy Grammar* test booklets - $4.95 each

Let's start with the teaching series. The *Easy Grammar* books, with the exception of *Easy Grammar: Grade 2*, are very similar to one another. I will begin with *Easy Grammar 2*.

This book is unique (in this series) with a format of daily lesson plans. It contains reproducible student pages with an answer key at the back of the book. Thus, you can either have students write in the book or you can reproduce pages for them. *Grade 2* can be used either as your primary teaching resource or as a supplement. Lessons need to be taught rather than used independently, although some students might be able to complete a good part of the work on their own.

Each daily lesson consists of four to five types of exercises that include capitalization, punctuation, alphabetizing, dictionary work, parts of speech, prefixes/roots/suffixes, synonyms, homonyms, antonyms, rhymes, and sentence combining. Rules or explanations and examples are provided within the lessons for each topic that is likely to be new or in need of review. The book has 180 lessons and is intended to be completed in one year. All principal parts of speech up through interjections and conjunctions are introduced although with only a very brief introduction for each of the more difficult parts of speech. My biggest hesitation with this book is whether or not it is necessary to go that far into parts of speech in second grade. Other than that, the coverage of other language skills is great.

Now we can move on to *Easy Grammar: Grades 3* and up. *Easy Grammar* books use the same approach and repeat much of the same material from book to book, albeit at slightly higher levels of difficulty. For example, the first book teaches a list of 28 prepositions while the two highest level books teach a list of 53 prepositions.

Each very large—the smallest volume is almost 500 pages—*Easy Grammar* book follows a pattern of brief, straightforward grammar instruction followed by examples then exercises. Most of the time, younger level books combine instruction and activity so that both together take up just one page per lesson.

Upper levels sometimes take a page or two for instruction followed by one page of exercises.

You will need a teacher's edition that includes everything in the student book plus answer keys. Student pages in the teacher's edition are reproducible, but that's a lot of photocopying. Instead of photocopying, you can purchase student workbooks that contain instruction and activity pages.

The layout makes *Easy Grammar* self-instructional for the most part. In the teacher's editions, one page is the reproducible student worksheet, while facing it is an identical student page with answers overprinted. This arrangement makes these answer keys very easy to use. Teacher's editions include reviews, tests, cumulative reviews, and cumulative tests, all of which help students retain previously-taught information. Separate test booklets are also available if you do not want to photocopy or use those in the teacher's edition.

This program is unique in presenting prepositions before other parts of speech. By teaching students to identify prepositions and prepositional phrases before other parts of the sentence, it eliminates such problems as confusing the object of a preposition with the subject.

Parts of the sentence are designated by underlining, circling, and making notations rather than by diagramming. In addition, it covers phrases, clauses, punctuation, capitalization, types of sentences, sentences (including fragments and run-ons), and letter writing.

Author Wanda Phillips strongly recommends that you teach the lessons in order since they include cumulative review of previously covered topics. The exceptions might be punctuation, capitalization, and letter writing, which can be taught whenever you choose.

Grammar topics are taught one at a time without significant integration of topics. You will find more grammatical detail taught in programs from Rod and Staff and A Beka than in *Easy Grammar*, but the essentials are here.

The format is repetitious. To add variety, you

might supplement with *Grammar Songs* (www. audiomemory.com), *Editor in Chief* workbooks (www.criticalthinking.com), or other resources.

Easy Grammar is especially good for students who struggle with grammar. In contrast to A Beka's *Language* series, sentences are fairly short which makes identification exercises easier. Once students figure out what is being done in the exercise, they can continue the pattern without much effort. Also, there are fewer exercises per lesson than you find in A Beka. Most students need more challenging grammar instruction after completing *Easy Grammar Plus*. The new *Easy Grammar Ultimate Series* now continues with instruction and practice that takes students through the end of high school and provides more-challenging instruction.

There are six books in the *Easy Grammar* series: *Grade 2, Grade 3, Grade 4, Grade 5, Grade 6*, and *Plus* (for grades 7 and above). These books are not really that specific to grade levels, so, for example, you might use the book for grade five with children in grades four through six. Also, you do not need to use all of these books since they contain so much repetition. You can use one volume then follow up with *Daily Grams* for a few years before switching back to a teaching volume.

Daily Grams

Daily Grams: teacher editions on CD-ROM - $24.95 each, student workbooks - $12.95 each

Daily Grams are a marvelous tool for reviewing and practicing grammar skills without boring students with an entire grammar course year after year. These books assume that students have already been instructed in the relevant grammar concepts and simply

provide reinforcement and practice without instruction. Each grade-level book becomes progressively more difficult reflecting what is assumed to have been taught in corresponding *Easy Grammar* books.

I love the easy-to-use, page-a-day format. It should take only about ten minutes per day. Each page has exercises in capitalization, punctuation, general review, and sentence combining. Answers are at the back of the book. You can make photocopies of the work pages or purchase student workbooks.

There are five *Daily Grams* volumes for grades three through seven plus a single book for junior and senior high. These are available as printed books or on CD-ROMs.

While you can use these alongside an *Easy Grammar* volume, I recommend using them in between *Easy Grammar* volumes. *Daily Grams* might also be used in the same way with other grammar courses since most repeat the same material year after year and *Daily Grams'* scope and sequence is similar to that of most programs.

Ultimate Series

Ultimate Series: teacher editions - $24.95 each, student workbooks - $12.95 each, test booklets - $4.95 each

Older students have yet another choice with 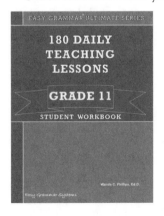 the new *Easy Grammar Ultimate Series*. While some students have used *Easy Grammar Plus* and *Daily Grams* in junior and senior high, the *Ultimate Series* offers more challenging material, but in a format similar to *Daily Grams*. The *Ultimate Series* books, one for each year for grades 8 through 12, require only about ten minutes per day. The format for each of the 180 lessons is the same with work on five topics per day. Every lesson has sections on punctuation, capitalization, and sentence combining. The other two sections cover other grammar concepts such as parts of speech, phrases and clauses, homonyms, analogies, and types of sentences. Brief instruction is provided. These texts do not assume that students have already attained a mastery of grammar. Students who already know the rules and concepts can simply complete the exercises to practice their skills while those who need explanations may read through them.

You need only purchase the teacher edition since it has reproducible student pages and an answer key at the back. Information for the teacher at the beginning of each book is brief, and scope and sequences at the beginning will help you find a lesson on a particular skill if you need to target an immediate issue. However, you may also purchase student workbooks to save the hassle of reproducing pages. Separate assessment booklets are available for grades 8 through 11. The *Ultimate Series* seems like an excellent way to provide just the right amount of grammar instruction for older students.

· · · · · · · · ·

Fairview's Guide to Composition and Essay Writing

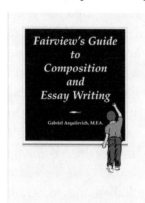

by Gabriel Arquilevich, M.F.A. Fairview Publishing PO Box 746 Oak View, CA 93022 805-640-1924 email: garquilevich@ roadrunner.com $20

Fairview's Guide to Composition and Essay Writing is a natural follow-up to use after *Writing for 100 Days* by the same author (another of my Top Picks). Although lessons cover basic essay structure, they go far beyond the minimal boring essay. Students create a reading journal in which they analyze many types of professional essays. Think of this as you would an artist who learns to paint by studying and analyzing great artists. Students begin to grasp the creative possibilities available to them as they identify effective techniques in these essays.

While Arquilevich covers some of the same territory as do others teaching essay-writing skills, he often uses unusual approaches. For example, in a lesson on paragraphs, he instructs students to, "Find an on-line essay…. After duplicating the essay, have someone eliminate all paragraphs so that it reads as a block. Now, locate the best places for paragraph breaks and compare your choices to the writer's" (p. 15).

You might have noticed that the parent or teacher will likely be the one reformatting the on-line essay into a solid block. Several lessons require either two or more students or else a parent/tutor who will interact with the student on assignments. For example, there is a two-part assignment that requires a writing partner. It says, "First, each person writes one page (any subject) using a lot of qualifiers, intensifiers, informal transitions, and slang. When you're done, exchange papers and rewrite each other's pieces, eliminating the excess. You be the wordsmith and decide what's appropriate" (p. 29).

Fairview's Guide is ideal for small group classes, but it can work with an individual student if a parent or teacher is willing to participate. While some research (e.g., locating professional essays on the internet or in magazines) is required, the lessons are very well explained and easy to follow. Students who meet periodically as a group should be able to work through lessons independently for the most part, bringing their work to exchange or share at class times.

The first half of the book works on preparatory skills such as those mentioned above, plus tone of voice, audience, word choice, use of quotations, and sentence structures. The second half shifts into actual essay writing, tackling four types of essays: argumentative, comparison and contrast, personal, and mock. For the mock essay, students either imitate an established writer's style or pretend to be someone else and create a style reflecting that personality. Each type is thoroughly developed, including a full-length sample essay of each.

An answer key at the back of the book has suggested answers for the applicable exercises. While there are a number of such short exercises, students primarily learn by doing lots of their own writing.

Fairview's Guide can be completed in a year, but it is more important to work through each of the skills, taking as long as necessary. It might be used with advanced junior high students, but it is best for high school level.

· · · · · · · · ·

First Language Lessons

by Jessie Wise
Peace Hill Press
18101 The Glebe Lane
Charles City, VA 23030
877-322-3445
email: info@peacehillpress.net
www.peacehillpress.com
Levels 1 or *2*: softcover - $14.95 each, downloads - $11.95 each; *Levels 3* or *4* instructors guide: softcover - $29.95 each, downloads - $23.95 each; *Student Workbook Level 3*: softcover - $18.95, download - $15; *Student Workbook Level 4*: softcover - $19.95, download - $15.95; *Audio Companion*: CD - $10.95, MP3 - $8.75

Jessie Wise, co-author of *The Well-Trained Mind (TWTM)*, has written *First Language Lessons (FLL)*, a series of four courses for grades one through four that supports classical education as described in *TWTM*. *FLL* actually combines Charlotte Mason's ideas and classical education elements.

FLL mimics many elements of resources such as *English for the Thoughtful Child* by Mary Hyde and Cyndi Shearer and Emma Serl's *Primary Language Arts* and *Intermediate Language Arts*, all of which have been popular among Charlotte Mason advocates. Common to all are the use of art reproductions as prompts for discussion, narration, and writing. Picture studies are intermixed with poems, fables, and other short writings. Also common to all of these resources is the presentation of questions for parents or teachers to use to guide the instruction that covers the broad range of language arts including reading and listening comprehension, grammar, oral expression, and composition.

However, *FLL* adds a much stronger emphasis on recitation, repetition, and memorization. This represents the "Dorothy Sayers" line of thought in classical education that young children in the first (or grammar) stage of learning should be learning in this way.

There is much more content in *FLL* books than in *English for the Thoughtful Child* or Emma Serl's books. *FLL* has 100 lessons each for *Levels 1* and *2*, 89 in *Level 3*, and 85 in *Level 4*. In *FLL*, grammar rules, usage, writing skills, listening and reading comprehension, and proper oral usage are all covered using four techniques: memory work, copying and dictation, narration, and grammar lessons.

Lessons follow a developmental sequence. For example, students do a minimal amount of copying for the first half of *Level 1*. They might copy their own name or a short list of pronouns. They continue with increasingly difficult copywork until *Level 2* when they begin taking dictation.

Let's look at each of the techniques used by this program. Children memorize poems, rules, definitions, and short lists. Poetry memorization helps children develop a familiarity with the rhythm and style of good language. Memorization of rules, definitions, and lists helps children acquire the "grammar" of English language.

Copying develops writing skills plus familiarity with spelling and proper usage. As Jessie Wise says, "Copywork engages both the visual and motor memory of the student. It gives the student models of properly constructed sentences" (*Level 4*, p. 1). After students have developed sufficient fluency in handwriting, spelling, and mechanics, they can begin taking dictation which is introduced in *Level 2*, lesson 22. Dictation exercises are never longer than a sentence for this level.

Narration practice prepares children for their own original writing. The parent reads a short fable or story to his or her child, or the child examines a piece of art reproduced in the book. Then the child relates key elements of the story or picture. Parents can use the scripted questions to help their children recall or elicit elements of the story or artwork. Artwork is often used as a springboard to grammar. For example, one piece is used to discuss prepositions and placement of objects in the picture.

The largest amount of attention seems dedicated to grammar lessons. These are scripted dialogues that call for repetition of rules and oral responses. Sometimes children are prompted to come up with their own examples for categories such as proper and common nouns.

Repetition is used much more than in other programs. For example, the third lesson on pronouns (*Level 1*, lesson 48) begins with recitation of the definition of a pronoun three times. Then the lesson continues with children continually repeating lists or sentences through the end of the lesson. I imagine you could take the lesson idea and use your own style of presentation if this sounds as boring to you as it does to me. (While the repetition seems excessive to me, I don't think it's as overdone as it is in *Shurley Grammar*.)

Grammar coverage focuses heavily upon parts of speech, covering all eight by the end of *Level 2*. *First Language Lessons* covers all of the other elements of grammar such as sentence formation, capitalization, punctuation, plurals, suffixes, contractions, and usage. Diagramming is introduced in *Level 3*. While much of this is taught explicitly, when children are copying and taking dictation, they learn much of it from the models and usage.

Children are not required to do much writing in the first two levels, but there are occasional enrichment activities for those able to do more than is required. Some of these include hands-on activities that I think would really appeal to all children. For example, one enrichment activity has a child use his body, furniture, toys, and a box to "act out" prepositions.

More writing is required in *Levels 3* and *4*. Because of this, *Levels 3* and *4* each have a separate student workbook with 345 and 380 pages, respectively. Large fonts and plenty of white space make the individual pages very manageable for children; these workbooks are not intimidating despite their size. The workbooks cannot be used on their own. They are adjuncts to lessons taught from the instructor's book.

The *Level 1* and *2* books and *Level 3* and *4* instruction books are non-consumable. For the first two levels, children should maintain a separate binder where they keep all of their work.

All of the books are available in either print or downloadable PDF versions.

An optional *First Language Lessons Audio Companion* might appeal to some families. Seventy-five minutes of recorded material on 48 tracks accompany the lessons in the first two *FLL* levels. Professionally produced, the recording includes dramatized readings by radio "actor" Mark Russo and sing-along songs by Mike Smith. The *FLL Audio Companion* is available on CD or by MP3 download.

I know that some parents greatly appreciate

the detailed lesson presentation, the script that tells them what to say, when to have children repeat things, etc. Other parents will find this approach much too structured and controlled. The elements that make it so structured (i.e., memorization of parts of speech, excessive repetition) almost overwhelm the elements reflecting Charlotte Mason's ideas. In my opinion, more narration activity and free flowing discussion would better reflect Mason's philosophy, but those looking for a Dorothy Sayers style of classical education should find this a good fit.

· · · · · · · ·

Jump In

by Sharon Watson
Apologia
Educational
Ministries, Inc.
1106 Meridian
Plaza, Ste.220
Anderson, IN
46016
888-524-4724
www.apologia.com
student worktext
$30, Lifeguard's Locker - $10

Jump In is a two-year writing program for middle school students. While most appropriate for grades 6 through 8, it can also be used with high schoolers who need more work on basic writing skills or need a user-friendly approach to motivate them to improve their skills. Written particularly for Christian home-schoolers, it is designed for students to work independently most of the time, and it assumes a Christian audience with references to favorite Bible verses, church activities, judgments about Greek gods and goddesses, spiritual motivations of characters in stories, and other Christian experiences and attitudes.

The course consists of a student book plus a teacher manual titled *The Lifeguard's Locker: A Parent/Teacher Manual for Jump In*. Both

are essential. The 248-page student worktext includes instruction, activities, and assignments plus helpful reference tools at the back. Assignments are presented in seven sections of varying length: prewriting skills, opinion, persuasion, exposition, description, narration, and poetry. Within each section, lessons are presented as a series of skills so that students approach each type of writing in bite-size chunks. For most of the activities student will write directly in their workbook, spending from five to twenty minutes per lesson on writing activities. I particularly like the way Watson has interspersed activities throughout the instruction to ensure that students are processing and applying as they learn. At the end of each section of skill lessons students are given a number of writing assignments from which to choose. These lengthier assignments might take anywhere from two to ten days to complete and will likely be done either in a notebook or on the computer.

Jump In is a fairly comprehensive course. It provides instruction from brainstorming, topic selection, and construction of a composition with an introduction, body, and conclusion all the way through the use of citations and creation of a bibliography. The exposition section of the workbook expands to include lessons on writing biographies, book reports, book responses, newspaper articles, how-to articles, and compare-and-contrast essays.

The student workbook itself can be completed in one school year. What transforms *Jump In* into a two-year program are the "10-Minute Writing Plunges" found in the teacher manual. These are a number of writing prompts—four per week for September through May—that are the basis for ten-minute writing assignments to be completed Monday through Thursday. You are free to substitute your own writing prompts if you wish. On Friday, students select their favorite of the four papers they have written that week and polish it to be turned in on the following Monday. The "Writing Plunges" are not intended to be used at the same time as students are working through their other lessons. They should be used on their own as the second year of the program or they can be used to break up the workbook lessons by spending a month or more on "Writing Plunges" between sections of the book.

The student workbook is very attractive. Printed in full-color, it includes illustrations and graphics that break up the print and keep students from getting overwhelmed. Students will also need a grammar reference book or additional instruction if they are weak in grammar; suggestions are included in the teacher manual.

The teacher manual has answers for the activities when they are predictable answers, and it also has an extensive section on evaluating lengthier student work with reproducible forms and samples of completed forms—very helpful for the inexperienced parent or teacher.

· · · · · · · · ·

Michael Clay Thompson
Language Arts

Royal Fireworks Press
PO Box 399
First Avenue
Unionville, NY 10988
845-726-4444
www.rfwp.com

Classical educators have brought attention to a language arts program that might otherwise have had little visibility in the homeschool marketplace. Michael Clay Thompson's language arts program should be viewed as collections of five books per level beginning about third or fourth grade level. There are six levels (or years) available. Although written with gifted students in mind, these might be used for a much broader range of students up through high school, adjusting the choice of levels appropriately. The program covers grammar, composition, poetics (poetry), and vocabulary, all at more challenging levels than

are typically found in other texts for comparable grade levels. Each book (or series) could stand on its own, but the integration of the five books for each level creates a synergistic effect: the whole is greater than the sum of the individual parts. The catalog shows the six levels divided into two sets with the first three levels designated "elementary" and the second three levels "secondary." However, "secondary" books are suggested for grades six and up. Despite the grade level recommendations, I would suggest starting at the beginning of the series in most situations since there is a cumulative "building" process that occurs with these books that might be difficult to plug into midstream.

Each book has both a student text and a teacher manual. However, in some cases you are able to get away with purchasing only the teacher manual if you are teaching a single student since the manual includes the student's text. Students always need to see the pages since artwork and layout are often as much a part of a lesson as the text. Thus, a student and teacher may work together in a book if need be, but the student DOES need access to each book. (Students definitely need to write in the *Practice* books, but these are the only ones that function like workbooks.) Teaching information is often separated into a section at the back of the teacher manual, but some of the teacher manuals have small boxes and circles with teaching suggestions overprinted on student pages. These are unobtrusive enough that you can still have a child reading from the book. (Less expensive Home School Parent Answer Manuals can be purchased instead of teacher manuals for *The Word Within the Word* and *The Magic Lens* series as well as for *Advanced Academic Writing 2*.)

Thompson's approach especially appeals to classical educators for a number of reasons. Most obvious is vocabulary study based upon Latin and Greek stems. (An interesting twist is Thompson's occasional references to Spanish vocabulary and grammar since Spanish, too, draws on Latin roots and is a "living" language with which students can easily connect.) Use of classical literary examples as lesson material and composition assignments based upon literature are just a few examples of how literature is incorporated. Thompson frequently uses a Socratic approach for teaching—using questions to help students discover answers or concepts for themselves. Socratic questions are really just part of a comprehensive teaching methodology that both expects and demands students to be mentally engaged with the learning process at a high level. It is very respectful of the student, but it will not work well for an unmotivated student.

Another critical element, sometimes missing in other classical resources, is poetics. Poetry instruction is included at each level.

Although the five books for each level have different titles from year to year, they cover five strands: grammar, grammar practice, writing (composition), vocabulary, and poetics.

Grammar books (in sequential order by level) are titled *Grammar Island, Grammar Town, Grammar Voyage, Magic Lens 1, Magic Lens 2,* and *Magic Lens 3.* In all six grammar books, Thompson strives to simplify the presentation of grammar by using four "lenses" through which a sentence might be studied: parts of speech, parts of the sentence, phrases, and clauses.

While grammar instruction is thorough, the core instruction is given at the beginning of each year, with practice and application during the rest of the year. Thompson calls it "front-loading."

All eight parts of speech are covered each year, with the level of complexity gradually increasing from year to year. Similarly, parts of the sentence are studied, with even the first level (*Grammar Island*) including subject complements, prepositional phrases, and identification of clauses.

Thompson teaches a variation on traditional diagramming. He begins by teaching a strong vertical break between complete subject and complete predicate. But after that, diagramming plays a minor role in comparison to "four-level analysis," a technique used at all levels as students analyze sentences for parts of speech, parts of the sentence, phrases, and clauses. The four-level analysis is introduced in *Sentence Island* at the first level then used in all the grammar books for the rest of the levels. The *Practice* books for each level (titled *Practice Island, Practice Town, Practice Voyage, 4 Practice 1, 4 Practice 2,* and *4 Practice 3*) provide pages with sentences for students to analyze at the four levels.

Writing is taught with a strong grammatical approach. Titles of the first three books—*Sentence Island, Paragraph Town, and Essay Voyage*—reflect the sequential development of composition skills. *Advanced Academic Writing* books 1, 2, and 3 (for the last three levels) teach students to write formal academic papers following Modern Language Association (MLA) guidelines. Depending upon the ability of the student, two to four such papers will be written each year. *Advanced Academic Writing* teacher manuals each include a CD-ROM with a library of Michael Clay Thompson's comments on student papers that he has accumulated over the years. These are comments that he has used repeatedly enough that he "recorded" them rather than rewrite them each time. A parent or teacher can use these comments to save the time it would take to figure out how to create his or her own comments.

Vocabulary study eschews the idea of grade level vocabulary. Instead, from the very beginning, students are introduced to interesting and challenging words such as aqueduct, suburbs, spectacular, spectrum, introduction, and reduction. The first book, *Building Language,* offers a gentle, artistic introduction to vocabulary by creating an analogy of architectural arches to word stems. This heavily illustrated book should be a fun exploration of language that includes reading, discussion, creative writing, oral review, and quizzes that may be done orally or in writing. *Caesar's English* books *I* and *II* ratchet up the academic challenge significantly with a number of interactive activities that challenge students to analyze and apply stems and words. Analogies play a prominent role. Vocabulary continues to transcend typical grade-level lists with words such as vulgar, undulate, tremulous, countenance, languor, and prodigious in book *I* and derision, vivacious, sanguine, inexorable, alacrity, magnanimous, and obsequious in book *II*. Spanish gets special attention in both *Caesar's English* books.

Classical home educators requested even more content than what is already in *Caesar's English I*, and Thompson obliged by greatly expanding that book into a two-volume *Enhanced Edition*—both the original and *Enhanced Edition* are available. The *Enhanced Edition* has 192 additional pages of material with many new photographs of Greek and Roman art and architecture, maps, word searches, a biography of Julius Caesar spread throughout both volumes, original poems by Michael Clay Thompson, more on English-Spanish language relationships, and fifteen essays by Dr. Thomas Milton Kemnitz on topics such as Roman architecture and methods of construction. A single Implementation Manual for the teacher includes reproduced student pages with answers and comments overprinted or inserted where appropriate. It retains the division into 20 lessons as in the original, but each lesson will obviously take longer to complete. I particularly like the way the *Enhanced Edition* reinforces and builds vocabulary through the poetry and essays.

The *Word Within the Word*, books *1, 2,* and *3* (vocabulary books for the last three levels), emphasize the Latin and Greek roots of words and may be used for more independent study than the lower level vocabulary books. Many activities can be done independently or through group discussion. Some written activities must be done independently. For example, one activity directs students to "translate the following ostentatious, ponderous passage into graceful, direct English." Lengthy passages follow that include sentences such as, "He had seen it all: mendacious miscreants, peripatetic mendicants in dishabille, philandering officials, hedonistic values, pulchritudinous youths wallowing in puerile narcissism, venial sins, dissembling sycophants, refractory recidivists, querulous neighbors—a world replete with sins and problems" (*WWW3*, p. 123). You can see how this type of assignment really challenges a student to understand and apply vocabulary.

If you want to instill in your children a love of poetry but find most teaching resources less than inspiring, you will likely love Thompson's approach that includes poetry study at every level. Poetry books are titled *The Music of the Hemispheres; Building Poems; A World of Poetry; Poetry and Humanity; Poetry, Plato and the Problem of Beauty*; and *Poetry, Plato and the Problem of Truth*. Even from the youngest level, students learn to appreciate the beauty of language and the skill of an outstanding poet who has carefully selected words not just for meaning and rhyme but also for the actual sounds the words make. All six books explore the technical and mechanical aspects of poetry as well as the aesthetical and emotional. The last three books, as you might surmise from their titles, delve further into philosophical questions such as the nature of man and whether beauty and truth are relative or absolute. Thompson presents the questions in a Socratic manner, encouraging thought without offering definitive answers. Those teaching a Christian worldview might want to expand such discussions within that context.

As I mentioned previously, the five books for each level work together although all but the *Practice* books can also be used on their own. However, grammar books provide an understanding of the structure of language used throughout all the books; vocabulary study prepares students to explore a wider variety of literature with understanding; poetry books feed the imagination for writing and allow students to experience the beauty of aptly chosen words they might have just learned in their vocabulary study; and all of this prepares students to be able to express ideas in their own writing. I suspect that most parents will be inspired by these books, just as I was, since they reveal aspects of language arts that offer beauty and meaning.

Following is a list of the five titles for each level with suggested grade levels.

- Level 1 - for 3rd grade and up: *Grammar Island, Practice Island, Building Language, The Music of the Hemispheres, Sentence Island*
- Level 2 - for 4th grade and up: *Grammar Town, Practice Town, Caesar's English I* (OR *Caesar's English I Enhanced Edition*), *Building Poems, Paragraph Town*
- Level 3 - for 5th grade and up: *Grammar Voyage, Practice Voyage, Caesar's English II, A World of Poetry, Essay Voyage*
- Level 4 - for 6th grade and up: *Magic Lens 1, 4 Practice 1, The Word Within the Word 1, Poetry and Humanity, Advanced Academic Writing 1*
- Level 5 - for 7th grade and up: *Magic Lens 2; 4 Practice 2; The Word Within the Word 2; Poetry, Plato and the Problem of Beauty; Advanced Academic Writing 2*
- Level 6 - for 8th grade and up: *Magic Lens 3; 4 Practice 3; The Word Within the Word 3; Poetry, Plato and the Problem of Truth; Advanced Academic Writing 3*

A new literature component is being added to this curriculum. Two courses are available thus far and they are not tied directly to any one level of the curriculum. Each consists of three complete books (all novels thus far) plus a parent manual. The first course (most appropriate for lower levels of the curriculum) includes the three novels *Alice's Adventures in Wonderland, Peter Pan,* and *The Wind in the Willows.* The second course (most appropriate for upper levels) includes *A Christmas Carol, The Time Machine,* and *A Connecticut Yankee in King Arthur's Court.*

The novels are annotated by Thompson and include original illustrations when they are critical to the text. Annotations include vocabulary definitions, four-level analysis of selected sentences, and comments on literary elements. Thompson places the emphasis on reading and discussion instead of worksheets and comprehension questions. He includes in the parent manual selected quotations for oral "quote quizzes" where students identify the speaker or they identify who or what is being described. He also provides "Creative Questions and Activities" that you will most likely use for discussion as well as "Study Questions" that may be assigned for written work. Written assignments should be made according to the knowledge and skill level of the child and following guidelines in *Paragraph Town, Essay Voyage,* or another of the composition-oriented books. Thompson provides many suggestions as to how you might use the various learning strategies with children of different ages.

In addition to the new literature component, you might want to consider using the "Self Evident Truth" series. This series demonstrates how the choice of words, grammar, poetics, and social/historical context together can produce language that changes the world. These three optional courses can be used whenever you wish. Each course is comprised of a student book and its companion teacher manual. *Jefferson's Truths* is a study of the "Declaration of Independence." *Lincoln's Ten Sentences* is an explication of Abraham Lincoln's "Gettysburg Address." *Free At Last* examines Dr. Martin Luther King's "I Have a Dream" speech.

Royal Fireworks Press offers either complete

or basic homeschool packages at discounted prices through their website with package prices ranging from $105 to $205 per level. Basic packages eliminate teacher manuals or student books when it is possible to work with only one or the other. The Royal Fireworks Press website has Michael Clay Thompson's free downloads, video clips and implementation slide shows to assist parents, and the publisher sponsors online support forums to which both the publisher and the author regularly contribute.

• • • • • • • • •

Saxon Grammar and Writing

by Christie Curtis and Mary Hake
Houghton Mifflin Harcourt
10801 North Mopac Expressway, Bldg. 3
Austin, TX 78759
800-289-4490
email: info@saxonhomeschool.com
www.saxonhomeschool.com
$75 per kit for each level

Saxon Grammar and Writing uses the same  educational methodology that has popularized the Saxon math books. Courses for grades five through eight are designed so that students can do much of their work independently. New concepts are taught in small increments. Also, continual review and building upon prior concepts in a spiral fashion helps students retain what they have learned.

There are three components for each level: student edition, student workbook, and teacher packet. Both the student edition and student workbook serve as worktexts with instruction, exercises, and assignments.

The student edition, the largest of the three books (with 107 to 112 lessons per volume) is the starting place. A brief introduction succinctly describes course content. In the student editions for grades 7 and 8, a few vital lines have been added to direct students to dictation and journal topics in the back of their books. At the top of the first page of each lesson is a box that says "Dictation or Journal Entry" followed by "Vocabulary"—a few words with definitions and sample sentences. Without instruction, students would not know that there are dictation passages for each week at the back of their student edition. They copy these on the first day they begin the next group of lessons and study them on remaining lesson days until they reach a test day. Then they write the passage out from oral dictation as part of testing. Spelling and punctuation are learned primarily through the dictation exercises.

Each student edition also has 100 journaling topics at the back. Students should write about these topics between the first day when they copy the dictation and test day, although they are not assigned for particular days. The bulk of the book is dedicated to instruction, examples, and exercises in grammar. Lessons follow a standard format of instruction accompanied by examples. This is followed by some practice exercises on the new concept and the vocabulary for that lesson. The review set is where students find the bulk of the exercises. These tackle previously-taught concepts. Italicized numbers next to each question indicate which lesson(s) taught the concept in case students need to review. While many students will like the variety in these exercises, others might prefer exercises all on one topic such as you find in *Easy Grammar*.

This is a fairly comprehensive English program covering grammar, writing, spelling, punctuation, and vocabulary. Literature and reading are the only areas missing. Grammar instruction is very challenging and includes sentence diagramming. Students coming into this program in sixth through eighth grades may need to back up a level to keep from getting overwhelmed. The program does review and repeat through each level, so it is possible for a student to begin at sixth, seventh, or eighth grade level.

Saxon Grammar and Writing has a stronger composition component than many other comprehensive programs. In addition to the dictation and journal assignments, the student workbook focuses mostly upon composition skills. A schedule for the lessons—showing which days students are to do lessons from either the student edition or the student workbook—is found in the teacher packet. I would recommend copying this schedule for students. As far as composition skills are concerned, in fifth grade, students work on sentences, paragraphs, essays, personal narratives, chapter summaries, and imaginative stories while also learning how to evaluate their own essays. Sixth grade adds outlining, writing research papers, and creating a bibliography. Seventh and eighth grades continue with the above skills at more challenging levels and add poetry.

In addition to the composition lessons, student workbooks also have "More Practice" lessons that are to be used in conjunction with student edition lessons. (Note that in the student editions it says "See Master Worksheets" when there is a companion "More Practice" lesson. Parents might need to come up with an easy system for students to locate the appropriate worksheets when they are required.)

The student workbooks also include a few supplemental activities that are similar to *Mad Libs* where students come up with a list of words that fit designations such as "abstract common noun," "preposition," or "nominative case personal pronoun (feminine)." They then slot these "parts of speech" into a pre-written story in the workbook, and the result is bound to be silly. This is a great way to review grammatical terms.

The content of the lessons sometimes integrates information about literature, history, geography, and character building. While U.S. history gets some attention at all levels, the eighth grade text brings in U.S. history and government even more through examples, exercises, dictation, and journal topics. This makes the eighth grade course an excellent companion for simultaneous study of U.S. history in social studies or history. Although the content is not Christian, it supports those with a Christian worldview.

Beginning after the first ten lessons in the student edition, there is a test after every five lessons. This does not follow a predictable schedule such as testing every Friday since there are five student edition lessons and sometimes one or more student workbook lessons between tests. Tests and answer keys for all components are in the teacher packet. (The teacher packet is actually a book rather than loose pages.)

All three components for each level are printed in black and white in soft cover books. There are no graphics other than those required for diagramming or other exercises. The weight and type of the paper in these books is close to newsprint quality, so these are definitely meant to be consumable books. Students can complete most of their exercises directly in the student edition, but occasionally they will need more space for such tasks as rewriting sentences or diagramming. Thus, students will also need to maintain a notebook for some of their exercises as well as for composition assignments.

Saxon Grammar and Writing seems comparable to A Beka in the grammar department, but better on composition. It is both stronger and more challenging than *Easy Grammar*. And the inclusion of diagramming distinguishes it from many other options. The distinctive Saxon incremental teaching and review approach will also attract fans as well as put off those who prefer more concentrated coverage of each topic in each lesson. I suspect parents will like this program since students can complete most of their work on their own, and even with composition assignments, students learn to self-evaluate to a certain extent. The content appeals to a broad audience that might be either secular or religious.

Note: a fourth grade level is scheduled to be added to this series in 2013.

• • • • • • • • •

Teaching Writing: Structure and Style seminar

Institute for Excellence in Writing
8799 N 387 Rd.
Locust Grove, OK 74352
800-856-5815
email: info@excellenceinwriting.com
www.ExcellenceInWriting.com
Teaching Writing Seminar - $169, seminar workbook alone - $35, *Student Writing Intensive Courses* (Levels A, B, or C) - $109 per set, *Continuation Courses* (Levels A, B, or C) - $199 per set

A few homeschoolers were so impressed with Andrew Pudewa's *Structure and Style* writing seminar that they went out of their way to make sure I reviewed it. My impression is that their enthusiasm was well founded.

Two things seem to be stumbling blocks for homeschooling parents when it comes to teaching composition skills: the difficulty of finding the right resources and lack of confidence in their own abilities to teach and evaluate. Andrew Pudewa presents writing seminars for parents and students that overcome the confidence barrier better than anything else I have yet seen. And his Institute for Excellence in Writing (IEW) resources give parents easy-to-use tools that work for a wide range of students.

Since attending Andrew's seminars is not practical for many parents and teachers, he offers those same seminars in the *Teaching Writing: Structure and Style* course on DVDs. The video course consists of seven discs (13 hours of viewing), a seminar workbook, and three *Student Workshop* discs.

Parents and teachers learn how to teach both creative and expository writing. The course teaches both structure and style in such a clear manner that parents and teachers learn how to easily teach students a repertoire of techniques. In addition, selected grammar skills are taught and applied periodically through the course so students better understand the relationship between grammar and good writing. Students continue to develop and apply techniques through actual writing activities taught throughout the course.

Parents may watch the entire course all at once or spread it out over weeks or months. Students might watch with them, but the DVDs really are focused on teacher training.

Pudewa does not try to cover all types of creative and expository writing but focuses on basic structures and approaches. Regardless, this foundational development should be excellent preparation for students to build upon as they explore other forms of writing.

For example, one of the strategies Pudewa uses is to have students begin by making notes from a model composition. Students come up with key words to convey main ideas. Then they work from their notes to reconstruct the piece, not attempting to copy it, but using their own words, expanding with their own ideas and expressions. This strategy works very well since it provides a secure starting place so students are not worrying excessively about what to say. Instead, they concentrate on structure and style. The basic strategy is then used for various types of writing assignments.

The course as presented to students consists of nine units: Note Making and Outlines, Summarizing from Notes, Summarizing from Narrative Stories, Summarizing References and Library Reports (2 units), Writing from Pictures, Creative Writing, Essay Writing, and Critiques. Once past the first few lessons, you can use the lessons in whatever order seems best for your students. The seminar workbook includes reproducible models that are an essential part of each lesson.

What I like most about this course is that Pudewa walks you through each strategy in detail. His teaching experience is very evident as he identifies and deals with problems that tend to crop up for both teacher and student. The lessons move along slowly enough for you to think and work through the process with his "live" DVD audience. This means you are more likely to end up with a really solid grasp of the course content.

As mentioned above, the seminar set includes three *Student Workshop* presentations. *Student Workshops* are recordings of hour-long classes conducted with different age groups: elementary (grades 2-4), intermediate (grades 5-7), and high school (grades 8-12). These serve as demonstration classes. You might have students work alongside a "video" class to introduce them to some of the methods of this course.

Even more help is available through *Student Writing Intensive* DVDs *(SID)*. There are three levels (*A*, *B*, and *C*), each consisting of four discs of actual classes, running about 7½ hours total. Each *SID* also includes a (new for 2012) *Structure and Style Overview* DVD which is a brief introduction to the various units so parents and teachers can get a quick overview of the *Structure and Style* course outline. *Level A*

is for grades 3-5, *Level B* is for grades 6-8, and *Level C* is for high school. Students shown in the classroom settings reflect the same age group breakdowns as in the *Student Workshops*. Video classes focus on selected lessons from the seminar. A binder and a set of reproducible papers (models, checklists, reference sheets, and worksheets) come with the set of discs. As with the *Student Workshop* videos, students may work through these along with the video classes.

Once you have worked through the basic seminar and *SID*, the *Student Writing Intensive Continuation Course* picks up where *SID* ends. It features 9 DVDs of video instruction, a CD-ROM with the teacher's manual, 10 class handouts, student samples, and a student packet with 162 pages of 3-hole punched, loose-leaf handouts that contain 32 weeks or more of writing assignments lasting one to two years.

For all of their courses, IEW allows parents to make copies of the printed material for their own children. However, each family in a co-op setting is expected to purchase their own set of student materials.

Older high school students (as well as college students) should benefit from the IEW *Advanced Communication Series*. The set consists of three DVDs of classes. Each DVD comes with a comprehensive booklet containing the models, exercises and samples presented in each class. The three titles are *Persuasive Writing and Speaking, Advanced Note Taking: A Dynamic Key Word Approach,* and *Power Tips for Planning and Writing a College Level Paper*.

IEW also offers other related resources in their catalog or through their website. Among them are some actual lesson books that will help you implement what is taught in the original seminar such as *Rockets, Radar, & Robotics; Following Narnia;* a variety of history-based lesson books; and more. These can be used in conjunction with the *Structure and Style* program or afterward. *Bible-Based Writing*

Lessons in Structure and Style has lessons that you can begin using from the very beginning of the *Structure and Style* program while most of the other books need to wait until a little later. Many of IEW's materials, including the core courses discussed here (except for *Bible-Based Writing Lessons*) are written from a secular, but "Christian friendly" viewpoint.

• • • • • • • • •

Winston Grammar

Precious Memories Educational Resources
18403 N.E. 111th Ave.
Battle Ground, WA 98604
360-687-0282
email: liz@WinstonGrammar.com
www.WinstonGrammar.com
complete course - $41 per level, extra student packet - $17.50, supplemental workbook - $11 each, supplemental workbook and answer key - $18

One of the toughest parts of most English language courses is the part that deals with structure and syntax—the sort of thing that diagramming teaches. However, for one reason or another many students just don't get diagramming. Instead of traditional diagramming, you might prefer to use *Winston Grammar*.

Winston Grammar has both *Basic* and *Advanced* sets. All students should begin with the *Basic* set. Although the *Advanced* set does some review, it assumes familiarity with the components and methodology introduced in the first set.

Winston Grammar uses key questions and clues for word identification. Rather than constructing diagrams, students begin by laying out color-coded cards in a horizontal fashion that correlates with the sentence under study. Then they use symbols and arrows to "mark up" sentences on their worksheets, showing parts of speech. There are larger colored cards that lead students through strategies for figuring out word functions within sentences. It begins by identifying only articles and nouns, but progresses up through prepositional phrases and predicate nominatives. Overall, it is a much more multi-sensory approach than most others.

The *Basic Winston Grammar* set teaches parts of speech, noun functions, prepositional phrases, and modifiers. It can be used with students at least fourth grade level or above. It includes a teacher manual, student workbook, and the cards, all of which are stored in a heavy-duty vinyl case. Four quizzes, a pre-test and a post-test are included in the student book. Extra student packets (student workbook and a set of cards) can be purchased since each student needs his or her own set.

In addition to the above, there is also a Supplemental Workbook for extra practice. This workbook corresponds exactly with the original in content and difficulty, offering "more of the same" for those students who need it. It comes with an answer key, but workbooks can be purchased without answer keys for additional students.

Once students have mastered the basic course, they should continue with *Advanced Winston Grammar*, but it should probably wait until students are in junior high. You might use *Winston Word Works* between the two courses if a student completes the *Basic* set in fourth or fifth grade or if you want to save the *Advanced* set for high school. The components are similar, but there is an additional quiz in the student book.

This level moves on to more complex noun

functions, reflexive pronouns, possessives, gerunds, infinitives, participles, and various kinds of clauses. Some of these sentences get very tricky! I think many of the lessons are fun for a parent and student to work through together, sort of like trying to solve a puzzle.

Precious Memories also publishes *Winston Word Works: A Usage Program* ($27). This is a complementary program that focuses on the most common usage errors such as subject-verb agreement, use of personal pronouns, use of who/whom, correct forms of indirect object pronouns, and comparative and superlative forms of adjectives. This course builds upon the basic *Winston Grammar* procedures for identifying sentence elements. It can be used any time after completing the *Basic* set.

• • • • • • • • •

Wordsmith series
by Janie B. Cheaney
Common Sense Press
Publisher sells only through distributors.
Contact them for distributor information.
352-475-5757
email: info@commonsensepress.com
www.commonsensepress.com

Wordsmith is a series of three books for developing writing skills. These are not age-graded, but they address skills at three different levels. My favorite book in the series is the original *Wordsmith: A Creative Writing Course for Young People*, which targets students around junior high or beginning high school level. My review begins with that book then discusses the other two volumes in relation to it.

Wordsmith: A Creative Writing Course for Young People (revised edition)
student book - $16, teacher's guide - $7

Many students in upper elementary grades and junior high have learned the basics in grammar and need some help transferring grammatical knowledge into their writing.

Wordsmith assumes the student knows basic grammar. It moves on from there to work with

grammar through written applications. For example, one assignment has them come up with vivid action verbs to replace weak verbs accompanied by adverbs. The goal is to sharpen writing skills by carefully choosing words for the best effect.

After working on grammar, they tackle sentence construction, again with the goal of writing more interesting yet concise sentences. Once grammar and sentence structure are under control, they can apply those skills to compositions.

Although *Wordsmith* does not teach all the different forms of writing such as reports, research papers, etc., it covers techniques that can be applied in almost any writing situation. Lessons work on skills such as describing people, narrowing the topic, and writing dialogue. At the end of the course, students write their own short story. Helps for proofreading and editing are included along with review quizzes.

The student book may be written in or used as a reusable text by doing the brief activities in a notebook. Lesson organization is clear and well designed. Most students should need a year or more to work through all of the lessons. Some teaching, primarily in the form of discussion and evaluation, is required, although students will do much of the work on their own. The author's humorous touches scattered throughout the book add special appeal.

Parents or teachers who lack confidence in their ability to teach students how to write will appreciate the inexpensive teacher's guide. It includes answers, lesson plans, teaching suggestions, and ideas for expanding lessons. Parents with strong writing skills will probably be able to manage without it.

Other books attempt to meet the same goals, but the presentation here is better than almost everything else at this level.

Wordsmith Apprentice
student book - $16

Wordsmith Apprentice is a "prequel" to

Wordsmith: A Creative Writing Course for Young People. Author Janie Cheaney translates the same enthusiasm, humor, and energy that so impressed me in the older-level book to this course for younger students.

Using a newspaper-writing approach, she creates interesting writing activities that develop both grammar and composition skills. For example, in the first section teaching about sentences, students learn the four types of sentences then write four sentences to describe a news photo, mixing declarative, interrogatory, and exclamatory sentences. Stretching beyond the limitations of the newspaper format, students also write invitations, letters, and thank-you notes. "Comic-strips" introduce each new section.

Topics covered are nouns, verbs, sentences, modifiers, prepositions, paragraphs, synopsis writing (often neglected in other courses!), dialogue, opinion writing, and more. These are covered within the context of newspaper tasks such as writing classified ads, travel articles, book reviews, articles, and headlines, as well as editing. Examples and some forms are included, not to stifle or limit students, but to help stimulate their imaginations and give them organizing tools.

Cheaney writes from a Christian perspective, although it comes through subtly. For example, students learn to recognize good synopses by deciding which one of three synopses most accurately conveys the story of David and Goliath. Then an assignment follows to write three synopses, one of which is for the story of The Good Samaritan.

This study is designed for students in grades four through six, and it can be used by students working independently (with parents or teachers reading and responding to exercises and assignments) or by a mixed age and ability group. There is a two-page answer key at the back of the book. There is no teacher manual since none is needed.

Students who have already been introduced to grammar basics will find this a great way to apply what they have learned. Those without prior grammar instruction will need supplemental study defining and identifying grammatical concepts. All students will need a thesaurus and they should also have a newspaper to consult for examples. It need not be current, so you can carefully screen a newspaper for objectionable content.

Wordsmith Craftsman
student book - $16

Designed for high school students, *Wordsmith Craftsman* can be used after completion of *Wordsmith: A Creative Writing Course for Young People* or any other courses that have built up a basic foundation in grammar, mechanics, and composition. High school students who have done a great deal of grammar but little composition should probably complete the *Creative Writing Course* before jumping into *Wordsmith Craftsman*.

This book is divided into three parts which can be used over a span of anywhere from one to four years depending upon the student.

Part One draws students into the writing process with practical, everyday writing tasks like note taking, outlining, summarizing, personal letters, business letters, and even business reports (although the last topic is addressed very briefly).

Part Two gets more technical with exercises on paragraph writing (narrative, descriptive, persuasive, and expository), word usage, and style. Part Three concentrates on essay writing but builds on paragraph writing skills to create five types of essays: descriptive, narrative, expository, critical, and persuasive.

Cheaney does an excellent job of pointing out different organizational strategies you might use to construct different types of essays. Plentiful examples help students visualize their goals. Cheaney's emphasis on style encourages students to move beyond mechanical correctness to excellence in communication skills.

The book is written for a student to work through independently, receiving feedback and encouragement from a parent or teacher as needed. There is no teacher manual or answer key since they are unnecessary. Students should work through the lessons at a pace slow enough to allow time for them to practice and master the various skills. A ninth or tenth grader should not expect to complete the book in one year, although an eleventh of twelfth grader might do so.

. . . .

WriteShop: An Incremental Writing Program

by Kim Kautzer and Debra Oldar
WriteShop
5753 Klusman Ave.
Alta Loma, CA 91737
909-989-5576
email: info@writeshop.com

website: www.writeshop.com
Basic Set (teacher's manual and
WriteShop I) - $99.95,
WriteShop I student workbook - $45.95,
WriteShop II student workbook - $45.95,
teacher's manual - $55.95,
Handbook for Teaching in a Group Setting
- $11.95,
Copying and Dictation Exercises - $4.95

WriteShop is another great resource for parents who lack confidence in their own ability to teach their students to write. It takes the guesswork out of the process.

The program is presented in a single teacher's volume and two student volumes, *I* and *II*. *WriteShop* provides detailed daily lesson plans and instructions for teachers, and the student volumes have all the worksheets and forms they will need. The teacher's manual offers more than lesson plans. It also has instructions on how to edit and make comments as well as descriptions of typical student errors and probable solutions. Student sample writings are accompanied by sample, edited versions and check-off lists with teacher comments so you can get a feel for how you might write your own responses to student work. Other helps in the manual are answer keys; reproducible check off lists, reference sheets, and forms; supplemental activity ideas; story starters; essay topics; and suggestions for writing across the curriculum. These features walk you all the way through activities, evaluation, and grading.

Not only do these features make the program easy to use but the authors have structured lessons to build from the ground up, covering sentence and paragraph structure and style before tackling lengthier assignments. The subtitle, "An Incremental Writing Program," refers to the way the program incorporates and builds upon skills taught in previous lessons. Because of this you should not skip lessons or change the order.

WriteShop is a great starting place for parents

who have done minimal writing instruction with their children. *WriteShop I* targets students in grades 7 through 10, though it can be used with students as young as sixth grade. Lessons in descriptive, informative, and narrative writing include describing a person, food, and place; explaining a process; writing a short report; and learning about tense, omniscience, and point of view in narratives. *WriteShop II* is written for students in grades 8-12, picking up where *WriteShop I* leaves off. Following a brief review of *WriteShop I* concepts, *WriteShop II* lessons cover advanced descriptive narration, point of view, narrative voice, and essay writing (including how to write a timed essay).

None of the writing assignments are very lengthy. High schoolers will still need to practice writing lengthier papers and research reports than are required by *WriteShop*. (Keep in mind that this program is not intended to cover all types of writing assignments. For example, there are no lessons on poetry or writing business letters.)

If you start this program with younger students, move through it more slowly, taking at least three years rather than two. Older students might be able to complete both volumes in a single year if they are very diligent and have already developed basic writing skills.

The program works well for parents working with one or more of their own children, but it will also work in a group class situation. Co-op teachers will find the *Handbook for Teaching in a Group Setting* a helpful supplement to the teacher's manual; this is sold only as an e-book.

WriteShop does need to be taught. It is not designed for independent study even though students do much writing on their own.

Lessons—each of which might take about two weeks to complete—include "skill builder" exercises that focus on a particular skill, usually related to grammar or vocabulary. The "skill builder" activity feeds directly into the main lesson. For example, the second lesson is

"Describing a Pet." The "skill builder" teaches students to use a thesaurus to come up with more interesting words to replace overused adjectives and weak verbs. This skill is then incorporated into the pet description. Many of the grammar-oriented skill builders help students finally see the use of some of their grammar lessons.

Two weeks per lesson sounds like a lot of time, but the authors have incorporated more than the "skill builder" focus into each lesson. For example, the pet description also works with mind maps, topic sentences, metaphors, similes, and concluding sentences. In addition, *WriteShop* focuses on teaching students to self-edit. Using lesson-specific "Writing Skills Checklists," students work through their original assignment to edit, revise, and rewrite. The parent or teacher also has a unique "Teacher Writing Skills Checklist" for each lesson so you know what to look for when it's your turn to edit their papers. An evaluation form helps you come up with an objective grade for each final draft.

Students should also be completing the copying and dictation assignments that build skills of observation and attention while working on various sentence constructions and broader vocabulary. The *WriteShop* guides direct parents and teachers to select their own copying and dictation selections from the Bible or exemplary literature. (While this is fairly easy to do, WriteShop also has published a small booklet, *Copying and Dictation Exercises for WriteShop I*, with excerpts from well-known literary works that relate to each of the sixteen lessons. This saves parents and teachers from having to come up with their own passages.) I think the authors have actually resolved a critical problem some of us have encountered with copying and dictation by *requiring* copying first, followed by dictation of the same piece. This way, students have already encountered unusual punctuation or sentence breaks that otherwise might be unpredictable when encountered only through dictation.

The program is written by Christians; you will find occasional biblical references, primarily in the teacher's manual. However, the authors' Christian perspective also appears very subtly in lessons such as writing a description of a person where the authors caution the student to remember to be gracious and focus on a person's positive features.

WriteShop sells a Starter Pack at a slightly discounted price that includes the Teacher's Manual and *WriteShop I* student workbook plus *The Blue Book of Grammar and Punctuation* by Jane Straus, *Copying and Dictation Exercises for WriteShop I,* and a poster showing the five steps of the writing process. Older students need to have a grammar handbook for reference, and there is no specific recommendation or requirement for a particular book. However, the Starter Pack does include a Tips sheet that gives parents and teachers suggestions for how to incorporate the *Blue Book* with *WriteShop* lessons, so this should be a great package for getting started.

Overall, *WriteShop* is one of the best resources I've seen for group classes and for parents who need lots of help to teach writing.

Note that WriteShop also publishes a series of three books for grades K through 3 called *WriteShop Primary* and *WriteShop Junior* for grades 3 through 6. These two resources were written by Nancy I. Sanders and are structured differently. See my review of *WriteShop Primary* and *WriteShop Junior* on my website at www.CathyDuffyReviews.com.

• • • • • • • •

Writing for 100 Days: A Student-Centered Approach to Composition and Creative Writing

by Gabriel Arquilevich
Fairview Publishing
PO Box 746
Oak View, CA 93022
805-640-1924

email: garquilevich@roadrunner.com
$20

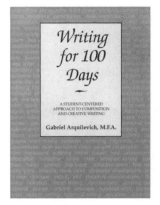

Individual lessons for 100 days address four areas: composition, fiction, poetry, and writing in action. Assuming the student has a foundation in basic grammar and composition, this book goes on to tackle elements that produce excellent writing. It should work best for high school level students, but many of the lessons could also be used with junior high students. I would begin using some of the lessons for seventh and eighth graders, then go back through many of those same lessons again a year or two later as I use the entire book with older students.

Composition lessons work on both style and grammar by focusing on skills such as word economy, word choice, use of dialect and slang, transitions, sentence variety, use of parentheses and dashes, tone, and organization. The strategy is often humorous; sometimes students are instructed to produce a negative example then a positive example.

In each lesson, instruction is followed by an exercise. Answers to the exercises are provided at the back of the book when appropriate. You need not use all the lessons in order; you can select those that best meet the needs of your students.

The fiction section walks students through the actual writing of a story. Poetry lessons address selected forms such as haiku, limericks, sonnets, and free verse. "Writing in action" lessons tackle a variety of real-life applications such as business letters, writing news reports, conducting an interview, writing a television commercial, technical writing, and travel writing. For fun, a few "word games" are added. A list of additional assignments is provided at the end of the book, but I think students will find some of the lesson activities worthwhile enough to tackle more than once. This means that even though the book is only 103 pages in length, it is packed with so many ideas that it can be used well beyond 100 days. Also, you are free to expand, skip, or repeat lessons as you choose.

Ideally, these lessons should be done in a group. Even two students will do! However, most lessons can be used by a single student working independently as long as there is a parent or teacher to interact with and to evaluate the work. Interaction between two or more students in many of the lessons ranges from helpful to essential, so *do* try to have at least two students work through the lessons if possible.

This book offers a well-balanced combination of skills instruction, motivation, and practice. I often compare it with Janie Cheaney's *Wordsmith: A Creative Writing Course for Young People* because it has a similar playful but effective approach to writing for this age level.

Language Arts: Spelling, Vocabulary & Handwriting

Spelling and vocabulary are lumped together because many spelling courses actually serve more as vocabulary courses as they move to upper grade levels. Also, if you have a child who is born with the "perfect-spelling gene" or a child who masters phonic and spelling rules in the early grades, it makes more sense to work on vocabulary than to waste time in a spelling program.

Handwriting recommendations follow spelling and vocabulary recommendatons in their own section at the end of this chapter.

· · · · · · ● · · · ·

Spelling and Vocabulary

All About Spelling
by Marie Rippel

All About Learning Press, Inc.
615 Commerce Loop
Eagle River, WI 54521
715-477-1976
www.allaboutlearningpress.com
Basic Interactive Kit: $29.95, Deluxe Interactive Kit - $49.95 - Level 1 teacher's manual and student packet - $29.95, Levels 2-7 teacher's manual and student packet - $39.95 per level

All About Spelling (AAS) is an incremental spelling program based on the intensive phonics approach of the Orton-Gillingham methodology. It uses multisensory activities that should work well with most learners. Each lesson focuses on a single concept, such as a particular phonogram or spelling rule, and includes a spelling word list that reinforces that concept. Although the program shares many features with reading programs, and students will learn to read and write words, it is specifically geared toward teaching spelling. You might want to use it alongside *All About Reading* (also reviewed in this book) from the same publisher since the lessons will reinforce one another.

Because *Level 1* teaches foundational spelling rules that apply to more advanced words in higher levels, most students should begin at *Level 1* regardless of what grade they are in. A placement test on the publisher's website will help you determine the correct level for your child.

Each level of *All About Spelling* requires three essential components: the teacher's manual, the student packet, and either the Basic or Deluxe Interactive Kit.

The student packet for *Level 1* contains four sets of color-coded flashcards: Phonogram Cards, Sound Cards (for dictation), Key Cards (spelling rules), and Word Cards (spelling words). It also includes tokens for segmenting words, a progress chart, and a certificate of completion. Flashcards are printed on perforated cardstock, so you'll need to separate them and store them in your own 3" x 5" index card box or the Spelling Review Box offered by the publisher. With the exception of the Word Cards, the *Level 1* flashcards are all used again in *Levels 2* through 7. Student packets for subsequent levels include additional flashcards, level-specific materials, a progress chart, and a certificate of completion.

The Basic Interactive Kit includes *The Basic Phonograms* CD-ROM, a set of letter tiles, magnets for the letter tiles, and spelling divider cards for your index card box. (As the child moves through the program, flashcards are sorted behind dividers labeled "Review" and "Mastered.") The Deluxe Interactive Kit adds the Spelling Review Box, sparkling bee stickers

for use on the progress chart, and a custom tote bag for storing all the components.

The Basic Phonograms CD-ROM is an interactive computer program that gives students practice in seeing, hearing, and identifying the phonograms. The letter tiles are one-inch square laminated tiles of all the letters and phonograms. The adhesive magnets go on the back of the letter tiles so you can use them on a magnetic white board. Author Marie Rippel recommends using a 2' x 3' magnetic, erasable white board that you can also use for storing the tiles. If you don't magnetize the tiles, you can either store them in baggies and set them out for each lesson or organize them on some other surface where they can remain undisturbed between lessons. Labels for various groups of tiles and an organizing diagram are included to help you arrange the tiles into categories. Some children may not need or enjoy the hands-on work with letter tiles, and for those students Rippel suggests that you write out words on paper or a white board instead.

AAS lessons are presented as "Steps." The Steps are fully customizable and designed to be completed at the student's pace, so depending on the needs of the student, each one might take a couple of days or weeks to complete.

Step 1 in the *Level 1* book teaches the sounds of the individual letters, including the various possibilities for vowels and consonants such as "g." Flashcards are used for teaching the phonograms, and children learn all the sounds of each phonogram (e.g., the two sounds of the letter "g" and the various sounds for each vowel). If you aren't familiar with the sounds of the phonograms, you can learn them from *The Basic Phonograms* CD-ROM.

After introducing the letters and their sounds, *Level 1* teaches students how to "segment" words by identifying the individual sounds within them. Color-coded letter tiles are introduced, first for learning how to alphabetize the letters, then for constructing words. Dictation begins early in the program beginning in Step

4 when students are asked to listen to the sound of a phonogram and then point to the letter tile that makes the sound. In later lessons, students write the phonogram on lined paper then listen to and spell words with letter tiles. By the end of Step 11, students are writing spelling words and several phrases such as "big dog."

Step 12 introduces consonant digraphs "th, sh," and "ch," with subsequent Steps continuing to build on prior knowledge to add more challenging phonograms and concepts like compound words and syllabication.

Level 2 quickly reviews *Level 1* content in Step 1 then adds 11 more phonograms. The program emphasizes rules and generalizations for spelling, and syllabication plays an increasingly important role. For example, students learn rules such as those on Key Card 5, which teaches that the vowel in a closed syllable is usually short and the vowel in an open syllable is usually long. The student packet includes "syllable tags" that students use in conjunction with the letter tiles to identify types of syllables. "Rule breaker" words like *of* and *was* are taught at this level, but there are very few such sight words. The amount of dictation expands to several phrases and sentences per day. The vocabulary in *Level 2* ranges from simple words like cake, late, and car to a few more challenging and possibly unfamiliar words like compost, humid, and prevent. As in *Level 1*, the Steps in *Level 2* might take more or less time to complete depending on the student.

Level 3 adds suffix tiles and more syllable tags to the letter tile collection. In addition to work on suffixes and syllables, silent-e words receive more attention as students complete the Silent E Book that comes in the student packet. More challenging phonograms like the sounds of "oo" and ways to spell /k/ are taught along with contractions and homophones. Spelling words taught in *Level 3* are generally longer and more complex, with words like childhood, graceful, we'll, and giggle being representative.

Level 4 adds prefix tiles to the tile set, then continues to advance with more challenging phonograms like "eigh" and the four sounds of the letter "y." The six syllable types, syllable division rules, and spelling strategies are also taught at this level. An example of a dictation sentence from the beginning of this level is, "None of the students took the test today." Examples of some of the more difficult words taught are chimney, eighteen, and unhinged.

Level 5 adds phonograms such as *si* and *ough,* while continuing work on other phonograms such as those that make the /er/ sound. Students also work on plurals, including irregular plurals. One sample from the dictation is, "What flavor is the cake you're baking for us tonight?" (p.62). Some more challenging spelling words from *Level 5* are encouraged, equipment, gnome, particular, perfection, and volcanoes.

Level 6 teaches phonograms like "mb, gu," and "augh;" exceptions to the i-before-e rule; suffixes such as "able" and "ible;" some "rule breakers"; and other advanced facets of spelling. Examples of the more challenging words are agreeably, collectible, encouragement, nourishing, sheik, and sheriff. Many of the words are familiar words with suffixes that are often misspelled.

Level 7 provides coverage through high school. The program covers advanced sounds, Latin roots, Greek word elements, French endings and silent letters, and some Spanish and Italian words. Examples of some of the words are extinguish, convenient, solemn, bankruptcy, transformation, and psychology. Students work on word analysis and learn to identify prefixes, suffixes, and roots. Letter tiles are frequently used for word analysis and word building.

Although *AAS* is a rules-oriented program, the multisensory approach helps students to be successful. *AAS* addresses the three learning modalities in these ways:

Visual: spelling rules are demonstrated with

color-coded letter tiles. Flashcards for phonograms, rules, and spelling words also provide visual cues.

Auditory: lessons are taught aloud and flashcards are reviewed orally. When learning new words, students hear themselves say the sounds as they write the corresponding phonograms.

Kinesthetic: children build new words with letter tiles; write phonograms, words, phrases, and sentences from dictation; and handle flashcards.

While *AAS* is not as multi-sensory as a program that includes songs and games, it should meet the needs of most children. And it uniquely incorporates multi-sensory learning all the way through high school.

AAS does not teach handwriting or letter formation. If you are teaching a young child who has not yet learned to write, you might choose a handwriting program to use in conjunction with *AAS*.

With the exception of the stickers and progress chart, all items are non-consumable, so you could use them with another student. However, if you are teaching two or more students simultaneously, each student will need his or her own student packet so you can customize the review portion of the lesson.

One of the most impressive features of this program is the instruction for teachers. Lessons are explained thoroughly and include teaching tips and cautions about common problems at pertinent points in each lesson. Because you learn as you go, the layout eliminates the need for you to first read through a separate manual whenever you need information. If you should need additional help, the publisher offers free phone and email support.

. . . .

Building Spelling Skills

Christian Liberty Press
502 W. Euclid Ave.
Arlington Heights, IL 60004
847-259-4444

email: custserv@homeschools.org
www.christianlibertypress.com
student books - $8.99 each,
answer keys - $3.99 each

It doesn't get any more affordable for solid

spelling coverage than the *Building Spelling Skills* series. However, you can't describe these books as "fun" or "colorful." Instead, I would use words like "comprehensive," "thorough," and "businesslike." Illustrations are mostly clip art, and books are printed in two colors.

They begin in the early grades with a strong basis in phonics, shifting toward word origins and language principles in upper grades. The level of difficulty is higher than in most other series and even more so at upper levels. Also, there is Christian content throughout.

Each book is a self-contained, consumable student worktext. Students should be able to work independently through these books for the most part, especially past the early grades. Inexpensive answer keys are available for all but the first book. There are no separate teacher guides. These last features coupled with cost effectiveness make these books very appealing for busy families with limited budgets.

Book 1

This first grade workbook serves as much for phonics reinforcement as it does for spelling. All but the last two lessons are each designed around a phonics rule. (The last two lessons work on syllables.) The first five lessons cover the short vowels, working only on words with the designated short vowel sound. Almost all of the phonograms are covered in *Book 1*. A variety of exercises induce the child to practice writing words over and over. The number of words per lesson seems a little large in comparison to other programs, and the difficulty level also is advanced. Examples of the more difficult words are voyage, poison, grudge, because, awkward, and laundry. Space for children to take their weekly tests is provided at the back of the book. Teaching instructions are at the front. Some content and inserted verses and quotations identify the curriculum as Christian. No answer key is available or needed.

Book 2

Book 2 accelerates the emphasis on phonics rules with some intense phonics vocabulary. Weekly word lists are introduced with definitions of the phonetic concepts such as consonant digraphs and voiced/voiceless consonants, or rules of syllabication. Some of the lessons deal with root words, prefixes, and suffixes. The newest editions have dropped challenging work with accented syllables that used to be in two lessons, substituting more work with words with the digraphs "ch, sh, th," and "wh." The new spelling words in the revised lessons are more age-appropriate than were the words in the previous edition. There is plenty of practice in *Book 2*, but as in *Book 1* the word lists are generally more advanced than in other second grade programs. Examples of the more difficult words: adage, foreign, cyclone, musician, disappear, although, exodus, and accomplish.

Book 3

This book seems to build on *Book 2*, assuming that much of the phonetic vocabulary is familiar. Phonics "Rules and Definitions" appear at the back of the book for reference. Like *Book 2*, it is very rule-oriented, reviewing previously-covered phonetic rules, then moving on to still more rules. The difficulty level still seems advanced with words such as audience, dynamite, and luncheon, but not quite as much so as the first two books.

Book 4

Book 4 continues in the same vein but moves on to accents, more complicated prefix and suffix work, contractions, and possessives, plus calendar and measurement words. Interestingly, it has a lesson on computer-related terms. The newest 2011 edition was updated with current terms.

Book 5

Book 5 is subtitled *The World of Words*. The first nine units deal with geography-related words. Remaining units feature individual topics such as birds, sports, anatomy, economics, and terms related to church. Exercises are very eclectic rather than following similar formats each time. One might have students practice with antonyms or suffixes, while others concentrate on the unit topic with vocabulary and practical usage. There is a great deal of practical and academic usage in this book. For example, in Unit 2 students learn the names given to citizens in various countries (e.g., The Danish live in Denmark). In another example from Unit 19 on "Titles for Civil Officers," students learn job descriptions for mayor, notary, auditor, magistrate, constable, assessor, etc. *Book 5* strikes me as one that might be used whenever this type of study seems appropriate for a student rather than at a particular grade level.

Book 6

Book 6 reviews the basic spelling rules students most likely encountered in the early elementary years. This is a good time to review because most students have forgotten there are patterns to help them figure out the spelling of unfamiliar words even if they use that knowledge without realizing it. Review does not take students back to one-syllable words but introduces challenging words. Suffixes and prefixes (including Latin and Greek prefixes) are also addressed in depth. Spelling rule coverage is not as thorough as that found in *The Writing Road to Reading* or other resources dedicated specifically to spelling rules. However, this book should be very useful for the student who either never learned the rules or does not use them as a tool when needed. Many junior high students would do well to go through these lessons.

Book 7

Book 7 is obviously more difficult than *Book 6* with its smaller, more abundant print. Suffixes and prefixes are the organizing themes for all lessons, but vocabulary development is the overall emphasis. Students become familiar with many new and challenging words. Since spelling is practiced rather than taught in this book, students lacking spelling skills (rule familiarity) should use *Book 6* first. *Book 7* can also be used with students at older grade levels. Typical of words in the lessons are psychic, infirmary, apologize, and noticeable. Examples of some of the more challenging words: prerequisite, antediluvian, expatriate, ostentatious, and recapitulate.

Book 8

Word origins are the theme of *Book 8*, and this does not mean studying only Greek and Latin roots. Instead, lessons explore words from many languages and cultures including African languages, Arabic, Celtic, French, Hebrew, Italian, Persian, Scandinavian, Spanish, and more. Students need an unabridged dictionary to use alongside the lessons. Lessons are both fascinating and challenging—maybe too challenging for some eighth graders. I would also consider using this book with high school students.

· · · · · · · ·

English from the Roots Up: Help for Reading, Writing, Spelling and S.A.T. Scores

by Joegil Lundquist
Literacy Unlimited
PO Box 278
Medina, WA 98039-0278
425-454-5830
email: joegilkl@aol.com

www.literacyunlimited.com
$29.95 each, Word Cards - $18

In *English From the Roots Up*, Greek and Latin words are the foundation for vocabulary study in the broader sense of word derivations. Children are unlikely to find the majority of the vocabulary words they learn here in their everyday reading, but they will be well prepared for new vocabulary they'll encounter in high school and college. Even more important than the actual vocabulary words they learn is the skill children develop in analyzing new words they encounter and being able to figure out their meanings.

Each lesson begins with one Greek or Latin word, teaches its meaning, then gives children a list of from three to ten English words derived from the root word. For example, lesson ten introduces the Greek word *kinesis* meaning movement. The lesson then teaches five words derived from *kinesis*: kinetic, kinesiology, kinescope, cinema, and cinematographer. The words *photos* (light) and *graph* (write or draw) were introduced in the first two lessons, so children are connecting the last word to two Greek words they have already learned. This can create a picture in students' minds of someone who can "draw" with "moving light," making it easier for children to understand that a big word like cinematographer refers to the person who decides how to compose the scenes that he wants a movie camera to capture. Children each need a set of 100 cards, one for each lesson. Each card has the Greek or Latin word with a border of green for Greek words and red for Latin words. On the reverse are the derived words and their meanings. You can purchase sets of pre-made cards or make them along with your students.

The goal is similar to that of *Vocabulary from Classical Roots* (also reviewed in this book) although the vocabulary words here are less commonly used than those in *Vocabulary from Classical Roots*. This program requires teacher presentation and interaction. There is no workbook. Instead, index cards (or purchased sets of cards), a file box, and a good dictionary are the primary learning tools.

The program might be used with students from middle elementary grades through college, but I think junior high through high school the best time to use it.

Actual teaching information provided is brief but loaded with activity suggestions. The teacher is on his or her own to implement the ideas. Here are some examples of activity ideas: for the root *graph*, a number of related words are presented with accompanying ideas: "Telegraph—Let someone present a research report on Thomas Edison's early days as a telegrapher. Let someone do a report on Morse code and give a demonstration of it." "Lithograph—Discuss the process of lithography and talk about Currier and Ives. Their lithographs are still used every year as Christmas cards. Make potato or linoleum block prints." These activity ideas could be turned into great unit studies. This resource is especially suited to the creative teacher who prefers general guidelines rather than detailed lesson plans.

A second volume is also available. It targets a slightly older audience, so it makes a good follow-up to the first volume. It teaches an additional 100 Greek and Latin root words with new activities and teaching notes.

· · · · · · · ·

Spelling Power

by Beverly L. Adams-Gordon
Spelling Power
PO Box 520
Pomeroy WA 99347
888-773-5586
www.spellingpower.
com
book - $64.95,
*Activity Task
Cards* - $29.95,

student record books - $5.95 each

Spelling Power is a single volume that can be used to teach spelling to all of your children, ages eight through adult. It serves as instruction manual for the parent or teacher with all of the word lists needed for all grade or ability levels making up the bulk of the book. Students complete work with their word lists each day on two forms: Daily Test Sheets and 10-Step Study Sheets. These are then compiled in a binder or record book.

Spelling Power might seem overwhelming at first. There is a great deal of material for parents or teachers to read. However, the "Quick Start Steps" at the beginning of the book walk you through placement and instructions for using the program. Once you understand how the program works, it is relatively easy to use.

The newest (2006, fourth) edition of *Spelling Power* comes with the Quick Start DVD and the Teacher's Resource CD-ROM. The Quick Start DVD makes getting started easier than ever since it walks you through actual lessons with a student so that it is very understandable. Watching at least the first few segments on the DVD is the best way to start, and you should have your book in hand so you can follow along.

This very comprehensive spelling program uses a base list of about 5,000 frequently used words. A list of the 12,000 most-frequently-used and most-frequently-misspelled words is included on the Teacher's Resource CD-ROM. This list is used to choose words for review as well as for supplementing the basic 5000 words already taught in the program. These 12,000 words are coded to show when each is taught by grade level and in correlation with *Spelling Power*.

The 5000 word list in the teacher's manual is broken down into eleven levels of frequency. Each level is further divided into 47 possible groups based on common elements such as phonetic principles or spelling rules.

Diagnostic tests place each student at his or

her proper beginning point in the list. From that point, rather than working on predetermined, weekly word lists as in other spelling programs, *Spelling Power* has children pretest words but then study only those with which they have trouble. This should be much more efficient and effective than typical classroom programs although it does require more parental direction. Each student progresses at his or her own rate. Frequently misspelled words are reviewed periodically to insure retention. There are six levels of built-in review in the program.

A ten-step study process is used to study each word to be learned. This ten-step process should help even poor spellers improve their skills.

The book itself has been rearranged for this latest edition to make it easier to use. I especially appreciate the pictures of student pages/worksheets placed in the instructions where they are discussed. The majority of the book is made up of the word lists, resources for teaching, and helpful suggestions for dealing with children with specific needs. This is not a student workbook. You still need to present each lesson's spelling pretest of the words and select the skill building activity designed to reinforce spelling words and skills.

Direct instruction will be required at first, but children will be able to work more independently as they learn how it works. Even after students become familiar with the program, parents or teachers still need to spend five minutes per day in direct instruction. Students should spend about fifteen minutes total per day on their *Spelling Power* lessons. The interaction required between teacher and child in the early grades actually makes this program more ideal for homeschoolers than for the regular classroom.

Suggestions for games and activities are included in the book. In addition, optional *Spelling Power Activity Task Cards* provide drill activities, games, skill builders, writing prompts, dictionary skill work, and other types of activities. Within each category of activities, cards are color coded into four categories corresponding to age and skill level groupings covering all grade levels. Most activities can be completed by a student working alone, although a few require a partner. The *Activity Task Cards* come with a very helpful teacher's manual. The manual tells you how to use the cards, offers suggestions for making your own letter tiles, cross references to *Spelling Power* lessons, and includes answers for the appropriate cards. *Activity Task Cards* might also be used along with any other phonic-based spelling program. I highly recommend purchasing the *Activity Task Cards* since they help address the needs of various learning styles.

The companion Teacher's Resource CD-ROM is installed directly onto your computer. The CD includes the *Spelling Power Digital Tutor*, a spelling tutorial program for independent study. Parents or teachers need to enter word lists for students, but then students can work with the words—listening, repeating, and typing them into the computer. The CD also features a huge library of printable resources that include student worksheets, record keeping pages, rules charts, and teaching aids, and printable "cards" with skill building activities. (Note that the activities are the same as those in the book but do not include all those on the separate set of task cards.) The printable forms make it easy to create your own student record books, but you still might want to purchase the pre-printed, bound versions from a *Spelling Power* distributor that are designed with lines appropriately spaced for different ability levels. When used properly, the student record books eliminate extra record keeping by the teacher.

Note that the Teacher's Resource CD-ROM is not compatible with Mac systems. Those with Macs may contact Spelling Power for an alternate way to access skill-builders and printable forms, but they will not be able to run the *Digital Tutor*. Since the *Digital Tutor* is not essential to the program, this should not be a significant drawback. Also, the DVD and CD-ROM are sold separately and will work with older editions of *Spelling Power*.

The DVD and CD-ROM plus the improvements in the book itself make a great program even better. I think parents who were overwhelmed by the explanatory information in previous volumes will find the latest edition far more user friendly.

. . . .

Spellwell Series

by Nancy Hall
EPS School Specialty
PO Box 9031
Cambridge,
MA 02139
800-225-5750
www.eps.
schoolspecialty.com
student books -
$8.25 each, teacher
keys - $4.85 each

The *Spellwell* series targets grades 2 through 5 with two worktexts per grade level. Books are designated *A* and *AA* for second grade level, *B* and *BB* for third grade level, *C* and *CC* for fourth, and *D* and *DD* for fifth. Teacher keys are single books that each cover the two books for a grade level. This series designs lessons around spelling rules or generalizations. Some of these are discovered by students as they look for patterns, while others are specifically identified. One or more "outlaw" words appear in each lesson, and space is provided for you to add your own words to be studied.

Lessons begin with a pretest. Students who get most or all words correct might be given an additional list of more-challenging words to study or the "alternative homework" I describe below.

A variety of age-appropriate activities help students recognize spelling patterns. Other

thinking skills come into play in activities such as identifying rhyming words, words that fit the same categories, and antonyms and synonyms. Some assignments take students outside the workbook. They might be instructed to "find as many words with *ow* as you can." To do so, they can use spelling words, ask friends or relatives, or consult a dictionary. There are occasional composition assignments. There are also puzzles, scrambled letters, crosswords, and other more-entertaining activities.

A really nice feature is the "alternative homework" option at the bottom of many pages. If a student does well on the pretest, he or she should tackle the alternative homework option rather than the regular lesson activities. Of course, parents are always welcome to use alternative homework assignments whenever they seem appropriate. Alternative homework suggestions are very diverse. For example, page 23 in *Book CC* says, "Choose two of your longest spelling words. Make as many words as possible using these letters." Page 33 of that same book instructs, "Write synonyms or antonyms for eight of your spelling words."

All worktexts have lists of all spelling words covered at the back of the book. Some books have progress charts for recording spelling test grades.

Because of the variety, these worktexts might require more teaching or interaction than some others, but even using the most challenging activities does not require a lot of input from the parent or teacher. Generally, these are very easy to use and will not require any lesson preparation.

Worktexts are printed in black-and-white, but they have some cartoonish illustrations and creative page designs that make them more visually interesting than books like *Building Spelling Skills*.

The flexibility and variety within *Spellwell* lessons is likely to make these especially appealing to Sociable Sues, although they should work well for all students. Another plus is the very low cost for both the student worktexts and the teacher keys.

· · · · · · · · ·

Vocabulary from Classical Roots Books A-E

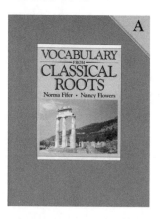

by Norma Fifer and Nancy Flowers
EPS School Specialty
PO Box 9031
Cambridge, MA 02139
800-225-5750
www.eps.
schoolspecialty.com
student books A-C - $12.70 each, D-E - $13.65 each; teacher's guides - $22 each

General vocabulary study makes sense for the younger grades, but the type of more specialized study with Greek and Latin roots we find in *Vocabulary from Classical Roots* becomes more useful for older children since they have already built up a foundational vocabulary and can start to make connections with prefixes, suffixes, and roots. The publisher recommends this vocabulary series of *Books A* through *E* for grades seven through eleven, although the letter designations make them easily adaptable to students above and below the recommended levels.

The series draws upon both Greek and Latin roots simultaneously to expand students' English vocabulary. For example, the second lesson in *Book A* begins by introducing the Greek word *tri* and the Latin word *tres*, both meaning three. It goes on to a study of the words trilogy, trisect, and triumvirate. Greek and Latin words are not always this similar. Lesson four introduces the Greek word *pan* and the Latin word *omnis*, both meaning all, plus the Greek word *holos* and the Latin word *totus*, both meaning whole.

Students with some exposure to Greek or Latin will immediately recognize the derivation of words from those languages. Other students without prior knowledge of those languages will develop some familiarity with Greek and Latin simply by using these workbooks.

Each book is written at an increasingly difficult level. Words with similar roots are grouped thematically for ease of study. A variety of exercises, including work with synonyms, antonyms, analogies, and sentence completion, helps students develop full understanding. Two unusual extras are included: literary, historical, and geographic references help develop cultural literacy; and suggestions for extended writing activities help students to apply new vocabulary. *Books D* and *E* add exercises for testing vocabulary within the context of short articles. One student, who has used earlier levels of this series, pointed out that *Book E* contains creeping elements of political correctness, even though they are subtle and sporadic rather than obvious and pervasive.

While students can work independently through most of the lessons, group or teacher discussion really helps most students.

A teachers guide and answer key for each level has teaching suggestions, exercise answers, and glossaries of some of the literary and historical references.

· · · · · · · · ·

Vocabu-Lit series

Perfection Learning
PO Box 500
Logan, IA 51546
800-831-4190
email: orders@perfectionlearning.com
www.perfectionlearning.com
student workbook (softcover) $10.95 each, teacher edition on CD-ROM: $19.95 each for grades 2-4, $15.50 each for grade 5-12

The *Vocabu-Lit* series begins each lesson with an excerpt from a book, story, essay, poem, or speech. Within each literary piece, ten vocabulary words in bold become the focus of each lesson as students encounter the words in a number of ways to develop a nuanced understanding of each word's meaning. After the literary piece, the layout in the first three books (*B* through *D* for grades 2 through 4) differs from that of the rest of the series (Books *E* through *L* for grades 5 through 12).

In *Books B* through *D*, students first copy definitions for each word from the dictionary in the back of their books. The next exercise focuses on context clues as students fill in the blanks with the correct words; in books for grades 3 and 4 students also circle the context clue within the sentence. Students identify synonyms and antonyms and work with word relationships in the next two sections. There are still two more activities for each lesson! One of them uses a graphic organizer to work with words. For example, one graphic organizer presents a word web for students to identify words or phrases from the story that relate to a particular topic. The final activity is a puzzle of some sort that uses the words from that week's list. Grade 2 exercises differ from those in the other two lower-level books. They are simpler with students doing such things as circling yes/no answers or selecting one of two answers by checking a box. They skip the graphic organizers, but they do include puzzles and some composition activities.

In books for grades 5 and up, the first exercise challenges students to provide a definition of the word working from prior knowledge and context. This serves as sort of a pre-test. Students then look up and write the definitions from a dictionary, comparing these with their own definitions. The next exercise works with antonyms and synonyms; students are encouraged to consult a dictionary. Work with analogies stretches students beyond synonyms

and antonyms into cause-effect and other types of word relationships. The next exercise seems easier as students fill in the blanks of ten sentences with the correct word. The final exercise varies with crossword puzzles, word spirals, word association games, story writing, drawing, and other activities.

There are either three or four review lessons within each book that test students on words learned over a number of lessons. Separate tests are available but they are sold in classroom sets and are likely too expensive for most homeschoolers to user. The review lessons should give students sufficient accountability.

The teacher editions, available only on CD-ROM, are a copy of the student text with overprinted answers. You can easily skip the teacher edition for second grade, but you will probably want them for other levels to save you time even if you can easily figure out the answers yourself.

I particularly like this series for a number of reasons: the use of literary excerpts, the variety of activities, the selection of words (challenging yet more practical than in some other resources), and reasonable cost.

Sample pages are available at the publisher's website.

• • • • • • • •

Wordly Wise, Original series and 3000 series

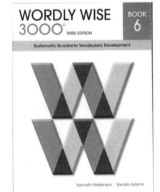

Educators Publishing Service
PO Box 9031
Cambridge, MA 02139
800-225-5750
www.eps.
schoolspecialty.com
student books -
about $12 each,
answer keys - less than $10 each

I've seen many vocabulary resources over the years, but my favorite for general use remains the original *Wordly Wise* series, *Books 1* through 9. (*Books A* through *C* in the original series are also available, but I think other academic priorities preclude their use in the early grades.)

I suspect the popularity of *Wordly Wise* stems from its effectiveness and reasonable cost as well as the fact that students can work independently most of the time. *Books 1* through 9 are intended for grades four through twelve. However, vocabulary is somewhat advanced, so choose lower level books if your children are average in their vocabulary skills. I suggest starting average to bright students at fourth grade level with *Book 1*.

In this series, students use one list of words through four or five different types of exercises to become familiar with the word's usage in different contexts as well as its various meanings. Exercises include definitions, recognition of proper usage, word origins, prefixes and suffixes, analogies, and synonym substitution. Crossword puzzles at the end of each unit reinforce learning from earlier lessons. Children must truly understand meanings to complete the activities.

The answer key for each level is relatively inexpensive and you will certainly want it to save time and energy since the exercises are often quite challenging.

One issue that might be viewed as a drawback occurs in *Books 4* through 9 of the original series. While *Books 1* through 3 include glossaries in the back listing all vocabulary words and their definitions, from Book 4 on students must use a separate dictionary.

EPS/School Specialty has continued to sell the original series, but they will eventually take it out of print. They have already replaced it with the *Wordly Wise 3000* series, and that series is already in its third editions. *Wordly Wise 3000* retains many of the features of the original series. It teaches multiple meanings of some words. A variety of activities encourages students to think about vocabulary words and their meanings in ways that are more likely to

help them recall them. A major difference is that the new series has added reading passages and some questions that require complete-sentence, original responses. Because some of these answers are more subjective, they require more time for parents to evaluate responses.

Book 1 requires direct teaching and differs significantly from the rest of the series. As with the original series *Books A* through *C*, I would probably skip it. However, I like *Books 2* and *3* of *Wordly Wise 3000* and consider them more useful than the original *Books B* and *C*.

The first editions of *Wordly Wise 3000* were labeled similarly to the original series with *Book 1* targeting students at fourth grade level. With the second edition, EPS renumbered the books so that *Book 1* is for first grade with the series concluding with *Book 12* for twelfth grade. The three editions of *Wordly Wise 3000* have not changed significantly, so purchase whichever you please, just making sure that you get the right level.

The inexpensive answer keys for home educators for any of the *Wordly Wise* editions are not listed on the publisher's website, so you would do best to order through any of the homeschool distributors who carry *Wordly Wise* such as www.ChristianBook.com, www.RainbowResourceCenter.com, and www.ExodusBooks.com. You do not need the expensive teacher's resource books that are listed at the publisher's website.

Handwriting

There are quite a few factors to consider when selecting a handwriting program, factors such as which method to use, when to introduce cursive, the format for practice, and the content of the practice exercises.

Among the methods to consider are traditional handwriting with ball-and-stick manuscript and cursive with simple loops, the method that is most common. Another option might be programs that use slant print or manuscript forms that are very similar to their cursive forms. These make the transition between manuscript printing and cursive little more than learning how to join the letters. Italic style is similar to a simple calligraphy. Some styles such as *Handwriting Without Tears* do not fit neatly into any of these three categories.

Some methods work better for left-handed writers, another factor to consider. The style you choose does not matter as long as it works for your child. After all, by the time we reach adulthood, most of us have modified whatever style we learned to create our own personal style of handwriting.

While, traditionally, publishers have structured programs so that students make the transition to cursive writing in second or third grade, there are many who prefer to teach cursive earlier, perhaps even omitting manuscript and beginning with cursive.

Programs vary in the amount and style of practice activities. You need to select a program with the correct amount of practice for each of your children.

Some programs have fairly bland content for handwriting practice, some provide more interesting content or strong Christian content.

Some parents question the need to even teach their children to write cursive, especially when they have resistant learners. They rationalize that much writing will be done on computers or other devices. However, circumstances inevitably arise in life where you need to make quick notes, and there might be times where you need to take lengthy notes without mechanical assistance. Printing can be too slow a process in such instances, so you will likely handicap your child by not teaching cursive.

Handwriting is another area where it is difficult to select Top Picks since there are so many good options. I have selected programs representative of different styles to help you keep in mind the range of options. Keep in mind

that many comprehensive language arts programs incorporate handwriting—programs like *Primary Arts of Language: Reading & Writing* (www.excellenceinwriting.com) which teaches a style that is somewhere between traditional and slant print and *My Father's World's from A to Z* kindergarten program (reviewed in chapter 13) which uses a traditional style manuscript. Also, you might not need to continue with a separate handwriting workbook if students have mastered the forms and get plenty of practice through dictation or other writing.

· · · · · · · ● · · · ·

Handwriting Without Tears

Handwriting Without Tears
8001 MacArthur Blvd.
Cabin John, MD 20818
301-263-2700
www.hwtears.com
$7.75 per book, see the publisher's website for prices for multi-sensory products

Handwriting Without Tears (HWT) teaches handwriting for children PreK through about fifth grade. Some distinctives of this program are:

• it teaches upper case letters before lower case

• it teaches groups of letters together that have similar strokes for their formation or the same starting points for their formation

• letters are not slanted for either printing or cursive

• multi-sensory learning methods are used for instruction

HWT's style is simpler than traditional cursive, but it differs from most of the other "simplified cursive" forms in that there is no slant and some of the letters such as "e", "f", and "k" change form from printing to cursive.

I mentioned multi-sensory learning methods in the list of distinctive features. Preschoolers and kindergartners work with wooden shapes (lines and curves) to form letters on Capital Letter Cards. They use the magnetic Stamp and See Screen to form letters. Adding yet another tactile activity, preschoolers use the dough from the Roll-A-Dough Letters set to roll out letters to match to laminated cards. Kindergartners begin using the 4" x 6" Slate Chalkboard to write individual letters. They might also use the 10" x 17" Blackboard with Double Lines as they learn to write words. Auditory learners can listen to the *Rock, Rap, Tap & Learn* CD as they learn.

There are a teachers' guide and student workbook for each level pre-K through fourth grade.

Get Set for School, the pre-K workbook, teaches shapes, strokes to be used in letter and number formation, numbers, letters, and capital/lower case recognition. *Letters and Numbers for Me* teaches kindergartners both capital and lower case letters and numbers. It also covers beginning handwriting instruction in such skills as paper placement. *My First Printing Book* for first grade introduces the correct use of either lower or upper case letters in sentences along with punctuation as students continue to practice letter and word formation.

Up through first grade students learn to print on double-line pages. This approach differs from the traditional triple-line format normally used. It eliminates the top line but leaves more space between lines. Children then focus more on formation within the double lines with extensions going above and below. In second grade, students begin to write on single lines.

The second grade book, *Printing Power*, reviews basic formation of letters and continues with word and sentence writing. *Cursive Handwriting*, the third grade workbook, introduces cursive writing. It begins with the letters requiring the simplest joins to make the transition easy. *Cursive Success* provides fourth graders plenty of practice to develop fluency in cursive.

(All of the student workbooks for grades K through 4 are also available in Spanish and French.)

Can-Do Print and *Can-Do Cursive* are books that might be used by students fifth grade or above who still need additional work in either area. There are no teacher guides for either of these books. Students originally taught another handwriting system but who need remediation might need to start in one of the lower level books.

Additional items you might want are Wall Cards, Desk Strips, HWT Double Line Paper (in wide, regular, and narrow line widths), Big Sheet Draw and Write Paper (large 11" x 17" pages with lines on the bottom half), and the Magic C Bunny Puppet. Of special interest to those with struggling printers might be the Gray Block Paper. The packet includes 26 pages each of four different styles of blocks on each page: Starting Corner Dot, Center Starting Dot, Alphabet/Number Review, and Blank Gray Blocks.

Lessons are designed to be presented by the parent or teacher although most work can be done independently once children have learned the basic forms. *HWT* is a great choice for homeschoolers since the instruction is very child-friendly. There's a reasonable amount of practice, but not so much that children feel overwhelmed. Also, the cost of the books is very low. The other items provide more multi-sensory learning but are not essential for every child.

HWT includes some broader language arts skills within its handwriting lessons. However, they have also introduced an additional resource for kindergarten called *Sentence School*, which is to be used alongside *HWT. Sentence School* is a 248-page, spiral-bound teacher guide that comes with a set of 215 laminated word cards. It teaches spelling, grammar, composition, vocabulary, and reading comprehension (at levels appropriate for kindergartners) through brief, multi-sensory lessons.

. . . .

Peterson Directed Handwriting

315 South Maple Avenue
Greensburg, PA 15601-3218
800-541-6328
e-mail: mrpencil@peterson-handwriting.com
www.peterson-handwriting.com
homeschool basic kits: preK & K -
$22.60, grades 1-4 - $16.55 each

Peterson Directed Handwriting is another resource that should appeal to home educators since it is both inexpensive and thorough. Homeschool handwriting kits include the teacher and pupil books plus a self-adhesive Position Guide and pencils or pen (depending upon the level).

The teacher's handbooks offer step-by-step teaching instruction as well as extra strategy helps and explanations about some of the research and theories behind the methodology. It covers types of pencils, how to hold them, desks and sitting positions, tips for teaching left-handed students, and more. This is one of the few handwriting programs where the teacher's manual is a necessity because it contains so much useful information.

The methodology is standard ball-and-stick, based on learning basic movement patterns to reinforce left-to-right tracking. "Printwriting"

begins with the traditional one-stroke-at-a-time process. In second grade, slant print is introduced using a "no-lift" rhythm called "threading" in the jargon of motor control specialists. Transition to a traditional cursive takes place in third grade. Form, slant, size, spacing, smoothness, and control are continually emphasized. Songs and rhythms that assist in teaching handwriting skills are available upon request in MP3 format. An optional CD-ROM (included in the "complete" kit) offers animations for all letters—print, slant print and cursive. Your student can see the strokes written by an invisible hand on your computer screen. Peterson has materials for preschool through eighth grade, but I expect that the courses for grades K through 4 will be of primary interest.

In addition, Peterson offers printable e-workbooks, reproducible lesson-sheets, wall alphabets, pencil grips, and special education materials. Of particular interest might be *Shirley's Books* ($4.95 each), a four-book series of vertical manuscript, slant print, and cursive reproducible practice books. *The Left-Handed Writer* (e-book for $9.95) might be of special interest to those with left-handed students.

Peterson's website offers many how-to videos and an extensive resource library with research information and practical ideas for teaching handwriting. They also offer free online support.

. . . .

A Reason for Handwriting

by Carol Ann Retzer and Eva Hoshino
The Concerned Group
PO Box 1000
Siloam Springs, AR 72761
800-447-4332
www.areasonfor.com
teacher guide
- $24.95,

student books - $17.95 each

A Reason for Handwriting uses ball-and-stick manuscript and a traditional style cursive, with scripture as the writing material. Scripture verses are modified to be understandable for children—more at younger levels than older. One of the most popular features is the set of decorated border sheets in the back of the books for children to color and write their Verse of the Week. These completed pages are attractive enough to hang in prominent places, use as family memory verses, or send to grandparents and relatives.

Eight different books are offered with schools in mind: levels *K* and *A* through *F*. Plus there is a *Transition* book that has no letter designation.

The first book, level *K*, is an introduction to manuscript (printing) for kindergarten level. The next two books, *A* and *B*, teach manuscript covering the same skills but with different scripture selections. Lines have more space than in upper level books, so children don't become frustrated by lack of space.

The *Transition* book covers the transition from manuscript to cursive and would typically be used in second or third grade. Books *C* through *F* all cover cursive skills, using different scripture verses each year. Scripture for the four books is drawn from these areas: *C* - Epistles, *D* - Gospels, *E* - Psalms, and *F* – Proverbs. I would likely use book *C* for the first year of cursive (after *Transition*). After that, you might select books according to scripture content since it is unlikely that you will need to use all of the books.

The *Handwriting Teacher Guidebook*, which covers all levels, includes brief lesson plans, principles of handwriting, teaching tips, vocabulary and skill lists for each student workbook, reproducible master forms for skill development and evaluation, plus supplemental exercises, games, and ideas. Initially, you should purchase a set of one student worktext and the teacher guide. After that you need purchase

only student worktexts.

. . . .

The Getty-Dubay Italic Handwriting series

by Barbara Getty and Inga Dubay
Allport Editions
2337 NW York St.
Portland, OR 97210
800-777-2844
www.allport.com
teacher guide - $12.75, student books - $11.75 each

The Getty-Dubay Italic style handwriting, typically thought of as our third option, can be taught with this series of inexpensive handwriting worktexts for grades K through 6.

Italic is somewhat similar to slant print in appearance, but letters are formed differently. The method is more like a very basic calligraphy than anything else, although the writing instrument is lifted far less often than in calligraphy. Italic letter forms for printing and cursive are basically identical, with entrance and exit strokes added to the "printed" forms for joining letters in cursive. This makes transition from printing to cursive almost effortless.

These books teach students to use a "look, plan, and practice" approach to evaluate and improve their own work, beginning with the first step in *Books A-C*, then using all three steps in *D-G*. The books have full-color covers, and the print explaining lessons matches the Italic style.

The teacher's manual (one book for student *Books A-G*) contains the scope and sequence for the series; discussion of materials; tips for teaching left- or right-handed writers; and techniques for teaching and evaluating shape, strokes, size, slope, spacing, and speed of writing. It also has blackline masters for various sizes of ruled-line paper, three letter formats, and an envelope.

Italic style handwriting looks impressive without requiring extraordinary effort. This method might be a good choice for children who have struggled with or have very sloppy handwriting and need a new approach. Introducing italic style to children with handwriting difficulties has proven very successful in some cases. It gives them a fresh start, and the results can look good with little skill. Students need not begin in *Book A* (kindergarten level) but can start with the book for their grade level.

Blackline masters on CD-ROM ($12.75 per level) are available for use with children who need even more practice than that supplied within the workbooks. Each half sheet references the page number in the corresponding book. Writing practice contains single letter and/or short letter combinations.

To make teaching Italic style easier, there is a DVD video ($29.95) titled *Write Now! Italic Handwriting*.

For those who prefer more efficient instruction within a single book rather than child-oriented worktexts, the authors have produced *Write Now* ($19.95). Although written for adult learners, children from about ages eight or nine should be able to learn from it even though they might need some adult assistance. *Write Now* teaches basic Italic handwriting with plenty of examples and practice exercises. Unlike the workbook series described above, it goes beyond simple italic into the use of different types of pens and more complicated calligraphy. Following the instruction is a brief, illustrated history of the alphabet. Lined guide sheets are also included.

Mathematics

My top picks for math are a diverse assortment to suit different situations and learning styles. Since I've had to be selective, I have narrowed my choices to resources that fit the largest number of students.

You might have noticed that I have not included programs from A Beka or BJU Press, and I should explain why. A Beka's math program is very traditional, does an excellent job developing computation skills, and has more than enough review and practice. Explanation of new concepts is included within student worktexts, so students can work independently most of the time. However, the series is weak in developing conceptual understanding, especially in comparison to programs like *Math-U-See* and *Singapore's Primary Mathematics*. Curriculum Guides offer some teaching assistance, but my experience is that homeschoolers rarely use them. Instead, they are more likely to purchase only the teacher editions that serve as answer keys. Some children are strong enough conceptual thinkers that A Beka still works very well for them.

In contrast, BJU Press's math program is strong on conceptual development. The drawback with BJU Press's program is that it needs to be taught from the teacher's edition. This is not a program for independent study. The teacher's editions include teaching strategies that explain concepts and address different learning styles. While this is very helpful, it also means that it takes longer to get through a lesson, either in planning and selecting what to use or else in actually doing the lesson with your child. Consequently, I find that too many homeschoolers try to shortcut by just handing their children the workbook without adequate instruction. If you have time to use the program correctly, it is very good.

I have also had to leave out other math programs that would be great in just the right situation but are not practical for most home educators.

Math Supplements

Narrowing down to the top 101 resources also meant skipping all of the helpful supplemental items. This was especially frustrating when it came to math since there are so many great supplements that you really might need to use.

Check www.CathyDuffyReviews.com where I have such a large number of reviews of math supplements that they have their own index page! Meanwhile, here are just a few ideas to consider. All of these types of supplements can be found at teacher supply stores, homeschool distributors, and online sources.

- Focused Topical Books: When children struggle with a particular topic or skill, they often need to get a better understanding of the concept itself. Supplemental books are often the solution. The *Key to...* series workbooks from Key Curriculum Press are an example of this sort of thing. They have excellent series on *Fractions, Decimals, Measurement,* and *Geometry* (www. keypress.com). Other publishers offer single books on such topics.
- Computer-based computation drill programs: I won't mention any single program since there are so many good ones. This is one area where computers are really useful. Drill can be sooooo boring, but the computer can jazz things up, put it into a game format, add color, and make it fun.
- Cuisenaire Rods, Base Ten Blocks, and other manipulatives can be used as supplements alongside more traditional programs. If your children do not need *Math-U-See's* immersion in manipulatives, it can be relatively inexpensive to purchase a set of one of these other manipulatives and a resource book on

how to use them to teach particular concepts. Cuisenaire actually has some activity books for working with the rods that are just plain fun.
- Games: many traditional games like Monopoly and Life have quite a bit of math built in. Other games have been developed specifically to focus on math skills. Check homeschool and educational product distributors such as those listed below for ideas.
- Supplemental Activity Books: Some children love to do activity pages when the math practice is linked to a dot-to-dot picture, puzzle, or something that provides a motivation for figuring out the correct answers. Drill and review in such formats is much more appealing than what is generally offered in math textbooks.

Some of the best sources for math supplements are:
- Activity Resources, www.activityresources. com
- Educational Learning Games, Inc., 727-786-4850, www.educationallearninggames. com
- Learning Resources, 888-489-9388, www. learningresources.com
- Nasco Math, 800-558-9595, www.enasco. com/math/
- Rainbow Resource Center, 888-841-3456, www.rainbowresource.com
- WCA Games That Teach, 800-559-9206, www.wiebe-carlson.com

Core Curriculum

Note that I have arranged my Top Picks for math in a progression from lowest to highest grade levels rather than alphabetical order, although there is some overlap with programs covering many levels.

Horizons Math

Alpha Omega
Publications
804 N. 2nd Ave. E.
Rock Rapids,
IA 51246
800-622-3070
www.home-
schooling.com
sets for each level
include a teacher
handbook and two
student workbooks: K - $69.95, grades
1 through 6 - $79.95 each, optional
student worksheet pack - $9.95 each

Those familiar with Alpha Omega's *LIFEPAC* curriculum are often surprised when they check out Alpha Omega's *Horizons Math* because they are so different in both format and methodology. Whereas *LIFEPAC* courses are comprised of ten (for most courses) individual worktexts through which students work independently, *Horizons Math* follows a more traditional format. In *Horizons Math*, the teacher handbook is the main part of the program although each level does have two full-color student workbooks.

The teacher handbook outlines every step of each lesson, listing objectives, materials needed, stories, poems, and games. Some preparation time is needed, and lessons must be taught. However, lessons are purposeful; they don't waste time on peripheral topics as occurs in some other math programs like the Saxon K-3 program.

Horizons uses a variety of manipulatives throughout all levels, although far more in the early grades than fifth and sixth grades. Among manipulatives used are dominoes, counters, play money, place value materials (might be as simple as popsicle sticks or something similar), flannel board and numbers, abacus, beads, and flash cards, along with household items such a calendar, an egg carton, a ruler, and straws. For the most part, these are things you can easily find or make yourself or they are relatively inexpensive items. Base Ten Blocks used at upper levels would be one of the more costly items. Charts at the front of each level's teacher handbook list manipulatives to be used and lessons for which they are to be used as well as which manipulatives are essential and which are optional.

Each lesson has instruction on a new concept and practice or review of previously learned concepts. This continual practice and review marks this as a "spiral" curriculum.

Each lesson includes a number of activities that require interaction between teacher and student, often with hands-on materials. For example, one lesson in the first-grade program includes paper-and-pencil work with a hundreds chart, regrouping demonstration with place value manipulatives, oral number-chart work, time-telling practice using small clocks, written place value practice, addition practice, writing the words for large numbers, and word problems.

Alpha Omega explains their scope and sequence and course layout in great detail at the beginning of each teacher handbook. A readiness evaluation is also found there, so you can make sure that each child is ready for the selected level and also spot weaknesses. Readiness evaluations are also available for free on the publisher's website.

The teacher handbook is very well designed with each part of the lesson clearly labeled. Activity instructions are numbered and spaced so they are easy to locate and read quickly. All instruction is provided through one-on-one teacher instruction, demonstrations, and hands-on activity.

Students have two separate workbooks (each about one-half inch thick) to cover each level. This is a lot of workbook pages—two to four per lesson depending upon grade level—especially for kindergarten, but they are appealingly designed with full color, large print, and variety in the layout. Illustrations, puzzles, and lesson explanations take up some space. Simple instructions are included with each activity in the workbooks.

I suspect that many parents will be tempted to hand their children the workbooks and ignore the teacher handbooks, but there are important teaching instructions in the handbooks you should not skip. You should review the lesson plans and determine how much of each presentation is useful for each student.

Supplemental, reproducible worksheets are also included in the teacher handbook with clear indication of lessons to which they correlate. You can purchase the worksheets as a separate packet if you prefer not to photocopy pages from the teacher handbook. Periodic tests are in student workbooks. Answer keys to workbook pages, including tests, are in the teacher handbook.

Each level goes beyond most other programs by spending more time on development and practice of concepts and skills. The scope and sequence is purposely advanced. While I have not seen that Alpha Omega has created a chart showing correlation with the Common Core Standards, the curriculum seems to cover them but sometimes at a grade level earlier than required by the standards.

Alpha Omega's educational philosophy is also very evident in this program. They believe repetition and review are essential until a subject has been mastered to the point where it becomes second nature. They view math as both a basic functional skill and a communications skill that develops precision in thinking. Within this framework that emphasizes mental discipline, they have done an excellent job of breaking tasks down into manageable increments while also building in methods that address the needs of various learning styles.

However, this also means that you might not need to use everything in each lesson with each of your children; they might not need all of the multi-sensory instruction and they might not need all of the practice and review

(in spite of instructions to the contrary in the teacher handbooks). You will need to exercise some discretion as to what you might skip. You might also need to proceed more slowly given the advanced nature of the curriculum.

Quarterly tests and a final in grades four hrough six, plus answer keys for workbooks, worksheets, and tests are all in the teacher handbook. Except for level K, there is also a test after every ten lessons in the student workbooks.

This program was designed very much with home educators in mind, so there are very few classroom-only type activities that must be adapted or skipped.

Horizons Math K

The *Horizons Math K* program follows an advanced scope and sequence, closer to some publishers' first grade programs. Students are doing addition and subtraction (two digits plus or minus one digit) with no regrouping by the end of the year. However, lessons are taught with visual aids and manipulatives to better help young children grasp concepts. Time, money, measurement, ordinal numbers, and introductory fractions are among other concepts covered. For home educators who want an advanced academic math program for kindergarten, this is a practical solution.

Horizons Math 1

The first grade program begins with concepts such as place value and counting by twos and fives—all within the first ten lessons. Addition works up through addition of triple-digit numbers with carrying from the ones column. Subtraction works up through three-digit numbers but without borrowing. In addition to basic number concepts (e.g., counting, addition, subtraction, place value), this level teaches time, money, the calendar, measurement, fractions, sets, shapes, bar graphs, and estimation.

A solid foundation in number recognition and number values along with other concepts such as colors and shapes is essential before beginning this level. (This foundation is laid in *Math K.*) Readiness assessment tools in the teacher handbook will help you evaluate readiness. If children are weak in some areas, extra lessons in the handbook can be used to cover some topics. However, some children in first grade might need to start with *Math K.* Choose levels according to appropriate skill levels rather than equating them to grade levels.

Horizons Math 2

Mathematics 2 expects that children have learned two-digit addition and subtraction with carrying, but it still reteaches the concepts then moves on to larger numbers. Multiplication facts for 1-10 are taught along with place value, sets, correspondence, cardinal and ordinal numbers, shapes, graphs, fractions (1/2, 1/3, 1/4), measurement, temperature, estimation, ratio, the calendar, time, money, area, perimeter, volume, and decimals (in money).

Horizons Math 3

Mathematics 3 covers the same topics as *Mathematics 2* but at more challenging levels; e.g. multiplication teaches up through four-digit multipliers, division works up through two-digit divisors with remainders. Algebraic thinking is introduced with equations like n + 5 = (7 + 2) + 4.

Horizons Math 4

The readiness test at the front of the book will help you know whether or not your child is able to work at this level. It asks students to reduce fractions, multiply four-digit numbers by multiples of 10, perform short division, compare values of fractions with unlike denominators, round off numbers, understand ratio, add fractions with common denominators, and solve simple, algebraically-expressed addition equations.

Among concepts covered by the end of the course are long division with two-digit divisors, adding and subtracting fractions with unlike denominators, converting fractions to decimals, adding and subtracting decimals, metric measurement, and multiplying or dividing to find equal ratios. Time, money, geometry, and graphs are also covered.

Lessons are designed to be presented by the teacher as with lower levels, but students should be able to do much of their work independently. Materials or supplies needed are listed, and you might have to plan ahead to procure some of these. One lesson describes a bingo game for the teacher to construct, but other than that, most materials are much more standard—counters, flash cards, rulers, Base Ten Blocks, a clock, and play money. While much of the lesson activity takes place within the two student workbooks for this level, there are additional activities such as mental math or manipulative work described in the lesson plans. About every other lesson uses a worksheet for which reproducible masters are found in the teacher handbook.

Horizons Math 5

Among concepts on the readiness test for *Math 5* (which students are expected to know *before beginning* this course) are division of two-digit divisors into dollar amounts with decimals; acute angles; diameters and radii of circles; similar and congruent figures; simple perimeter, area, and volume; ratios; addition of fractions with unlike denominators, addition and subtraction of mixed numbers, decimal values, and metric measurements. As with earlier levels, there is a great deal of review, so if your child has not yet covered all of these concepts, he or she might be able to pick them up easily through the review that is built into *Math 5.*

Among concepts taught by the end of this course are multiplying three-digit by three-digit numbers, values of numbers with exponents, finding averages, division by two-digit divisors, types of triangles, least common multiples, multiplying and dividing fractions, all four functions applied to decimal numbers, percents, and probability. Calculators are used, primarily for checking answers. This course continues to stress both computation skills and understanding of concepts.

Horizons Math 6

Students *beginning* this level are expected to know how to work with fractions, decimals, and percents. Some other concepts covered in *Horizons'* earlier levels might not yet have been taught in other programs: congruency/similarity; diameter, chords, and radius of a circle; and different types of averages. However, the continual review and spiral approach used throughout the program mean that these concepts are reviewed or retaught at this level. Still, the program moves beyond the level of most others. For example, *Saxon's Math 7/6* introduces the idea of ratio while *Horizons Math 6* goes further, teaching cross multiplication to solve for "n." Geometry coverage is more complex with students learning to construct geometric figures using a compass and straightedge. Students continue to work with fractions, decimals, and percents. Consumer math topics such as check writing, banking, budgeting, and computing interest are covered along with more advanced equations, graphs, measurement, and problem solving.

Students who complete this course should be prepared for *Horizons Pre-Algebra*.

· · · · · · · · · ·

Mathematical Reasoning

The Critical Thinking Co.™
PO Box 1610
Seaside, CA 93955
800-458-4849
www.criticalthinking.com

A combination of challenging content, very attractive layout, variety, significant incorporation of thinking skills, and relatively low cost merited this series inclusion among my Top Picks.

This relatively new series (2006-2011 copyrights) should work very well for home educators since it works best taught one-on-one or in small groups. While the worktexts might be used as supplements, these books are comprehensive enough to serve as your core texts. There are fewer problems to solve in these books than in other programs—fewer problems per page although the books are quite large. So you might supplement with additional hands-on activities, games, or practice problems, and you might also use the *Mathematical Reasoning Supplements* I describe at the end of this review. The first three books include a suggestion that you check out the National Library of Virtual Manipulatives http://nlvm.usu.edu/en/nav/vlibrary.html, a free-online site where students can work on math activities with simulated manipulatives. This site has activities up through high school level so you might also want to access it if you are using upper level courses or any other math program for that matter.

The *Mathematical Reasoning* series uses a spiral approach, introducing a concept then revisiting it a number of times at intervals. Students who like variety should love this series since there are seldom two pages that look similar. Pages always have at least one illustration and are so colorful that there is little white space on a page.

As one would expect of anything from The Critical Thinking Co. (TCTC), this series emphasizes critical thinking in ways you seldom encounter in other math courses. It includes some grid-type logic puzzles (like those in the *Mind Bender* series from TCTC) as well as puzzles from *Balance Benders* and *Cranium Crackers* books from TCTC. Other puzzles of many types are incorporated into exercises to challenge thinking skills as well as to make it more fun.

The authors teach proper nomenclature from the beginning. For example, they use the term "line segment" rather than "line" and the term "numeral" rather than "number," even in the preschool books.

Conceptual development is exceptionally strong since the program uses numerous ways of explaining and applying each concept. Concepts are often introduced with visual representations, sometimes representations of Base Ten Blocks or other manipulatives. You might actually use manipulatives if that is helpful for your child, but they are not required.

At the beginning of the book are very brief teaching instructions. Each lesson has directions and brief instruction on a new concept when needed. Parents and teachers might need to work with students with more explanation, examples, and practice on a new concept before expecting them to solve problems or complete activities. Even for lessons on concepts that students already understand, they might sometimes need assistance to know how to complete an unusual activity.

Answer keys are included at the back of each book from *Level B* (Grade 1) and up. You should not need them for the first three books.

Books are challenging and sometimes move into topics that are beyond what is typically taught at each level. Be especially cautious to select the correct level, and do not be concerned if your child needs to start at what appears to be a lower level than you would expect.

Following are a few observations on the coverage of each book.

Beginning 1 (Age 3)
$32.99

Beginning 1 introduces the numbers 1 through 5, both visually and with numerals. It even introduces the concepts of addition and subtraction (e.g., 2 owls + 2 owls shown with pictures) at the end of the book! Other topics are size comparisons (e.g., smaller and larger), shapes, colors, identifying similar objects, counting, one-to-one correspondence, patterns, order (first, second, …fifth), measuring inches, the number line, numeral recognition,

beginning logic (via *Mind Bender* types puzzles), and the characteristics of triangles, squares, and rectangles. There is a great deal of repetition in this book, and many concepts are those that children will be exposed to in normal activities around the house, so you can skip this book without missing anything critical. All concepts also show up again in *Beginning 2*. Some concepts in this book will be beyond many three-year-old children. (236 pages)

Beginning 2 (Age 4)
$34.99

Beginning 2 is similar in design to *Beginning 1*, but it covers numbers 0 through 13 as well as the concepts covered in *Beginning 1*. It starts with activities where students match numerals and groups of objects, so children should already be at least somewhat familiar with what the numbers 1 through 6 look like. Other concepts introduced in this book are the idea of zero, how to write numerals, working with a number line, visual estimation (i.e., which group appears to have more or fewer items), prepositional placement (e.g., how many dogs are in front of or beside the dog house?), dot-to-dot puzzles, right and left, and halves. (282 pages)

Level A (Kindergarten)
$39.99

The *Beginning* books emphasize counting, while *Level A* really moves into addition and subtraction but with sums not higher than 8 and subtraction problems with minuends (the top number) no higher than 7. Other concepts taught are odd and even numbers, patterns, counting and writing numerals up to 20, identifying similar objects, order (first, second, etc.), geometric shapes, symmetry, attributes, equations for addition and subtraction, completing bar graphs, *Mind Bender* type logic problems, halves and quarters (only visual concepts), coins, and time telling. (250 pages)

Level B (Grade 1)
$39.99

Level B introduces place value, expanded

notation, counting by tens, coins, directions (including compass directions), measuring inches, the concept of measuring by other units, completing a hundred chart, visual analogies, transformations, bar graphs, lines of symmetry, fractions and their numerical expressions (1/2, 1/4, 1/3), thermometers, the calendar, time telling, and puzzles such as dot-to-dots, *Mind Bender* grids, and other logic puzzles. Base Ten Blocks might be especially helpful with *Level B* since they are shown visually in many lessons. (312 pages)

Level C (Grade 2)
$42.99

Level C teaches carrying and borrowing (regrouping) up through subtraction problems with two-digit subtrahends. It teaches multiplication via skip counting, arrays, and other visual methods while it also introduces multiplication equations. Division is briefly presented at the end of the book, but it is taught only as a function opposite to multiplication. Students start learning their multiplication facts this year but shouldn't be expected to have mastered them. Among other concepts in this level are surveys, probability, graphs, estimation, measurement, place value, odd and even numbers, metric measurements, fraction concepts, money with coins and bills, polygons, vertices, rounding numbers, writing number words, placeholders in equations, and many word and logic problems. An illustrated glossary and answer key are at the back of the book. (310 pages)

Level D (Grade 3)
$42.99

Level D continues with topics taught in *Level C* but with a heavy focus on multiplication and division up through the introduction of long division with single-digit divisors. It also teaches fraction algorithms including addition, subtraction, and multiplication of simple fractions; recognition of like and unlike denominators; and finding equivalent fractions. Among other topics new at this level are beginning

work with decimals, congruent figures, using the (x,y) form to identify locations on a coordinate grid, units of measurement, rays, angles, endpoints, perimeter, area, weight, least common multiples, reflections, translations, and rotations. There are also two pages of "Time Trials" on multiplication facts. (376 pages)

Level E (Grade 4)
$42.99

Students do lots of work with addition, subtraction, multiplication, and division in *Level E*. Multiplication and division are taken to higher levels including teaching about remainders in division. While decimals receive some attention, fractions are the main topic. Among other topics added this year are factors, prime and composite numbers, mean/median/mode, inequalities, negative numbers, order of operations, working with improper fractions, and the concept of functions. (374 pages)

Level F (Grade 5)
$42.99

Fractions and decimals receive the most attention in *Level F*. Students continue to move to more challenging levels of study on concepts introduced in lower level books. New concepts are the use of a protractor, measurement of angles, elapsed time, computing a bank account balance, volume of three-dimensional objects, and geometric shapes such as hexagons and decagons. (440 pages)

Mathematical Reasoning Supplements

Those who want more of a challenge for their students might want to use one of the *Mathematical Reasoning Supplement* books. Three are available, one for grades 2 through 4, one for grades 4 through 6, and the *Middle School Supplement* for grades 7 through 9. (The first two books are $24.99 each and the third is $19.99.) Each book is topically arranged with lessons under headings such as Geometry, Measurement, Fractions, Patterns, and Graphing. Topics vary by level. Books are printed in black and white but they include many math illustrations such as geometric shapes and patterns. These books stretch students to apply their math skills in non-routine problems. Many of the problems have "puzzle-solving" appeal. Each book is self-contained with a complete solutions guide at the back. Student pages are reproducible for one family or class group.

Sample pages from each book as well as the table of contents may be viewed at the publisher's website.

· · · · · · · · ·

Math Mammoth

by Maria Miller
Math Mammoth
www.
mathmammoth.com
price for full sets
for each grade
level: downloads
- $34 each,
CDs - $39 each,
printed versions
- $54.80 each
for grades 1-3 and $57.80 each for
grades 4-6; complete program for grades
1-6: downloads - $136, CDs - $141

Math Mammoth seems to be an underground, "overnight success" in the homeschool marketplace. With little fanfare and no significant marketing budget that I have noticed, *Math Mammoth* has garnered lots of attention along with many fans in a relatively short period of time.

Math Mammoth offers a few different options, but the primary thing to know is that the Light Blue Series is a complete core curriculum while the Blue Series is supplemental. The Blue Series' content is almost identical to that of the Light Blue Series, but it is arranged and sold in small, topical units rather than as grade level texts—great for those who need to focus on a single topic like fractions.

Math Mammoth can be purchased in printed-book format, on CD-ROM, or as downloadable files. Printed books are purchased through Lulu or Rainbow Resource Center on the internet. (Links are on the Math Mammoth web site.) Most users purchase the downloadable versions, probably because of both convenience and cost. The price for downloads is fantastic—or even better, if you buy the bundle for grades 1 through 6 it works out to less than $25 per grade level. For those with downloading problems, all grade levels can be purchased on CD-ROMs. Keep in mind that you can print out the pages from either the download or the CD over and over again to be used with all children in your family.

The price alone is enough to cause you to sit up and take notice, but the content is also top notch. Some people have compared *Math Mammoth* with *Singapore Primary Mathematics* since both programs teach for mastery and understanding. Both explain concepts thoroughly, generally using visual illustrations to present new concepts. Also, both programs employ a number of different ways to explain new concepts so they can reach different learning styles. *Math Mammoth* adds occasional use of simple, inexpensive manipulatives such as a $10 abacus, ruler, measuring cup, and printable fraction manipulatives for levels 1 through 4. Fifth grade introduces the calculator but teaches students to use it appropriately. Word problems and practical applications are used throughout the series so students gain a sense of how math might be used in real life.

While topics are presented in an order somewhat similar to most other programs, there are some purposeful differences. The scope and sequence is challenging, but not quite as much so as *Singapore Math*. For example both fractions and decimals are introduced at the end of third grade level, with both receiving additional attention in level 4 and extensive attention in level 5. However, decimals are more thoroughly developed before the presentation of multiplication and division of fractions so that the concepts are intertwined in a very sensible fashion. By the first half of fifth grade (5A), students are already prepared to solve problems such as $10,816/(47 + 5) = y!$ While this is really just a division and order of operations problem, it prepares students well for future work in algebra as they work with a variable.

Level 5 introduces plotting "number patterns" in a coordinate grid—a precursor for the concept of linear functions. Even though some topics could be challenging, the thorough explanations might make it possible for even math-challenged students to be successful. Or you may skip some of these topics and save them for later.

Level 6 covers ratios and rates, percents, decimals, factoring, fractions, positive and negative integers, coordinate graphs, geometry (area, volume, and perimeter), interpreting charts and graphs, and statistics. Here is an example of the word problems at this level: "The life spans of Mr. Short and Mr. Long were in a ratio of 3:7. Mr. Long lived 44 years longer than Mr. Short. How long did Mr. Long live?" (From the lesson on ratio problems, 6-A).

Most topics are taught for mastery although there is some "spiraling" where topics are taught first with some elements then revisited later with added elements. However, this is far different from Saxon's spiral approach where topics are taught in small increments coupled with continual, extensive review of previously-taught concepts. *Math Mammoth* generally concentrates on one topic at a time for a number of lessons.

If you want more practice and review of any topics, the download comes with links for generating hundreds (at least!) of worksheets by topic. Problems are randomly generated, so you can create a number of different worksheets for the same topic if needed.

At the beginning of each chapter *Math Mammoth* books include many weblinks to other sites on the internet for math games, tools, activities, tutorials, and worksheets.

While you can certainly copy the URLs from a printed book, the convenience of hyperlinks makes them much more likely to be used.

Time, money, measurement, graphs and other topics are included throughout the program. Grades 1 through 3 also include optional material about money in Canadian, British, Australian, and European (Euro) currencies.

Author Maria Miller encourages parents to choose when to use the various sections rather than just plow straight through each book. This is really an amazing amount of material and resources for so reasonable a price.

The worktext format includes teaching information directly on the worksheets. Pages are produced in full color, but it is not too vivid or distracting. You might choose to print these out on a black-and-white printer, but I did spot at least one instance with a number line (different colors used to reflect two numbers being added) where the color was very useful. There might be other such instances, but you can always look again at the lesson directly on the computer if you run into a problem. (The one preprinted book I received from Lulu has a color cover but is otherwise printed in black-and white, so I assume that Math Mammoth views the color as optional.)

The worktexts are presented as PDF files, but they are enabled for annotation which means students can type directly onto the pages on the computer. While the computer does not correct or score the pages, students may print them out or save them. (Be sure to save your original files if you want to reuse them!)

There are some brief teaching notes at the beginning of each chapter that shouldn't be skipped. Even using these notes, explanations on the worksheets might be too brief for some students, so a parent or teacher should probably be assisting as students tackle new concepts. Parents will likely need to be more involved with younger students than older. Once students have grasped concepts, they should be able to work independently.

The program features plenty of thought-provoking word problems. These problems, coupled with the other methods of lesson presentation, will certainly help students develop both conceptual understanding and critical thinking skills. However, some students might need help working through some of these problems.

Tests, cumulative reviews, and answer keys are all included in the download or on the CD. The Math Mammoth web site offers free placement tests, free worksheets, and other helps.

The 2013 editions of this program will be aligned to the Common Core Standards. The author will also be selling a version with DVD videos to match the curriculum.

In my opinion, *Math Mammoth* is an amazingly well-developed program for such a reasonable price. *Math Mammoth* has created a very high quality product that can function as a traditional program while also taking advantage of the internet and the computer to enhance the course with valuable extras.

• • • • • • • •

Math-U-See

PO Box 8888
Lancaster, PA 17604
888-854-MATH (6284)
www.mathusee.com
teacher packs: *Primer* - $30, levels *Alpha* through *Zeta* - $40 each, *Pre-Algebra* through *Geometry* - $55 each, *Algebra 2 & Pre-Calculus* - $70 each, *Calculus* - $90; student packs (include student text and test booklet except for *Primer* level): *Primer* - $20, levels *Alpha* through *Zeta* - $25 each, *Pre-Algebra* through *Calculus* - $30 each; Manipulative Block Set - $35, Fraction Overlays - $30, Algebra and Decimal Inserts - $20, *Skip Counting* CD with book - $10

Steve Demme, creator of Math U-See, combines hands-on methodology with incremental instruction and continual review in this manipulative-based program. It excels in its hands-on presentation of math concepts that enables students to understand how math works. It is one of the rare multi-sensory math programs that continue to use manipulatives up through *Algebra 1*.

Manipulative Blocks, Fraction Overlays, and Algebra and Decimal Inserts are used at different levels to teach concepts, primarily using the "rectangle building" principle. This basic idea, consistently used throughout the program—even through algebra—is one of the best ways to demonstrate math concepts.

One of the things I think makes *Math-U-See* so popular is that many parents and teachers find that author Steve Demme's presentations of math concepts helps them to finally comprehend much that they were taught in math but never understood. Parents and teachers with a new or renewed enthusiasm for math then do a much better job teaching their own children.

Math-U-See uses a "skill-mastery" approach, requiring students to demonstrate mastery of each topic before moving on. The program also builds in systematic review for previously learned concepts.

There are eight books for elementary grades titled *Primer, Alpha, Beta, Gamma, Delta, Epsilon, Zeta,* and *Pre-Algebra*. The Greek letter designations were chosen particularly to emphasize the order of learning rather than grade level designation. Students should move on to the next level once they've mastered the content of a book. These first eight books are followed by *Algebra 1, Geometry, Algebra 2, PreCalculus with Trigonometry,* and *Calculus*. Placement tests for the different levels are available free at the Math-U-See website.

Student books are perfect-bound, and the pages are perforated and punched so they can easily be removed, written upon, and placed in binders. (Test books have been redesigned in this same fashion.) Student books now have much more practice work than they did in earlier editions, and they include many word problems. Honors exercises have been incorporated into the student books for *Pre-Algebra* through *PreCalculus*. These optional, additional problems stretch students to higher levels of understanding and application of math concepts covered within the lessons.

Test booklets for each course have tests to be used at the end of each lesson plus four unit tests and a final exam. Neither student work-text pages nor tests are reproducible; you need to purchase books for each student. Student workbooks and test booklets are the only consumable items in each course.

Instruction manuals are printed in hardcover books with full-color covers so they might be used a number of times. *Calculus*, the only exception, has a softcover, comb-bound book, although that will likely change to hardcover with the next printing. Complete answer keys with solutions are now included for all problems at all levels, an especially helpful feature at upper levels.

All books are printed in black and white with no illustrations other than mathematical ones. This is not a particular problem in the first four levels if students are working with the colorful manipulatives, learning the skip-count songs, and possibly watching the DVDs. In other words, the other multi-sensory experiences make up for the bland worktext. However, as upper levels use manipulatives less and less, the "plainness" of the worktexts is a point to consider with some students.

The program covers all basic math concepts and all of those in the elementary-level Common Core Standards, but it does not try to correlate the teaching of concepts at the same grade level or in the same order as the Core Standards. Everything gets covered eventually, but in a more sensible order than the standards, in my opinion.

For each level you need both the student kit and the instruction pack. The student kit for each level includes a student workbook and a test booklet for most levels.

For *Primer* through *Algebra 1*, you will also need to purchase the set of Manipulative Blocks, but these are very reasonably priced. Math-U-See's manipulatives are primarily plastic blocks somewhat similar to Base Ten Blocks and Cuisenaire Rods, color-coded to correspond to each number. The blocks snap together like LEGOS because of their raised surfaces. Fraction Overlays are added at *Epsilon* level and Algebra/Decimal Inserts are added at the *Zeta* level. That means, the same sets of manipulatives are each used over at least a few years.

The instruction pack for each level includes an instruction manual plus one or more DVDs that "teach the teacher." Note that DVDs have subtitles for the hearing impaired. Parents must watch the DVDs to understand the basic concepts that are the foundation of the program. On the DVDs, Demme works through each level, lesson-by-lesson, demonstrating and instructing. Demme's presentation is enthusiastic and engaging as he clearly explains why and what he is doing. He throws in lots of math tricks, the kind that make you scratch your head and ask yourself why they never taught us that in school.

The DVD presentations are critical components of the courses although instruction manuals have briefer lesson presentations of the same material covered on the DVDs. I expect that most parents will have their children watch the DVDs with them, although it is intended that parents watch the DVDs then do their own presentations to their children. (DVDs below high school level are not intended for students to watch on their own.)

After the initial viewing or lesson presentation, parents and children work through lessons together for as many days as it takes for children to master the concepts. Once students have grasped a concept, they practice and do problem pages on their own with occasional assistance. Typically, children should be spending about a week per lesson, but you need to take as long as necessary for your child to learn each lesson.

Primer will generally be the starting place for most kindergartners. The *Primer* level begins with essential number concepts and continues up through adding to make 10, telling time, and an introduction to subtraction. Children use manipulatives more than in upper levels of the program (and far more than in most kindergarten math programs).

There is no test booklet for the *Primer* level. At the early levels, you will also want to use the *Skip Counting and Addition Songs* audio CD. Both a "Bible" version and a "Science and Literature" version are included on the CD.

Alpha level focuses most heavily on place value, addition, and subtraction. *Beta* level teaches regrouping for both addition and subtraction. *Gamma* primarily covers multiplication while *Delta* moves on to division. Fractions are the main topic in *Epsilon,* while *Zeta* tackles decimals and percents. Of course, other topics are included alongside these primary themes—topics such as money, measurement, geometry, time telling, graphs, estimation, prime and composite numbers, Roman numerals, and solving for unknowns. *Pre-Algebra* topics are similar to those in other such courses: positive and negative numbers, exponents, roots and radicals, order of operation, geometry, ratio and proportions, and other such topics. One unusual topic for this level is irrational numbers.

While manipulative use remains essential for understanding new concepts, the amount of time spent using the manipulatives decreases in *Epsilon* and *Zeta.*

There are plenty of practice problems in the latest editions of *Math-U-See,* but students who need more practice have free access to a computation drill program on the Math-U-See website. Parents need to choose which math concepts students will practice, then students use the program on their own. You can also use the website's Worksheet Generator to generate and print additional pages of practice problems for courses up through *Pre-Algebra.* Problems are randomly selected so you can produce a number of different worksheets for the same lesson, even though some problems might show up on more than one worksheet.

As you move into the high school level books, students are able to work more independently. The instruction manual for each level is written to the student. Students need to watch the DVD presentation then read  through the instruction manual before tackling the workbook. Workbooks include extra instruction for unusual problems, especially for some of the honors problems, but they do not serve as complete coursebooks on their own.

The honors exercises provide more challenging practice, more critical thinking, practical applications, more complex word problems, test prep practice, and preparation for the math required in advanced science courses. The addition of the honors exercises largely alleviates concerns I expressed in my review in the first edition of *Top Picks* about the program's ability to challenge advanced students. Students can also move through the texts more rapidly if they master the lessons quickly.

Even at high school level, Demme presents concepts simply and clearly, avoiding dense-sounding mathematical abstractions common to so many high school textbooks. The upper level courses feature many word problems and applications that make the lessons more interesting. The upper level instruction manuals include complete step-by-step solutions and answers for all the exercises and tests plus a glossary and an index.

While some students might be able to work through the courses independently, many will need parental or tutorial assistance. Math-U-See offers online co-op classes for those who might want to take a course with other students under the supervision of an experienced teacher.

In *Algebra 1, Manipulative Blocks* and the *Algebra and Decimal Inserts* are used, but less than in earlier levels. For example, manipulatives are used to demonstrate basic equations, including the use of unknowns and negative quantities. However, they are not used to teach "slope" since the graph itself is very visual and manipulatives would be cumbersome at this point.

Algebra 1 does not cover as much territory as do most other first year algebra courses. For example, complex work with radicals as well as motion problems are taught in *Algebra 2*, although they are included in most other first year courses. Slower students should find the pace very manageable. Honors lessons will challenge brighter students, but you can always speed up by moving students through the courses more quickly.

The rest of the upper level books no longer use manipulatives. However, *Geometry* students need a protractor, a compass, and a straight edge to draw constructions.

Math-U-See Geometry is fairly traditional in presentation and coverage, although it is an easier course than most. While it covers the standard topics, it does not go as far in depth as *Discovering Geometry*. For example, Demme deals only with regular polygons when teaching about interior and exterior angles of pentagons, hexagons, etc. There is not as much work with tangents as you find in both

Discovering Geometry and *Jacob's Geometry*. However, Demme introduces geometric proofs in lesson 24 and uses them through the end of the course. He also introduces trigonometry and transformations in the last three lessons. Algebra is reviewed frequently within the lessons. As with *Algebra 1*, the *Geometry* course should be manageable for average to slow students, and you can challenge advanced students with Honors exercises or move them ahead more quickly into *Algebra 2*.

Algebra 2 moves on to new material rather quickly (as compared to many other second year algebra courses), bringing the total of *Math-U-See's* combined algebra coverage close to that of other publishers. It introduces matrices and determinants in the honors section of the last lesson but does not get into functions at all. Students should be able to move on to either pre-calculus or trigonometry courses after completing *Algebra 2*.

Math-U-See's PreCalculus with Trigonometry course dedicates a significant amount of space to trigonometry as one might expect from the title. Vectors, functions, logarithms, and a few other advanced math topics are also covered. *PreCalculus* students need a protractor, ruler, and a scientific calculator. (Note that this course and *Calculus* are the only *Math-U-See* courses that require a calculator.) This is a straightforward, fairly traditional course.

The *Math-U-See* series culminates with *Calculus*. While *Calculus* teaches the content typical of calculus courses it also includes chapters on "Physics Applications" and "Economics Applications" that help students really grasp how useful calculus can be. *Calculus* does not include an honors component since the course already includes content that will challenge advanced students.

The DVD instructional component might make a huge difference, especially for these last two courses, since Demme does a great job of explaining and illustrating concepts. However, I very much appreciate the fact that the newest editions' instruction manuals for these and other high school level courses now include a teaching component so that students do not have to rely entirely on the DVDs.

• • • • • • • • •

Singapore Math/Primary Mathematics

SingaporeMath.com, Inc.
404 Beavercreek Road #225
Oregon City, OR 97045
503-557-8100
email: customerservice@singaporemath.com
www.singaporemath.com
U.S. editions textbooks and workbooks - $10.80 each, home instructors' guides - $17.50 each

Everyone has heard how well Asian students do in math compared to U.S. students, but few people understand why this is so. You will have a better idea of why Asian students excel if you check out this math program. Also called *Singapore Math, Primary Mathematics* is published (in English) by Times Publishing Group and approved by the Curriculum Planning & Development Division of the Ministry of Education in Singapore.

Primary Mathematics has taken the homeschool market by storm, and with good reason. This program teaches children to think mathematically rather than just having them memorize the mechanics of problem solving. And it is very reasonably priced.

Primary Mathematics is more advanced than just about every other math program used in the U.S. There are three different versions: the Third Edition that retains the British spellings and conventions used in Singapore (these are

sold only in Canada); U.S. Editions that were adapted directly from the Third Editions but substitute U.S. measurements, spellings and conventions; and Standards Editions that align with the math standards for California, changing the order of presentation for some topics and adding units on topics such as probability, graphing, data analysis, and negative numbers.

Since the U.S. and Standards Editions are those most of my readers will be considering, the question that arises is which of these two editions to choose. Standards Editions are printed in full color while others are printed in two colors. This might be important for some learners, but the cost is significantly higher with text and workbook prices ranging from $14.50 to $20.50 each compared to $10.80 each for workbooks or texts in the U.S. edition. The entire series is advanced so I, personally, would not be concerned about using the Standards Editions to try to stay on the same track as others. Nevertheless, this might be an important factor for some parents.

The scope and sequence of the U.S. Editions does not align with state or national standards. For example, they leave most work on graphs, statistics, and probability for upper levels rather than teaching these concepts in elementary grades. Instead they focus on laying a solid foundation in basic concepts and processes using a three-step process, taking children from concrete, to pictorial, then abstract approaches to learning. Since I prefer this approach over that of the standards, I would recommend the U.S. Editions rather than the Standards Editions in most situations.

The *Primary Mathematics* series has levels 1 through 6 which cover material for approximately grades one through seven. Each level has two textbooks (A and B). There is a student workbook as well as a home instructor's guide or teacher guide for each textbook. This is not as overwhelming as it sounds since these books range in size from only 80 to 128 pages each. In addition, textbooks and workbooks are each about 10 by 7 ½ inches, with uncrowded, large print. The amount of written work required of children is very reasonable.

While each level has both a teacher guide and a home instructor's guide available, the latter is designed specifically for homeschoolers, is less expensive, and is what I recommend. You do not need both. Teacher guides have additional teaching activities that might be useful, but most parents are not likely to use them. Both guides have answer keys, the component that you really need.

The program requires one-on-one teaching throughout most lessons for the younger grades. The textbooks use pictorial lessons to introduce new concepts that parents will need to work through with their children. Both the home instructor's guides and teacher guides help with lesson presentation.

Correlated workbook exercises are indicated at the end of each textbook lesson. The textbooks are not consumable and are not intended to be written in, although they are inexpensive enough that you might choose to have your children write in them. Children should be able to work through workbook exercises independently once they can read directions without a problem.

SingaporeMath.com, Inc. carries a number of supplemental books for extra practice and targeted work on particular concepts, all keyed to the *Primary Math* series. Check their website for more information.

Placement tests are available at their website. If your child is not starting at the beginning of the program, it is vital that you use the placement test to determine the appropriate level. **It is not unusual for a child to place one or two levels below their official grade level.**

Primary Mathematics 1A and 1B

The level 1 course begins with an assumption that children already have a basic sense and recognition of numbers. It begins with counting to 10, but by the fourth unit of the first book, students are learning subtraction.

Single-digit multiplication is introduced about half way through *1B*, with division introduced very briefly immediately after. (Students are not expected to memorize multiplication facts yet.) The text stresses conceptual understanding over math-fact drill at this level. (Drill suggestions are given in the guides, but you might want to provide opportunity for more practice with math facts using other resources.) Practical applications are used in lesson presentation and word problems. In addition to the arithmetic operations, level one teaches ordinal numbers, shapes, measurement, weight, time telling, money, and graphs.

Primary Mathematics 2A and 2B

The second level teaches addition and subtraction with renaming (carrying and borrowing), multiplication and division, place value, measurement, money, introduction of fractions, writing numbers in words, time telling, graphs, and very introductory geometric shapes and area.

Primary Mathematics 3A and 3B

This level has more advanced work on the four arithmetic operations including long division, fractions (equivalent fractions plus adding and subtracting), measurement, graphs, time, and geometry. It also teaches two-step word problems and mental calculation. It will be challenging for most students to begin this program at level 3 if they have been using a different math program. However, the pictorial lessons do help students pick up concepts they might have not yet been taught. Make sure that if you are just starting this program, you watch for this problem, and provide the necessary teaching before expecting your child to do the lessons.

Primary Mathematics 4A and 4B

At the fourth level, students learn all four functions with both fractions and decimals. Geometry coverage is also very advanced as students compute the degrees in angles and complex area and perimeter questions. Students also work with advanced whole number concepts (e.g., factors, multiples, rounding off), money, other geometric concepts, graphs, and averages. *Primary Mathematics* introduces two-digit multipliers at this level but doesn't really concentrate on two-digit multipliers and divisors until the fifth level. While students complete quite a few computation problems, the number of word problems seems to gradually increase at this level. There is still quite a bit of pictorial lesson presentation, but not as much as in earlier levels.

Primary Mathematics 5A and 5B

At the fifth level, students do advanced work with decimals plus multiplication and division with two-digit multipliers and divisors. They learn to work with percents and continue with advanced work on fractions, geometry, and graphs. Time/rate/distance word problems, as well as other types of word problems are given a great deal of attention. At the end of the course, students are working on beginning algebra concepts. Some of the geometry taught at this level is rarely introduced before high school level. For example, a workbook problem asks students to find the ratio of the area of one triangle to another, with only dimensions for the triangles given. The rate and distance problems are not quite as complex as the time/rate/distance problems typical of high school texts, but they get close.

There are many time-consuming word problems and fewer drill type problems at this level which accounts for the reduced number of workbook pages. Pictorial lesson presentations continue to decrease.

Primary Mathematics 6A and 6B

Because of this series' advanced scope and sequence, at the sixth level much of the work is more typical of other publishers' high school level texts. Students work with fractions, but a typical problem requires students to perform three different operations on four different fractions within a single problem, much like an advanced Algebra 1 type problem, although without variables.

Common geometry problems are set up in proof-style format, although you need not require students to present their solutions in that format.

Among other concepts covered at this level are graphs, algebraic expressions, geometry (e.g., radius, diameter and circumference of circles plus the volume of solids), advanced fractions, ratio, percents, tessellations, and lots of word problems including time/rate/distance problems. It might be challenging for parents with a weak math background to use this level without some assistance.

· · · · · · · · ·

Teaching Textbooks

by Greg Sabouri and Shawn Sabouri
Teaching Textbooks
PO Box 60529
Oklahoma City, OK 73146
866-TOP-MATH (867-6284)
www.teachingtextbooks.com

I knew that *Teaching Textbooks* were going to be added to my Top Picks next time around as soon as I reviewed the first few courses. These fantastic courses were designed specifically for homeschoolers to solve some of the issues that make math challenging for them.

The textbooks are written directly to the student and do not assume the presence of a teacher. Explanations are clear and complete, with plenty of practical examples. Companion CD-ROMs actually teach the lesson for *Math 3*, *Math 4*, *Math 5*, *Math 6*, *Math 7*, *Pre-Algebra*, and *Algebra 1* while upper level students might work either from the textbooks or the CDs. (CDs will run on either Windows or Mac systems for all courses.) For *Math 3* through *Algebra 1* it is actually possible to work only with the CDs. However, as students encounter more difficult problems such as long division, they will then need to copy problems and work them on paper. The text saves the copying step, and it also provides an easy way for either student or parent to review a lesson.

In the textbooks, a light-hearted touch avoids silliness but gives the texts a user-friendly feeling. This is evident in everything from the typeface and layout through the occasional cartoon illustration and the wording of the text itself.

Lessons are taught in a traditional fashion. The new concept is presented, followed by examples then practice problems. Next, students work through a set of problems on their own (about 18-25 problems per lesson). Problem sets include continual review of previously-learned concepts. In addition, key points are highlighted for quick student review. There are from 95 to 142 lessons per course, with lessons grouped into smaller numbers of chapters that concentrate on different topics. In all these texts, students should aim to complete approximately one lesson per day. Adding in test days still should leave you at least 20 days in the school year for extra work on troublesome concepts, review, or "mathless" school days.

The textbooks are soft-cover, plastic-spiral-bound, ranging from 612 to 872 pages in length. The paper is a bit thin for textbooks, but the books are already more than an inch thick. (*Pre-Calculus* is two inches thick!) Durability might be a concern. I know that is a lot of pages for each course, but there are two obvious reasons: each page is less crowded than pages in many other courses, and expanded explanations that make the material much more understandable take up extra space, particularly in high school level books.

Problem sets in each lesson are laid out such that students can actually do some of their work directly in the textbook. However, in high school level books, it is not practical for students to solve lengthy problems in the textbook, so you might want to have students solve and answer all problems in separate notebooks. I would encourage the latter approach, because you really want to see the work—how a student arrives at his or her answer—alongside the answers.

One complaint I have about the textbooks is the lack of an index. Sure, you can look up things in the table of contents, but you won't be able to locate everything, and it takes much longer to scan through lesson titles. This omission has been remedied in the new 2.0 editions of *Pre-Algebra* and *Algebra 1*.

The *Teaching Textbooks* series is a college prep curriculum even though it is not as rigorous as some other courses. However, textbooks for the elementary grades move at a slower pace than other series such as *Horizons* and *Saxon*. Of course, you can always move ahead more quickly with a child who is able. You might even select a grade level higher than the student's actual grade level. Placement tests on the publisher's website will help you select the correct level.

There are some very important differences between courses up through *Algebra 1* (i.e., *Math 3* through *Math 7*, *Pre-Algebra* and *Algebra 1*) and *Algebra 2* and up. I'll first address the lower level courses.

Each *Math 3* through *Math 7* course comes with a set of four CD-ROMs; *Pre-Algebra* and *Algebra 1* each have ten CDs. CDs include lectures, problems, quizzes, and complete solutions. Students actually enter answers on the computer. The CD will track student responses. They can have a second try if they miss a problem, but the program will report this. This automatic gradebook feature enters reports for practice problems (which are optional), assigned problems, and quizzes. The final score (expressed as a percentage) does not include the practice problems. The program also reports whether or not students view the step-by-step solutions to problems. The gradebook can be edited, so the parent or teacher can delete the record for a problem or an entire lesson if students need to redo them.

Significantly, students begin by watching the lectures on the CD then read the summary in the textbook. Next, they work the practice problems in the workbook, entering their answers in the computer. For problems they miss, they should watch the solution on the CD. Then they are ready to tackle the problem set, again beginning in the workbook then entering answers on the computer. They can still view solutions if they continue to make errors. Voice hints are available for the hardest problems. Parents should review progress before students go on to the next lesson. Each chapter concludes with a quiz. These courses also each come with an answer booklet that is strictly an answer key for practice problems, lesson problems, and quizzes.

Math 3 and *Math 4* have an extra bonus—a game that drills students on basic math facts. This pops up every five lessons. Parents can erase game scores if they wish to give students more practice time with the game.

Families are given permission to install the CDs on as many computers as they like, which means that two or more students might be working in the same course at the same time. Even better, each time a student completes the course, you can simply reinstall for a new student. That means that all of your children can use the course over subsequent years. (Note: after two installations, you will have to contact Teaching Textbooks for new activation codes.)

Math 3 complete set
$119.90

Math 3 covers addition, subtraction, multiplication, division, fractions, money, time, geometry, and measurement, plus a final lesson introducing the concept of percent. Much of the addition and subtraction instruction might review concepts already learned at earlier levels since it begins with simple addition and very gradually builds toward carrying in lesson 47 and borrowing (regrouping) in lesson 87. Both concepts would generally already have been taught in second grade. Other instruction moves from beginning to more advanced concepts, but multiplication covers only through single-digit multipliers and division only through single-digit divisors. Fractions begin with basic concepts up through adding and subtracting fractions with common denominators. Numerous word problems help students with mathematical thinking and practical application. This level also includes plenty of pictorial representation in the textbook (e.g., number lines, fraction circles, multiplication arrays, clocks, coins, geometric shapes, different types of graphs), another reason to not work only with the CDs.

Math 4 complete set
$119.90

Math 4 reviews and re-teaches concepts taught in *Math 3* then continues to build new concepts. Reflecting the slower pace of *Teaching Textbooks*, concepts that generally appear earlier in other courses don't show up till near the end. Some examples would be multiplication by two-digit multipliers, long division, division with a remainder, and changing improper fractions to mixed numbers. Roman numerals are taught at this level.

Math 5 complete set
$119.90

Math 5 again reviews the basics with the first 29 lessons heavily focused on addition, subtraction, and multiplication along with review of Roman numerals (taught at the end of *Math 4*), and introduction of rounding and estimating. Interestingly, more time seems to be spent on decimals before complete coverage of fractions, but both topics are covered extensively at this level.

Math 6 complete set
$149.90

Math 6 reviews the four basic arithmetic operations, place value, and time. It spends a great deal of time reviewing and teaching new concepts with fractions, decimals, and percents. It also covers geometry (points, lines, line segments, angles, both area and perimeter for polygons, circumference for circles, and introduction of geometric solids), units of measure (including the metric system), and graphing concepts (e.g., number line, thermometers, bar graphs, circle graphs). A section of "additional topics" at the end includes order of operations, decimal remainders, equations, and probability. A student with weak math skills might be able to pick up what he or she is missing since this course is fairly comprehensive on arithmetic basics. It might be too repetitive for a student who already has developed strong skills in the basic operations. (In my opinion, *Math 6* is closer to *Horizon Math 5* in concepts covered. It is easier than *Saxon Math 7/6*.)

Math 7 complete set
$149.90

Math 7 covers many of the same topics as *Math 6*, but review is briefer. Then each topic is tackled at a distinctly more challenging level. For example, fraction instruction moves on to ratios, percents include work with fractions and decimals plus real life applications like commissions and sales tax, and geometry gets into computing the volume of solids. Statistics, probability, graphing, equations, and inequalities are also taught this year. "Additional topics" delve into powers, exponents, square roots, Pythagorean theorem, and negative numbers.

Pre-Algebra complete set
$184.90

Pre-Algebra briefly reviews whole number operations, fractions, decimals, percents, and measurement. Review has been greatly condensed from the first edition of this text, a commendable improvement since the first edition spent too much time on review. The rest of the book covers beginning algebra, negative numbers, exponents and roots—topics typical

of all pre-algebra courses. *Pre-Algebra 2.0* has now added 37 lessons that tackle plane and solid geometry, functions, relations, graphing, statistics, probability, and other more challenging concepts. "Additional Topics" covered at the end of the text include equations and the distributive property, absolute value, distance formula, and more on formulas. Note that the 2.0 versions of *Pre-Algebra* and *Algebra 1* also have smaller improvements. Every exercise problem now has a reference number telling the student in which lesson the relevant concept was first introduced. Extensive appendices with all important formulas, graphs, and other reference information have been added to both books. Backup chapter tests and supplemental exercises for each lesson are available upon request; however, these will not have step-by-step audio solutions to go with them.

Algebra 1 complete set
$184.90

Algebra 1 seems to have more review of basic operations and pre-algebra concepts at the beginning than do some other texts. *Algebra 1 version 2.0* has raised the bar a bit higher by adding sixteen new lessons covering functions, relations, statistics, probability, graphing with a calculator, the quadratic formula, absolute value, two-variable inequalities, and other more-challenging topics. These additions address concerns that version 1.0 was not challenging enough. With version 2.0, overall, topic coverage is similar to that of many other first year algebra courses, but with more thorough explanation. It is not as advanced as courses such as Saxon's new *Algebra 1*.

Algebra 2 through Pre-Calculus

Now, I'll focus on the courses for *Algebra 2* and above. Note that these courses are gradually being revised in the same fashion as *Pre-Algebra* and *Algebra 1* with version 2.0 of *Algebra 2* due out in August 2012.

CD sets are not essential as with the lower level courses, but they are a very positive feature. All courses have optional CD packages—none of which require installation as do the courses below this level. Let's look first at the Lecture & Practice CD sets. There are four CDs each for *Algebra 2* and *Geometry*, and seven CDs for *Pre-Calculus*. Pop one in a computer and it comes up with an easy-to-use interface listing lessons and your choice of lecture or specific problems.

The lecture is an audio presentation accompanied by a step-by-step written explanation showing how to work each problem. The screen design is colorful and nicely illustrated without being too busy. The audio follows the same presentation and wording as the lesson in the book. Students can actually choose to use either the CD or the textbook—they will get the complete presentation either way with the exception of solutions and explanations to the practice problems which are only on the CDs. Students might work through the lesson in the textbook then use the lecture and practice problem CDs only when they need help working out the sample problems. It is very easy to quickly access a single problem.

The Solutions CDs—six each for *Algebra 2* and *Geometry*, and seven for *Pre-Calculus*—provide complete solutions for all problems except those on the tests. An audio track explains while the screen shows each step. The screen interface is similar to that in the other CD set. Again, students can go directly to the lesson and a particular problem very quickly, so it is very easy to get just the help they need. These solution CDs make it possible for students to work independently, even when parents lack familiarity with the subject matter.

Both sets of CDs are packaged together for each course along with the separate Test Solutions CD and come as part of the complete package. I highly recommend purchasing the complete package with CDs, even if only for the solutions. However, if you choose to purchase only the books, you still have a complete, high-quality course, albeit without a solutions manual.

Each textbook comes with an Answer Key & Test Bank book. The first part is strictly answers (without solutions) for all problems sets. The second part has chapter tests with 24-25 problems per test. Finally, there is an answer key for the test problems.

Although tests are not reproducible according to language on the back of the title page, tests are printed with pages from different tests printed back to back so you cannot simply tear out a single test to give to a student. I checked with the publisher about this problem since the only apparent alternative is to give students the book (containing the answer key) while they take the test. They said that this was an oversight and customers DO have permission to photocopy tests.

Algebra 2 complete set
$184.90

Algebra 2 version 1.0 reflects fairly typical second-year algebra course content, but not advanced. It gets into functions at the end of the book, but matrices and determinants are not covered. More advanced programs include all these topics. While *Teaching Textbooks* algebra courses are not as advanced as some, they do include practical applications in areas such as banking and physics that make them more practical than others. Word problems in all lessons also help students grasp how they might actually use algebra in real life. [Note that advanced topics such as matrices and determinants are covered in *Teaching Textbook's Pre-Calculus* course. For students who want to cover those extra topics (i.e., matrices, determinants, log and exponential functions, statistics and probability) without going to the next book, lessons and problem sets covering those topics are posted on the website. Students can access these without charge.]

Note that version 2.0 of *Algebra 2* will have all of the improvements described for *Pre-Algebra* and *Algebra 1* and should definitely be more challenging than version 1.0. It will add about twenty lessons of new material, including logarithms, exponential functions, matrices, determinants, statistics, probability, and arithmetic and geometric sequences.

Geometry complete set
$184.90

Geometry uses a traditional Euclidean approach, beginning with a chapter on logic and reasoning, then moving on to definitions, postulates and theorems. Formal proofs are introduced very early at the beginning of chapter three. However, constructions are not really incorporated into the text; they're in the "Additional Topics" at the end. Analytical geometry using the coordinate plane is also reserved for the end of the book. As with the algebra courses, practical applications and occasional word problems help students understand how they might make use of geometry.

Pre-Calculus complete set
$184.90

The *Pre-Calculus* course includes problems modeled after those on the SAT II Math test and the CLEP Pre-Calculus test which should help students prepare for either exam. This is a challenging course that begins with functions and moves on from there. Topics covered are polynomial functions, rational functions, exponential and logarithmic functions, radical functions, power functions, triangle trigonometry, trigonometric functions, trigonometric identities, vectors and polar coordinates, systems, matrices, determinants, analytic geometry (advanced), sequences, probability, statistics, and introduction to calculus. "Additional topics" include Pascal's triangle, the binomial theorem, synthetic division, more on sines and cosines, more on complex numbers, De Moivre's theorem, and fitting a graph to data.

You can access a free demo at the publisher's website.

. . . .

Saxon Math Intermediate 3 through Calculus
Houghton Mifflin Harcourt

10801 North Mopac Expressway, Building 3
Austin, TX 78759
800-289-4490
e-mail: info@saxonhomeschool.com
www.saxonhomeschool.com

The Saxon math program for upper elementary grades through high school has retained high popularity among homeschoolers year after year because of its comprehensive content, reasonable price, and its instructional methodology that allows for and encourages independent study. Saxon has added courses for the lower grades, with a series by Nancy Larson for the primary grades that is very different from the rest of the Saxon courses. Most recently, they have introduced *Math Intermediate 3* that is similar in format and approach to *Math 5/4*, *Math 6/5*, and the rest of the series.

Saxon's two-digit grade level designations can help you figure out the correct grade level for each book, although free placement tests are available at their website. Typically the second of the two digits indicates the grade level usage for average to bright students. The first digit indicates the grade for students working a little below level. For example, *Math 7/6* would be for average to bright sixth graders or for slower seventh graders.

Homeschool kits include a non-consumable student edition textbook, either an answer key or solutions manual, and tests with their answer keys. Some student books are hardcover and some softcover. For some high school courses, solutions manuals are available separately. There are no teacher editions for the Saxon program since each lesson in the student text provides the explanation of the concept to be learned. Each lesson includes an introduction and explanation of the new concept, examples and practice problems, then a set of problems that not only reinforces the new lesson content but also reviews previously-learned concepts. Parents might help students work through the beginning of the lesson, but most students will be able to work through the rest of each lesson independently. Parents need to check daily assignments and tests, ensuring that students understand what they are learning. The program requires virtually no preparation time.

While most parents appreciate not having to directly teach this program, the newest editions have added a valuable feature that does require some interaction at the younger grade levels. The "warm up" box at the beginning of each lesson should be used orally. In that box typically are math fact drills, mental math problems, and a thought-provoking problem to solve. This interactive time should also give parents an informal tool for assessing student performance and understanding of concepts. Warm-ups at high school level can be completed independently by students.

One significant feature of the Saxon series that sets it apart from many other math programs is the incremental method in which concepts are taught. Once a concept is introduced it is not dropped but is incorporated into the mixed practice that students encounter every day. In later lessons, the concept is developed more fully. Over time and through repeated exposure to a developing concept, students gain understanding and mastery. Unlike most traditional math texts where one content strand is taught and fully explained over a few consecutive lessons, Saxon has students work with a concept many times over the course of study. (Note that some students prefer this approach while others would rather have the entire concept fully explained all at once.)

At levels *Math Intermediate 3* and above, Saxon Math has a rules orientation in its presentation, more like A Beka's rather than a hands-on conceptual orientation like *Math-U-See's*. Saxon's own program for grades K-3 by Nancy Larson is more conceptually oriented than these upper levels. In a very simplified nutshell, that means that younger Saxon students use manipulatives to see what actually happens when they multiply, while older students generally memorize the rules and facts for multiplication.

Even though the program is not strong on teaching concepts, thinking skills get a good workout. This means that the program works best for students who do not need manipulatives and who tend to figure out mathematical concepts without a great deal of explanation. It is also good for those who like "brain teasers" like those troublesome time/rate/distance problems.

The latest editions of the texts correlate well with the new math standards, having incorporated more on topics like statistics and probability, additional word problems to develop mathematical thinking skills, and topical investigations. Up to this point, Saxon has resisted teaching the use of calculators before *Algebra 2 Third Edition*, but they have bowed to the standards a bit and included calculator instruction in the fourth edition of *Algebra 1* .

Another helpful addition to the revised editions of Saxon's textbooks is reference numbers in the mixed problems sets. If a student misses a problem, the reference number next to the problem provides the number(s) of the lesson(s) where the concept was taught. Reference numbers are also included on the assessments. The new editions have also added a second color to the black-and-white presentation, but the Saxon books still lack visual pizzazz compared to texts from major publishers like Scott Foresman.

The situation with *Math 8/7* and *Algebra 1/2* is a little confusing. *Math 8/7* was a late addition to the Saxon lineup, and was considered optional for a few years. However, with revisions to the other texts, *Math 8/7* really replaces *Algebra 1/2*. Ideally, students will complete *Math 8/7* in seventh grade and *Algebra 1* in eighth. If a student is not ready for algebra in eighth grade, consider using *Algebra 1/2* at that point. There will be some repetition of content but struggling students will be better prepared to tackle *Algebra 1* if they complete both courses.

Math Intermediate 3 Homeschool Kit
$103.50

Saxon Math Intermediate 3 differs a little from the upper level books in course layout and requires a little more teacher involvement than *Math 5/4*. Parents might need to work through presentation of new concepts with students in each lesson, but some students might be able to work independently through most or all of many lessons.

There are four components to the homeschool kit: the student text, a solutions manual, *Power Up Workbook*, and *Homeschool Testing Book*.

Each lesson begins with the Power Up activities. These are a bit more involved than the "Warm Up" activities that begin each lesson in *Math 5/4*. Power Up activities include four categories of problems each time: math fact review, "jump start" (which might include oral counting by increments, drawing hands on a clock, thermometer reading, writing a fact family for three numbers, etc.), mental math, and problem solving. The separate *Power Up Workbook* is used for the written activities for the Power Up section of each lesson with one page to accompany each lesson. The top half of each page is for math fact review problems. Then sections for each of the other three type activities might each contain some content (e.g., clock faces in jump start) or simply provide blank space for students to write their responses.

After the Power Up activities, a new concept is introduced along with sample problems and lesson practice problems that focus only on the new concept. Written Practice problems follow

with 15 to 20 problems per lesson that review previously taught concepts. Students will need to work in a notebook or on other paper to complete lesson practice and written practice problems. The Written Practice problems are wide ranging in approach, really challenging students' thinking skills as you see in *Primary Mathematics* (Singapore). Occasionally, students encounter an open-ended question that asks for both an answer and an explanation. Some lessons add an extra problem for "Early Finishers." These are usually word problems that are either more time-consuming or more challenging than the other lesson problems and that also make real-world connections. These aren't the only real-world word problems since lessons generally have quite a few of them.

The textbook refers to several lesson activity worksheets not found in the homeschool package. These are available on a password-protected page at the Saxon Homeschool website.

In keeping with national math standards, this course covers addition and subtraction review, multiplication through one-digit multipliers times three-digit multiplicands, division through one digit divisors into two-digit dividends, measurement, rounding, estimation, number concepts, geometric shapes, area, perimeter, time, money, calendar reading, graphing, and probability.

After every ten lessons there is an "investigation" lesson. Each of these will likely take an entire class period. For example, one investigation teaches about bar graphs, directs students to collect survey data by asking questions, then has them create their own bar graph. Investigations will require parental or teacher oversight.

Instead of a teacher manual, *Saxon Math Intermediate 3 Solutions Manual* has answers and complete solutions (when applicable) for all textbook problems. There is no need for a teacher's manual beyond this since the text is self-explanatory. There is no answer key for the *Power Up Workbook*, although parents or teachers should be able to check the answers fairly easily without a key.

Math 5/4 Third Edition Homeschool Kit
$86.05

This textbook should be appropriate for most fourth graders and those fifth graders who lag slightly behind grade level. Among topics covered in *Math 5/4* are addition (review), subtraction, multiplication (up to multiplying a 3-digit number by a 2-digit number), division (up through dividing by 2-digit numbers), time, measurement, money, area, perimeter, fractions, mixed numbers, arithmetic algorithms, geometry and measurement, negative numbers, powers and roots, two-step word problems, decimals, averaging, estimation, patterns and sequences, statistics and probability, and Roman numerals. Saxon also sells *Basic Fact Cards*, an optional set of flash cards for working on addition, subtraction, multiplication, and division that might be useful at this level.

Math 6/5 Third Edition Homeschool Kit
$86.05

This text continues developing arithmetic skills through multiplication and division of fractions and decimals while reviewing and expanding concepts of place value, addition and subtraction, geometry, measurement, and probability. Powers and roots, prime and composite numbers, ratios, and order of operations are also taught. Extra math drills for each lesson are at the back of the book. A few students might have difficulty with this text because it requires them to work in more abstract ways than they might be ready for.

Math 7/6 Fourth Edition Homeschool Kit
$95.75

Math 7/6 is for average sixth graders or slower seventh graders. This text is especially good at providing cumulative review and expansion upon topics covered through earlier grade levels. Among topics covered at this level

are fractions, mixed numbers, decimals, percents, ratios, rounding, estimating, exponents, working with signed numbers, square roots, beginning algebraic expressions, surface area, volume, angles, circles, prime factorization, ratios and proportions, and statistics and probability. Especially notable are word problems that cause children to think of math concepts in a number of different ways to ensure understanding. These features make this a great choice for many students at this level.

Math 8/7 Third Edition Homeschool Kit
$95.75

Math 8/7 reviews material introduced in the prior texts, especially *Math 7/6*, and provides pre-algebra instruction. The new edition covers word problems, scientific notation, statistics and probability, ratios and proportions, simplifying and balancing equations, factoring algebraic expressions, slope-intercept form, graphing linear inequalities, arcs and sectors, and the Pythagorean theorem.

Algebra 1/2 Third Edition Homeschool Kit
$74.70, kit with solutions manual - $107.15

This pre-algebra text can be used after completing *Math 8/7*. Plenty of review, a spiral learning process, thought-provoking word problems, and clear instruction that works for independent study make this one of my favorite options available for this level, even if it is no longer needed. As is typical of the upper-level Saxon books, the level of difficulty rises sharply toward the end of the text. If your student starts to have more difficulty toward the end of the book, consider doing only half a lesson each day.

Among topics covered are fraction, decimal, and mixed number operations; scientific notation; exponents; radicals; algebraic expressions and solving equations with one variable; order of operations; ratios; geometry fundamentals; and graphing. Saxon has resisted the inclusion of calculator instruction even though most other texts for this level include it. While students can use calculators to solve problems when it is appropriate, they are not instructed to do so.

Saxon Math High School Options

It is important to consider the design of the entire Saxon lineup of high school math courses before starting into *Algebra 1*. Fortunately, Saxon now has two options with two parallel series of textbooks.

Originally, Saxon took an approach that, while common to other countries, is uncommon in the United States. They integrated algebra, geometry, and trigonometry into three textbooks, titled *Algebra 1*, *Algebra 2*, and *Advanced Mathematics*. Most high schools teach one course in algebra, then geometry, then return to algebra. Saxon has continued this integrated approach with *Algebra 1* and *Algebra 2*, *Third Editions*, now also referred to as the "Classic Editions." But they have recently published a brand new *Geometry* text and *Fourth Editions* of *Algebra 1* and *2* that follow the more typical sequence. I will discuss the *Third Editions* first.

Algebra 1 and Algebra 2 Third "Classic" Editions Homeschool Kits

$74.70 each; Kits with Solutions Manuals: *Algebra 1* - $114.80, *Algebra 2* - $111.45

In Saxon's *Algebra 1 Third Edition*, coverage is comparable to that in other first-year algebra texts, although Saxon teaches the use of a graphing calculator sparingly compared to many other courses. The spiral method of presentation and constant review help students work fairly independently, a major advantage for parents who lack time and expertise.

Saxon seems to work fine for students who grasp math fairly easily but not so well for those who struggle with the abstract thinking required. Overall, *Algebra 1* is fairly easy for students to work through on their own. Interestingly, I have yet to find a text that does a better job with distance/rate/time problems than does this one, even though I know that students still struggle with them in Saxon.

If students have used *Math 7/6* and *Math 8/7*, they might be ready for this book in eighth grade. Although many eighth graders will have no problem with this book, there are many who will not be developmentally mature enough to begin algebra for another year or two. If you feel that your child is not ready for *Algebra 1* at eighth grade level, either academically or developmentally, alternatives might be to use Saxon's *Algebra 1/2*, a consumer math program such as A Beka's *Business Mathematics* or Barron's *Essential Math,* or a specialized topic study such as one or more of the *Key to...* series (Key Curriculum Press) before continuing with algebra. Or you might have your teen begin *Algebra 1* in eighth grade, but move at a slower pace, taking a year and a half or two to complete it.

In the *Third Editions*, Saxon does an excellent job with algebra, but the geometry is weak in my opinion. Geometry is scattered throughout *Algebra 1* and *2*, and it is presented very briefly in both books. By the time students have completed both books they will have studied about one semester's worth of geometry. They complete their geometry requirement with the *Advanced Mathematics* book. Explanation of geometry topics is fairly brief, and does not begin to compare with the quality of presentation in such texts as *Discovering Geometry*.

A student planning to take only one year each of algebra and geometry (not recommended for college bound students!) could use Saxon's *Algebra 1 Third Edition*, possibly skipping over geometry instruction and problems, and then using Saxon's or another publisher's

Geometry text instead.

Students who complete both *Algebra 1* and *Algebra 2*, but who do not intend to continue through *Advanced Mathematics*, need to use another resource to complete geometry requirements. So they, too, might skip geometry activities within Saxon's first two books.

However, if a student is going to go through *Advanced Mathematics*, tackling a separate geometry course is likely to be redundant and overwhelming, so it would be better to stick with only the Saxon texts.

Algebra 2 Third Edition covers standard second-year algebra topics, although its inclusion of a significant amount of trigonometry is not a standard feature of all second year courses. Students will need a scientific calculator for this course. You might want to invest in a graphing calculator while you are at it so it will be useful for future math courses.

Algebra 1 Fourth Edition Homeschool Kit with Solutions Manual
$115

The *Fourth Edition* of *Algebra 1* is a total rewrite rather than just a modification of the *Third Edition*. Both appearance and content are improved. The text has two-color printing throughout with more graphic design. Each lesson begins with a "warm up" that includes one vocabulary question and five review problems. "Investigations" follow every ten lessons. One of the most significant content changes is the early introduction and frequent use of a graphing calculator with graphing calculator labs. Also, probability and statistics receive far more attention in keeping with national math standards. In addition, the *Fourth Edition*

introduces trigonometry and more extensive work with quadratic equations and functions than does the *Third Edition*.

One feature lost in the transition is the tongue-in-cheek humor of some of the word problems. John Saxon often incorporated historically anachronistic references or offbeat content such as "In a picaresque novel about the Spanish Main, the ratio of rascals to good guys was 13 to 5" (p. 149 *Second Edition*). The *Fourth Edition* has plenty of word problems and real life applications, but the humor has disappeared.

Other elements of Saxon's methodology remain. Lessons are taught in increments followed by examples and a few practice problems. After that, students works on "Distributed and Integrated" practice problem sets with 30 problems per lesson.

The homeschool package includes the student text, a solutions manual with complete solutions for the warm ups and all practice problems, and a Homeschool Testing Book. The Testing Book has 23 cumulative tests plus your choice of three, reproducible test answer sheets. In addition, a Test Analysis Form helps you identify the pertinent lessons for concepts tested in each problem in case review or re-teaching is needed. It also has the answers for all the tests. Note that the *Classic Editions* have answers to odd-numbered problems in the back of each student text, but there are no answers in the *Fourth Editions*. All answers and solutions are in the solutions manuals.

Algebra 2 Fourth Edition Homeschool Kit with Solutions Manual
$115

The *Fourth Edition* of *Algebra 2* is very similar in layout to *Algebra 1* with the same course components. In keeping with the slightly advanced content of *Algebra 1*, *Algebra 2* does much less review in the early chapters than in the *Classic Edition*. (A Skills Bank at the back of the book provides some review if needed.) Instead of a thorough review, this text jumps quickly into functions, matrices, and determinants. More attention is given to functions, while matrices and determinants are not even taught in the *Classic Edition*. Geometry is reviewed through problems and incorporated into lessons that apply algebra and trigonometry. There is more practical application of concepts through word problems than we find in many other Algebra 2 courses. A graphing calculator is used in every lesson with frequent Graphing Calculator labs ensuring that students become familiar with their use. This text should be a great option for those who need a challenging course that prepares them for more advanced math.

Saxon's program has tended to be strong on skill development, but weaker on conceptual explanation and application. The inclusion of investigations in the *Fourth Editions* of *Algebra 1, Algebra II*, and the new *Geometry* book (as well as in the newer texts for younger levels) reflects Saxon's awareness of this problem. This particular feature along with other improvements would make the new *Fourth Editions* my recommended option.

Geometry Homeschool Kit with Solutions Manual
$120.65

Geometry might be used with either the *Third* or *Fourth Editions* of Saxon's Algebra courses, but it works best with the *Fourth Editions*. For those using it with *Third Editions*, the publisher recommends using *Saxon Geometry* after *Algebra 2* since a significant amount of geometry is taught at the end of that text. It makes a natural point at which students can switch over to the full-year course, possibly skipping geometry lessons in *Algebra 2*. Students taking *Algebra 1 Third Edition* in ninth grade might want to use *Saxon Geometry* in tenth grade in preparation for the PSAT test in their junior year or possibly for other test situations. This, too, will work, but not quite as easily as after *Algebra 2*. All of this sounds a bit awkward, and it is. Using *Geometry* between or after *Fourth Editions* of *Algebra 1* and *2* will both

work much more easily.

As with the other Saxon texts, *Saxon Geometry* is written to students so it is possible for them to work independently. Since it has also been written for classroom use, there are a few issues that come up. The text sometimes refers to "working with a partner," although those situations are easily adapted. The text is missing a few points of explanation: asterisks next to some questions indicate problems that should be done in a "classroom setting" with the parent or teacher nearby while other problems can be assigned for independent homework. Obviously, this makes little difference for most homeschoolers. Also, "Geometry Sketching Software" is referenced in a number of the lab activities with instructions for its use, but it is not part of the homeschool kit. This is *The Geometer's Sketchpad* from Key Curriculum Press. (See description within the review of *Discovering Geometry*.) The publisher tells me that it is not essential—students can skip those lab activities. However, students going on to higher math would benefit from use of the software. Also, one lab activity uses a graphing calculator. It walks students through step-by-step for this particular assignment having to do with scatterplots, but it does not really teach broader use of the calculator. Again, you could skip this lesson, but for students continuing on to higher math courses, it might be a useful time to introduce a graphing calculator.

One feature that assists students with self-instruction is the inclusion of sidebars with helpful instructional tips. There are plenty of word problems and practical applications throughout the text, and many problems incorporate algebra to help keep those skills current.

The content coverage is similar to other geometry courses, although it has a bit more trigonometry than some. Proofs are taught very early and used throughout the course. Constructions with straight edge and compass are taught as labs within the pertinent lessons. Other labs have students do such things as make and use a hypsometer, cut and trace triangles to investigate symmetry and patterns, create and use a spinner to conduct a probability experiment, and use *The Geometer's Sketchpad* Software.

Saxon Geometry is a challenging course. It really draws on higher level thinking skills more than some other courses—another reason why it might better suit students who have already completed *Algebra 2*.

Although *Saxon Geometry* lacks John Saxon's humorous touch, it does provide much more solid geometry instruction than is found in the other Saxon texts. In addition, the extensive work with proofs, challenging applications and skill development suit the needs of students. While the classic Saxon series will retain all the geometry and not require the use of this text, it is great to have this option.

Advanced Mathematics, Second Edition Homeschool Kit with Solutions Manual
$116.85

Advanced Math should follow *Algebra 2* for both the *Third* and *Fourth* editions. This text is one of the easiest for most homeschoolers to work with to cover advanced algebra, geometry, and trigonometry. Originally designed to be a one-year course, Saxon now recommends that students take at least a year and a half to complete the course unless they are very bright. However, students who have worked through the *Fourth Editions* of *Algebra* and the new *Geometry* course should find more material to be at a "review" level and might be able to get through the text more quickly.

Advanced Math includes the equivalent of the second half of geometry, plus advanced algebra, pre-calculus, and trigonometry. In the revised *Second Edition*, much of the geometry was moved to the front of the book rather than being spread out. This should make it easier for students who need to get through the geometry in preparation for PSAT tests in their junior year. In addition geometric proofs are taught early on then used throughout the

first half of the book.

Students will need a graphing calculator to use with this text, although the calculator is not used as much as in other texts for this level. Parents might decide to allow students to use a calculator more than is required.

Among other topics covered are logarithms, conic sections, functions, matrices, and statistics. This text moves even more into the theoretical math realm than do earlier Saxon texts.

By the time students complete Saxon's *Advanced Mathematics*, they should be on a par with students who have completed a pre-calculus course. This course should be particularly good for preparing students to do well on college entrance exams.

Calculus

Saxon also has a text titled *Calculus with Trigonometry and Analytic Geometry*. Since few students seem to be tackling calculus on their own, I will simply mention that the text is available. The review of that text is posted at www.cathyduffyreviews.com/math/calculus-saxon.htm.

DVD Teaching Help

Some students do better when the Saxon courses are actually taught to them, so *Saxon Teacher* CD-ROMs ($97.35 per course) might be the solution. These supplemental CDs are to be used alongside each course. Instruction is presented by an experienced teacher for selected Saxon textbooks.

· · · · · · · ·

Horizons Pre-Algebra

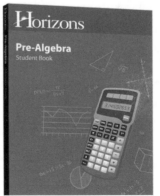

Alpha Omega Publications
804 N. 2nd Ave. E.
Rock Rapids,
IA 51246
800-622-3070
www.home-schooling.com
boxed set with
student book,
teacher's guide,

and tests & resources book - $87.95

Horizons Pre-Algebra course uses a traditional approach that also includes some use of manipulatives. Students who do well in math and who do not need the manipulatives might be able to work independently through most of the lessons. Some concepts and skills are taught directly from the teacher's guide. Among those are the use of algebra tiles, fraction-decimal flashcards, a scientific calculator, and how to use a compass and protractor to draw a circle graph. There might be other concepts I've missed in this list, but at least the latter two would need to be taught to the student since they aren't taught within the student text. This course would probably work best for most homeschoolers using a combination of some lessons being taught and others completed independently.

This is a challenging course. While it reviews the basics of addition, subtraction, multiplication, division, and number theory, it quickly moves into signed numbers, exponents, factoring, square roots, and order of operations. It continues through work with fractions, decimals, and percents including much practical application. A good deal of attention is given to graphs, probability, and statistics. Geometry covers perimeter, area and volume as well as topics like congruent triangles, and nets of solid figures (two-dimensional representations of three-dimensional objects as if they were opened up and laid flat), lines, angles, graphing points on a coordinate plane, and slope-intercept form. It even introduces trigonometry. Algebra topics include performing addition, subtraction, multiplication, and division of polynomials, including factoring. Other topics such as the metric system and measurement are taught.

The teacher's guide is useful. It lists concepts, objectives, and materials needed, but most useful are the teaching tips. Designed for a classroom situation, it mentions such things as students working on the board or students explaining problems for the class. Nevertheless, this course will work well for homeschoolers. Ideally, a parent working with a single child will use the teaching tips to teach the lesson with more concrete examples and explanations as well as the extra topics mentioned above.

Students will need a scientific calculator, protractor, straight edge, one die, colored pencils, and graph paper. (Three pages of graph paper are included at the back of the student text.) Other items such as blocks, scissors, tape, a party hat, and coins are used rarely and are open to makeshift substitutes.

While other simple manipulatives are used from time to time, the most important manipulatives for concept development are the algebra tiles. These are printed in full color in the Tests and Resources book and need to be cut out. I recommend that you laminate these for easier handling. The algebra tiles teach algebra concepts using the "rectangle-building" method, similar to what is taught in *Math-U-See*. Personally, I very much like to use this visual representation for algebra to help students really grasp what is happening when they manipulate equations.

This book also has "formula strips" that are to be given to students for use in some lessons. These restate some basic formulas such as that for finding the area of a circle or measurement equivalents such as 1 mile = 5,280 feet and metric-English equivalents. There are 24 of these strips to be used with different lessons, and formulas are sometimes repeated on more than one strip. The reason for presenting formulas this way rather than in the textbook is that the strips are sometimes used with quizzes and exams where it would not be appropriate for the student to have access to the text. Of course, students need to memorize some formulas. The teacher's guide indicates which formulas are not given on the ACT/SAT tests (and therefore not on the formula strips) and must be memorized.

Fraction-Decimal Flashcards are used in

a number of lessons, but these must be purchased separately. Some students will not need to use them and can skip them. Their use is directed from the teacher guide, so students will not notice they are missing if they are working independently.

In the Test and Resources book are a total of 80 worksheets for the year, some of which may be used as quizzes. Only half of the lessons have a worksheet or quiz. These are noted in the individual lessons in the teacher's edition and are marked there as to which ones are appropriate for use as quizzes.

Every tenth lesson includes an interview with a Christian who uses pre-algebra skills in his or her career. Word problems in that lesson and some subsequent lessons are then based on the interview. Also in every tenth lesson, students are given a set of questions in multiple-choice, standardized-test format to help with test preparation skills.

A reproducible "Horizons Pre-Algebra Readiness Evaluation" and answer key is in the front of the teacher's guide. Sixteen tests and four exams are included in the Tests and Resources book. The teacher's guide has reduced pictures of student text pages and quiz and test pages with answers overprinted.

The student text is very attractively printed in full-color. The number of activities and problems to solve does not appear overwhelming compared to some texts that are dense with problems. However, some of *Horizon's* problems will take some time to complete. For example, one problem on p. 170 instructs the student to "Find the mean, median, mode, and range. Then draw a histogram and a box-and-whisker plot. Football scores one Saturday were 14, 0, 7, 26, 13, 27, 36, 37, 24, 7, 7, 31, 20, 19, 24, 27, 17, 10, 31, 24, 24, 27, 41, 34, 16, 13." Many times there are charts to complete. Frequent word problems help student to understand practical applications for what they are learning. So there is plenty of work without pages appearing cluttered with problems.

The text is clearly written for a Christian audience with many references to church, pastors, a gospel magic show, designing shirts for a youth retreat, missionaries, and other church-related activities.

· · · · · · · · ·

Kinetic Books: Pre-Algebra, Algebra I, Algebra II, Geometry

Perfection Learning
PO Box 500
Logan, IA 51546-0500
800-831-4190
email: orders@perfectionlearning.com
www.perfectionlearning.com
$79.95 per course

Kinetic books is producing math courses that really take advantage of the computer as a delivery system by including multi-sensory teaching methods, games, interactive exercises, and student tracking. You enroll a student in a course for an annual subscription. The program is installed on your own computer (either Mac or Windows systems), but records are kept on their server so you can easily reinstall on another computer and still access your student's data.

A "Pacing Guide" serves as guide to the amount of material to be covered per lesson. A student clicks on a lesson to immediately move to where they need to begin. Students may also use a more detailed listing of chapter topics to navigate if they choose. The Pacing Guide divides material into lessons within which there are at least a few segments. For each segment students can learn from both a video presentation and a text segment on the same topic. Students can skip the video presentation but they must do the text segments. The videos feature a teacher working on a whiteboard, walking through the lesson, referring to the text segment being covered as they teach. This feature is great for students who need an actual teacher. The text lessons are based on a digital text which you can print out if you wish. However, the text segments add features not available in the print version. The text segments frequently have buttons to "listen to explanation"—great for auditory learners. The auditory segments repeat key points from the printed material. Text segments also have practice and Quick Check problems that students answer online. A help button next to every question provides step-by-step help or the answer if students get stuck. The help on some of the problems walks the student through the steps, entering some numbers at each step rather than just showing the solution. Students get immediate feedback as to whether or not they answered correctly. They can try to answer the problem again and still get full credit, but if they check the solution, they won't get credit. Quizzes and tests are also online. Scores are recorded and tracked. Parents can check on student progress whenever they wish. Because the program tracks the student, only one student can use a course subscription.

There are still more features that might be useful to some students. Clicking on buttons at the bottom of the screen allows them to highlight and insert notes as well as to enlarge or shrink font size on the display and set other preferences.

I reviewed the *Algebra I* course and found it comparable to other text-based courses in coverage and general style, even though it uses multi-media forms of presentation. It teaches a concept, offers practice problems, then has the student complete exercise problems. Quick Check problems cover only the skill taught

in that lesson. At the end of each unit is a section of Kinetic Homework problems that cover topics from the past group of lessons. As with the Quick Check problems, students also have a second try, and help/solutions are available but give no credit. However, in Kinetic Homework, when a student misses a problem or looks up the solution, the same type of problem is presented again at the end until they get it correct. So this is very much a mastery type program.

For even more variety, there are mental math activities as well as interactive problems that combine math challenges with games. For those who want students to have traditional paper and pencil activity, End of Unit Problems can be printed out and solved. There are many problems in these sections so you might choose to use some rather than all of them. Answer keys to End of Unit Problems can be viewed online or printed out.

At the end of each chapter (each of which encompasses quite a few lessons) are a practice test and a "standardized test," both of which are completed online with immediate grading after submission. The standardized test uses the multiple-choice bubble format while other quizzes and tests frequently require students to enter complete mathematical expressions. Since mathematical language is difficult to write from a standard keyboard, the screen pops up mathematical symbols and functions for students to use.

There is more material in this course than most students will use. The digital text has 752 pages! But students need not use everything—only those elements that are helpful.

At the end of the digital text are supplemental lessons that some students might find useful. The supplemental lessons are available as appendices accessible from the main table of contents. Extra lessons cover Arithmetic Review; Fractions, Decimals, and Percents; Advanced Data Modeling; and Trigonometry Fundamentals. There is also an Initial

Assessment with 97 questions. The answers for the Initial Assessment problems are available within each problem screen by clicking "Study Solution."

Kinetic Books courses' alignment with National Council of Teachers of Mathematics standards is available on the publisher's website along with correlation to some of the state standards. The *Algebra I* course has been adopted into several states, so it is clear that the publisher intends for these courses to compete with those from the major publishers to the traditional school market. The relatively low cost for course delivery makes Kinetic Books courses strong competitors against traditional printed texts, both in the traditional and homeschool markets.

A 30-day money-back guarantee allows you to make sure a course will work for your student.

• • • • • • • • •

YourTeacher.com Pre-Algebra, Algebra 1, Algebra 2, and Geometry

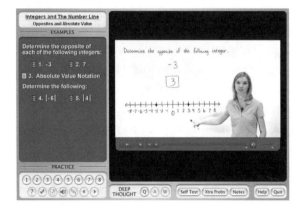

713-807-0470
email: sales@yourteacher.com
www.yourteacher.com
$49.50 for a one-month pass or
$199 for a one-year pass

I selected *Algebra Classmate* as one of my Top Picks in 2005, but the company has undergone some major improvements since then. One of the most significant is their name change to YourTeacher.com. Also, at the time of my

initial review, only *Pre-Algebra* and *Algebra 1* courses were available, and those were sold only as CD-ROM sets. Now, they have added *Geometry* and *Algebra 2*, and they have moved exclusively to online delivery for their multimedia courses.

A free demo lesson at YourTeacher.com's website will give you a good idea how the courses work before you subscribe. Subscriptions for homeschoolers are by the month or the year. With a single subscription you get access to all four courses, so this might be a super bargain if you have two or more high schoolers and need more than one of the courses. However, subscriptions provide only a single student name and access code, so cannot distinguish and track student progress if more than one student tries taking the same course at the same time. This isn't a problem if they are taking different courses. Still, keep in mind that two students will not be able to sign in to the account simultaneously, so they would have to schedule their lesson times to accommodate each other.

These are complete courses. However, YourTeacher.com has provided a correlation of lessons to texts commonly used in public schools for students who might use YourTeacher as a supplement. These include correlations for most of the pertinent Saxon textbooks. At YourTeacher.com, click on the text you are using, enter the page number where the topic appears, and YourTeacher will show which of their lessons address each topic covered on that page of the text.

Lessons are presented in a video screen on the computer with course creator Mike Maggart or another teacher leading each lesson on a whiteboard. (You will need your computer speakers or a headset to listen to the audio for the presentation.) A notes section, viewed by pushing a button on the lesson screen, details the primary concepts of the lesson and can be printed out for reference and review. Practice problems are also provided (along with answers for self-checking). Then there's a self-test for each lesson that is automatically corrected. Scores for these self-tests are recorded and can be referenced by the parent or teacher. In addition, each lesson has a "deep thought" problem for those needing an extra challenge.

Lessons are grouped into chapters and units, with another quiz at the end of each unit. Lessons are very thorough and offer a number of ways for students to learn and practice the material. Explanations are excellent. All these features make this one of the most truly independent-learning high school math courses.

On a personal note, a friend of mine who teaches continuing education for older students who struggle with learning in the regular classroom raved about these courses and has now used them with a number of students.

. . . .

Elementary Algebra

by Harold Jacobs
W.H. Freeman
Homeschool orders should be directed to MPS High School Customer Service
16365 James Madison Highway
Gordonsville, VA 22942
888-330-8477, press "1" for order entry, then "3" for high school orders
[Note: All orders placed by homeschool parents must be placed on a credit card. All homeschooling orders that include teacher's materials must be accompanied by (via fax or mail) a current certificate from the State or other source documenting homeschooling status.]
student text (#9780716710479) - $93.95, instructor's guide (#0716710757) - $30.95, test bank (#0716710773) - $30.95

This is an atypical algebra text that, unlike most, has been around for many years in the same edition. *Elementary Algebra* covers all concepts typical of a first-year algebra course, but it invites students to explore algebra concepts in a friendlier environment than other texts. Cartoons, comic strips (e.g., *Broom Hilda,*

B.C., Wizard of Id, and *Doonesbury*), interesting and creative applications, puzzles, and even poetry capture the interest of students who struggle with abstract mathematics.

For example, a lesson on mixture problems opens with the story of Archimedes and the King of Syracuse's golden crown that the king suspected was not really solid gold. Jacobs then sets up a volume and weight equation based on the problem.

In addition to stories and practical applications, Jacobs uses the rectangle-building concept throughout the text to demonstrate how concepts work. This is the same rectangle building idea used by *Math-U-See* and some other manipulative systems. While Jacobs' book shows pictures and doesn't require use of manipulatives, students can still use them if they are helpful. I think most students really benefit from this approach when they are learning to multiply and factor polynomials. (This last feature makes this text a particularly good one to use after *Math-U-See's Pre-Algebra* level. If you don't already have manipulatives, check out either the very inexpensive Algebra Tiles or Algebra Base 10 Kit from Nasco (www.enasco.com/math/).

The book is divided into seventeen chapters, with each chapter subdivided into a number of lessons. A summary and review section is at the end of each chapter. Four exercise sets are at the end of each lesson, with problems ranging from simple computation through word and application problems to challenging thought problems. Generally, you will choose two of these sets for students to work on. By assigning appropriate problems, you can use the text with students of varying capabilities.

Answers to questions from one of the sets from each lesson are in the back of the student text so students can see if they are getting the correct answers. The instructor's guide is the source for the rest of the answers. A test bank is also available.

• • • • • • • • •

Geometry: Seeing, Doing, Understanding, 3rd edition

by Harold Jacobs
W.H. Freeman
Homeschool orders should be directed to
MPS High School Customer Service
16365 James Madison Highway
Gordonsville, VA 22942
888-330-8477, press "1" for order
entry, then "3" for high school orders
[Note: All orders placed by homeschool
parents must be placed on a credit card. All
homeschooling orders that include teacher's
materials must be accompanied by (via fax or
mail) a current certificate from the State or other
source documenting homeschooling status.]
student text (#9780716743613) - $112.95,
instructor's guide (# 0716756072) - $37.95,
test bank: book (#0716775948) - $37.95
or CD (#071677593x) - $82.95

Harold Jacobs has managed to write a user-friendly geometry text that is heavy on logic and proofs. This is one book where you don't want to skip the introduction that fills students in on the influence of Euclid and teaches them the basics of construction with a straight edge and compass.

In the third edition, the first chapter is an introduction to vocabulary, tools, and basic ideas of geometry. However, it ends with a lesson titled, "We Can't Go On Like This," a lesson that takes students through some intriguing problems to demonstrate the necessity for a logical approach to geometry.

Then, in the second chapter, Jacob begins to teach logic. Many people cite the value of geometry as being the development of logical thinking skills. Jacobs takes this idea seriously, ensuring that students are truly tuned in to logical thinking before tackling other geometry topics. Given the foundation in logic, students then immediately begin work with proofs, which continues throughout the text.

Jacobs uses entertaining illustrations (including cartoons), as well as practical applications and engaging word problems. For example, the lesson on similar figures and ratio begins with a comparison of movie and television screens, including the letter-box option that changes the ratio.

Topic arrangement is different than I have seen in most texts. For instance, work with circles follows introductory lessons on trigonometry. The trigonometry is introduced as a natural progression in the study of triangles, so this is not really an outlandish arrangement. Even if the arrangement is unusual, there is a clear continuity to topics, building one upon another.

There are sixteen chapters in the book, with each chapter divided into a number of lessons. Each lesson has three problem sets. All students should try to complete the first two sets, but skip the second set for struggling students. The third set frequently features intriguing investigations, but these should be used as a challenge for better students who have the time. A summary and review at the end of each chapter includes specific algebra review.

Construction activities (using straight edge and compass) are minimal. Because of this and the emphasis on logic, I recommend this text for abstract thinkers rather than hands-on learners. But I suspect that even some students who struggle with the logic will like this text because the presentation is so appealing.

Problems from SAT tests are interspersed throughout the exercises. They are labeled as such so students preparing for the test can be sure to master these.

Selected answers for about one fourth to one third of the problems from each lesson (selected in no numerical sequence) are at the back of the student text. All answers are in the instructor's guide. A separate test bank is available in either book or CD-ROM format (both Windows and Mac versions on one disk).

· · · · · · · · ·

Discovering Geometry: An Inductive Approach, Fourth Edition

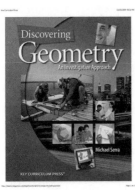 by Michael Serra
Kendall Hunt
Publishing
800-542-6657
email: orders@
kendallhunt.com
www.kendallhunt.
com
student text (either
print or PDF version)
- $72.95, teacher's
edition - $92.95, solutions manual -
$39.95, assessment resources - $69.95

I used this text twice, each time with groups of three students with widely diverse mathematical aptitudes. Amazingly, after completion of the course, all my students actually thought geometry was fun! That's because *Discovering Geometry* truly uses a different approach to teaching the subject. This is a complete, college-preparatory course that is more inviting than any other I have seen. It is now in its fourth edition, although the fourth is very similar to the third edition. Some chapters have been reorganized. An illustrated glossary and "Dynamic Geometry Explorations" have been added along with a few more projects, investigations, and opportunities for students to apply algebra skills in every chapter.

The first thing that students encounter in the book is art—geometric art. The art leads students into their first investigations about lines and shapes. Investigations by students help them discover postulates and theorems by inductive reasoning. Many investigations involve students in activities, especially making and working with constructions using a straightedge and compass.

Word problems are imaginative, and real-life applications are true-to-life. Mathematical thinking is the goal of this text rather than mere memorization of postulates and theorems.

The text moves from the concrete to the abstract—a strategy essential for many students to be able to succeed in geometry. In the teacher's edition, the author explains his philosophy of gradually working through levels of thinking to the point where students are able to deal with proofs.

Paragraph proofs are introduced in chapter two as a means of getting students to organize data and explain their thinking process. Flowchart proofs are taught in chapter four, and two-column proofs are saved for the last two chapters (12 and 13) after students have mastered concepts and understand relationships between theorems. Even though formal proofs are not taught at the beginning of the course, students are applying both inductive and deductive reasoning and working with logic and language leading up to use of two-column proofs. In fact work with proofs is probably stronger and more effective than in many other texts. The fourth edition has added even more exercises that are specifically focused on reasoning and proof skills. The text continually challenges students to explain why.

While I love this text, there's a reason why more homeschoolers are not using it. It was definitely designed for classroom use. It requires cooperative learning with two or more students working together. It is possible that a parent could function as a second student for some of the activities, but it is more than a bit tricky for a parent to function simultaneously as teacher and student. Lest you view the cooperative learning requirement as a negative, I must tell you that it is one of the features that make it so enjoyable. This is primarily where students have the many "Aha!" experiences of this course. It will be well worth your while to pull together even a small group class to make this course work.

You need both the student text and the teacher's edition. The full-color student text is available in hardcover or as PDF files that include weblinks. The text has "Hints for Selected Exercises" and answer keys for chapter reviews.

In addition to the aforementioned straightedge and compass, students will need a protractor and a ruler. Numerous other items are used to make this a hands-on course, although most of the time their use is optional. Among these items are drinking straws, interlocking cubes, geometric shapes, geoboards and rubber bands, meter stick, modeling clay, patty paper (the lightweight paper used to separate burger patties), toothpicks, and uncooked spaghetti.

The teacher's edition is a larger hardcover edition that includes reproductions of student pages, with some answers overprinted in magenta. Other answers don't fit on student pages, so those are in the margins at the bottom of the page of the teacher's edition along with teaching information and other helps. Additional teacher information is in the forematter and at the beginning of each chapter. One valuable part of this information is course outlines that will help you schedule lessons, tailoring the course for "standard," "enriched," or "block" schedules. Answers to all problems are found either in the chapter or at the back of the teacher's edition. A separate solutions manual shows the steps leading to the answers. Parents who are not strong in math might want to have this on hand in case they get stuck.

Every exercise set in the student book includes some review questions. Reviews at the end of each chapter consist of about 50 or more problems. Assessment resources (quizzes and tests) are available separately.

The fourth edition has upped the number of opportunities to incorporate technology into learning, although use of technology is not absolutely required. Students can access "Dynamic Geometry Explorations" that help demonstrate concepts; these are free online and are often well worth exploring. The student text notes when and where to access these Explorations.

The author suggests that students have a graphing calculator and/or software such as *Geometer's Sketchpad* ($9.95 for a student edition for one year, Key Curriculum Press, www.keypress.com), a computer program (either Macintosh or Windows versions) that can be used in conjunction with *Discovering Geometry* or other geometry courses. I expect that *Geometer's Sketchpad* might help compensate if you absolutely cannot find a second student. Students can create numerous constructions quickly on the computer and compare results, whereas it would be too time consuming to do many of them manually. However, you would not want to use the software as a total substitute for a student learning to create constructions with compass and straightedge. *Fathom Dynamic Data* is another computer-based tool you might want to utilize with this text. Some projects using it have been added to the fourth edition.

You can see an entire chapter online to preview the text and a free, online 30-day trial is also available.

Note that Kendall Hunt Publishing acquired *Discovering Geometry* from Key Curriculum Press in 2011. Older editions from Key Curriculum are still great.

11

History, Geography, & Social Studies

Some of us cringe at the term "social studies," equating it with the watered down mush that passes for history education in some textbooks. But the "social studies" label is not the culprit. The problem lies in emphasis and philosophy. "Social studies" is a comprehensive term which includes history, geography, and cultural studies. The public school system (in general) has overemphasized cultural studies, especially politically-correct cultural studies, at the expense of history and geography. With the increased emphasis on reading, math, and science, public schools are rarely accomplishing much even with cultural studies.

Social studies has often been used as a tool for social engineering rather than to provide an education in history. Christians have been particularly aware of the secularization of history—the sort of thing that translates our Thanksgiving holiday into a mutual admiration day between the Pilgrims and the Indians without any mention of God. In reacting against the secular bias in textbooks, Christians have sometimes erred in moving to another extreme, rejecting cultural studies and reducing the subject to memorization of history and geography data. Neither approach is correct.

I think a great way to resolve this is to approach social studies as a newspaper reporter. Reporters look for the answers to the questions: Who did what? When did they do it? Where did they do it? and Why did they do it?

So, imitating a reporter, we look at the interrelationships of the three areas: history, geography, and cultural studies. The reporter's first two questions are answered by the names and dates or time periods (history). The third question "Where?" is answered by describing the location (geography). The last question deals with the background of the event and other influences, essentially putting an event in context (cultural studies). Our social studies should be like a good newspaper article, combining all the necessary ingredients.

A few history/social studies textbooks manage to pull all these elements together, but then you have to deal with the biases of the authors. It is impossible to write an entirely neutral textbook.

Even if the language is not slanted, every textbook will exhibit bias in the choices of what is or is not included. For Christians, textbooks that cover all of world history while paying little or no attention to the impact of Judaism and Christianity reflect a bias that paints a false picture of a world that has developed without interaction with God. If you are a Christian and want to help your child develop a Christian worldview, then you will probably want to use resources that help rather than hinder that goal by discussing God's actions and impact through history.

In regard to resources, there are at least three approaches to social studies. You might use any of these approaches exclusively or mix two or more of them. The three most common approaches are:
- History textbooks
- History through unit studies (which might use texts or real books)
- Real books (and I would include internet research in this category)

History Textbooks

Most history textbooks are rather boring. They try to cover lots of information, and that usually means they can allot only a few lines or a few paragraphs to each event. Textbook authors don't usually have space to make the interesting connections between events. Other than in the occasional sidebar, they can't tell us the personal history behind extraordinary events such as 21-year-old Nathan Hale's heroic declaration, "I only regret that I have but one life to lose for my country." (Check the Wikipedia entry if you're curious: www.wikipedia.org/wiki/Nathan_Hale.)

Learning history as sets of facts to be memorized and regurgitated for tests might even do more harm than good. It might teach children to despise history if they never get to experience the delight or amazement that comes from reading the "whole stories" of history.

The dumbed down language of some history texts for primary grades is another turn off. Increasingly, upper-elementary level history texts are showing signs of the same malady. Publishers, seeking to make their books more visually appealing, add lots of large color illustrations as they update history textbooks. They steal space for the illustrations from the lines of text, reducing them to short, choppy sentences, for the most part devoid of literary beauty or human interest. I rarely encourage parents of children in the elementary grades to use traditional history textbooks, especially since we have so many better options available to us. Junior high level history books generally are little better with more content and fewer pictures. By high school, history textbooks have much more written material than do earlier levels, and there are some that are worth using.

I know I've made some sweeping generalizations here. There are a few exceptions. I've included reviews of a few history texts for elementary grades, but you will note that these exceptions are not the typical written-by-committee, state-approved textbook series.

Geography textbooks might be even worse than history textbooks. I have included only one resource that exclusively targets geography—*The Ultimate Geography and Timeline Guide*. This unusual book is so much better than traditional geography texts that, in my opinion nothing else comes close.

History through Unit Studies

Most unit studies have a strong historical component. Sometimes history is the primary theme with other subjects branching off from the study of history. Studying scientific investigations or literary works within their historical and geographical settings is a great way to make history as well as science and literature more interesting.

Unit studies generally recommend real books as sources of historical information. Some unit studies include historical information within their own material, but even then they generally direct you to other resources for further reading.

A few unit studies recommend history texts as the source of information, but they enhance the textbook information with stories, real books, and activities.

Some unit studies are structured in chronological order, so if you follow the publisher's sequence of study, students study history in its proper order. However, some unit studies are organized around other themes, and their history coverage jumps around—you might be studying ancient Rome one month, then South America the next. In such instances, timelines are essential for children to be able to grasp the actual chronology of events. If they can visually see events on a timeline it helps them put things in proper context.

Don't forget to check out the reviews of unit studies to see if you might want to use one of these for coverage of history. Increasingly, publishers are creating history programs that function like limited unit studies. Their primary focus is history, and they incorporate other subject areas to a very limited extent. *Mystery of History* (one of my Top Picks) and *BiblioPlan* (www. BiblioPlan.net) are examples of this type of program.

Real Books

I'll never forget a television talk show interview with the Colfax family, homeschool pioneers whose sons were probably the first homeschoolers to receive scholarships to Harvard University. One of their sons was talking about his transition from homeschooling to the academic demands of the university. The host was probably trying to get him to acknowledge some deficiencies by asking about his history studies through high school. The young man admitted that he had never read a history textbook before going to Harvard. But, he continued, he had read many real books—biographies, historical fiction, and non-fiction. He surprised even himself when he discovered that through his reading he actually knew more history than his classmates who had each been through ten or more history textbooks. He attributed his acquired knowledge to his love for the subject that blossomed as he read about history in a way that brought the subject to life.

I have had opportunities to ask groups of veteran homeschoolers what actually worked best for them. The unanimous response is always, "Real books." Most did not start out with a real books approach, but after experimenting with it, they gradually shifted from exclusive reliance on textbooks to real books or a combination of both.

Because I believe so much in the value of real books for history, I am including lists of books by historical periods first, followed by reviews of my Top Picks. Real books in the following lists are a mixture of historical fiction, biography, and even some legend.

I have also included some "fact books" such as David Macaulay's intriguingly illustrated books (e.g., *Cathedral* and *Pyramid*) and a number of colorfully-illustrated information books such as those from Usborne and DK Publishing. See my review of *History of the World* (MFW edition of the original DK Publishing book) to get a general sense of what these fact type books are like.

I suggest using these fact books along with other books that give more complete coverage of at least some topics. Fact books often do a great job on the introductory or supplemental level. But keep in mind that they generally strive for religious neutrality, and religious neutrality often means omission of important religious information and ideas as well as the occasional inclusion of problematic content such as nudity, praise for non-Christian gods, and distortion of religious beliefs.

I have *not* read all the books in these lists myself but have compiled the lists from my own experience and the recommendations of others. So I cannot vouch for the content of every book.

You can choose an assortment of such books as the core of your curriculum, adding discussion, writing, and activities to accomplish your educational goals, or you can purchase a guide such as one of the *Literature Approach to History* guides from Beautiful Feet Books (www.BFBooks.com) that recommends particular books and provides questions and assignments for students in relation to the books.

This is not intended to be a comprehensive list, but it should be enough to get you started exploring history through real books.

I've included some titles that are written for adults but might be read aloud to older children. When I know the audience level for certain I've used (y) to indicate books written for younger children up through about fourth grade level and (o) to indicate books written for at least fifth grade level and older. "FB" after a title indicates that it is a fact book. I've also used some notations for books that are part of well-known series:
- Landmark = Landmark Books
- CFA = Childhood of Famous Americans,
- Sower = Sower series

I have noted specific dates or time periods by many titles to help you choose books in a chronological sequence if you so desire. Also, I have sometimes mentioned the geographical area where a story takes place when I think it might be helpful.

"Real" Books by Time Periods/Topics

Ancient Egypt
- *Adventures in Ancient Egypt* by Linda Bailey (Kids Can Press)
- *The Cat of Bubastes* G.A. Henty (o)
- *Golden Goblet* and other titles by Eloise Jarvis McGraw
- *Into the Mummy's Tomb* by Nicholas Reeves
- *Moses* by Leonard Fisher
- *Motel of the Mysteries* by David Macaulay (FB)
- *Pharaohs of Ancient Egypt* by Elizabeth Payne (Landmark)
- *Pyramid* by David Macaulay (FB)
- *The Riddle of the Rosetta Stone* by James Cross Givlin

- *Shadow Hawk* by Andre Norton
- *Tales of Ancient Egypt* by Roger Lancelyn Green
- *Usborne Internet-Linked World History: Ancient World* (FB) (y,o)
- *The Usborne Time Traveler* (FB) (y)

Ancient Greece and Rome
- *Adventures in Ancient Greece* by Linda Bailey (Kids Can Press)
- *Alexander the Great* by Andrew Langley (Oxford) (y)
- *Alexander the Great* by John Gunther (o)
- *Ancient Greece (History in Art)* by Andrew Langley (o)
- *Archimedes and the Door of Science* by

Jeanne Bendick
- *Black Ships before Troy* by Rosemary Sutcliff
- *The Children's Homer* by Padric Colum (o)
- *Classic Myths to Read Aloud: The Great Stories of Greek and Roman Mythology* by William F. Russell
- *D'Aulaires' Book of Greek Myths* by Ingri and Edgar Parin D'Aulaire (y)
- *The Iliad* translated by Richmond Lattimore (o)
- *The Librarian Who Measured the Earth* (Ptolemy) by Kathryn Lasky
- *The Odyssey* translated by Richmond Lattimore or another translation by Robert Fitzgerald (o)
- *Tales of the Greek Heroes* by Roger Lancelyn Green (o)
- *Tales of Troy and Greece* by Andrew Lang (o)
- *The Trojan Horse* by Emily Little (y)
- *Usborne Internet-Linked World History: Ancient World* (FB) (y,o)
- *The Wanderings of Odysseus* by Rosemary Sutcliff
- *You Wouldn't Want to Be in Alexander the Great's Army!* by Jacqueline Marley (y)

Bible Times and Ancient Rome
- *The Aeneid of Virgil* translated by Robert Fitzgerald
- *Against the World: Odyssey of Athanasius* by Henry W. Coray (Inheritance Publications)
- *Augustus Caesar's World* by Genevieve Foster (63 B.C.-14 A.D., World) (o)
- *Ben Hur, a Tale of the Christ* by Lew Wallace (1st Century A.D., Rome, Judea) (o, use this as a read aloud book for the family)
- *Beric the Briton: A Story of the Roman Invasion* by G.A. Henty (61 A.D., Britain & Rome) (o)
- *Bronze Bow* by Elizabeth Speare (32 B.C., Judea)
- *Cleopatra* by Diane Stanley and Peter

Vennema (1st Century B.C., Egypt)
- *Classic Myths to Read Aloud: The Great Stories of Greek and Roman Mythology* by William F. Russell
- *Cultural Atlas for Young People: Ancient Rome* by Mike Corbishley (Facts on File) (FB)
- *The Eagle of the Ninth* by Rosemary Sutcliff (119 A.D., Rome)
- *Eyewitness Books: Ancient Rome* (Knopf) (FB)
- *For the Temple* by G.A. Henty (70 A.D., Judea) (o)
- *Hittite Warrior* by Joanne Williamson (1200 B.C., Judea)
- *The Ides of April* by Mary Ray (60 A.D., Rome)
- *Jason's Miracle: A Hanukkah Story* by Beryl Lieff Benderly (o)
- *The Lantern Bearers* (Britain at the end of the Roman occupation) by Rosemary Sutcliff (450 A.D., Britain)
- *Pearl Maiden* by H. Rider Haggard (1st Century, Judea)
- *Quo Vadis* by Henryk Sienkiewicz (60A.D., Rome) (o-read aloud)
- *The Robe* by Lloyd C. Douglas (read aloud) (1st Century A.D., Rome & Judea) (o)
- *Runaway* by Patricia St. John (1st Century, Judea)
- *Saint Valentine* retold by Robert Sabuda (3rd Century A.D., Rome)
- *Spring Tide* by Mary Ray (o)
- *Usborne Internet-Linked World History: Ancient World* (FB) (y,o)
- *The White Stag* (Attila the Hun) by Kate Seredy (400s, Asia & Europe)
- *You Wouldn't Want to Live in Pompeii!* by John Malam (y, o)
- *Young Carthaginian* by G.A. Henty (220 B.C., North Africa) (o)

World History from the Fall of Rome through the Middle Ages
- *Adam of the Road* by Elizabeth Gray (1294, England)

- *Adventures with the Vikings* by Linda Bailey (Kids Can Press)
- *The Apple and the Arrow* by Mary and Conrad Buff (1300s, Switzerland) (y,o)
- *Augustine Came to Kent* by Barbara Willard (600, England)
- *Beorn the Proud* by Madeleine Pollard (800s, Ireland & Denmark)
- *Beowulf the Warrior* by Ian Serraillier (1100, England)
- *Big John's Secret* by Eleanor M. Jewett (o)
- *The Black Arrow* by Robert Louis Stevenson (1400s England)
- *By Right of Conquest or With Cortez* in Mexico by G.A. Henty (1500s, Mexico) (o)
- *Cathedral* by David Macaulay (1200s, Europe)
- *Columbus* by the D'Aulaires (1492, Exploration) (y)
- *D'Aulaires' Book of Norse Myths* by Ingri d'Aulaire and Edgar Parin d'Aulaire (Norse mythology) (y)
- *The Dragon and the Raven or the Days of King Alfred* by G.A. Henty (800s, England) (o)
- *Dragon Slayer* (Beowulf) by Rosemary Sutcliff (1100, England)
- *The Hidden Treasure of Glaston* by Eleanore M. Jewett (1171, England)
- *If All the Swords in England* (Thomas Becket) by Barbara Willard (1100s, England)
- *In Freedom's Cause* (William Wallace and Robert the Bruce and the battle for Scottish independence) by G.A. Henty (1300, Scotland) (o)
- *Ivanhoe* by Sir Walter Scott (1300s, Europe) (o)
- *Joan of Arc: Heavenly Warrior* by Tabatha Yeatts (1400s, France) (o)
- *Joan of Arc* by Diane Stanley (1400s, France) (y)
- *The King's Shadow* by Elizabeth Alder (1000s, England) (o)
- *The Lances of Lynwood* by Charlotte M. Yonge (1000s, Europe)
- *Leif the Lucky* by the D'Aulaires (1000, Exploration of America)
- *The Lost Baron* by Allen French (1200, England)
- *Magna Charta* by James Daugherty (1200s, England)
- *Men of Iron* by Howard Pyle (1300s, England)
- *The Merry Adventures of Robin Hood* by Howard Pyle (1200, England)
- *The Minstrel in the Tower* by Gloria Skurzynski (1195, Europe)
- *Otto of the Silver Hand* by Howard Pyle (1400s, Europe)
- *The Red Keep* by Allen French (1165, Europe)
- *The Road to Damietta* (St. Francis of Assissi) by Scott O'Dell (1200, Italy)
- *St. George and the Dragon* by Margaret Hodges (Legend, England)
- *Sir Gawain and the Green Knight* by J.R.R. Tolkien (1400, England) (o)
- *Son of Charlemagne* by Barbara Willard (780, Europe)
- *The Story of King Arthur and His Knights and Other Arthurian Tales* by Howard Pyle (Legend, England)
- *The Story of Rolf and the Viking Bow* by Allen French (1000, Iceland)
- *The Talisman* by Sir Walter Scott (1300s, The Crusades) (o)
- *Tristan and Iseult* (Ireland and Britain) by Rosemary Sutcliff (Legend, England)
- *The Trumpeter of Krakow* by Eric P. Kelly (1400s, Poland)
- *Usborne Internet-Linked World History: Medieval World* (FB) (y,o)
- *The Usborne Time Traveler* (FB) (y)
- *Vikings* by Elizabeth Janeway (Landmark Book) (1000, Exploration)
- *What Do We Know About the Middle Ages?* by Sarah Howarth (Peter Bedrick Books) (FB)
- *Where Do You Think You're Going,*

Christopher Columbus? by Jean Fritz (1492, Exploration) (y)
- *William Tell* by Leonard Everett Fisher (1300s, Switzerland) (y)
- *Winning His Spurs* by G.A. Henty (1190, The Crusades) (o)
- *Wulf the Saxon: A Story of the Norman Conquest* by G.A. Henty (1066, England) (o)

Renaissance to Modern Day— Other than U.S. History
- *By Pike and Dike* by G.A. Henty (1500s, Europe) (o)
- *Don Quixote* by Miguel Cervantes retold by Michael Harrison (fiction, Spain)
- *Edmund Campion* by Harold Gardiner, S. J. (1500s, England)
- *The Hawk that Dare Not Hunt by Day* (Tyndale) by Scott O'Dell (1494-1536, England)
- *Ink on His Fingers* (Gutenberg) by Louise Vernon (1400s, Germany)
- *Isaac Newton* by John Hudson Tiner— Sower series (1642-1727, England)
- *Johannes Kepler* by John Hudson Tiner— Sower series (1600s, Germany)
- *A Knight of the White Cross* by G.A. Henty (1480, Europe) (o)
- *Leonardo da Vinci* by Diane Stanley (1400-1500, Europe)
- *Lysbeth: A Tale of the Dutch* by H. Rider Haggard (1500s, Netherlands)
- *Martin Luther: A Man Who Changed the World* by Paul L. Maier (1483-1546, Germany) (y)
- *Red Hugh: Prince of Donegal* by Robert T. Reilly (1500s, Ireland)
- *St. Bartholomew's Eve: A Tale of the Huguenot Wars* by G.A. Henty (1500s, France) (o)
- *The Scarlet Pimpernel* by Baroness Orezy (1700s, France) (o)
- *A Tale of Two Cities* by Charles Dickens (1700s, Europe) (o)
- *This Was John Calvin* by Thea B. Van

Halsema (1509-1564, Europe) (o)
- *Under Drake's Flag: A Tale of the Spanish Main* by G.A. Henty (1500s, England & Exploration) (o)
- *With Pipe, Paddle and Song* by Elizabeth Yates (1750, Canada)
- *The World of Captain John Smith* by Genevieve Foster (1580-1631, World)
- *The World of Columbus and Sons* by Genevieve Foster (1400s-1500s, World)

U.S. History
- *American Girls* series
- *America's Paul Revere* by Esther Forbes (y,o)
- *Amos Fortune: Free Man* by Elizabeth Yates (o)
- *And Then What Happened, Paul Revere?* by Jeanne Fritz (y)
- *The Last of the Mohicans* by James Fenimore Cooper (o)
- *Ben and Me* by Robert Lawson (y,o)
- *Ben Franklin of Old Philadelphia* by Margaret Cousins (Landmark) (y,o)
- *Benjamin Franklin* by the D'Aulaires (y)
- *By the Great Hornspoon* by Sid Fleischman (y,o)
- *Cabin Faced West* by Jeanne Fritz (y)
- *Caddie Woodlawn* by Carol Ryrie Brink (o)
- *Can't You Get Them to Behave, King George?* by Jeanne Fritz (y)
- *Carlota* (Mexican War) by Scott O'Dell
- *Carry on, Mr. Bowditch* by Jean Lee Latham (o)
- *Clara Barton: Founder of the American Red Cross* by Augusta Stevenson (CFA) (y)
- *The Courage of Sarah Noble* by Alice Dagliesh (y)
- *Crispus Attucks: Black Leader of Colonial Patriots* by Dharathula H. Millender (CFA) (y,o)
- *Daniel Boone Frontiersman* by Janet and Geoff Benge (Heroes of History) (o)
- *Diary of an Early American Boy* by Eric Sloan
- *Dragon's Gate* (Chinese immigrants and

the railroads) by Laurence Yep (y,o)
- *Fourth of July Story* by Alice Dagliesh (y)
- *Gold Fever: Tales from the California Gold Rush* by Rosalyn Schanzer (y,o)
- *George Washington's World* by Genevieve Foster (o)
- *A Hunger for Learning* by Gwenyth Swain (Booker T. Washington) (y,o)
- *If You Traveled West in a Covered Wagon* by Ellen Levine (y)
- *Iron Dragon Never Sleeps* by Stephen Krensky (y)
- *Island of the Blue Dolphins* by Scott O'Dell
- *Jed Smith: Trailblazer of the West* by Frank Latham (y,o)
- *Johnny Appleseed* by David R. Collins (Sower series)
- *Johnny Tremain* by Esther Forbes (o)
- *Make Way for Sam Houston* by Jeanne Fritz (y)
- *The Matchlock Gun* by Walter D. Edmonds (y)
- *Meriwether Lewis: Boy Explorer* by Charlotta Bebenroth (CFA) (y)
- *Minn of the Mississippi* by Holling C. Holling (y,o)
- *Mr. Revere and I* by Robert Lawson (y,o)
- *Mother Cabrini* by Frances Parkinson Keyes (y,o)
- *Patty Reed's Doll* by Rachel Laurgaard (y,o)
- *Paddle to the Sea* by Holling C. Holling (y,o)
- *Pioneers Go West* by George R. Stewart (Landmark) (y,o)
- *Pocahontas* by the D'Aulaires (y)
- *A Pocketful of Goobers: A Story of George Washington Carver* by Barbara Mitchell
- *The Reb and the Redcoats* by Constance Savery (o)
- *Sam the Minuteman* by Nathaniel Benchley (y)
- *Samuel F.B. Morse* by John Hudson Tiner (Sower series)
- *The Siege of the Alamo* by Janet Riehecky and Valerie Weber (o)

- *The Sign of the Beaver* by Elizabeth Speare (y,o)
- *Sing Down the Moon* (Navaho Indians) by Scott O'Dell (o)
- *Sitting Bull: Dakota Boy* by Augusta Stevenson (CFA) (y)
- *Streams to the River, River to the Sea* (Sacagawea) by Scott O'Dell (o)
- *Tree in the Trail* by Holling C. Holling (y,o)
- *Treegate's Raiders* by Leonard Wibberly (o)
- *Why Don't You Get a Horse, Sam Adams?* By Jeanne Fritz (y)
- *Witchcraft of Salem Village* by Shirley Jackson (Landmark) (o)
- *The World of Captain John Smith* by Genevieve Foster (o)

Civil War Period and Slavery

- *Abe Lincoln: Log Cabin to the Whitehouse* by Sterling North (Landmark) (o)
- *Abraham Lincoln* by the D'Aulaires (y)
- *Across Five Aprils* by Irene Hunt (o)
- *Black Frontiers: A History of African-American Heroes in the Old West* by Lillian Schlissel (o)
- *Booker T. Washington* by Christine Taylor-Butler (y)
- *The Drinking Gourd* by F.N. Monjo (y)
- *Freedom Train* by Dorothy Sterling (y,o)
- *Freedom's Sons: The True Story of the Amistad Mutiny* by Suzanne Jurmain (y,o)
- *Gettysburg* by MacKinlay Kantor (o)
- *Go Free Or Die: A Story about Harriet Tubman* by Jeri Ferris (y)
- *Hang a Thousand Trees with Ribbons: The Story of Phillis Wheatley* by Ann Rinaldi (o)
- *If You Traveled On the Underground Railroad* by Ellen Levine (y)
- *Incidents In The Life Of A Slave Girl* by Harriet A. Jacobs (o)
- *Iron Scouts of the Confederacy* by McGriffon (y,o)
- *The Life of Stonewall Jackson* by Mary L. Williamson
- *The Life of J.E.B. Stuart* by Mary L.

Williamson
- *Little Women* by Louisa May Alcott (o)
- *Mary McLeod Bethune* by Eloise Greenfield (y)
- *The Negro Cowboys* by Philip Durham (o)
- *Perilous Road* by William O. Steele (y,o)
- *A Picture Book of Frederick Douglass* by David A. Adler (y)
- *Pink and Say* by Patricia Polacco (y)
- *The Red Badge of Courage* by Stephen Crane (o)
- *Rifles for Watie* by Harold Keith (o)
- *Robert E. Lee, The Christian* by William J. Johnson (o)
- *Robert E. Lee* by Lee Roddy (Sower series) (o)
- *The Slave Dancer* by Paula Fox (read aloud) (o)
- *Sojourner Truth; Ain't I A Woman?* by Pat and Patricia McKissack (y,o)
- *Stonewall* by Jeanne Fritz (y)
- *The Story of Harriet Tubman: Conductor of the Underground Railroad* by Kate McMullan (y)
- *Tales from the Underground Railroad* by Kate Connell
- *Uncle Tom's Cabin* by Harriet Beecher Stowe (read aloud) (o)
- *Up From Slavery* by Booker T. Washington (o)
- *Virginia's General: Robert E. Lee and the Civil War* by Albert Marrin (o)
- *Walking the Road to Freedom: Sojourner Truth* by Jeri Ferris (y)
- *With Lee in Virginia: A Story of the American Civil War* by G.A. Henty (o)

Modern U.S. History
- *Amelia Earhart* by Beatrice Gormley (y,o)
- *American Girls* series
- *Andrew Carnegie: Builder of Libraries* by Charnan Simon (y)
- *The Bracelet* (Japanese internment in WWII) by Yoshiko Uchida and Joanna Yardley (y)
- *Children of the Dust Bowl: The True Story of the School at Weedpatch Camp* by Jerry

Stanley (o)
- *Counting on Grace* by Elizabeth Winthrop (Industrial Revolution) (o)
- *Farewell to Manzanar* (Japanese internment in WWII) by Houston and Houston (o)
- *Henry Ford: Young Man with Ideas* by Hazel Aird and Catherine Ruddiman
- *Rocket Man: The Story of Robert Goddard* by Tom Streissguth (y,o)
- *Roll of Thunder, Hear My Cry* by Mildred D. Taylor (read aloud,o)
- *Ronald Reagan* by Montrew Dunham (y,o)
- *Rosie the Riveter: Women Working on the Home Front in WWII* by Penny Colman (o)
- *Smokestacks and Spinning Jennys: Industrial Revolution* by Sean Stewart Price (y,o)
- *The Story of the Wright Brothers and Their Sister* by Lois Mills (y)
- *To Kill a Mockingbird* by Harper Lee (read aloud,o)
- *Understood Betsy* by Dorothy Canfield Fisher (o)
- *The Yearling* by Marjorie Rawlings (o)

Modern World History
- *America and Vietnam: The Elephant and the Tiger* by Albert Marrin (o)
- *The Collapse of Communism* by Stewart Ross (o)
- *The Crystal Snowstorm, Following the Phoenix, Angel and the Dragon, The Rose and Crown* (19th century European politics) by Meriol Trevor (o)
- *Hitler* by Albert Marrin (o)
- *The House of Sixty Fathers* (China) by Meindert de Jong (y,o)
- *The Land I Lost: Adventures of a Boy in Vietnam* by Huynh Quang Nhuong (y,o)
- *Number the Stars* (Danish Resistance) by Lois Lowry (o)
- *Stalin: Russia's Man of Steel* by Albert Marrin (o)
- *Sweet Dried Apples: A Vietnamese Wartime Childhood* by Rosemary Breckler (y)

- *Teresa of Calcutta* by D. Jeanene Watson (Sower series) (y,o)
- *Twenty and Ten* (WWII refugee children in France) by Claire Huchet Bishop
- *The Wheel on the School* (Netherlands) by Meindert de Jong (y,o)
- *When Jessie Came across the Sea* (Jewish Immigrant) by Amy Hett (y)
- *The Winged Watchman* (Netherlands) by Hilda Van Stockum (o)
- *The Yanks are Coming* (WWI) by Albert Marrin (o)

Help for Figuring Out Which Books to Use When

Many home school distributors sell such books as these for various historical periods. Some homeschool distributors list books under time period headings so you can easily find those you want to use for history studies. In addition to distributors' websites and catalogs, there are other resource books you can use to help you select your own books for historical studies. Some home educators glean ideas from books like *The Well-Trained Mind* by Susan Wise Bauer and Jessie Wise (Norton) or *For the Love of Literature: Teaching Core Subjects with Literature* by Maureen Wittmann (Ecce Homo Press).

I know of one book totally dedicated to selecting literature for history. *All through the Ages: History through Literature Guide* by Christine Miller (Nothing New Press, www. nothingnewpress.com) is a 300+ page reference guide for selecting literature by time period. The largest section of the book features listings divided by chronological periods. Selections reflect a strong western civilization and Reformed Protestant perspective. In addition to chronological divisions, titles within those divisions are further broken down by age groups covering grades 1 through 12. Within age groups there are sometimes further

divisions under headings such as overview of the era, specific events, biography, historical fiction, and culture. Other smaller sections follow a similar format, listing books for geography, science, math, the arts, and "Great Books of Western Civilization & the Christian Tradition."

Below are examples of the many websites that list historical literature by time periods that you might want to explore:

A Book in Time
www.abookintime.com

This secular list is arranged by time periods and levels, and it includes descriptions of books.

GuestHollow.com
www.GuestHollow.com

This is a personal website with the author's own schedules and recommendations plus extensive lists (although not covering all eras) of books, videos, and activity resources. It reflects a Christian approach but can easily be used by all.

Mater Amabilis
www.materamabilis.org/ma/subjects/history/

This site has free lesson plans and helps for a Charlotte Mason approach for all grade levels for both U.S. and U.K. Real books for history are listed by topic and level.

Paula's Archives
www.redshift.com/~bonajo/history.htm#WMID

Un-annotated lists on this site come from a Protestant homeschool perspective. The lists include movies for each time period.

University of Delaware
www.udel.edu/dssep/literature.html

A secular university published these lists of recommended literature for social studies that are arranged by level.

Reviews of History Resources

All American History

by Celeste W. Rakes
Bright Ideas Press
PO Box 333
Cheswold, DE 19934
877-492-8081
email: contact@brightideaspress.com
www.brightideaspress.com
Volume I OR *Volume II* set - $68 each,
extra student activity books - $16.95
each, *AAH Junior, Vol. I* - $44.95,
high school test packet - $7

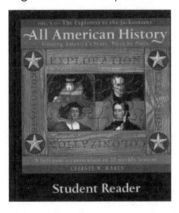

All American History (AAH) is a two-year, two-volume course in American History. While it can be used by students in grades five through twelve, it can be used by either one student or multiple students working at one or more grade levels. The two volumes are titled *Volume 1, Explorers to the Jacksonians* and *Volume 2: The Civil War to the 21st Century.*

This is a distinctly different United States History course that should work very well in homeschool settings. Developed through use in co-op classes, it easily adapts for use with individual children at home as well as for regular classroom use. Each volume stands alone, but you need both for complete coverage of U.S. History.

The content should be acceptable to almost all home educators since it is presented objectively and without editorializing in comparison to most other options used by home educators. *AAH* purposely emphasizes social and cultural aspects of history as we often find in mainstream history texts for the elementary grades. However, it includes religious developments often ignored by other texts. God and Christianity receive occasional mention but not nearly as much as one finds in history books from Christian publishers such as BJU Press, A Beka Book, and Christian Liberty Press. Those wanting a secular text should be comfortable with the minimal treatment of religion in this book. However, the student activity book's "For Further Study" suggestions and "Family Activity Ideas" in the teacher's guide occasionally offer some more overtly Christian topics. For example, one "For Further Study" question directs students to "Find out about John Eliot, the Puritan missionary who was known as the Apostle to the Indians" (*AAH* student activity book, p. 81). Almost all assignments and suggestions are not specifically Christian, so this arrangement allows the parent who prefers a secular approach to skip any topics with which they are uncomfortable. While Christian parents have occasional opportunities in *AAH* to make faith connections, they might want to supplement with more faith-based resources or raise questions about biblical principles and historical characters and events.

There are three components to the course for each volume: the student reader, student activity book, and teacher's guide. The core book is the hardcover, student reader. Similar to textbooks, student readers present historical information accompanied by black-and-white illustrations. A brief summary of key points concludes each chapter. The text of the Declaration of Independence and the Constitution are included in an appendix in both volumes. These are substantial books with 442 pages in the first volume and 557 in the second.

Questions and assignments are all found in the consumable student activity books. Here you find activity pages, map forms, review questions, "For Further Study" assignments, and "Images for Required Forms." The last item is a collection of illustrations (primarily of people) and flags to be used on activity pages. The illustrations in the student activity book are intended to be beneficial to both visual learners as well as kinesthetic learners, providing cut-and-paste activities to keep their hands engaged.

The "required forms" are one or more worksheets per chapter for students to complete that summarize key information from each chapter. The student activity book forms are intended to be filled in as the student is either reading the text or listening to the text being read. This is training in note-taking skills, and it encourages them to be active readers/ listeners.

Activity book pages are perforated and three-hole-punched so they can be easily removed and put into a binder. At the end of the activity book are Optional Forms for Further Study. These forms require students to do more in-depth research on topics such as a Native American tribe, a Revolutionary War or World War battle, or a United States President. Some forms might be used more than once. While these are great for students in grades five through eight, high school students should probably be working at a more challenging level than is posed by these forms.

The course for each volume is broken down into four units, with eight lessons (chapters) per unit. The activity book has review questions for each lesson, but it also has a test at the end of each unit. An additional set of high school level tests are available.

The teacher's guides include reduced reproductions of all student activity book pages with completed answers and information to serve as your answer key for all but the "For Further Study" assignments. "For Further Study" suggested answers are included in the instruction pages for each lesson. Answer keys include lengthy suggested responses for open-ended questions which are very helpful for parents who cannot keep up with the student reading themselves.

The teacher's guides have additional activity suggestions, recommended reading lists for three levels: grades K-4, 5-8, and 9-12. They also have checklists at the end of each unit to help you plan, showing which activities are required and which are optional. In addition, the teacher's guides include masters of the optional forms and all of the images. These images might also be used for a timeline as well as for a game as described in the teacher's guides.

Part of the reason this course is so suitable for homeschooling is that while the ideal audience is probably junior high, it easily expands for use with younger and older students. Younger students listen to highlights and key ideas from the chapter presented by the parent. They read real books related to the time period— annotated lists of age-appropriate books for each chapter are in the teacher's guide. And younger students participate in creating timelines, map work, and other hands-on learning activities. Bright Ideas Press has also come out with an optional *All American History Junior* for *Volume I* that gives students smaller amounts of material to read, adds five age-appropriate literature study guides, and provides alternative map work, activity pages, folder book projects, puzzles, and notebooking and coloring pages. This substitutes for the student activity book, but you still need the student reader and the teacher's guide. (*AAH Junior, Vol. I* is available as a download, and *Volume II* should be available late 2012.)

It's even easier with high school students. While you would choose from among the optional activities for students in elementary grades, older students would complete most of the optional activities, especially the For Further Study questions and the optional forms or something equivalent. The student readers cover most topics very briefly, so it is essential that high school students delve deeper into some topics. They need to read at least one book per unit from the recommended reading lists. Optional test packets for high school students are also available for $7 each. The biggest drawback for high school students is that they might need to complete both volumes in one year because of other credit requirements.

Another plus regarding this course for homeschoolers is that the components are very reasonably priced, especially the teacher's guide. To teach an additional student in the same family, you might share the student reader and purchase only an extra student activity book.

The books are very professional in appearance and presentation, but other than the covers, they are printed in black-and-white throughout. This should not be a big issue for most students.

Note that *Year 4* of Bright Ideas Press' new *Illuminations* is a wrap-around program that uses *All American History* as a spine. *Illuminations* integrates history, Bible, language arts, literature, science, fine arts, geography, and life skills. You might want to consider using *AAH* within the *Illuminations Year 4* program.

· · · · · · · ·

A Child's History of the World
by Virgil M. Hillyer

Calvert School
10713 Gilroy Rd., Ste. B
Hunt Valley, MD 21031
888-487-4652
www.calvertschool.org
book - $28, complete course with textbook - $62, course without text - $48, online interactive book - $25 for one year

Hillyer's classic, elementary-level world history, *A Child's History of the World*, is available as a beautiful, hardbound edition or through online subscription to an interactive version. For years homeschoolers scrambled to find out-of-print copies of this book, paying premium prices for well-used copies. Finally, recognizing the demand, Calvert School republished it in an updated edition, and now also as an interactive, online version. The update included the addition of events through the twentieth century as well as some minor content changes to archaic expressions and ideas.

The primary appeal is the writing style. Hillyer speaks to children in ways they understand, yet he doesn't talk down to them in the short, choppy sentences typical of most texts written for middle elementary grades. The difference is obvious in the page count—625 pages. Illustrations are minimal: a few maps, line drawings, and, occasionally, words arranged to convey an idea. (Can you imagine any modern publisher offering a textbook this length for fourth graders without color illustrations?)

In spite of these "limitations," Hillyer's book is far better than most of its modern counterparts in my estimation. It offers depth and interest lacking in most textbooks. History coverage reaches beyond Europe, the Middle East, and North America with selective topics on other countries and cultures. Children's imaginations will be engaged by the stories of history told in their proper settings with enough detail to make them come alive.

Hillyer clearly asserts Christian belief, although his biblical references imply a questioning of the truthfulness of Old Testament stories. Also, he sometimes slightly misinterprets the biblical text. For instance, he says, "King Saul had a daughter, and she fell in love with this... David the Giant-Killer, and at last they were married." This version overlooks the fact that Saul had promised his daughter in marriage to whoever killed the giant—it wasn't really a matter of falling in love. The beginning of the book also discusses cave men and prehistory in a manner with which some might disagree (e.g., cavemen talked in grunts).

A Child's History of the World really should be read aloud together so such things as I've mentioned can easily be discussed when you encounter them. There are no chapter questions or assignments in the book.

This book and associated lessons are included in Calvert's fourth grade curriculum, but Calvert also sells the book by itself or as part of a history course. The course adds a lesson manual and a workbook. Lessons include outlines, activity ideas, and discussion questions. The student workbook has two parts. The first part is fill-in-the-blank comprehension questions for each chapter. The second part consists of activity pages with word scrambles, crosswords, projects, recipes, map work, and more.

There is also an online interactive version of the book with the complete text plus original art, music, review questions, and computer-scored games. This version is recommended for students in grades four through six. You subscribe for access for a full year at a time.

The book itself is a good choice for the first world history text for younger students, and the course and online options make it easy for parents to expand learning beyond the reading itself.

· · · · · · · ·

Genevieve Foster books

Beautiful Feet Books
1306 Mill St.
San Luis Obispo, CA 93401
800-889-1978
www.bfbooks.com

William Penn - $14.95, all others - $21.95 each

Beautiful Feet Books has brought back into print some of my favorite books for world history for upper elementary grades through high school. This is a series of books by Genevieve Foster that were written around the 1940s. Titles published by Beautiful Feet are *Augustus Caesar's World*, *The World of Columbus and Sons*, *The World of Captain John Smith*, *The World of William Penn*, *George Washington's World*, *The Year of the Horseless Carriage 1801*, and *Abraham Lincoln's World*. They reflect a Christian culture although they don't have explicitly Christian content.

The beauty of these books is the storytelling approach to history. Foster begins with the day the key person was born and traces "goings-on" around the world throughout his lifetime. Foster makes the connections between people and events all around the globe that are usually lacking in textbooks. Because of this approach, even *George Washington's World* is a world history study. If you read these in chronological sequence you cover world history fairly well for the time periods they reflect.

These are great for read-aloud time, but only with older students, probably at least fifth grade, except for *The World of William Penn* and *The Year of the Horseless Carriage 1801*. These two are briefer books which should work fine as read alouds for children as young as fourth grade. With most of the books, younger children will be overwhelmed with the information and will not have enough background to make the necessary connections. Often the information comes "rapid fire," and even older children will need you to stop from time to time and discuss or explain what you have read. You might even take time off in the middle of a Foster book to read a biography or historical fiction that narrows down to a single person or event for a change of pace.

For the adventurous parent, I suggest creating your own unit studies by jumping off on one or more topics within each section of any of Foster's books. While there are no suggested assignments, study or discussion questions in these books, you could easily come up with some of your own for independent reading and research. Note that all of the books have indexes that are very helpful when you want to locate information.

The author provided her own hand-drawn illustrations for all of these books. The illustrations are often helpful visualizations of the story content, including maps and drawings of key characters.

Beautiful Feet Books, publisher of the Foster series, also publishes "history through literature" study guides, some of which include study questions for the Foster books. For example, their *Early American and World History* guide for junior high uses the Foster books on Columbus, John Smith, George Washington, and Abraham Lincoln along with other books. Their *Ancient History* guide uses *Augustus Caesar's World*. *The World of William Penn* is used with Beautiful Feet's new *Western Expansion* guide, and *The Year of the Horseless Carriage 1801* is used with their newly revised *Early American History* study guide for primary grades.

Whether you read these on their own, in conjunction with a Beautiful Feet history guide or as part of another unit study, I expect you and your children will enjoy Foster's books.

· · · · · · · ·

Guerber History Series

by H.A. Guerber, edited by Christine Miller
Nothing New Press
1015-M South Taft Hill Rd. #263
Fort Collins, CO 80521
info@nothingnewpress.com
www.nothingnewpress.com
print editions - $21.95-$27.95,
ebooks - $13.95-$19.95

Christine Miller authored *All through the Ages: History through Literature Guide*, which I described earlier in this chapter. Christine recommends using at least one overview or "spine" type book for each historical era in addition to titles that might focus on particular people and events. (An overview or spine book functions like a history text in covering the broad range of events in chronological order.) Because it can be difficult to find appealing overview books written from a Christian perspective, Christine has updated and rewritten a series of books originally written by H.A. Guerber (first published in 1898). These new books vary from minimal rewrites of Guerber's work to incorporation of her material into new books. The seven books in this series all begin *The Story of* …. The titles continue: *the Ancient World, the Greeks, the Romans, the Middle Ages, the Renaissance and Reformation, the Thirteen Colonies,* and *the Great Republic* (U.S. history to 1900). It is important to note that all of the material does not derive solely from Guerber's original work. For *The Middle Ages*, Miller also drew upon some historical works by Charlotte Yonge.

The Story of the Ancient World is based upon Guerber's *The Story of the Chosen People*, a biblical history focused on key figures and events of the Old Testament. Miller has added some history of ancient civilizations that are closely related to the Old Testament, so you learn about Egyptians, Phoenicians, Philistines, Assyrians, Babylonians, and Persians to better understand the historical context of scripture. Miller has also made a few changes to Guerber's wording. Most particularly she changes Guerber's original wording about the days of Creation that allowed for "day" to mean a longer period of time to an explanation that supports a literal 24-hour-day viewpoint.

Guerber writes with a lively style that reminds me of Joy Hakim (author of *The History of US* from Oxford University Press). Christine Miller has retained that same engaging style in her adaptations and additions.

Part of what makes this type of writing more enjoyable is that the author's feelings and opinions show through the narrative. That means we also get some of Guerber's original thoughts and attitudes, and there might be a few of these with which you disagree. However, Christine Miller has added explanations in the forewords regarding topics most likely to be problematic.

None of these volumes strive to be comprehensive. Instead they focus on key events and characters. This works fine for an overview in the first four volumes, but I find the topics covered in *The Story of the Great Republic* curious from our 21st century perspective. Because the book was originally written in 1899, events closer to that time period loomed large in the author's consciousness. Thus the Civil War and the Spanish-American War both get more attention proportionately than they do in more recent books. In spite of the original 1899 copyright of this book, it actually continues up through the assassination of President McKinley in 1901. Personally, I would be likely to use something else instead of this last volume.

The reading level would make these most appropriate for junior high level for independent reading. However, they can be read aloud with children from about fourth grade and up. There are no questions or exercises with any of these volumes. But if you use them as read-aloud books, following up with discussion, narration, writing, or other activities of your own, they will work fine with younger students. Older students could be assigned outlining, notetaking, or other written tasks to demonstrate comprehension.

Of particular note is the religious perspective. This series is Christian, and it does a surprisingly good job of fairly presenting both Protestant and Catholic positions. Even in the *Renaissance and Reformation* volume, you read about the good and bad from both sides.

All books are available in either print or ebook versions.

• • • • ● • • • •

History of the World (MFW edition)

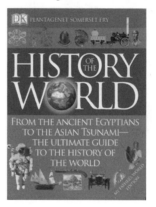

by Plantagenet Somerset Fry and Simon Adams
DK Publishing in cooperation with My Father's World
Order from MFW
573-202-2000
www.MFWBooks.com
$39.95
(discounted to $32.95 by MFW)

My Father's World (MFW), whose complete courses are also featured among my Top Picks, uses many "real books" as part of each course. They often use books from secular publishers, alerting parents to potentially problematic topics such as evolution and the age of the earth. Obviously, this is a problem that crops up frequently in world history books. DK Publishing's *History of the World* is a classic example of a very useful book with problem areas. MFW was selling so many of these books that they were able to work with the publisher to produce an edited edition. The most significant edit is the elimination of the first two chapters, "Introduction to Human History" and "Early People." These two chapters reflect belief in an old earth and the theory of evolution, making statements such as, "… life began 4,600 million years ago …" (p. 10).

The MFW edition, instead, begins with 5000 BC and continues with the original text up through 2006. Pages and chapters are renumbered so that you cannot tell that the book has been edited.

This is a large, 378-page, hardcover book that might be used across a wide span of grade levels. It covers world history across time and around the world, introducing each time period with a two-page visual timeline. The timeline is divided into color-coded sections for Africa, Asia, Europe, the Americas, and Oceania, so you can see at a glance what was occurring during the same time period around the world. Timeline bars at the bottom of each page highlight where in time the events on each page fit in.

The book is heavily illustrated with photos, drawings, and maps taking up at least half of the space on each page. Every paragraph is preceded by a heading or subheading so that it is easy to scan through the content.

Coverage of each topic is necessarily brief and selective given the limited space to cover so much information. Because of this, *History of the World* works best when used alongside other books that provide more in-depth coverage. Students as young as about fifth grade are likely to enjoy exploring this book, "reading the pictures," and selectively reading the paragraphs on topics that interest them. Yet, this is the type of book that interests older students and even adults because it is so visually appealing and unintimidating compared to a text. While MFW includes it among books used with their high school level *World History and Literature* course, they also sell it separately.

History of the World is an excellent example of the "fact books" that I include in my list of real books for history. MFW is working with a few publishers to create more of these "edited" fact books that should work well for Christian home educators.

· · · · · · · · ·

The Mystery of History

by Linda Lacour Hobar
Bright Ideas Press
PO Box 333
Cheswold, DE 19936

877-492-8081
email: contact@brightideaspress.com
www.BrightIdeasPress.com
Volumes I or II - $49.95 each; Volume III: Student Reader - $59.95, Companion Guide - softcover $39.95 or CD $29.95

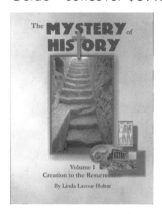

Volumes I, II, and *III* of the projected four-volume *Mystery of History* series are a great resource for homeschoolers. They are designed so that even inexperienced parents can break free from traditional textbooks. They combine read-aloud information with age appropriate activities to create a multi-sensory curriculum for history and geography with a very strong biblical base. They are designed to be used with children in grades K through 8 for the first two volumes, although the reading level is about sixth grade. *Volume III* stretches into high school level. Some families have adapted lessons in the first two volumes for use with high schoolers.

Titles for the volumes are:
- *Volume I: Creation to the Resurrection*
- *Volume II: The Early Church and the Middle Ages* (A.D. 30-1460)
- *Volume III: The Renaissance, Reformation, and the Growth of Nations* (1455-1707)
- *Volume IV: Revolutions to Rising Times* (1708-the present) (will not be available before 2014)

Volume I relies heavily on scripture since the Bible is a source for much of what we know about ancient times. Other than that, the historical information is all presented within this book as it would be in a textbook. No other reference works are required for this study except for research activities older students might pursue. However, a large list of other books and videos that expand upon subjec is in the appendix, presented lesson by lesson and broken down by age level.

Beginning with creation, the study follows biblical history, incorporating other sources as they fit into the chronological story. Thus, Stonehenge, early Egypt, and the Minoans are taught before Abraham, Jacob, and Joseph. The little we know about world civilizations is represented by inclusion of lessons such as those on Chinese dynasties, India and Hinduism, and early Greek City States up to the point where the historical record broadens and we have more sources for learning about early civilizations. Although eastern civilizations are given some attention, the focus is much stronger on western civilizations.

Each volume is structured for a school year with four quarters divided into two semesters. Lessons are arranged in sets of three with the expectation that you will complete three per week. Each quarter begins with "Around the world" background and introductory information that you will want to read aloud with your children. Each week includes a pretest designed to spark interest, so you want to present these in a light-hearted fashion (à la a *Trivial Pursuit* game) rather than as a test.

Three lessons follow, each with a similar format: read-aloud information is presented from the book then you choose an activity for each child to complete. An activity is given for each of three levels. For example, the lesson on Noah suggests that young children play a Concentration card game. Middle grade to older students might use their Bibles to find answers to a list of questions regarding the account of the Flood. Older students might instead tackle the third option, which requires research about the supplies needed on the ark for Noah, his family, and all the animals.

At the end of every third lesson is a reminder for students to create "memory cards." These are 3" x 5" notecards with key information on each event. A color-coding system helps students group events by time periods. These are used for oral drill, games, or independent review. (Downloadable files for these cards may be purchased if you want to save students from having to create these cards themselves.)

Review activities are always included at the end of the three lessons, sometimes including field trip suggestions. Activities include work on timelines, maps, and a review quiz. Nine reproducible map masters are at the back of the book along with answer keys for the geography assignments. Author Linda Hobar recommends that you have both a Bible atlas and a historical atlas for reference for map work.

Hobar also shares creative and inexpensive ideas for making timelines with detailed instructions for using folding sewing boards as the base for portable timelines, although any timeline will do.

You can see how all of this can break out easily into three days of lessons with their activities, a fourth day for timeline, mapwork, and quiz, and a fifth day for a field trip or focus on other subjects. Other possible scheduling suggestions for different levels are at the front of the book.

I appreciate Hobar's explanation of the shift toward increasing student responsibility that should take place over the years. She has a simple diagram that shows high teacher involvement with minimal grading for young children that gradually reverses to low teacher involvement and thorough record keeping and grading at high school level. This approach to education is reflected in the activities suggested for the different levels. Younger children will spend more time working one-on-one with a parent. They have more arts-and-crafts type activities that are not graded. Older students do more independent research and writing that is graded.

While this is essentially a study of history, it is also a Bible study of sorts with an apologetic flavor in spots. The appendix of *Volume I* includes an adaptation of Campus Crusade's booklet used for leading people to accept

Christ. A letter to students at the beginning of the book direct students to that section of the appendix if they don't already have a relationship with God.

For *Volume I*, you can now purchase a set of eight audio CDs with all the stories in this volume read by the author to the accompaniment of appropriate background music. This is a great time saver for busy parents, and it might be especially helpful for those children who like to hear the stories more than once.

Other extras for *Volume I* are:

- Reproducibles CD-ROM - PDF files for all pre-tests; post-tests; quarterly worksheets; semester tests; individual maps; Appendices A,B,C,D,E & F; the suggested reading lists; and more.
- 36 Coloring Pages - downloadable PDFs that correlate with lessons
- Challenge Cards - downloadable file for creating the memory cards
- Notebooking Pages - downloadable set of more than 400 PDF pages appropriate for both younger or older students
- Folderbook files for creating folderbooks for each quarter of the course—full year available on CD or each quarter available as a download
- *History Through the Ages* timeline figures - sets for *Volumes I* and *II* are not specific to *Mystery of History*. For *Volume III*, History through the Ages created a custom set.

Volume II: The Early Church and the Middle Ages follows the same layout as the first volume although it no longer follows a biblical chronology past the first few weeks of the course. There are 28 weeks worth of lessons instead of 36 as in *Volume I*, but each lesson has more content. You will want to have access to an atlas for this volume, and some recommended atlases are listed in the introduction. Bright Ideas Press' new *WonderMaps* (www. BrightIdeasPress.com) should work especially well with *MOH*. (*WonderMaps* is a customizable

collection of over 350 different maps available either on CD-ROM or as downloadable files.) Lists of additional resources you might use are at the back of the book.

Hobar's selection and presentation of topics is fascinating. Given the huge time period she covers in *Volume II*, she does a great job of pulling out key people and events so students get the big picture.

For *Volume II*, you can also purchase a set of 12 audio CDs with the "stories" as for *Volume I*. All the other extras described for *Volume I* are also available for *Volume II*.

Volume III is formatted differently than the first two volumes. It is divided into a *Student Reader* and a *Companion Guide: Curriculum and Student Activities*. The *Reader* is a colorful, 441-page, hardcover book, while the *Companion Guide* is a black-and-white, 600+ page "book." Pages of the *Guide* come three-hole punched for insertion into your own binder. The *Companion Guide* is also available on CD-ROM.

The *Volume III Student Reader* has more text than *Volume II* and significantly more than *Volume I*. Author Linda Hobar says the target audience is primarily grades four and up, but *Volume III* seems to me best for junior high and high school level simply because of the breadth and depth of information covered. Hobar suggests that younger students in grades K through 3 might listen in on parts of lessons and participate in age-appropriate activities—there are plenty of activities for all ages! I suspect that the quantity of material as well as the depth of the content might still be too much for even some fifth and sixth graders. The writing style is very engaging, and this certainly helps to offset difficulty in the level or amount of content. Occasionally, the author suggests that "younger" or "middle" students stop rea___ ing at a certain point, and that older stud__ continue with material that is deeper or ___ detailed. This helps, but, ultimately, p___ have to decide how much of the mat___ cover with children in elementary grades.

Even given the amount of material in the reader, Hobar says that high school students should be reading additional books from the 49-page "Supplemental Books and Resources" section of the *Guide's* appendix. Hobar says that the combination of reading and activities for *Volume III's* "core curriculum" should take about one to three hours per week to complete. For a high school credit, students should likely be spending four to five hours per week. To fulfill the hours requirement, students might also tackle a research paper or a number of shorter reports. For example: the *Guide* describes this activity for an older student:

> I mentioned in the lesson that grueling serfdom was a common way of life in Russia until 1861. Investigate what happened in that year that changed the system. Write a short report following a "Who, What, When, and How" format. Fold a sheet of notebook paper into fourths. Use each quadrant to write a few sentences answering the questions Who? What? When? and How? Research Hint: Sift through the history of Russia in an encyclopedia with your focus on 1861. File your short report in your Student Notebook under "Europe: Russia."

This type of assignment could be expanded beyond the single sheet of notebook paper into a longer report. You can draw plenty of ideas such as this for expanding assignments for older students directly from the *Guide*.

Alternatively, high school students might complete more than one volume of *Mystery of History* per year, but that might preclude the entire family working through volumes together since younger students would likely need a slower pace.

Note that those pursuing a classical form of education will likely want to select more of the primary resources and "Great Books" from the supplementary reading list, and this would certainly be another way to "fill the hours."

Map activities in *Volume III* require at least two Atlases: *Rand McNally's Answer Atlas* and *Rand McNally's Historical Atlas of the World*. Both are available through www.themysteryof-history.com or www.brightideaspress.com. The new *WonderMaps* can take the place of both atlases, so be sure to check out that option.

Volume III covers the time period of the Reformation. Although Hobar does a better than average job of trying to present the Catholic side of issues (e.g., indulgences), the content is strongly Protestant.

Volume III currently has Coloring Pages, Challenge Cards, and Timeline figures available with other extras in the works. Check the Bright Ideas website for availability of other ancillary resources.

I think this combination of self-contained history and multi-sensory activities should really appeal to many homeschooling families.

· · · · · · · · ·

The Old World's Gifts to the New

by Sr. Mary Celeste
Neumann Press
21892 County 11
Long Prairie, MN 56347
800-746-2521
email: sales@neumannpress.com
www.neumannpress.com
$28.95

Originally published (and reprinted) in eight printings from 1932 to 1939, this is a delightful Catholic presentation of world history, similar in some ways to Hillyer's *A Child's History of the World*. It is probably best for students in the upper elementary grades. This hardcover book is over 500 pages in length, but it has fairly large print, a number of black-and-white illustrations, and a lively writing style that actually make it read rather quickly.

Refreshingly, it begins with Adam and Eve rather than "millions of years ago." It continues up through exploration and settlement of the Americas, including the early colonial period.

As with most history books of the era, this one focuses on the roots of western civilization with little attention to Africa and the Orient. However, it does an exceptional job of connecting people, places, and events in a meaningful way, explaining why things happened as they did, so that it reads like a story rather than a collection of information. I found the illustrations—particularly the photos—quite interesting, but occasionally an illustration had little to no reference within the text—a curious situation.

There are a good many questions and activities, but they are presented in a somewhat random fashion. Sometimes they are presented as "test yourself," sometimes as recall type questions, and sometimes as discussion questions. Some activities ask students to retell events in their own words (i.e., narration, even if it's not described with that word). Among other exercises and activities are drawing or cutting projects and acting out historical scenes. Comprehension questions range from matching to writing a few sentences. These questions and activities appear with no predictability—sometimes in the middle of a unit, sometimes at the end. No teacher guide or answer key is available, but this isn't a significant problem.

I really enjoyed reading this book and found myself reading more than skimming as I frequently do when reviewing such books.

· · · · · ● · · · ·

The Story of the World: History for the Classical Child

by Susan Wise Bauer
Peace Hill Press
18021 The Glebe Lane
Charles City, VA 23030
877-322-3445
email: info@peacehillpress.com
www.PeaceHillPress.com
texts for *Vols. 1-4:* paperback

$16.95, hardcover - $21.95, or PDF downloads - $13.50 each; activity books for *Vols. 1-4:* paperback - $34.95-$36.95 or PDF downloads - $27.95-$29.50 each; student page packets: print - $9.95-$11.95 or PDF downloads - $7.95-$9.50 each; test packets: print - $11.95-12.95 or PDF downloads - $9.50-$10.35 each

The Story of the World by Susan Wise Bauer presents world history through narration and storytelling in this four-volume series. While these books are written at increasing levels of difficulty, they might be read aloud to younger children and read independently by older. The *Story of the World* books are available in your choice of hardcover, lay-flat perfect binding (softcover), or as PDF downloads.

Many will recognize Bauer as one of the authors of *The Well-Trained Mind*—an exceptionally good book on providing a classical education. This history series is intended to be used within the context of just such an education, even though it will also work within more traditional approaches.

Volume 1: Ancient Times addresses the time period from the earliest nomads (given a date of about 6000 BC) up through the last emperor of ancient Rome—no cave men or Neanderthals included! The book's size of 338 pages means there's actually quite a bit of material in comparison to most world history texts for the target audience for this volume which is grades one through four. Nevertheless, coverage is not comprehensive because chapters are devoted to lengthy stories about key characters or events rather than tidbits about everything. On the other hand, the book does span civilizations around the world, including India, China, and West Africa in addition to the usual cast of western civilizations.

As in *The Well-Trained Mind*, the presentation is not overtly Christian, although it recognizes and includes Christianity. For example, stories of gods and goddesses from other civilizations are retold without value judgments as to their validity. However, the author's own Christianity is still evident in the heavy weighting of biblical stories—lengthy accounts about Abraham, Joseph, Moses, and the beginnings of Christianity, as well as the birth, death, and resurrection of Jesus.

This and other *Story of the World* books have only a few black-and-white illustrations and a good number of maps. These are not colorful, history picture books for browsing since they are intended to either be read aloud or used for independent reading by older students. Those who might have seen only earlier editions of the first two books should know that the newer, revised editions have all-new illustrations that are very professional, unlike those in the earlier editions.

Story of the World books are intended to be used as spine books around which you can build a complete study. To help you do just that, Susan Wise Bauer has also created activity books for each volume. Activity books serve as curriculum guides, providing parents with detailed information for creating multi-sensory lessons that can be used with a wide spread of grade levels. For each lesson there is a compilation of questions, narration exercises, reading lists (for both history and literature), map work, coloring pages, and activities to accompany each section of the text.

Reproducible student pages in this and other activity books are segregated from lesson plans into their own section, which makes copying easier. The entire activity book for the first volume is 320 pages in length, and the reproducible pages account for 127 of those pages.

You are given permission to copy these pages for your family but not for other group classes. However, Peace Hill Press sells separate packets of only these reproducible pages which might be worth purchasing even for other children in your own family.

You will find some very unusual project ideas in the activity book, for example, mummifying a chicken and making Greek tattoos with pure henna. Reproducible blackline masters are used for all sorts of things—mapwork, "board" games, paper dolls, making a lighthouse, and more. Another useful feature is "Review Cards"—reproducible pages with illustrations and blocks of information on each card. These are to be copied onto card stock and cut out. (I would probably enlarge each page slightly before copying.) Cards can be used as flashcards to review key ideas.

I particularly like the review questions that begin each section. These help children focus on the reading from the text. The narration exercises are also very helpful for parents who have trouble figuring out how to implement narration techniques. The guide truly supports the grammar stage of classical learning with its focus on information and comprehension.

Cross references are included to *The Kingfisher Illustrated History of the World, The Kingfisher History Encyclopedia, The Usborne Book of World History,* and *The Usborne Internet-Linked Encyclopedia of World History*. You would do well to purchase at least one of these additional basic resources; these same reference books are also used with the other three volumes of *Story of the World*. These books supply the colorful illustrations lacking in the core history book as well as more complete historical information on some topics. Other recommended books should be available through the library, but they are optional.

An activity book (available in either softcover or downloadable PDF versions), extra sets of looseleaf student pages, and test booklets with answer keys are available for each of the four

Story of the World books.

Volume 2: The Middle Ages - from the Fall of Rome to the Rise of the Renaissance is very much like the first volume but is written for an audience in grades two through five. In her delightful style, Bauer covers a huge amount of territory with selective highlights that actually provide good introductory coverage. She hits touchy territory when it comes to the Reformation although she tries to balance her presentation better than do most authors. However, I suspect some Catholics might want to skip or "edit" her chapter on Martin Luther.

The activity book for *Volume 2* is even larger than the activity book for the first volume with 280 lesson plan pages *plus* another 182 student activity pages as compared to the 320 total pages of the activity book for *Volume 1*.

Volume 3: Early Modern Times - From Elizabeth the First to the Forty-Niners continues in the same fashion, targeting grades three through six. However, it seems a little "scattered" because it ambitiously tries to cover a huge swathe of worldwide history in about 420 pages. It seems even more selective and limited in topics covered than previous volumes, although featured topics each get enough attention to present an engaging story. Of course, the activity book offers suggestions for expanding on any topics you wish with supplemental books and activities. There's much to be said for this approach in contrast to history texts that cover far more information but with little or no depth on any of the topics.

Volume 4: The Modern Age covers 1850 up to through the 1990s. The target audience is grades four through eight. This volume is more like a history text than the other books. It uses storytelling within the context of tracing and relating historical events rather than telling selected stories, making it more comprehensive in coverage than earlier books. In my opinion, this is one of the best options for world history for upper elementary through junior high levels. I noted only one issue that might give some

parents pause. On pages 285-286, Bauer discusses Franklin Delano Roosevelt and the New Deal, concluding that the New Deal brought the U.S. out of the Great Depression. Many people would reject that conclusion. One other issue is one of omission. Religion and its influence are seldom mentioned. Nevertheless, this is a very engaging history resource that should work for most families.

The activity book for *Volume 4* teaches students to outline their reading in the text. Halfway through the book, students begin to write from the outlines, recalling and writing details to expand their outline into a composition. This activity book also adds *The Usborne History of The Twentieth Century* as another reference resource.

Both the *Story of the World* texts on their own and the activity books are valuable contributions that fill a need for Christian-friendly but classically-oriented history study.

The publisher's website has samples you can view as well as information about ancillary products.

. . . .

Take A Stand!

by John De Gree
The Classical Historian
1019 Domador
San Clemente, CA 92673
714-623-6104
www.classicalhistorian.com
$24.95 per set of one student edition

and one teacher booklet, student books - $18.95 each, *Teaching the Socratic Discussion in History* set - $99, individual DVDs for *Ancient* or *Medieval Civilization* - $19 each

Take A Stand! is one of the most unusual but practical resources I've seen lately. Written by a homeschooling dad who is also a public school teacher, this is a series of books designed to be used as supplements for both World and U.S. History for students in junior and senior high. While history textbooks, biographies, and other fact books provide the "information," Take A Stand! books guide students in their reading as well as through discussions and extensive writing activities, using elements of classical education in the process.

The books assume that students have a basic history textbook plus access to other sources of information. Students are presented with very brief statements about a key event in their Take A Stand! book then challenged to research and write in response to questions such as, "Which government of ancient Greece was the best?" They must also defend their conclusion(s) after completing their research. Students might use their core history text or any other resources for their research. (The more research they do, the more well-developed their information is likely to be.)

Originally written for classroom settings, lessons in the books also direct students to compare their own conclusions with those of classmates and reconsider whether or not they want to change their own conclusions before writing their papers. Students begin by writing one-paragraph responses and progress through five-paragraph essays to multi-page essays. Note that the new DVDs available for some of the courses were created particularly for homeschoolers and show how to teach in that setting. Classical educators will note that the methods used are those appropriate for both the dialectic and rhetoric stages.

Students are given plenty of assistance with skill development and prewriting activities. The last section of each student book consists of skills assignments. These can be used prior to or integrated between the topical essay lessons. (The author assumes that students already have basic writing skills.) Teachers must use the skill assignments as needed for their own students, skipping those that are unnecessary. The types of skills addressed in these sections are distinguishing fact and opinion, finding supporting evidence, taking notes, paraphrasing, using quotations, writing a thesis statement, writing a conclusion, outlining the essay, writing a rough draft, documenting sources, and creating a works-cited page. Rough draft and outline forms are included for the various essays.

In addition, there are other forms in the student books that help students direct and organize their research. For example, the first lesson in the second book has to do with the fall of the Roman Empire. The "take a stand" question is, "Based on the evidence you researched, what were the two most important reasons for the fall of the Roman Empire?" Three prewriting forms follow. One is headed "Reasons for the Fall of the Roman Empire." A first reason is given as a freebie followed by six more blank lines for students to add six more reasons they discover in their reading and research. The second prewriting activity is headed "Explain your reasons for the fall of the Roman Empire." Here students use a brief statement to explain each of the reasons they came up with in the first activity. Again, one explanation is supplied then there are lines for the student to add six more explanations. The third activity is a more complicated chart that has the student rate the reasons, ranking them as to relative importance. All of this helps them arrive at their two most important reasons.

"Classroom discussion" is a vital component of each lesson. In a homeschool setting this will be more challenging to accomplish because it really requires at least two students or family members comparing their research and ideas. The more students the better... up to a point. If you are working with only one student at this level—and even if you have more than one student—these questions would be great to use for a discussion involving dad, mom, and appropriate-aged children after dinner.

There are a few reasons why I think the Take A Stand! approach works so well. When students read and research with the questions in mind, they pay much closer attention than when reading simply to cover the material. When they have to analyze information, thinking about cause and effect and relative importance, they have moved to a much deeper level of thinking. Discussing their research and ideas with others forces them to think logically and critically.

After students have worked through these steps, they are ready to write their essay where they pull it all together. The instructions for each of the essays says, "In your essay, include a thesis, evidence, and explain how your evidence supports your thesis."

Assignments each have a chart for recording due dates for various assignments. In addition, grading rubric forms are included for the different essays. These can be used by both student and teacher.

All of this sounds like fairly high level work for high school students, but this series was originally written for grades 6, 7, and 8. As I was reviewing these books I was concerned that students in middle school might not have enough historical knowledge to use this approach, but author John De Gree assured me that he has used these very successfully with students, many of whom were ESL students with very weak knowledge of history. De Gree says that the format motivates students to read and think more than they would with just a textbook. Arguments and essays from some students might be shallow or poorly informed, but the learning experience itself still takes

them beyond where they would be with only a textbook. Students with a better knowledge base are able to form more complex arguments. If you use these books with high schoolers you should expect more depth of research and argumentation than you would from a sixth or seventh grader. It's also important to note that assignments gradually become more challenging, eventually requiring the use of at least three sources, then five sources.

Another concern of mine was that a few of the assignments are simply too broad. For example, the eighth grade book on U.S. history has one assignment on westward expansion that seems like it should it should be broken down into a number of separate topics. The question is, "[D]id the 1800's expansion of the U.S. bring about more accomplishment or tragedy?" Then it instructs students to include in their essays thirteen specific people and terms among which are "manifest destiny, Mexican-American War, Trail of Tears, California Gold Rush, Northwest Ordinance," and "Laura Ingalls Wilder." Any of these terms could be the focus of a complete essay on westward expansion. Trying to put them altogether in one assignment sounds overwhelming to me. However, De Gree tells me that younger students take more of a general overview of these events rather than going into detail on all of them. On the other hand, high school students would do well to apply the same question to each topic individually. You can decide for yourself how to use lessons such as this.

The curriculum is aligned with California state standards (which are very similar to those of other states). It actually succeeds quite well in meeting the standards without being anti-Christian or exhibiting other biases because it uses a historical inquiry method. For example, state standards include study about religions, so the curriculum includes questions that relate to religions, albeit without expressing belief or unbelief. For instance, the final lesson in the sixth grade book is on the rise of

Christianity and poses the question, "What made the relationship between the Roman Empire and Christianity change so much from the death of Jesus to the year A.D. 395?" Students might come up with a wide range of answers and opinions depending upon their research resources and parental or teacher directions. Also, remember that the parent or teacher can always add other ideas to those presented in the book.

There are six books in the series, but they need not be used in order. Titles are as follows:
- *Ancient Civilizations*
- *Medieval Civilizations*
- *Modern World History* - opens with a review of western political thought then covers the "Age of Revolution" beginning in the 1600s and continuing through the Cold War
- *American History from the American Revolution to 1914*
- *Modern American History* - Reconstruction then selected topics up through "Nixon and Watergate" and "Technology as a Cause for Change"
- *American Democracy and Economics* - classical approach to government and economics

The modern history books both include a Create Your Own Assignment lesson since students might well come up with another topic of great interest they wish to pursue.

There are 11 to 13 lessons per book. Each of these should take at least a month to complete as students work through the various stages of researching, outlining, writing a rough draft, and writing a final draft. That means you are unlikely to use every lesson every year—unless your children never get a break from school! De Gree tells me his students write six essays per school year.

The Take a Stand! books are a perfect tool for those wishing to use either a classical or a real books approach to history. You might forego use of a core textbook if students are already familiar with the key events of history. They can then focus more deeply on particular events rather than covering everything. However, if they do not yet have enough general knowledge, you will still want to use a core book.

I also can see how this approach could be the basis of your entire high school history curriculum. I would add a few more topics, possibly breaking down some of the present topics into a number of separate assignments as I mentioned with the westward expansion question. I would also get into more current events and issues with U.S. history if it were for high school level. To make this work in the limited time available, I might require reading, research, and discussion on some questions with very short summary papers. Then I would integrate some of the lengthier assignments in these books, requiring perhaps six lengthy papers per school year. This might sound time consuming, but you will be fulfilling requirements for English instruction along with history.

Each book has its own teacher's booklet with instructions on how to use the books, how to lead Socratic discussions, how to teach analytical writing, sample essays, extensive help for grading, and suggested answers. The teacher's booklet comes bundled with the text but you may also purchase extra student texts.

Some parents learn better from audio-visual presentations than from a teacher's edition, so DeGree has developed *Teaching the Socratic Discussion in History*, a set of four DVDs with a binder that help parents, teachers, and students learn this approach. On the first DVD, DeGree introduces the program and explains how it works. On the three other DVDs, you watch DeGree working with different homeschool families through actual lessons. The binder includes instructions and forms so you can actually teach your own students through a complete lesson on the Fall of the Roman Empire, including the composition assignments. The last two DVDs are great for families using either *Ancient Civilizations* or *Medieval Civilizations*, the two books from which the lessons are drawn. The last two DVDs are essential for parent or teachers who want to become certified Classical Historian Teacher's. (Requirements and instructions are in the binder.) These two DVDs are also available individually if you do not need the entire instruction set. DVDs are not professional, but they are helpful for showing how this approach actually works in homeschool settings.

The Classical Historian has produced two supplemental products that should be useful. Go Fish Card Games in your choice of Ancient, Medieval or American History ($11.95 each or a set of the three games for $29) can be used to play at least four games: Go Fish, Continents (identifying cards with continents), Collecting Cards (uses a series of three hints on each card for a quiz/review game), and Chronology (arranging cards in time sequence). Cards are illustrated, color-coded, and numbered.

American History Flash Cards ($9.95 per set) are three separate sets of cards covering from early American history up through the beginning of the 20th century. Specifically tied to the California State Standards, each card has two questions with the answers on the reverse. These can be used for review, but I think they would also serve well as "trivia" questions used with any game board with a path.

I expect Take A Stand! will be popular among homeschoolers who want to engage in discussions with their children and who also want their children to both know historical information and know how to think about and analyze that information.

. . . .

TruthQuest History
by Michelle Miller
TruthQuest History
PO Box 2128
Traverse City, MI 49685

email: info@TruthQuestHistory.com
www.TruthQuestHistory.com
$24.95 - $34.95 each

Many parents are insecure about using real books without some sort of guidance. *TruthQuest History* (TQH) is a great solution since it is a series of eleven volumes that serve as guides for a real books approach to history. While the series can be used for grades 1 through 12, some guides target a younger audience and some target older students.

Guides recommended for grades 1-5 are:
• *American History for Young Students I*
• *American History for Young Students II*
• *American History for Young Students III*

Guides recommended for grades 5-12 are:
• *Beginnings: Creation/Old Testament/ Ancients/Egypt*
• *Ancient Greece*
• *Ancient Rome*
• *Middle Ages*
• *Renaissance, Reformation, and Age of Exploration*
• *Age of Revolution I (America/Europe, 1600-1800)*
• *Age of Revolution II (America/Europe, 1800-1865)*
• *Age of Revolution III (America/Europe, 1865-2000)*

Each guide is divided into many chronologically-organized topical sections rather than the typical chapter arrangement. Michelle Miller introduces each of these topics with background information written in a lively, informal, conversational style.

After reading the background information for context, you and your children read from real books to learn more information about the topic. Michelle recommends books, and sometimes chapters or pages within books, for each topic. She recommends a few spine books—books that are broad overviews of history such as Hillyer's *A Child's History of the World*, Wise Bauer's *Story of the World*, Dorothy Mills' series, and Guerber's history series. Then she lists many other books that cover specific topics. You can use spine (or overview) books, topical books, or both. However, using at least some spine books will save you time. Video recommendations are generally added after the book lists.

Michelle recommends some out-of-print books that you might still be able to find at a library, but she also includes many that are in print and available if you choose to purchase them. There are far more book recommendations than you will ever be able to use!

A unique aspect of *TQH* is a primary focus on the central questions of life: Who is God, and who is man in relation to God? How different people and civilizations answer these questions is reflected in the way they live and the choices they make. So these questions are the underlying focus of background information that Michelle Miller writes as she introduces each topic of study. This is probably most apparent in the *Beginnings: Creation / Old Testament / Ancients / Egypt* guide. You will be reading most of the Old Testament to your children through this study. The Bible might serve as your only spine book! This book probably has more of Michelle's commentary than do the other guides, especially in the first section dealing with Genesis. Michelle does a fine balancing act of presenting the key truths while leaving doctrinal interpretations up to parents. She does stress biblical truths that undermine evolutionary presuppositions, and she recommends many resources that support a creationist viewpoint. It will be up to parents how far to investigate that topic. Note that Egypt used to be covered in *TruthQuest*

History's Egypt and Greece, but study of Egypt was shifted and expanded into the *Beginnings* guide since it correlates historically with the story of the Bible.

TQH very much reflects a Francis Schaeffer approach to history based on his book *How Should We Then Live?* (In his book Schaeffer examines religious beliefs and philosophies, showing how historical events, scientific discoveries, artistic endeavors, literary pursuits, etc., were all shaped by beliefs and philosophies.) In addition, Michelle supports a limited-government perspective. Although Michelle writes from her own Protestant viewpoint, from time to time she discusses conflicting Protestant and Catholic viewpoints on history, acknowledging right and wrong on both sides. I was pleasantly surprised to see this respectful balance, especially in the *Renaissance, Reformation* volume.

As you might have gathered by now, there is a very definite philosophy to these books. However, if you disagree with some of Michelle's philosophy, you can still use these guides by skimming through the introductory material, sharing whichever parts of it you wish with your children, then moving on to the recommended reading and occasional video viewing. Some of the recommended books, particularly some of the spine books, reflect the philosophy described above. For example, *The Light and the Glory for Children* (providential view of history) and *How Should We Then Live?* (described above) are recommended spine books with a strong philosophical orientation. On the other hand, some of Guerber's history books and *Famous Men of Rome* are among others that are more neutral in their presentation. Since recommended spine books reflect a number of different philosophies, your choices of spine books will be particularly important in determining the tone of your study.

Enough on the philosophy of *TQH*. Let's get back to how they are structured. First, all *TQH* guides are available in either print or e-book format. Topical sections are further divided into subsections that address important people or events within a time period. For example, the section on The Roaring 20s has an introduction with a list of general resources. This is followed by subsections with their own resource recommendations on topics such as the Scopes Trial; Eric Liddell and the 1924 Olympics; Prohibition, bootleggers, and gangsters; women's suffrage; baseball and Babe Ruth; Charles Lindbergh; Bessie Coleman; literary authors; scientists; music; and sports. You won't have time to cover every topic with real books, so it makes sense to either use a spine book for broad coverage along with a few narrower topic books OR use as many topic books as you can reasonably get through and forgo efforts to cover very many topics.

Scattered throughout each book are a number of ThinkWrite exercises. These are writing assignments that require students to analyze the historical information they have learned from a worldview perspective. For example, ThinkWrite 5 in *American History for Young Students* says, "Please tell us your thoughts about America winning the Revolutionary War. How did Amerca's Big 2 Beliefs shape the war? Do you think you can see God's hand in it?" (p. 91). ThinkWrite 6 in the *Renaissance* volume asks, "What do you think Henry VIII's actions reveal about his Big 2 Beliefs? What would it have been like to live under a king who held those beliefs?"

These questions are not intended to solicit only objective information. They require children to make spiritual and practical connections. However, they also tend to support the philosophy of these guides. As long as you are aware of this and agree with Michelle's philosophy, this is not a problem. If you disagree, then you might want to come up with your own ThinkWrite questions. Suggested responses to the ThinkWrites at the end of each book should help parents evaluate student work.

TruthQuest History has collaborated with A

Journey through Learning to create customized resources that help reinforce learning while providing hands-on and creative activities. Three downloadable PDF packages are available for each *TQH* guide. The first one, *AJTL Binder Builder for TQH* helps students create a fancy lapbook with lots of mini-booklets. The second, *AJTL Notebook for TQH,* provides notebooking pages for students to record information on most topics about which they are reading. *AJTL Map/Timeline/Report Package for TQH* includes maps, a timeline, historical figures to color, timeline markers, mini-timeline cards, and various report forms. These are optional, and you may choose one package or all three of those designed to accompany each guide.

You will have to watch the level of difficulty in these guides. The three *American History* books are suggested as starting places for children in the primary grades. That does not mean they are only good for the primary grades since recommended books within these guides are for all levels up through grade 12. However, all the other guides shift to a higher level in their ideas and presentation. The publisher's website suggests all the other guides as ideal for grades 5 through 12. However, these guides also include book recommendations for all grade levels. The TruthQuest History website has an extensive discussion about how you might select the appropriate guide(s) to use at www.truthquesthistory.com/howtochoose.php. Note that you would probably not want to substitute the *American History* guides for *The Age of Revolution* guides since the latter cover the same time spans as the *American History* guides (including the same book recommendations) while also adding the study of Europe. American History is also covered at a much deeper level in *The Age of Revolution*.

My impression is that all except the *American History* guides will work across the entire span of grade levels as long as parents are judicious about how much information they give to each child—don't overwhelm the young ones, and *do* give the older ones plenty to work with. Ultimately, parents need to decide which assignments as well as which books to use with each child.

• • • • • • • • •

The Ultimate Geography and Timeline Guide

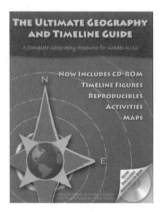

by Maggie Hogan and Cindy Wiggers GeoCreations, Ltd. PO Box 51 Cheswold DE, 19936 800-426-4650 email: contact@ brightideaspress.com www. Geomatters.com or www.BrightIdeasPress.com $39.95

Maggie Hogan, author of *Hands-On Geography*, and Cindy Wiggers of Geography Matters have combined their wisdom and experience to put together this resource book for teaching geography to children in grades K through 12.

It takes a little time to explore the wealth of options found here. The first section, "Planning Your Destination," suggests basic teaching methods, describes notebooks that students might create, and recommends basic supplies. Chapter two is sort of a primer course in geography—hopefully a refresher for most of us. It covers basic terminology and concepts, including the five themes of geography identified by the national standards group for geography. Hogan and Wiggers show you how to incorporate the five themes into your studies. Next is a section on maps: different types, how to use them, map games, and more. All this is in just the first of six units!

The second unit focuses on fun, games, and food as tools for teaching and enjoying geography. Here's where you can learn about letterboxing, geocaching, and trucker buddies—all of which sound like great fun.

Unit three teaches you how to teach geography through other subject areas. This is especially important since Hogan and Wiggers are unit study fans and see the inclusion of geography as an important element of such studies. To help you get into unit studies, the authors include two complete unit studies, one on volcanoes and one on the book *Hans Brinker or the Silver Skates*. At the end of this section are tips on teaching geography through the internet, including a list of great websites.

Unit four presents what most people think of as the nuts and bolts of geography: lesson directions and data on geographical features, climate, vegetation, etc. Lesson ideas are divided into those for middle school and those for high school.

Reproducible maps and activity sheets for games, weather reports, research and other activities described in this book comprise the next two sections. The final unit is all about creating a timeline and includes hundreds of reproducible figures created by Liberty Wiggers to use for your own timeline.

A CD-ROM that comes with the book has PDF files of all the pages you are likely to want to print, including timeline figures, game cards, vocabulary lists, maps, worksheets, record keeping pages, and much more.

An especially fun feature of this book is the "Who Am I?" game that uses the reproducible pages of game cards. In addition to all this, the book includes an answer key, glossary, an index (very useful with a book such as this), and lists of additional resources you might want to use.

In my opinion, this approach to geography will be far more interesting than a standard text on the subject. The fact that one book does it all for every grade level makes it even more appealing.

Science

Let me pose a few questions about your own experience learning science before we begin with reviews and recommendations. First, did you enjoy science classes when you were in school?

If you are like most people, your answer is, "No." That was probably because you primarily learned from a textbook. Almost every textbook for the elementary grades takes the same mile-wide, inch-deep approach to science. They cover numerous topics but not with enough depth or interest to encourage curiosity or a love for science. At high school level, it switches to another extreme: vocabulary and memorization ad nauseam. High school texts stay focused on one subject but only provide depth through tons of dry factual information. Both approaches are a real turn-off to science.

On the other hand, if you are one of the few who found science enjoyable, what was it about those classes that made the subject enjoyable? I suspect the reason is that your teachers did not stick with the textbooks. You learned science by really digging into a topic, perhaps doing experiments or activities that made it fascinating.

Unfortunately, forgoing textbooks is a challenge for those of us who love the security of a textbook that boils a subject down to predictable, manageable, and measurable information. So how do we get past this problem?

Science can be an intimidating subject unless you develop a proper perspective. Science, in terms of Christian education, means the study of God's creation, its purposes, its functioning, and its beauty. We sometimes limit our idea of science education to memorization of plant structure, the names of bones, the periodic table and other such laborious data without seeing beyond to God's purposes for each aspect of creation. Obviously, we do not have a total understanding of all of God's purposes, but even with our limited understanding we can develop a sense of awe for God's creative genius that has nothing to do with the labels we have come up with for his creation.

It seems to me that it is more important for children in the early elementary grades to develop an appreciation for God's creation—our bodies, the earth, plants, animals, the weather, and so on—than it is for them to begin memorizing details. Doing this does not preclude children learning some of the vocabulary of science, but it shifts the emphasis. Field trips, experiments, observations, and nature collections are all likely to generate interest in science. I believe that these activities should continue to be a major part of the science curriculum for all ages.

I also believe that attention to vocabulary and acquisition of facts become more important around eight to ten years of age. For those trying to use a classical approach to education, think of this as part of the grammar stage. You want children to develop foundational knowledge and skills in science, but you begin by making it interesting so children more easily acquire the knowledge and skills.

Consequently, I propose the following goals for teaching science for elementary levels (kindergarten through sixth grade):

1. Turn children on to science so they develop inquiring minds
2. Expose children to many topics in science
3. Teach children the foundations of scientific method—orderly thinking as well as forming, testing, and evaluating hypotheses

In my opinion, using science textbooks is not the best way to meet these goals. Instead, you can turn your children on to science by teaching them to observe, experiment, read, and think about the things that surround us.

Why do they find pill bugs under rocks? Why can they "see" their breath when it's really cold outside? Children are naturally curious about the different areas of science but not usually according to the textbook's scope and sequence. It is far better to respond to an area of interest with an immediate internet search, trip to the library, field trip, or an experiment that gives a child the information he or she is seeking.

If you limit science to a textbook, you will be missing "teachable moments" that are right in front of you. Although textbooks try to introduce a variety of topics each year at elementary levels, they have no way of predicting what will interest each child. Textbook authors cannot know that your family is taking its first trip to the ocean this year and that you want to explore seashells and ocean life in conjunction with that trip. They cannot know that your family just adopted a puppy and your children need to learn all about dogs. They cannot know that your family finally bought a house with a backyard and this will be the year to learn all about gardening. It is much better if you and your children choose your own topics for science study that relate to your particular interests and activities.

Scientific method is a vital part of science education, but we seldom equate it with the sense of wonder and curiosity that children have. When children look beyond the surface appearances and ask, "Why did that happen?" they are beginning to apply scientific method. Scientific method begins with observations and questions. It continues when you work with your child to form possible answers and ways of testing those possibilities. This is real science, but it is the sort of thing that cannot be easily controlled and explained via a science textbook—you might end up spending too much time on one topic and not get through all of the chapters. Horrors!

However, when you choose your own topics and allow more time to cover fewer topics, you will be able to follow the rabbit trails your child discovers into areas you might not have had on your agenda. This is the sort of learning that inspires great scientists. Think of Thomas Edison tinkering with all of his experiments and inventions, most of which came to nothing in themselves.

The time he spent following his own rabbit trails, learning what did not work, ultimately contributed to his amazing successes.

So How Do You Know If You're Doing Enough?

Even if you are willing to abandon the textbook approach, many parents feel insecure determining at what level their children should be working on a science topic. Does making a model of the body's systems equally satisfy the learning needs of both a seven-year-old and a twelve-year-old? Probably not.

Kathryn Stout's *Science Scope* (Design-A-Study, www.designastudy.com) helps you identify appropriate activities for different age groups within each science area. This is an extremely useful resource. Divided into four main areas—general science, life science, earth science, and physical science—it lists specific topics under each heading and suggests methods for use with students at various levels. This makes it much easier to select appropriate resources for topical science studies.

What To Do?

At high school, the course of study for required for college entry restricts science to fewer topics. For the elementary grades I suggest choosing only three or four science topics per year, taking into account the general topics you feel should be covered as well as your children's interests. Then use information books, experiment and activity books (such as those listed under the "Anything But a Textbook!" section in this chapter), and field trips to put together an interesting study for each topic. You can enhance textbooks for high school level by supplementing in this same fashion.

I can just imagine some parents reading what I've just written and saying, "Oh, great! I've got to go make it all up myself. Forget it!" Those of you who don't delight in creating your own courses can take heart. Others have done it for you. They have chosen one or just a few topics, found some real books that make the subject interesting, come up with activities or experiments, and put it all together in one place to make it easy for you to teach science through topical unit studies. If you are using a larger unit study that encompasses many subject areas, you are likely to find this approach to science already incorporated into your unit study.

It is impossible to narrow science resources down to "the best" while simultaneously covering all possible science topics. Therefore, the Top Picks for science reviewed in this chapter are representative of a wide range of useful resources. My Top Picks also represent a mix of resources that support my own approach to science as well as other more traditional approaches. Bowing to the fact that at high school level most parents are concerned about meeting requirements for lab courses that fit the widely used categories—biology, chemistry, and physics—I also review resources for those specific courses.

I hope that just thinking about possibilities will help you figure out what you might want to use with your own children. If you still need inspiration:
- check out the science section on my website at www.CathyDuffyReviews.com
- investigate the offerings of science specialty sources such as those listed under the "Science Beyond Books" section in this chapter
- check homeschool resource distributors' stores, catalogs, and websites—most of them

feature a stimulating assortment of fun and fascinating science resources.

"Anything But a Textbook!"

If you agree with my philosophy of science education, then you will probably be looking for real books on particular topics rather than textbooks. Many publishers specialize in heavily-illustrated, visually-appealing topical books. These are the kind of books children will pick up to read on their own. Some examples of this type of book:

- *Animal Lives* series (Teacher Created Resources)
- *The Awesome Forces of Nature* series - intermediate level (Raintree)
- *Blood and Guts* by Linda Allison - study of human anatomy and physiology (Little Brown and Co.)
- *Castle, Cathedral, City, Mill, Pyramid*, and *Underground* by David Macaulay - these cover both science and history (Houghton Mifflin)
- *DK Eyewitness* books and DVDs (DK Publishing)
- *The Magic School Bus* series: *Inside the Human Body, Inside a Hurricane, On the Ocean Floor, Lost in the Solar System* and other titles by Joanna Cole (Scholastic)
- *National Geographic Kids* series (National Geographic Children's Books)
- *The New Way Things Work* by David Macaulay (DK Publishing)*See How They Grow* series - great for very young children (DK Publishing)
- *True Books* series (Children's Press)
- *The Visual Dictionary of the Human Body* (DK Publishing)
- *The World of Science* (My Father's World/ Master Books joint edition) - see review in this chapter
- *What's Under the Sea, Why Do Tigers Have Stripes?, See Inside Your Body, The World of the Microscope, What's Chemistry All About?*, and many more titles (Usborne Books)
- *Zoobooks* - outstanding picture books with text available in magazine (subscription) or book formats (www.zoobooks.com)

This list is only a very small sampling of what is available. Don't forget to include field guides, biographies of famous scientists, and historical fiction about scientific discoveries. Field guides start to seem essential when you concentrate on particular topics. If you study birds, then you become curious about the species that you see in your area. The same thing happens with flowers, trees, rocks, and other topics—observing them closely makes you want to know more about them. I like the series of guides from Peterson and from Audobon Society best, but look for simpler guides if you start with young children.

As far as biographies and historical fiction, you will find plenty of choices at the library and from homeschool distributors. I've included a few such titles here to get you started.

- *Alexander Graham Bell: Setting the Tone for Communication* by Mike Venezia (Children's Press)
- *Archimedes and the Door of Science* by Jeanne Bendick (Bethlehem Books)
- *Albert Einstein, Young Thinker* by Marie Hammontree; *Thomas Edison, Young Inventor* by Sue Guthridge; *Wilbur and Orville Wright* by Augusta Stevenson; and other titles (all from the Childhood of Famous Americans series from Aladdin)
- *Benjamin Franklin* by Ingri and Edgar Parin D'Aulaire (Beautiful Feet Books)
- *DK Eyewitness Books: Great Scientists* by Jacqueline Fortey (DK Publishing)
- *Galen and the Gateway to Medicine* by Jeanne Bendick (Bethlehem Books)
- *The Mystery of the Periodic Table* by Benjamin D. Wiker (Bethlehem Books)
- *Pasteur's Fight Against Microbes* by Beverley Birch (Barron's Educational Series)

Science Beyond Books

Don't limit yourself to books. Science kits, equipment, games, DVDs, and software can help get your children excited about science.

Absolutely crucial are hands-on experiences with science. Many programs have experiments and activities built into them. Sometimes supplementary experiment and activity books supply the magic ingredient that draws children into science. I particularly like resources that pose questions and stimulate thinking rather than those that simply outline steps in an experiment or present an experiment for "entertainment" without any exploration of what is happening.

Again, most homeschool distributors usually carry these types of resources. But there are a few companies that specialize in science and have catalogs or websites devoted just to science "stuff." Some of the best of these companies are:

- Home Training Tools - 800-860-6272, www.HomeTrainingTools.com
- Nasco - they also have specialized catalogs for art and math - 800-558-9595, www.enasco.com/science/
- Nature's Workshop, Plus! - 888-393-5663, www.naturesworkshopplus.com
- Tobin's Lab - 800-522-4776, www.tobinslab.com

Curriculum

Some science programs are similar to unit studies, combining a variety of activities and resources for topical science study. Media Angels books, Noeo Science, *A History of Science*, and Living Learning Books are among resources reviewed below that fit this description. They vary in the amount of information they include, sometimes sending you elsewhere for resource material. This type of curricula best reflects my own ideas about how children should learn science. For parents who want to use a more traditional approach, I have also included a few such resources.

• • • • • • • •

Apologia Science series for Junior and Senior High Levels

by Dr. Jay L. Wile
Apologia Educational Ministries
1106 Meridian Plaza, Suite 220
Anderson, IN 46016
888-524-4724
email: mailbag@highschoolscience.com
www.apologia.com

Dr. Jay Wile is the primary author of most of Apologia's *Exploring Creation* science curricula for junior and senior high. These Apologia courses are among the few options for college-prep lab science courses that do not require a parent to teach the courses. Another factor that makes them popular is their very reasonable cost.

Apologia offers courses for general science, physical science, biology, chemistry, and physics. Among them are both standard courses and supplemental ones that provide the equivalent of Advanced Placement (AP) courses. I appreciate the options that accommodate a range of student goals—from the non-science oriented student who just wants the basics through the ambitious, college-bound student who wants AP level courses. Some courses also offer choices of lab experiences to provide more activity for ambitious students or more limited options that might fit a family's limited financial resources.

Most courses are available in your choice of traditional textbook or CD-ROM versions. Textbook courses come as two-volume sets ($85 per course). The first book is the hardbound student text with color illustrations. The second book is a softbound solutions and tests manual with complete answers and explanations for questions from the student book as well as for the tests. Step-by-step instructions for lab experiments appear in each chapter alongside the concepts they illustrate.

CD-ROM versions ($65 per course) contain all the textbook and solutions manual content plus multimedia video clips, animations, pronunciation guides, and other helpful tools. They also have nifty indexing so you can simply click on an index entry to go to that topic in the correct module on the CD.

Students who benefit from auditory input might prefer to listen to the textbooks being read aloud. You can purchase CDs with MP3 files with the complete student text content read aloud for each of the courses ($19 per course). Students still need the print textbook to read along with or refer to as they study and complete their work.

Most courses also have an optional Multimedia Companion CD-ROM available for those who select the textbook version of one of these courses. These CD-ROMs have only the extras not already contained in the textbook ($19 per CD per course). Icons in the textbook alert students to available video clips they might want to pull up on each CD-ROM.

Since lab work is often a challenge for home educated students, Apologia is developing optional "Experiment Only" DVDs for the high school level courses. Check the publisher's website for availability.

A Christian worldview permeates these courses. Dr. Wile brings in not just creationist views, but also other scientific issues and ideas in relation to Christianity (e.g., geocentric versus heliocentric viewpoints).

All of these courses were written for independent study. Dr. Wile's conversational style of writing makes these texts much easier reading than most others. He speaks directly to students, assuming they will be working through the courses on their own—a realistic expectation in most families. Brief information for parents or teachers is at the beginning of the solutions and tests books. Free support is available via email, phone, fax, and snail mail.

Students who need more oversight or outside prodding might want to enroll in one of the internet courses based on these texts. Apologia has information about such courses in their catalog and on their website.

In student textbooks, the text font is large compared to other science texts, but this makes it easier to read and less intimidating. (That also means there has to be slightly less content than in an equivalently-sized book with smaller type.) Books are divided into modules which are similar to units—each module is divided into a number of topics and activities. Within each module are "on your own" questions and problems. Students are to answer these as they proceed through each section, and answers can be self-checked within the textbook. At the end of each module is a study guide that has questions and problems. Answer keys are in the solutions and test book for each course. Students also need to keep a separate lab notebook to record observations and conclusions from their experiments.

All textbooks have glossaries and indexes plus other helpful tools such as the periodic table and lists of the elements and their symbols. At the beginning of the book are lists of lab materials needed. Dr. Wile specifies lab materials that, for the most part, can be found at grocery and hardware stores. However, the biology and chemistry labs do require some more specific equipment like a scale, microscope, and test tubes. Using some non-traditional lab equipment means students will not be familiar with all of the more complex scientific equipment, but this should be a small liability given the practical advantages of these type labs. Lab equipment and resources for high school level courses are available from Apologia.

Exploring Creation with General Science and *Exploring Creation with Physical Science* are junior high courses targeted at grades seven and eight. *Exploring Creation with Biology, Exploring Creation with Chemistry,* and *Exploring*

Creation with Physics meet requirements for high school lab courses. However, Apologia also offers advanced courses in biology, chemistry, and physics that, combined with the corresponding foundational course, cover the content of AP courses.

The advanced courses are titled *Advanced Chemistry in Creation, Advanced Physics in Creation, Advanced Biology: The Human Body, Fearfully and Wonderfully Made,* and *Exploring Creation with Marine Biology* ($85 per course). These are similar in format to the foundational texts, but *Advanced Physics* is illustrated only in black and white. CD-ROM versions of all of the advanced courses are planned but only *Advanced Biology* and *Marine Biology* are available as I go to print with this book in 2012. (Note I have not reviewed *Advanced Chemistry, Advanced Physics,* or *Marine Biology.*)

Exploring Creation with General Science

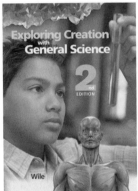

This is a broad general science course for junior high students that includes a significant amount of lab work. The course is set up in 16 modules that should take about two weeks each to complete.

Topics covered include the history of science, scientific method, how to perform experiments, simple machines, archaeology, rocks, minerals, fossils, geology, paleontology, evolution and interrelated theories (uniformitarianism and catastrophism), living organisms, organisms and energy, classifications, and the human body. A new student notebook that can be used with this course should be available by Fall of 2012.

Exploring Creation with Physical Science

This large, 490-page text is the foundation for the most user-friendly, yet academically challenging physical science course for homeschoolers of which I am aware. It qualifies as a lab course with extensive experiments and recording activity. In fact, Dr. Wile begins the first lesson with an experiment. He carefully details how to perform the experiment as well as the expected results. He describes possible corrections if it's not working as it should. Then he uses the results as a platform to provide a basic explanation of molecules, atoms, and chemical reactions.

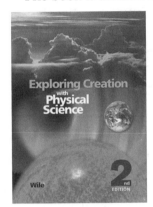

The book is divided into 16 modules, each of which should take about two weeks to complete. Topics covered include air, atmosphere, water, the hydrosphere, earth and the lithosphere, weather, motion, gravity, electromagnetic force, electrical circuits, magnetism, atomic structure, radioactivity, waves and sound, light, and astrophysics.

While the content is appropriate and challenging, it is not as difficult as some physical science texts. For example, in discussing chemical bonds, it addresses overall positive and negative charges without going into valences as do some physical science courses.

A new student notebook that can be used with this course should be available by Fall of 2012.

Exploring Creation with Biology

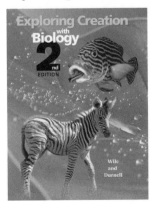

Dr. Wile coauthored this text with Marilyn F. Durnell. It is very similar in format and presentation to the *Physical Science* course. While it is traditional in its approach for the most part, it does not include study of the human body. Instead, human anatomy and physiology are covered in a separate course, *Advanced Biology: The Human Body*. Students preparing for AP exams or wanting to list an AP course on their transcript need to complete both courses.

Clear explanations present concepts in a friendly fashion without oversimplification. Questions provoke thought rather than just recall of information.

With this text, lab activity becomes more demanding, although you have a choice about how much of it your student needs to complete. There are three levels of lab activity: household labs require minimal equipment and should be completed by all students; optional microscope labs require a microscope and slide set (kit available for $316); dissection labs are also optional, but the dissection kit is only $55. Instructions for all labs are found in the text.

Exploring Creation with Chemistry

This text covers essentially the same content as most high school chemistry courses. Algebra 1 is a prerequisite. While Dr. Wile assumes that the student has this math background, he does do some math review.

The text presents concepts and guides students through practice exercises before leaving them to work on problems. Solutions to test questions include the math work, so students weak in math can figure out what they might have missed. This sort of help is very rare in chemistry courses. Dr. Wile has done a great job constructing lab activities with low-cost equipment while providing enough experience for a solid college-prep course. The labs are exacting in detail, achieving a great deal of precision with minimal equipment. Apologia sells a Chemistry Glassware Set for this course ($60)

that provides the basic equipment you need. All the chemicals you need are available at the grocery, drug, or hardware store. However, the second edition of the text for this course has added optional extra lab work for which you need to purchase a "secondary lab set" ($157) that includes more specialized chemicals.

One negative point: chemicals are frequently introduced by formula but not by common names. This seems odd in a text that is generally good at making practical connections for students. However, Dr. Wile explains the reason for this: "When you introduce every chemical with its name, the student is quickly overwhelmed by the names and thus ceases to remember them. Therefore, I only introduce the names of practical chemicals that the student will encounter in everyday life. As a result, the student remembers the important names and does not get overwhelmed with chemical names he or she will never encounter."

Apologia's *Advanced Chemistry* course combined with this foundational course is equivalent to an AP chemistry course.

Exploring Creation with Physics

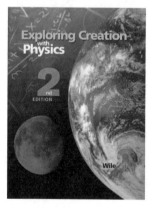

This course will be quite challenging for students who attempt to work independently unless parents are knowledgeable and can help from time to time. However, it is still a good course for the student who does not intend to take much science in college. Coverage is adequate but not as complete as in some other high school physics texts. For example, there is no treatment of the properties of matter, heat transfer, atomic and nuclear physics, relativity or quantum physics. (Such topics are covered in some, but not all, high school level physics courses.) These shortcomings not withstanding, Dr. Wile's casual and illustrative prose goes a long way toward helping both teacher and student grasp inherently difficult subjects.

Lab activities are fairly simple for a high school physics lab course. Lab experiments seem to be designed to illustrate principles more than to provide opportunities for serious scientific work. Nevertheless, this course will satisfy most college entry requirements for a physics course with lab.

Science oriented students should consider adding Apologia's *Advanced Physics* course. Together the two courses are equivalent to an AP course.

This is a math-based course; prerequisites are algebra and geometry up through beginning trigonometry. However, the math is not overly complex, and example problems are worked out in clear and thorough detail. A primer on the subjects of conversion of units, scientific notation, and measurement precision is available for free by mail or on the internet in case students need to review these topics.

Apologia offers a Video Instruction DVD ($140) that might make this course more practical in some situations. The DVD (which plays only on computers that can handle .wmv files and open PDF files) features more than 20 hours of lecture and presentation of experiments. It also has printable notes from the lectures. It does not replace the print or CD-ROM textbook.

Advanced Biology Course - The Human Body: Fearfully and Wonderfully Made

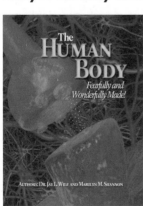

Dr. Jay L. Wile co-authored this text with Marilyn M. Shannon, M.A.

Many parents will want to cover human anatomy and physiology as part of their teen's biology instruction even if students do not intend to take the AP exam. However, be forewarned that this is a challenging course with some content (especially the large amount of vocabulary to be learned) more likely to be encountered in a college course rather than a high school course. That's why it is suitable for AP test preparation!

Along with the student text and the solutions and tests book, students will need a microscope (available through Apologia for $262), a set of prepared slides ($73), a dissection specimens kit (cow's eye, cow's heart, and fetal pig) ($44), and *The Anatomy Coloring Book* by Kapit and Elson. All of these resources are available through Apologia. If students opt not to do all the lab work, they should still purchase *The Anatomy Coloring Book* since it has far more detailed illustrations than does the text. As with other Apologia courses, students need to keep a separate lab notebook.

Although this is a very challenging course, it is designed such that students can complete all work independently. The publisher recommends it for twelfth grade but says it can also be used from tenth grade on if students have the prerequisites—first year courses in both biology and chemistry.

(Note that a new edition of *Advanced Biology* is due out in 2013. It will use the *Kaplan Anatomy Coloring Book* by McCann and Wise rather than *The Anatomy Coloring Book* by Kapit and Elson.)

• • • • • • • • •

Behold and See Science series

Catholic Heritage Curricula
PO Box 579090
Modesto, CA
95357
800-490-7713
www.chcweb.com

Catholic Heritage is developing a beautiful series of science textbooks for homeschoolers that features solid science content and plenty of hands-on activity.

Books for grades 1 through 5 are available thus far, with a sixth grade book in the works. While *Behold and See 4* is an older book now in its sixth edition, all the other books were published in 2010-2011. Books are written by different authors and they differ in style quite a bit. Books for grades 1 through 4 are self-contained, each in a single, spiral-bound worktext, while *Behold and See 5* has two soft-cover books. All books except *Behold and See 4* and the workbook for grade 5 are printed in full color. Each course has an answer key—at the back of the worktext for grades 1 through 4 and at the back of the workbook for grade 5.

Many lessons include hands-on activities that are an important part of the learning process. You should really try to complete all of them if possible.

Books are written from a Catholic perspective and include scripture references. They present a strong belief in God as Creator, a pro-life position, and an attitude of love and concern for people as well as the environment. Within the "Note to Parents" at the beginning of *Behold and See 3* is a summary of official church teaching regarding evolution. The author follows with comments that point out a few of the unproven claims of evolution. Aside from an indirect comment in *Behold and See 5* mentioning millions of years in regard to geological movements, I could not find evolution discussed in the textbooks themselves.

The entire program is relatively easy to use. Activities and experiments require some pre-planning and supervision. Parents should plan to teach these texts rather than use them for independent study. Overall, this seems to me one of the best science programs for Catholic families.

Behold and See 1 and 2
$26.95 each

The first two books are co-authored by Nancy Nicholson and Mary Piecynski. The books share a similar format featuring two children, Josh and Hanna, who interact with their parents and each other in story dialogues throughout the books. Much of the scientific information is imparted within the stories but some is presented in a more traditional fashion.

Behold and See 1 is subtitled, *On the Farm with Josh and Hanna*. The text follows through each season on the farm as they learn about seeds, plants, mammals, weather, reptiles, fish, birds, vertebrates, invertebrates, skeletons, exoskeletons, evergreen and deciduous trees, insects, and spiders. The final chapter shifts to the human senses. You will need to complete about two lessons per week to finish this text in one year.

Each lesson includes an activity. This might be a worksheet, a cut-and-paste activity, an experiment, a drawing, or something similar. Many activities for first graders aim at developing observation skills. Toward the end of the book, students record data from experiments as they begin to apply scientific method.

This book does not require much in the way of experiment supplies, and they are listed in a box at the beginning of each lesson. Some supplies you will need are a magnifying glass, seeds, soil, plastic wrap, dry oats, and magazines or catalogs with pictures of various types of leaves. The only challenging item might be the suggestion that you catch or purchase crickets to observe and keep as pets.

Behold and See 2, subtitled *More Science with Josh and Hanna*, shifts into the physical sciences with lessons on tools, machines, and energy. It also studies the water cycle, natural resources, conservation, erosion, the earth, rocks, volcanoes, the ocean, and marine life. The reading level is actually a little easier than the first grade book; students might be able to read parts of the lessons, although they should not try to work independently. There are more experiments and they are more complex than in the first grade book. You will find some of the standard types of experiments such as testing the qualities of different types of rock and construction of a baking soda and vinegar volcano. There are a few activities that use foods. I particularly like the one for modeling the creation of sedimentary rock with raisins, coconut, nuts, graham cracker crumbs, butter, and other ingredients. Children do only a little more writing at this level.

Behold and See 3
$44.95

Behold and See 3, written by Suchi Myjak, is intended to be used as a general introduction to science. It begins with a chapter about the nature of science and scientific method, introducing the foundational concept that science is the study of God's creation. The remaining nine chapters are divided into groups of three under the headings "Physical Science," "Life Science," and "Human Body." Physical science covers matter, force, energy, the sun, the moon, and the stars. Life science teaches about animals, plants, and interdependence. The section on the human body begins with a correlation between the parts of our bodies and Christians as members of the Body of Christ. This is followed by an overview of body systems, the senses, and nutrition and health.

This book is loaded with investigations and experiments. Many of these use an inductive approach, leading students through an experiment and their observations to arrive at conclusions or generalizations. For example, students construct a simple balance with balloons on each end to try to answer the question, "Does air have mass?" Each chapter ends with a substantial section of review questions and a beautifully illustrated page for students to write pertinent scripture verses.

Behold and See 4
$24.95

Subtitled *Human Anatomy and Health,* this book was originally published in 1998 and is now in its sixth edition. The current 2009 edition is up-to-date and includes website addresses for investigation of some topics.

There is quite a lot of overlap in content with the last third of *Behold and See 3*. The first half of this book covers body systems while the second half teaches about nutrition, health, and first aid. *Behold and See 4* was written by Katherine Rode, R.N. and Dr. Mary Ann Grobbel, and the content is presented quite differently than the content of the third grade book. Even so, I would be unlikely to use these two books one right after the other because of the repetition.

Behold and See 4 has fewer activities, although it does include patterns for creating a child-size body with a skeleton and some of the organs. The book directs you to "make organs" using felt pieces that you sew together and stuff with batting. (The skeleton and ureters are only one layer of felt.) All of these are then to be sewn onto a cardboard outline of each child. You could simplify this project by using construction paper (and overlapping organs) and glue if the sewing is intimidating.

The two halves of the book were each written separately by one of the authors, and they are presented quite differently. The first half seems much more interesting—this is where you find the hands-on activities. Both sections have vocabulary lists. In the first half, vocabulary words are accompanied by their definitions. In the second half, definitions are in a glossary at the end. The first half includes optional Suggestions for Supplemental Activities for each section. Review activities for the first half are a series of word puzzles, a few activity sheets, and a Jeopardy type game. Many questions at the end of the chapters in both sections require full sentence responses.

Behold and See 5
text - $36.95, workbook - $10.95

Behold and See 5, by David Beresford, Ph.D., takes a large step up in the amount of content and the level of difficulty. It addresses a broad range of topics but selects a narrow subtopic within each one, providing a more in-depth study than one usually finds in books for fifth grade. For example, chapter 3 is titled, "Food Webs, Resistance to Disease, and Conservation of Energy. While information throughout the chapter is interrelated, eleven pages focus specifically on the pesticide DDT under the subtopic heading, "Immunity in Insect Populations and Making Wise Choices." Using the story of DDT, graphs, charts, and data, it helps children (and adults!) understand how creatures can build up immunities or resistance, how improper use of pesticides or other control measures can create unintended consequences, and generally teaches them to think through the complex interactions. Of course, this lesson applies far beyond the story of DDT. Chapter 6 in this text is titled, "Logic: Deduction, Induction, and Scientific Reasoning." While this chapter directly teaches about logic and reasoning, the entire book applies it.

Among other topics covered are metamorphosis, photosynthesis, the circulatory system, competition among plants and animals, seasons, atmosphere, the weather cycle, the earth and its composition, genetics, and taxonomy.

I found this text very interesting to read, even as an adult. Some fifth graders might find it challenging, but Dr. Beresford has done an excellent job of presenting complex ideas with stories, photos, examples, and diagrams that make it understandable.

The text is a non-consumable 226-page book. The 115-page student workbook includes experiment data sheets, written activity sheets, review questions, tests, and answer keys.

Behold and See 6

I was able to preview the sixth grade book, although it is not yet complete. *Behold and See 6* is written by RoseMary Johnson B.A. in collaboration with Dr. Richard P. Olenick, Nancy Nicholson, and Mary Catalano B.S. This gorgeously illustrated text is much larger than the others at 350 pages. The student workbook will be 125 pages. The text is written as conversations rather than direct presentation of lesson material. This makes it much more interesting to read. It will include experiments, activities, and website addresses for further exploration.

The text has three units focusing on physical science, biomes, and space respectively. As with the fifth grade text, topics are narrower than in traditional texts, and the authors explore each area more expansively. The result is high level science that is enjoyable to read.

Summary

Catholic Heritage Curricula has done a great job of enlisting experienced scientists to write in an engaging manner about topics they obviously love. Even with their diverse approaches, the entire series is excellent.

· · · · · · · · ·

Science series, third editions

BJU Press
Greenville,
SC 29614
800-845-5731
www.bjup.com
homeschool kit -
$157.50 for each
level

If you want a traditional style of textbooks for science in the elementary grades, BJU Press's series is one of the better choices. Recognizing that children have different learning styles, they have incorporated activities to suit different learners.

Both textbooks and activity manuals are attractively printed in full color with plenty of illustrations. BJU Press sells the same editions to both schools and home educators, so you will sometimes have to adapt activities that expect that you have a class group.

Scientific thinking is heavily stressed with the scientific method introduced at first grade level. Scriptural principles are incorporated with science applications in the curriculum.

Activities are at the heart of many lessons

rather than being presented as optional—especially at the early grade levels. Most activities are outlined in the teacher's editions but data recording and some activities are done from the activity manual. That means these courses need to be taught—you cannot just hand your child the text to use independently.

Each grade level has a homeschool kit that includes the student text, teacher's edition, an activity manual, answer key for the activity manual, tests, and an answer key for the tests. You need all components unless you choose not to test your children. You will still need to gather resources for experiments and activities.

The teacher's editions are well organized and easy to use. All except the sixth grade course include a CD-ROM Teacher's Toolkit in the back of the teacher's edition that will run on either Windows or Mac systems. Toolkits include reproducibles, rubrics, extensive science fair information, and similar resources—most of which are optional.

Each chapter has a number of lessons and concludes with a review lesson to reinforce concepts taught throughout that chapter. Chapters are also color coded so you can easily tell which lessons are included within a chapter in both the text and activity manual.

These courses require lesson preparation and presentation time, but if you follow the lesson plans in the manuals, you and your children should find the courses very engaging.

While courses are written for specific grades, you can use one level for children over a two- or three-year span of grade levels with a little adaptation to suit their abilities. (It will be most challenging to do this for first and second graders who are still developing reading and writing skills.) Courses are challenging enough that when you stretch to cover a range of grade levels, you should probably choose a level below that of your oldest student.

Grade 1 kit

The text for first grade covers the following topics on an introductory level: senses, weather, seasons, health and safety, wild and tame animals, matter, sound, plants, "pushes and pulls", and the sun, moon, and stars. The Teacher's Toolkit CD-ROM includes sound files that are used with some lessons.

Grade 2 kit

Topics taught in second grade include the nature of science and basic science methodology, living things, plants, fossils, earth, natural resources, how the earth moves, light, matter and how it changes, movement, and the human body.

Grade 3 kit

Topics at this level include cold-blooded and warm-blooded animals, plants, ecosystems, matter, sound, energy in motion, soil, rocks, minerals, weather, the solar system, and the human body.

Grade 4 kit

In grade 4, students study living things, insects, spiders, forces and machines, electricity and magnetism, light, the moon, water and oceans, weathering and erosion, the earth's resources, bones and muscle, and digestion.

Grade 5 kit

Topics studied in fifth grade are minerals and rocks, fossils and dinosaurs, matter, energy and heat, weather, biomes, ecosystems, sound, light, the respiratory system, and the circulatory system.

Grade 6 kit

Sixth graders study earthquakes and volcanoes, weather and erosion, natural resources, cells and classification, animal classification, plant classification, atoms and molecules, electricity and magnetism, motion and machines, the stars, the solar system, plant and animal reproduction, heredity and genetics, the nervous system, and the immune system.

• • • • • • • •

Christian Kids Explore series
by Stephanie L. Redmond
Bright Ideas Press
PO Box 333

Cheswold, DE 19936
877-492-8081
email: info@brightideaspress.com
www.brightideaspress.com
$34.95-$39.95

I like the balance of information and activity in the *Christian Kids Explore* science series. Rather than grade level specific books, each of the four books in this series might be used with children spanning at least four grade levels.

All four books are divided into a number of units, with multiple lessons per unit. These books are ideal for use in two 90-minute block sessions a week rather than shorter, more-frequent classes. This gives children enough time to get into the activities and think about the concepts. Working on this schedule, you should be able to complete one book per year.

While parents or teachers will need to do some lesson preparation, it is minimal for the first two books and very manageable for *Chemistry* and *Physics*. Lessons are laid out so clearly that these courses should be very easy to use. There are numerous activity pages within each book that you are welcome to reproduce or print from either CD-ROMs or downloadable files for your family. Students should each maintain a three-ring binder in which they keep all of their science work.

At the back of each book are answer keys plus lengthy lists of recommended resource such as books, DVDs, computer games, multimedia resources, and kits that you might use to supplement your studies or challenge older students. You don't have to use other resource books, but each study will be much richer for students if you use some of the colorful picture books available on the different science topics.

Since the *Christian Kids* books are printed only in black-and-white, this might be especially important for some learners.

All of these courses include learning activities that help meet the needs of different learning styles—hands-on activities for the Wiggly Willys, interaction for the Sociable Sues, predictable vocabulary study and testing for Perfect Paulas, and independent reading for Competent Carls.

Christian Kids Explore Earth and Space and Christian Kids Explore Biology

Christian Kids Explore Earth and Space and *Christian Kids Explore Biology*, both written by homeschooling mom Stephanie L. Richmond, are very similar in design to one another. Both books target grades 3 through 6 but can be used selectively with children as young as kindergarten—especially the hands-on activities. However, *Biology* is slightly more challenging than *Earth and Space*. While two ninety-minute sessions per week are best, you can break lessons down into more frequent lessons for younger students with shorter attention spans.

Both *Earth and Space* and *Biology* have optional downloadable student activity books (available only as downloadable files for $7.95 each) with reproducible student pages that you can print from your computer. These pages include "Review-its," wrap-ups, activity and experiment forms, and coloring pages.

The first session each week is "teaching time." It begins with reading and discussing the information from the text. Students complete a Daily Reading Sheet, write words and definitions for their vocabulary list in a notebook, and possibly work with flashcards. Younger students might do less writing, and older students need to do extended reading or research from real books and other resources from the lists provided at the back of each book.

The second session is "hands-on time" for experiments or activities. These don't require expensive or exotic materials, but it will take a little work to gather the necessary items. For example, *Earth and Space* requires items like clay, a funnel, sun-sensitive paper, an atlas, a globe, vinegar, baking soda, chewing gum, and a paper plate. For *Biology*, among resources you need are pipe cleaners, a magnifying glass, old T-shirts, face paints, and alligator stickers.

There are also some artistically-created coloring pages—one per unit. Colored pencils are the perfect medium to use for these. The book also has numerous black line illustrations that children might color.

Vocabulary words, timeline entry items, and lists of materials needed are at the beginning of each unit. Each unit concludes with a quiz. *Biology* also includes a writing assignment at the end of each unit while *Earth and Space* suggests either a writing assignment or creation of a "folderbook" (directions in an appendix).

Other reproducible pages in the appendices include a Field Trip Journal form, "Checking it Out" experiment form, "Write About It!" worksheet for unit wrap-up composition, maps, scripture memory cards, recipes, supplemental activities such as word searches, and numerous other worksheets pertaining to the lessons.

A biblical worldview is presented throughout both books and is reinforced by scripture memory cards. Unit 2, lesson 3 of *Earth and Space* advances a creationist/young earth perspective, although it does present the broader context of scientific disagreement as well as disagreement among Christians. Most recommended resources for the lessons are secular and present alternative explanations. In *Biology*, the first lesson advances a creationist perspective, although it takes no position on the age of the earth. However, recommended resource books tend toward a young earth position.

Christian Kids Explore Chemistry and Christian Kids Explore Physics

The next two books in the series are similar to each other, and both differ in format from the first two books. *Christian Kids Explore Chemistry* and *Christian Kids Explore Physics*

were written by Robert W. Ridlon, Jr. and Elizabeth J. Ridlon. They are both recommended for students in grades four through eight, and the level of content is more advanced than in the first two books. There are significantly fewer reproducible student activity pages, and the coloring pages in these two books are limited to a smaller selection in an appendix at the back of each book.

Christian Kids Explore Chemistry is more than a simple introduction to chemistry. In 356 pages, the authors cover the basics of chemistry, including some topics often reserved for high school courses. But they do so in a way that is very understandable for younger students. They use a conversational style and familiar examples to which children can relate. While you might occasionally find topics like "covalent bonds" that are beyond your fourth or fifth grader, most of the presentation is so clear and concrete in the way it is taught that most students will understand AND enjoy the lessons. You might even use this if you've got a high schooler who struggles with chemistry.

The book begins with lessons on matter, measurement, elements, mixtures, compounds, atoms, molecules, the periodic table, mass, and atomic number. Then it advances into chemical bonds, formulas, names of compounds, acids, bases, and chemical reactions. The next section deals with states of matter, and the final section gets into organic chemistry.

While older students might read the lessons directly from the book on their own, you will want to at least read the lessons to younger students, perhaps paraphrasing or skipping difficult sections as needed.

Following the lesson information is a "Review It" section with fill-in-the-blank questions that depend only upon listening and comprehension at this point. You should photocopy or print out these pages as well as those for unit reviews, worksheets, and coloring pages.

"Think About It" questions that come next in most lessons might be used as follow-up for a hands-on activity, or they might require written work or discussion. These challenge students to understand and apply some creative thought to the lessons. Each unit concludes with a "Unit Wrap-Up" test.

At the beginning of each unit you will find a list of objectives, vocabulary words, and materials needed for all activities for the unit. Materials are mostly common household items, with the exception of things like styrofoam balls, Alka Seltzer, and safety glasses for *Chemistry;* and a stopwatch, various types of balls, and a horseshoe magnet for *Physics*.

Hands-on activities are used to reinforce or help teach each lesson. These are frequently experiments but sometimes they are things like building models of molecules, creating cards for elements of the periodic table, completing observation forms, doing word searches, or coloring pages.

The second editions of both *Chemistry* and *Physics* each include a CD-ROM in the back of the book that has printable lesson plans, all reproducible student pages ("Review-its," wrap-ups, activity and experiment forms, and coloring pages), materials lists, and a bonus literature study guide for a science-related biography. Literature study guides offer substantial activities—written work, discussions, and hands-on activities—but they are an optional part of each course.

Although the books are intended for a Christian audience with occasional scripture verses in the sidebars, I found only scattered references to God, and they were so generic that the books should be fine for any family who shares a belief in God as Creator. It would be very easy for parents or teachers with other beliefs to use these books with very minimal adaptation.

The CD-ROM for *Chemistry* includes a literature study guide for Joyce McPherson's biography of Blaise Pascal, *A Piece of the Mountain*. While the rest of the study has minimal Christian content, this book centers around the spiritual life of this great thinker.

Christian Kids Explore Physics has 405 pages divided into six units on the foundations of physics, matter, mechanics, matter in motion, energy in motion, electricity, and magnetism.

The relatively simple activities and experiments should be appealing, although some of the math (used in only a few activities) will be challenging for younger students. Examples of the activities include: creating atomic models, determining the volume of a solid, observing balloon expansion and contraction in various temperature settings, plotting trajectories for a tennis ball rolling off a table, calculating bicycle wheel speed, and creating a compass. Simple household items are used for most of these. The optional literature study for *Physics* is based on the book *Ben Franklin of Old Philadelphia* by Margaret Cousins. This study takes a secular approach.

Those with earlier editions of *Chemistry* or *Physics* can purchase the downloadable content of the CD-ROMs (those that come packaged with new editions of the books) for either course for $9.95.

• • • • • • • • •

Exploring Creation Young Explorer Science Series (Grades 1-6)

by Jeannie Fulbright
Apologia Educational Ministries
1106 Meridian Plaza, Suite 220
Anderson, IN 46016
888-524-4724

email: mailbag@ apologia.com
www.apologia.com
books - $39 each, notebooking journals - $24 each

At first glance, the Apologia *Exploring Creation Young Explorer* books look like standard hardcover textbooks for the elementary grades. They're nicely printed with full-color illustrations. But the focus on a narrow area of science for each text and the methods of lesson presentation make these significantly different from standard texts.

The *Astronomy*, *Botany*, and *Human Anatomy and Physiology* volumes, with 176 pages each, address only those topics, digging much deeper into each than is possible in a typical textbook that aims to cover many different topics. *Zoology 1* teaches about flying creatures (birds, bats, flying reptiles, and insects) in its 240 pages. *Zoology 2* covers only creatures that live in water (235 pages), while *Zoology 3* (288 pages) tackles various orders of land animals including reptiles, amphibians, spiders, insects, worms, gastropods, and dinosaurs.

The Young Explorers series is clearly Christian in outlook, continually reaffirming God's role as creator. Occasionally, evolutionary beliefs are addressed directly, but these texts mostly take a positive approach of teaching truth rather than attacking evolution.

Author Jeannie Fulbright writes as if she is chatting with her children, so the writing style is very conversational and personal.

This series uses an "immersion approach," emphasizing depth over breadth with information, activities, writing, field trips, experiments, and other avenues to immerse the student deeply into each topic. Students gather enough information on each topic to begin to appreciate science, ask deeper questions, and look for applications.

Regarding methodology, Charlotte Mason's ideas are most evident in the use of narration. Periodically, after a section of text there will be a narration prompt written in italics such as "Explain what you have learned about flight muscles and birds in flight" (*Zoology 1*, p. 61). You might even want to prompt for narrations more frequently than does the text.

"What Do You Remember?" questions at the end of each chapter help to assess whether or not children are grasping the information. Parents can require students to write out answers or respond orally. Answer keys are at the back of each book.

To keep things interesting, the text is also broken up with "Try This!" activities. These are generally fairly simple activities in contrast to the full-fledged experiments with data recording and the projects that come at the end of each chapter. Two of the projects for each course are actually term projects. Term projects as well as some of the other experiments and projects are quite involved, but they don't require esoteric resources. Lists of the necessary resources are at the front of each book, shown chapter by chapter, making it easy to plan ahead. Types of resources are matches, wires, empty soda bottles, red food coloring, plaster of Paris, plants, glycerin soap bars, and a pinecone. At the front of each text is a reproducible "Scientific Speculation Sheet" to be used for applying scientific method and recording experiment information.

One other unusual aspect of this course is the creation of a notebook. Students can either use an Apologia Notebooking Journal or a binder to collect their notes, drawings, and records of experiments, projects, and field trips. Since the text tries to address the needs of students from grades K through 6, notebook activities are frequently suggested under separate headings for younger and older students.

Notebooking Journals are hefty (about 200 pages each), plastic-spiral-bound books that actually become the student's notebook. While it is certainly fine if you want to create your own notebooks with resources from the website and elsewhere, these Notebooking Journals make the process much easier.

The Notebooking Journals include a number of activities and resources for each lesson. Four sections directly support essential textbook material and activities. "Fascinating Facts" provides space for students to write a "narration" of information from the lesson. "What

Do You Remember?" reprints the review questions from the text, allowing space for students to write their answers. The notebook assignments, activities, and projects in the text are supported with template pages in the journal. In addition, there are "Project Pages" for recording observations and other information, as well as for inserting photos from activities and experiments within the text. The other "tools" in the journals include scripture copywork pages; vocabulary crossword puzzles; cut-and-fold miniature books printed in full color and in which students can write key information; "Dig In Deeper" assignments that expand lessons with additional experiments, activities, research, recommended reading and multimedia resources; field trip sheets for recording information about each trip; and a 50-question final review for the entire course. These extra tools, including the final review, are all optional. Use whatever is useful and then remove the pages not being used from each student's journal so they are left with their own personalized notebook.

Younger students with less developed writing skills should probably use the new Junior Notebooking Journals for each course. These require less writing, have fewer crossword puzzles with vocabulary that might be too difficult, and omit the written review questions and final reviews. They add two more coloring pages per lesson and primary-level writing lines to make the shorter writing assignments easier.

The resulting notebooks, whether the standard or junior versions, will have much more content than could be compiled into a lapbook. If you would rather have children create lapbooks, both Knowledge Box Central (www.knowledgeboxcentral.com) and A Journey Through Learning (www.ajourneythroughlearning.com) sell lapbooks that correlate with these textbooks. (Check either website to see what lapbooks look like.)

The intended audience is probably my biggest area of concern with the textbooks. The books are written at a reading level well beyond that of children in the primary grades. The texts include Latin and scientific names, sometimes including explanations of word derivations. There seems to be even more of this in *Botany* and *Zoology 1* than in the other books. While this should be fine for students in the middle grades, it might be too much information for younger students. Personally, I would probably start with the Astronomy text if my children were on the younger end of the spectrum, then follow with *Botany*, then with the lengthier *Zoology 1, 2,* and *3* books. Parents will likely read the text aloud to younger students, while older students can do much of their reading and work independently.

An added bonus with each course is a password to a dedicated website with extra helpful tools for each course. This information is provided in the front of the book with your course instructions.

Watch for forthcoming audio book CDs for each of the *Young Explorer* courses. These will soon be available as downloadable files, MP3 files on CDs, or audio CDs.

Overall, there is more activity and variety in these courses than in traditional textbooks. The format makes it easy for parents to provide an excellent balance of information and activity that should be very effective for science instruction in the elementary grades.

• • • • • • • •

God's Design Science

Answers in Genesis
PO Box 510
Hebron, KY 41048
800-778-3390
www.answersingenesis.org
$89 for each set of three courses (set
= 3 student books with 3 teacher
supplements), $299 for the entire series

When I first reviewed the original editions of the *God's Design* science series for grades 1 through 8, I was not very excited about them. However, the third editions (2008-2009) were totally redesigned with significant content improvements, resulting in an outstanding program.

There are four groups of books within the series. There are three textbooks in each group with a teacher supplement for each text that includes a resource CD-ROM with all of the printables, tests, and quizzes.

Titles for each of the four groups are:
• *Life: The Human Body, The World of Plants, The World of Animals*
• *Heaven and Earth: Our Planet Earth, Our Weather and Water, Our Universe*
• *Chemistry and Ecology: Properties of Matter, Properties of Atoms and Molecules, Properties of Ecosystems*
• *Physical World: Heat and Energy, Machines and Motion, Inventions and Technology*

You can purchase the books in sets for each group—the three texts plus the three teacher supplements or as a complete set of all the books.

There are a number of features that set these books apart. First, the books are ungraded—both "Life" and "Heaven and Earth" groups are designated for the entire range of grades 1 through 8 while "Chemistry and Ecology" and "Physical World" groups narrow to grades 3 through 8. If your children are in the early elementary grades, you should start with either of the first two series, saving the latter two for the upper elementary grades or junior high.

According to the authors, you might complete any of the groups of three texts in a single school year. With three books per group, you would complete three lessons per week, spending about 20 minutes per lesson for younger students and 45 minutes per lesson for older students. The books are approximately 150 pages each, so I would recommend to families with younger children that they take their time and use only one or two books per year, allowing time for further exploration when they hit topics of particular interest.

Each of the 12 student textbooks has a teacher supplement book with a CD-ROM that serves as the teacher guide and answer key. The philosophical and theological information at the front of the supplement—a must read for teachers—is critical for understanding the unique perspective and design of these textbooks. The CD-ROM contains PDF files with worksheets for some of the lessons—some are required as part of the expanded activities for older students. Many of these are data recording sheets or other means of recording observations. The CD also has quizzes for each unit and a final exam.

Brief teaching instructions are also found at the beginning of each textbook. They point out the color coding system used to indicate lessons and activities targeted for younger and older students. Older students generally are given more information and expanded, more-challenging activities to complete in addition to (or sometimes in place of) the lessons and activities completed by younger students.

The books in this series all reflect a Christian worldview, including a young-earth view of creation. Contrasts are made between evolution and creationist views when pertinent to the topic, especially in the texts related to life science and earth science.

Hands-on experiments and activities are built into every lesson. These are worthwhile and relate well to the topics. The activities and experiments include step-by-step instructions and are designed to teach scientific method as children observe, record information, discuss, and form conclusions. Lists of supplies needed for each lesson are in the teacher supplement for each text. Supplies are generally not too difficult to obtain, although it does vary from book to book. *The World of Plants* requires things like yellow gelatin, bean seeds, flower bulbs, corn meal, dried moss, and bread slices—fairly easy items to find. Heat and Energy is a little more challenging, requiring items like copper wire, iron filings, steel BBs, a compass, and a magnifying glass. Even the chemistry books mostly use easily available items like Epsom salt, ammonia, and rubbing alcohol. Rarely, the supply list also mentions a reference book that you will need such as a tree field guide to be used with *The World of Plants*.

Activities are followed by a "What did we learn?" section. These are just a few key questions for the teacher to ask to ensure that students understand the main points of the lesson. Suggested answers are provided in the teacher supplement.

Next is a "Taking it further" section with questions that will help children extend their thinking to draw some conclusions or make additional connections or applications.

Interesting biographical sketches of scientists and inventors plus articles on special topics such as chemotherapy, artificial islands, and rattlesnakes appear sporadically.

At the end of each book is a unit final project. These often encompass many topics covered within other lessons, so you should check out the unit project before beginning and consider having your child start work on the project early in the school year. They can then add to it whenever it seems appropriate.

Textbooks are printed in full-color with numerous, high-quality illustrations and excellent graphics. The publisher has also made good use of color to highlight different portions of the lesson, making it easy to spot sections to be used with different students.

These features make this series a practical choice for Christian homeschooling families as well as for classroom teachers in Christian schools. However, there are a few issues that you might want to consider as you use this series.

Textbooks are written to address a very wide age span. Even with the delineation of sections appropriate for older and younger students which help a great deal, I have some concerns. Many sections of text are dense with new vocabulary. Even following the guidelines of which material to use with each age group, you might find that some children will have a hard time just listening to and absorbing so much detail. For example, in the second lesson in *Our Weather and Water* (on the structure of the atmosphere) the text reads, "The earth's atmosphere consists of 78% nitrogen, 21% oxygen, and 1% other gases including hydrogen, helium, argon, and carbon dioxide. This combination of nitrogen and oxygen is the ideal atmosphere for life. Nitrogen is a relatively nonreactive gas. Its purpose in the atmosphere appears to be to dilute the oxygen. If the oxygen concentration was more than 21 % fires would easily burn out of control." Note that within just these few sentences, you are introducing a number of vocabulary words and concepts unfamiliar to most children: the various chemical elements, the idea of percentages, nonreactive gases, dilution, and the relationship between oxygen and fires. This quote is from a section for students in grades 3 through 8. The above sentences might sound like gibberish to young students. For this reason, I urge you to use discretion as to which sections of text to read with young students. Sometimes you might need to explain lesson material so that students can grasp concepts.

As I read through some of the lessons, I thought that I would very likely use the experiments and activities as the basis from which I would present the lesson information rather than presenting information first. If younger children can see and touch things as they are learning they will be able to understand better than if they are listening to what (to them) sounds like abstract information. For example, in *Our Planet Earth*, a lesson on identifying different minerals includes experiments for children to identify four or five minerals themselves. I'd have the minerals on hand and would talk about their different characteristics for identification while the children compared and tested the different samples. This might help solve the problem I mentioned regarding information overload.

Overall, I like this combination of information with experiments and activities plus questions to ensure understanding. The variety of activities effectively reaches children with different learning styles.

· · · · · · · · ·

A History of Science

by Rebecca Berg
Beautiful Feet Books
1306 Mill St.
San Luis Obispo,
CA 93401
800-889-1978
www.bfbooks.com
guide: print
version - $13.95
or downloadable
file - $11.95,
complete package - $149.95,
complete package without *The New Way Things Work* - $119.95

A History of Science is a guide for a literature-based introduction to science for children in the elementary grades. The guide takes students through a number of real books for a one-year study.

The complete package includes *The New Way Things Work*, *The Picture History of Great Inventors*, *Explorabook*, *Along Came Galileo*, *Archimedes and the Door of Science*, *The Story of Thomas Alva Edison*, *Albert Einstein: Young Thinker*, *Marie Curie's Search for Radium*, *Ben Franklin of Old Philadelphia*, *Pasteur's Fight Against Microbes*, *Scientists Card Deck*, *A Science*

Experiment Pamphlet, *A History of Science Time Line*, and the guide. These are almost all items that I would recommend to you even aside from this particular study!

A collection of five *Your Story Hour* audio CDs ($20 for the set) are also recommended materials, although these are not essential.

Lessons start with *The Picture History of Great Inventors*, a colorful picture book along the lines of so many of the Usborne books. It's strictly introductory in content. I suspect you will need to provide extra explanation for some of the pictures with younger children. This book serves as a "spine book" throughout the study—start here then branch off into more depth on different topics. The selected biographies in the package make this very much a "story approach" to the history of science.

Explorabook, *A Science Experiment Pamphlet*, and seven activities at this back of the Beautiful Feet guide combine to provide substantial hands-on activity. (Note that *Explorabook* will soon be going out of print and be replaced by a different resource.)

In addition to completing activities and reading, students record information in a science notebook they create, color pictures provided in the *Time Line* kit and place them appropriately, do additional research in an encyclopedia, copy related scripture verses into their notebooks, create and label sketches, and do reports and presentations. Of course, you will need to choose activities appropriate for the ages and abilities of your children.

This is a wonderful introduction to science. It teaches some basic principles, but even better for children in the elementary grades is that it connects science to people and real life in fascinating ways.

· · · · · · · · ·

Living Learning Books

Sandi Strenkowski
112 Heather Ridge Dr.
Pelham, AL 35124

205-620-3365
email: info@livinglearningbooks.com
www.livinglearningbooks.com
Individual units: teacher's guides $6.50
each, student pages - $5.50 each;
bundle packs: see website for prices;
Chemistry (print or e-book): teacher's guide
- $30, student activity pages - $12 each

Many home educators like the idea of using real books for science, but they find it difficult to turn the real books into lessons that ensure students are actually learning the information. Living Learning Books accomplishes this by incorporating narrations and adding questions, writing assignments, technology, vocabulary work, and hands-on activities to reading from beautifully illustrated books that are each devoted to a single topic. The curriculum provides parents with an effortless way to coordinate all of this into unified studies appropriate for grades K through 6. The emphasis is on teaching a child how to pursue information about a given topic through various media rather than spoon-feeding via traditional textbooks.

The three original books in this series made my first list of 100 Top Picks. These books were *Life Science, Earth Science and Astronomy*, and *Chemistry*. Of the original books, only *Chemistry* remains available. However, author Sandi Strenkowski has begun development of a series of individual units that is replacing the first two books of the original curriculum. The new version of Living Learning Books presents the curriculum as a wide variety of individual units, allowing parents the flexibility of selecting the units most appropriate for or most interesting to their child(ren). This approach still gives parents the ease and security of structured lesson plans, projects, and notebooking assignments but more flexibility on content. Each unit contains a teacher's guide and student pages.

The curriculum is available as either individual units or in bundles of related topics (at a slight discount) such as vertebrates, plants, and astronomy. Individual units are only sold as PDF downloads. Bundle packs are available as either downloadable PDFs or in black-and-white preprinted packets. Downloadable versions offer several benefits over their print counterparts. They are in full-color, so you can print full-color notebooking pages if you own a color printer. You are able to select only those pages that appeal to your child and print them as many times as you wish for your immediate family. But for those who don't mind the lack of color and prefer not to print themselves, the print format curriculum is the way to go. Pre-printed pages are three-hole punched, ready for placement into a binder for creating a notebook that will hold student pages, narrations, experiment observations, and other pages created through the course.

The new Living Learning Books units are not just a redesign of the original three books. These are newly written units. Thus far there are five units under "vertebrates," two units under "growing things," and four units under "invertebrates. More will be available soon. Inexpensive core texts have been selected—most are from Crabtree Publishing. These core texts are available individually or bundled for each broad topical area. However, the titles are also widely available at public libraries.

Each individual unit contains an average of ten days of lessons. The author recommends doing science two or three days per week so a single unit will provide you with an average of three to five weeks of study. The publisher's website explains how many days of study are in each unit. To make this your complete science curriculum, simply choose enough units to round out your school year.

The Living Learning Books curriculum supports a multi-faceted approach to the study of any topic, which includes the use of weblinks. While many resources provide website addresses in their printed versions, outdated links cannot be corrected until the next printing. To avoid this, Living Learning Books curriculum has chosen to support every unit with a wide selection of kid-friendly, educational weblinks (including some to videos) that can be accessed directly through the Living Learning Books website. All of the links have been screened for appropriate content and are regularly updated. (Access to the links is free to everyone.) The student pages in the units include forms for children to write about websites they have viewed which helps develop research skills.

In addition to the internet component, Living Learning Books has developed an Amazon site that makes it easy to locate additional materials such as books, stickers, craft kits, games and other resources to enhance any unit study. The materials are conveniently organized by topic.

The layout for each unit has been completely revised from the original books, making them much more attractive and easy to use. While many pages are created with full color, you can print in black and white without losing anything critical.

The teacher's guide contains lesson plans, project ideas, and answer keys for all of the student pages. There is a single answer key for each unit rather than answers imbedded into the lesson plans. Charts show weekly lesson plans at a glance. In addition, lesson plans are scaled for teaching children of different ages at the same time. Projects are presented in an easy-to-use fashion with complete instructions and checklists for planning.

The student pages have a wide variety of activities appealing to students of varying ages. "Reading Review Questions" worksheets can easily go into their notebooks. There are also student pages for reports—graphic organizers, report starters, and attractively formatted writing pages. Among other activity pages are some with space for drawings, puzzles, beautifully drawn coloring pages, and formatted pages for writing vocabulary words and definitions. There seem to me to be more coloring pages and an overall improvement in the artwork from the original volumes. Lists of vocabulary words are included in the lesson plans for each week whereas the first two of the original books left it to you to create your own vocabulary lists. Units conclude with reading and activity logs and an optional quiz geared for grades 4 through 6.

The books and units are written without scriptural or religious references. However, on the website there is a lengthy list of scripture quotes arranged by topics which anyone may access. In her introduction pages, Strenkowski urges parents to confront and study the question of evolution, but she does not address it herself within the curriculum.

I mentioned that *Chemistry* from the original series remains available—the full title is *Level 3: Chemistry*. This book was different from the other two original books and it differs from the individual units. *Chemistry* substitutes experiments and activities for reading because of the nature of the topic. Very few elementary level books are written on the topic of chemistry—fiction or non-fiction. In this course, children learn mostly by doing, although some reading material is included in the student pack pages. This level is recommended for grades 3 through 6.

In *Chemistry* lessons, students read or listen to the short introductory passage, conduct an experiment, record results of the experiment, review the reading passage, copy key words and definitions into their binders, and complete unit review pages. Children start to learn scientific method at this level, although the focus is primarily upon observation and comprehension rather than analysis. Parents will need to plan ahead to gather supplies for the experiments. Although activities don't require expensive or complicated equipment, it will still take some time to round up everything you need. I especially like the teacher guide pages. A left-hand column shows correlated student pages, reference pages in two Usborne and Kingfisher books that might be used, and a list of project supplies.

As you know, I liked the original Living Learning science courses, but the new, individual units make a great curriculum even better.

· · · · · · · · ·

Media Angels Science

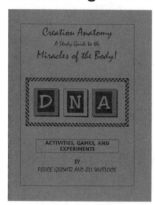

Media Angels
15720 S. Pebble Ln.
Fort Myers, FL
33912-2341
email: felice@
mediaangels.com
www.mediaangels.
com
all guides reviewed
here (print or
downloadable
versions) - $18.95 each

Media Angels publishes science unit studies as well as a guide to creating your own such studies. The guide, *Teaching Science and Having Fun!* is optional, but I will begin with it for those who prefer creating their own studies, especially those who are interested in science experiments and labs in the home.

Teaching Science and Having Fun!
by Felice Gerwitz

Felice Gerwitz provides detailed science scope and sequence for grades K through 12 while also explaining how to create either topical studies or comprehensive unit studies based upon science topics. She stresses the importance of knowing and applying scientific method at all grade levels, emphasizing the vital role that experiments play in learning scientific method. Because of this, Felice offers extensive suggestions for creating lab activities for high school level science where they are required, including lots of budget-conscious substitutes. She adds extensive resource lists with commentary so that you can use them to flesh out your courses.

Rather than attempting to offer complete course outlines, *Teaching Science and Having Fun!* addresses the big picture—Why teach science? How do you teach children of differing ages? What topics do you need to cover? Gerwitz also addresses problem areas such as what kind of microscope to buy. This is a very inspiring, practical, and helpful resource for teaching science to children of all ages.

The educational philosophy of this book is reflected in all Media Angels science books.

Creation Science Study Guides
by Felice Gerwitz and Jill Whitlock

This is a series of unit study guides titled, *Creation Science: A Study Guide to Creation, Creation Anatomy: A Study Guide to the Miracles of the Body!, Creation Astronomy: A Study Guide to the Constellations,* and *Creation Geology: A Study Guide to Fossils, Formations, and the Flood!*

This series very much reflects what I think science education should look like with its combination of real books, experiments, and other interesting activities that truly engage children in the study of science.

Each study should take about six to eight weeks to complete. The guides are set up for multi-grade teaching with activities divided into levels for K-3, 4-8, and 9-12.

These are actually unit studies that stretch beyond science, although they do not provide complete coverage of any of the other subjects. Activities for each level are divided under the headings of Science Activities and Experiments, Geography/History, Reading Ideas List, Vocabulary/Spelling List, Vocabulary/Spelling/Grammar Ideas, Language Arts Ideas, Math Reinforcements, and Art/Music Ideas. Science receives the most attention, with a good deal of background information for the teacher included in a Teaching Outline section in each guide. Read through this section in each guide before you begin to teach the unit.

Lots of extras are included in each guide although these vary from guide to guide. The newest editions have added complete lesson plans and extensive, annotated bibliographies of resources on each topic. The suggested books are a mixture of non-sectarian and Christian titles.

I want to particularly highlight *Creation Science: A Study Guide to Creation* since this is a unique course that might be foundational to your other science studies. The first part of the guide presents information to support a young-earth, creationist viewpoint as well as the problems with Darwinian theory. Lessons include study of the book of Genesis along with activities, reading, and investigation. While younger students might participate in hands-on activities (like experimenting with a prism) that help them learn about God's creation, older students might create an experiment to demonstrate sedimentary erosion (p.65) or "Write an argument against the earliest people being unintelligent, slow, and not very clever" (p. 118). Or you might read aloud as a family a book such as *Noah's Ark and the Ararat Adventure* by John Morris with up-to-date information about clues to the location of Noah's ark. This is a great study for the whole family to enjoy together.

All of the guides are loaded with activity suggestions—hands-on activities, experiments, reading, research, and writing. However, I think you will also want to use the Experiment and Activity Packs that complement the books. These, too, are available in either print or downloadable PDF files for $12.95 each. While there are separate packs for each of the *Creation Astronomy* and *Creation Anatomy* books, there is a single pack to be used with both *Creation Science* and *Creation Geology*.

These packs feature reproducible pages of activities and experiments with step-by-step instructions, questions, games, puzzles, a glossary, and more. Many of the pages are suitable for students to use to create notebooks. Experiments are most appropriate for the elementary grades up through junior high since they do not require any of the mathematical analysis necessary for high school courses. Activity instructions in the packs are fairly well spelled out—they are much more than lists or outlines of suggestions.

For both the guides and the packs you need to plan ahead to determine which activities to do and what resources you will need. All studies are presented from a young-earth perspective and rely on a literal interpretation of the Bible. Otherwise, the religious perspective is generically Christian rather than Protestant or Catholic.

· · · · · · · · ·

Noeo Science Curriculum

Noeo Science
7020 Barbuda Drive
Fort Collins, CO 80525
email: inbox@noeoscience.com
www.noeoscience.com

For years I've advocated avoiding traditional science textbooks and, instead, choosing fewer topics to cover using real books and experiments. Obviously, more and more homeschoolers agree with me since publishers are increasingly putting together courses that fit this description. However, I think Noeo Science has done the best job yet! You'll see why as you read on.

Courses are available for three levels. Level I courses target grades one through three, level II courses are for grades four through six, and level III courses are to be used in grades seven through nine. It should take one school year to complete each course. The titles of the eight volumes in the series and their prices (as of the printing of this book) are:

- *Biology I: Seeds, Scales, Feathers, and Tails!* $143.59
- *Chemistry I: Bubbly, Sticky, Bouncy, and Icky!* $165.22
- *Physics I: Zip, Zap, Zing, and Zoom!* $157.27
- *Biology II: Worms, Beans, Germs, and Genes!* $134.94
- *Chemistry II: Atoms to Alloys and Beyond!* $150.06
- *Physics II: Gizmos, Gadgets, Gears, and Gravity!* $155.70
- *Chemistry III: It's Elementary!* $211.42
- *Physics III: It's Forceful!* $160.18

You might have noticed that all courses are titled *Biology, Chemistry,* or *Physics.* Some science topics such as geology, weather, and astronomy overlap these three areas of science, so they are included at points within chemistry, biology, and physics where they fit most appropriately.

It doesn't really matter which order you use the volumes for each level. Choosing the most appropriate level is more important. However, you might easily shift a student at one end or the other of a level into a lower or higher level if it helps consolidate your teaching of more than one child together. While the titles of the books might sound similar, the content at each level changes to cover different topics within biology, chemistry and physics (as well as other areas of science) so that students will have a broad and thorough science education after completing a few levels of these courses.

Noeo Science has taken its name from a Greek word meaning "to understand." The first page of the introduction to each book reminds us that, "The essence of science is simply observing and describing God's creation. When scientists make a new discovery, they are seeing another part of creation revealed….

[Our children] should … be immersed in the sciences so that 'His invisible attributes, his eternal power and divine nature' will be clearly seen." So the curriculum is designed with lots of experiments and hands-on activity rather than in a traditional format.

The author describes the curriculum's approach as "mostly classical" with elements of Charlotte Mason and unit studies, although it seems to me that the latter two approaches dominate.

Each volume of Noeo Science targets a narrow range of topics under the general heading of biology, chemistry, or physics. For example, *Biology I: Seeds, Scales, Feathers and Tails!* covers weather, bacteria and fungi, sea life, amphibians, plants, insects, birds, and the human body. Despite the number of topics, extensive time is spent on narrower subsets of each of the above topics, using real books, observations, and experiments—all hallmarks of unit studies.

Charlotte Mason's influence is seen in the use of real books, the use of narration (oral and written), drawing, and creation of a notebook. While children learn some vocabulary, the curriculum does not rely on the memorization typical of many science courses, and neither does it use typical worksheets and tests. That doesn't mean students do no writing. Reproducible forms in each volume are used by students for notebooking, drawing, recording data from experiments, writing definitions, and taking notes. Samples of completed student pages are included in the instructor's guide to assist parents. (Note: The reproducible pages are also available for free download at the website.)

For each course, the key component is the instructor's guide that comes in a spiral-bound book. Each instructor's guide consists primarily of lesson plans that are laid out for each week in chart form for easy reference. They list the pages in books to be read, experiments to be completed, optional experiments or optional websites to explore. Notes at the bottom tell you when students need to makes notes or drawings for their notebooks or provide a narration.

Each instructor's guide also has a fairly brief explanation of how the curriculum works, the aforementioned reproducible pages, lists of required books and experiment kits, and a master supply list of items needed for other experiments and activities.

Noeo Science sells the instructor's guides with sets of the required books and experiment kits that save you money over buying items individually. However, you can purchase all items separately if you prefer. Experiment kits from the Young Scientist Club are included in levels I and II, while more extensive kits from Thames and Kosmos are used with level III courses. The Young Scientist Club experiment kits (between 5 and 7 kits per course) for younger levels come bundled in boxes for each course rather than individually. It is important to note that the Young Scientist Club Kits have a number of experiments within each individual kit so there's even more here than you might think. Each kit includes its own instruction book plus equipment and supplies for all the experiments. These kits are relatively small and inexpensive, but they do contain some unusual items like a spring scale, glycerol, and a Petri dish. You will need to collect some common household items (see the master supply list in each volume) to use with the kits, but all the difficult-to-get items are provided.

Chemistry III and *Physics III* come with larger experiment kits, each with its own substantial manual. Students are not required to complete every experiment in each kit, but they might enjoy them enough to tackle the optional experiments on their own.

Physics III has two kits. A *Physics Workshop* kit (with all sorts of gears, pulleys, rods, building components, and a battery-operated motor) has 38 workshop projects for students to construct things from the kit. Most workshop projects are accompanied by experiments

in which students use the workshop creation. For example, students build a force scale and type-two lever in a workshop then use it in an experiment to measure forces on a lever. The *Electronic Snap Circuits Kit* used in *Physics III* can be used for building 78 projects for learning all about electricity. *Chemistry III* has one large kit that includes chemicals and lab equipment as well as a complete manual with instructions for 251 experiments.

The books selected for each course are outstanding. For example, *Chemistry II* books are the *Usborne Internet-Linked Science Encyclopedia; Usborne Internet-Linked Mysteries and Marvels of Science; Fizz, Bubble & Flash; Adventures with Atoms and Molecules; The Mystery of the Periodic Table;* and *Geology Rocks!* These are mostly colorful, illustrated books that children will love to explore on their own. Even better, both *Chemistry II* and *Physics II* use the same two Usborne books so you can save on the second course by purchasing a less expensive package that does not include those two books. You will develop a great science library with the books from these courses.

Some parents using level III courses will be concerned about high school requirements. While there is plenty of lab work in both the *Physics* and *Chemistry III* courses, the labs do not require the mathematical measurements and calculations typical of high school level labs. The course material introduces ideas taught at high school level but does not go as far as usual for high school courses. For example, at least two of the books in the *Chemistry III* course—*Eyewitness Books Chemistry* and *Material Matters: Mixtures, Compounds & Solutions* (Raintree)—discuss covalent and ionic bonds, yet none of them fully develop the technical aspect of how atoms bond with each other. Consequently, these courses are perfect for junior high and might serve as introductory courses for ninth graders that would be followed up later with more challenging, math-based chemistry or physics courses.

Each course is laid out for 36 weeks—a full school year. Lessons are provided for four days a week. However, lessons for level I should take only 15 to 20 minutes a day, lessons for level II should take only 20 to 30 minutes per day, and lessons for level III should take 30 to 40 minutes per day. This means that you can easily double up your lessons and do science two days a week in longer sessions since even level III lessons twice a week would require no more than 60 to 80 minutes each. Of course, if students complete optional reading or experiments, that will take more time. In addition, many of the observations, activities and experiments in all of the volumes could be expanded beyond the minimal time required.

Check the website for information on various options for purchasing individual components.

While the author of the curriculum has a Christian worldview, most of the resource books do not. In the introduction the author suggests using encounters with secular or materialist viewpoints in the books as opportunities for discussion rather than skipping over them. I also suggest that since the resource books are your primary source of information, you might want to add discussion about God's design or presence when it seems appropriate.

· · · · · · · · ·

The Rainbow

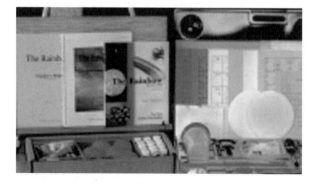

by Durell C. Dobbins, Ph.D.
Beginnings Publishing House, Inc.
328 Shady Lane
Alvaton, KY 42122

800-831-3570
email: dcdobbins@aol.com
www.beginningspublishing.com
complete year 1 - $257, complete year 2 - $150, text - $77, Teacher's Helper - $13, lab workbook - $16

Serious science is coupled with a light-hearted approach and lots of hands-on activity for this two-year course targeted at junior high level. Written specifically for Christian home-schoolers, *The Rainbow* has a beautiful full-color textbook (softcover) and huge lab set with all sorts of interesting items. The course is also unusual because the text is intended to be used for two years. In the first year, students study physics and chemistry, and in the second year they study biology and applied science.

The Teacher's Helper is a guide for the text as well as the labs, covering both years. The first year's lab set includes both durable equipment and consumable supplies plus a lab workbook. For the second year, you need additional equipment, supplies, and a new lab workbook, all of which is sold as a "year 2" set.

I really enjoy Dr. Dobbins personal, friendly writing style, and I think most junior high students will too. Here's a short excerpt to give you the flavor:

So you've given up on dissolving oil and vinegar together without killing people, but you are still convinced you are a smart chemist. So what do you do? Like every other good chemist in the world, you pick up the bottle of salad dressing and shake it really hard, then fret to remove the cap and pour the dressing before it separates again. But unlike the untrained non-chemists, you know the word for what you just did. You created a suspension. (p. 118)

Dr. Dobbins explains concepts simply, frequently relating concepts to familiar experiences such as the above. Each small section has "exercises"—questions that can be used for discussion or written assignments.

The Teacher's Helper outlines a schedule for three days per week for 32 weeks per year.

It also gives the purpose of each lesson as well as section review quizzes, answers, and troubleshooting ideas in case a lab experiment doesn't turn out as it should. A separate lab workbook for the student gives detailed (and often humorous) instructions for the weekly experiment.

The complete kit includes a neatly packaged set of lab materials with everything needed to carry out the experiments including such items as safety glasses, a marble roller assembly, a baseball, resistors, magnets, light bulbs, glass tubing, syringe, PVC tubing, dye, and much more. You could conceivably collect your own materials from the list provided on the publisher's website, but it's such an odd assortment that you would be better off purchasing the kit from the publisher.

If you have more than one student, you will need to add an extra lab workbook. Each lab workbook comes with a pair of safety glasses, an essential item for each student. Other than that, students should be able to work cooperatively on the experiments using what comes in the kit. Those using this program with a larger group need to order multiple kits.

The curriculum is obviously Christian with its numerous references to God. Dr. Dobbins' treatment of the theory of evolution is interesting. He says, "In this text we will attempt to teach the general theory of evolution because a good education in the sciences requires it. We present it as a theory… which we ourselves do not accept" (p. 136). However, it does not seem to me that evolution is taught in this text so much as it is undermined or argued against. Dr. Dobbins does not take a position on the age of the earth. Another sensitive subject might be human reproduction, but it is tastefully and conservatively explained.

Overall, I think this course prepares students with a solid foundation for more in-depth high school level science courses.

· · · · · · · ·

Supercharged Science

presented by Aurora Lipper
www.SuperchargedScience.com
subscriptions: $37 or $57 per month
Science Mastery Programs: Silver $599, Gold $1195, Diamond $1895

NASA rocket scientist, university professor, pilot, and mom Aurora Lipper is dedicated to making science intriguing and fun for children. To that end she has created both online science curriculum and packaged science programs (which include materials and equipment) for grades K through 12. In both the "e-Science" Online Science Learning Program and the Science Mastery Programs, the emphasis is on learning by doing. Hundreds of experiments are available to students in both types of programs. Even better, videos of Lipper demonstrating how to do each experiment allow all but the youngest students to work independently most of the time. However, parents with young children will need to pay attention to safety issues and oversee most experiments to ensure students are using proper procedures and reasonable caution. For parents who might not have a science background themselves, or perhaps don't have the time to teach it, these programs are a welcome solution.

Lipper's specialty is in physics and engineering—not surprising given her background. So there are lots of experiments with electricity, magnetism, mechanics, matter, energy, light, sound, thermodynamics and much more. Chemistry and life science are also covered;

experiments in both beginning and advanced chemistry are now available. While hands-on experiments are the mainstay of both programs, there's much more to Supercharged Science.

Online e-Science Curriculum and Learning Program

Supercharged Science offers the Online e-Science Curriculum and Learning Program with options to suit students in grades K through 12 plus optional "packages" that include all materials for those who would rather not search out all the resources themselves.

One thing that e-Science does better than almost everyone else is use hands-on activities to connect scientific concepts with practical applications in the real world. Experiments use mostly inexpensive, easy-to-find items. Once kids are excited by what they've built or experimented with, the course then introduces the academics. In this way, students have a deeper understanding of the material while enjoying it more than with traditional academic-focused approaches. Lipper explains that she has based this approach on how real scientists work in the real world.

For starters, a monthly subscription fee of $37 a month for students in grades K through 8, or $57 a month for high school students or advanced younger students (at least fifth grade) gives your family access to an amazing number of resources—more than 800 experiments plus enough educational material for at least two to three years of science education. For grades K through 8, you might need nothing more than what is on the website. Sign in on the website, select which lesson you wish to use and let your kids run with it. Science experiments are buttressed with easily-digestible information to convey the key points students should be learning. Quizzes will help you check whether or not that's happening. For high school (or junior high students needing more challenging material), you can access textbook readings, exercises, and quizzes for a

complete course with both academics and lab work. Even with all this, the video presentations and experiments provide an indispensable core. Beginning with a video presentation then completing the experiment is likely to create an excitement and curiosity about science that is difficult to achieve starting with textbook material.

In addition to this, author Aurora Lipper teaches a live tele-class on the computer every few weeks where students in e-Science can connect with her personally. While this component is offered live at a particular time, it is also recorded. Aside from the live tele-class, everything else can be accessed whenever it's convenient for you.

Unlimited support is provided for all students and parents. Whatever part of the course you're using, feedback or advice from Lipper or another expert in the field of science a student is studying is always available by email. There's also a place to share ideas and comments with other parents and students.

A 30-day trial period will allow you to sample the program with no obligation, and costs just one dollar. Even if you decide to enroll, you can still cancel at any time without any obligation. Also, there's no need to enroll for a full year at a time either; you just pay month-by-month with no long-term commitment.

Science Mastery Programs (include materials and equipment)

Science Mastery Programs are offered at Silver, Gold, and Diamond levels and include access to all the online resources for time periods of one, two, and five years, respectively. Each level includes parts and materials for 100 to 600 activities and experiments plus a nearly 200-page experiment manual. Extra kits for more specialized projects (e.g., robotics) are also included, with more such kits added as you move up to the Diamond level. All the video and audio material is provided on DVDs and CDs so you need not be reliant on an internet connection, but you still have both options. The larger programs for Gold and Diamond levels are serious science programs that include everything you need for two to three years of science education.

Supercharged Science takes a secular approach but should not have any content in conflict with religious beliefs. They describe themselves as "creation neutral."

Overall, Supercharged Science has put together some very comprehensive science education programs. Their online e-Science programs give students access to a high-quality curriculum that makes extensive use of hands-on activities and experiments to excite and motivate kids. The price is reasonable for all that you receive. If you want all of the extra parts and pieces too, you may want to consider their Science Mastery programs. Everything they sell comes with a full money-back guarantee and comprehensive technical support.

If you want to try out a free sample of the types of activities contained in these programs, you can download the "Science Activity Manual & Video Series" for free by going to: www.superchargedscience.com/affiliate/401_science_activity_manual1.htm.

• • • • • • • • •

The World of Science

My Father's World/ Master Books joint edition
Order from MFW
573-202-2000
www.MFWBooks.com
$24.99 (discounted to $16.25 by MFW)

The World of Science is a lightly "edited" version of an original pictorial science book published by Parragon Publishing in 2004. My Father's World (MFW) and Master Books

worked with the original publisher to keep this excellent introductory science book in print while also editing out references to and images of early (prehistoric) man and correcting outdated information.

While there are many pictorial science books from publishers such as Usborne and DK Publishing, many of the most interesting ones include controversial information. So it is very helpful to have such a book without such content. On top of that, *The World of Science* is a 248-page, hardcover book that you can purchase through MFW at a very reasonable price.

The World of Science, like many such books, dedicates about half of each page to full-color illustrations. This is the type of book that children (and maybe adults, too) are likely to explore for fun.

The book is divided into seven sections. The first six sections are topical, covering matter and chemicals; energy, motion, and machines; electricity and magnetism; light and sound; earth and life; and space and time. Each section is divided into numerous subtopics, each one presenting foundational information along with examples of real-life science applications, science discoveries, and biographies of famous scientists.

Section seven consists of 40 pages of science projects with illustrated, step-by-step instructions. Many projects are quite simple but some (such as creating a water turbine or making an electric motor) are more elaborate.

MFW includes this book in their *1850 to Modern Times* course for students in grades four through eight, and that grade range would also be my recommendation for this book's audience.

MFW and Master Books have created another similar special edition of *The World of Animals* that I would also recommend to you.

Unit Studies, All-in-One Programs, & Online Courses

This chapter includes some choices that are almost opposite each other in their philosophies of education. Unit studies are generally very hands-on and interactive while many computer-based or online courses such as *Switched-On Schoolhouse* and *Monarch* (reviewed in this chapter) are designed for independent study with most of the work done either on the computer or in traditional style textbooks. In my discussion of online courses on p. 287, I include a list of some online courses that vary in design. Some include live, interactive sessions, and many for younger students require significant parental involvement. While I love unit studies, there are times and situations where computer-based or online courses are the better choice.

Making Learning Come Alive

Traditional textbooks were created for classroom management purposes—not because authors prefer to write them. Too often textbooks are written by committees, warped by state and federal goals, censored by publishers' agendas, written with little sense of style, and boring beyond belief. Of course, there are some exceptions but not many. And even good textbooks reflect a compartmentalized approach to learning. Math stays in one book, while language remains in another. Spelling is in yet another compartment, and literature has to stay separate from both spelling and language.

Real life is not compartmentalized. Unit studies try to make learning more like real life by bringing a number of subjects together around a central theme for study. Unit study themes are infinite. Some follow historical timelines while others form their units around character traits, novels, geography, science topics, scripture, and other themes.

Unit studies can be narrow, topical studies such as a single unit on the theme of horses. In such a study, children might study breeds of horses, the history of their development, how horses have been used through history, horse anatomy and physiology, and famous horse stories. This sort of study might cover science along with some history and language arts.

Other unit studies are more comprehensive. Most of these larger unit studies are at least year-long programs that cover history and science completely, while offering varying degrees of coverage of language arts and math. Most have arts and crafts mixed in, and many have strong religious components.

Many parents, but especially Perfect Paulas, might like the idea of unit studies but find it overwhelming once they get into it. In many unit studies, parents have to choose which books to use, find those books at the library or figure out substitutes, choose among a number of activities, organize all of this, and then keep records of everything. The insecurity and worry about making "wrong" choices paralyzes them, and they quickly return to safe and predictable textbooks. Fortunately, some unit studies have taken this into account and provide much more direction and fewer choices—features that make it possible for those who prefer structure and predictability to still take advantage of unit studies.

Addressing Learning Style Needs

Unit studies can be a marvelous way of meeting all of the different learning style needs of children while providing an education vastly more interesting than what comes out of standard textbooks.

While unit studies vary in the types of activities they include, there are almost always some hands-on and multi-sensory activities to engage Wiggly Willys. Sociable Sues usually thrive on the interaction that is so much a part of most unit studies. Perfect Paulas might be uncomfortable with unit studies that change the lesson structure all the time, but they generally do well with those that follow a predictable format and spend plenty of time developing academic knowledge and skills rather than peripheral projects. Competent Carls usually love the independent reading and research required by many unit studies.

By selecting unit studies that have the elements that best fit your children, then selecting the appropriate activities for each child, you can bring everyone together to study the same topics.

Unit studies also help children overcome learning style weaknesses. After they have already been introduced to a topic or skill via a method that is best for them, choose other activities from the unit study that have them apply that knowledge or skill in ways that are not as comfortable. For example, Sociable Sue learns about a history topic as you gather everyone together to read aloud and discuss a biography related to the historical event. Sociable Sue learns the background and some interesting details of what happened in a way she enjoys. After that, you can assign her to do further independent reading on the same topic, requiring her to come to you to do a narration about what she has read. She would have a difficult time if she began with the independent reading, but sandwiching it between two interactive activities makes it more palatable.

These Are Not Your Only Choices!

I have selected some of the best unit studies on the market as examples of the different types available. There are many more excellent ones I could have included if I had unlimited space.

Unit Study and All-in-One Program Reviews

Connecting with History

RC History
PO Box 73
Andover, MN 55304
877-895-6627
email: Sonya@rchistory.com
www.rchistory.com
Volume 1- print, download - $26,
Volume 2 - print $45, download - $40,
Volume 3 -print - $40, download - $34

Connecting With History (CWH) is definitely one of my favorite options for Catholic families. It is a unit study designed for teaching children in grades K through 12, but it charts out lesson plans so that you can teach each child at his or her own level. It uses a classical education approach, focusing on the humanities and using real books with lots of reading and writing. I also appreciate that *CWH* follows a historical chronology.

In addition to complete coverage of history, *CWH* lessons can provide a major part of your geography and language arts curriculum. Grammar and composition skills are not taught, but there is plenty of practice in the application of grammar and composition skills along with plenty of reading and development of critical reading skills. While *CWH* is a Catholic-worldview based program, it is not a complete religion program. It will help children become very familiar with scripture,

Bible history, and Church history, and many activities are related to religion. But it does not attempt systematic coverage of topics such as the Mass and Sacraments.

The first three of a projected series of four volumes are available at this time. *CWH* volumes are bound with a plastic spiral so that they will lie flat (or you may purchase a downloadable version that you will probably want to print and put into a binder). Each volume functions as an outline and teacher manual rather than a text, although *Volumes 2* and *3* have added some text elements not present in the first volume.

CWH uses a six step model for teaching that is explained at the beginning of *Volume 1*. Those beginning with *Volume 2* really need the information and forms from the first volume, so the teaching guide from *Volume 1* is available as a free download for those who purchase *Volume 2* or *3*.

I will describe *Volume 1* then point out differences in *Volume 2*.

Volume 1: Old Testament and Ancient Cultures
by Sonya Romens and Andrea Chen

Volume 1 consists of one introductory unit that takes one week to complete and ten thematic units that will take three to six weeks each to complete.

For each unit, there are about eight to ten pages that provide background reading suggestions for parents. About a half dozen resources are listed at the beginning of the book, and parents are free to choose which ones they wish to use. One of the most important resources, although it is still optional, is a Bible timeline study course, *The Great Adventure: A Journey through the Bible* (TGA) by Jeff Cavins. *CWH* is structured around the time periods of *TGA*. A teen version of *The Great Adventure* is titled *T3: The Teen Timeline*. Both studies are available in your choice of DVDs or audio CD presentations with a study guide and timeline. They do a marvelous job of presenting the story of salvation history and familiarizing the audience with the layout of the Bible.

Other background resources such as *Making Sense Out of Scripture: Reading the Bible as the First Christians Did*, *You Can Understand the Bible*, and *Where We Got the Bible*, provide parents with foundational knowledge that will make it easier to lead discussions and answer children's questions. (Specific page numbers are given for each suggested background resource at the beginning of each unit.) Catechism references are also provided for parent preparation. While background reading is recommended, it is not a requirement. Parents can learn alongside their children as the family explores the books and resources together.

Parent information at the beginning of each unit also includes discussion prompts, an overview, notebook activity and exploration charts.

Discussion prompts are a lengthy list of questions that should be used to spark discussion and stimulate interest. The overview gives brief background information. You will probably want to pre-read this, then paraphrase ideas at a level your children can understand.

Notebook activities help children create their own notebooks that will include vocabulary words, timelines, maps, charts, and written assignments. Some copywork material is included in the book—primarily scripture passages and poetry. This material should also be used for memory work.

Exploration charts break down specific assignments for beginning (K-3), grammar (4-6), dialectic (7-9), and rhetoric levels (10-12). Reading assignments are divided into three categories: core texts, basic reading, and additional literature. Most essential is the reading from core books. Core books are from one to three books required for students at each of the four levels. For example, the grammar level requires *Bible for Young Catholics* and *Ancient World* (Usborne book) while the rhetoric level requires a Bible, *You Can Understand the Bible*, *Genesis: The Book*

of Origins, and *Exodus: Road to Freedom*. Basic reading assignments are from other books that expand the study as well as from Scott Hahn's *Salvation History* audio CD series (for rhetoric students). Examples of books used along with *Volume 1* are *Old Testament Days: An Activity Guide*, *Tut's Mummy Lost and Found*, *Science in Ancient Greece*, *Famous Men of Greece*, *Alexander the Great*, *Greek Lives* (by Plutarch), and *Mythology* by Edith Hamilton. This is just a sampling of the many titles used! Additional literature options appropriate for each level are provided for each topical unit. Page or chapter assignments from these books are listed for each unit unless the entire book is to be read.

At the back of *Volume 1* are eight forms that are used either for teacher planning or student reporting. Optional downloadable files of Ancient History Timeline Cards (114 cards for $16.95) and Illustrated Report pages ($7.95) are available for *Volume 1*. These are real time savers, and they are likely to be more visually appealing than something you create on your own. Nevertheless, you (or your children) can create your own timeline pages or a larger timeline on your wall, and children may write reports on the computer or use another format.

Volume 2: The Arrival of the King and His Kingdom
by Sonya Romens

Volume 2 covers the New Testament and the beginnings of the Church up to 1066 AD. It is heftier than *Volume 1* because of some significant additions. Built into this volume are quite a few novel discussion guides for books recommended for various levels of the program. The discussion guides (which have been used by permission from Hillside Education) include vocabulary lists, discussion questions, activities, and projects.

In addition to the discussion guides, one of the most significant improvements is that the project and writing ideas have been expanded, both in number as well as with far more explanations and suggestions.

Some core resources from *Volume 1* are also used with *Volume 2*. Among them are the Bible (in a version appropriate for each child), *Ancient World, Bible History* (by Johnson, Hannan, and Dominica), *You Can Understand the Bible, Usborne Time Travelers,* and *Roman Lives* (by Plutarch). Keep in mind that you will be using only those core books required for the level(s) at which your child(ren) will be working.

Among additional core books required for *Volume 2* are *2000 Years of Christian History, Life of Our Lord for Children, Facts on Acts of the Apostles, Heroes of God's Church,* and *57 Stories of Saints.* You will also need to select a core history text. Titles for the various levels are: *Founders of Freedom* (beginning level), *The Old World's Gifts to the New* (grammar level), either *The Old World and America* or *Light to the Nations* (logic level), and either *History of the Church* (from the Didache series) or *The Catholic Church: The First 2000 Years* (rhetoric level).

CWH offers choices of core books since some of the excellent newer options (e.g., Didache series and Catholic Schools Textbook Project history texts) are much more expensive than some older resources. Many books from *Volume 2* are also used with the third volume, so keep that in mind when deciding which books to purchase.

As with *Volume 1,* many other titles are on the list of basic books. Just a few examples are: *How to be a Roman Soldier, City, Famous Men of the Middle Ages, Pompeii: Buried Alive, The Great Heresies,* and *Augustus Caesar's World.*

There are only seven units in *Volume 2,* but they will each take longer to complete than those in *Volume 1.* Downloadable files for Illustrated Report Pages ($9.95) and Timeline Cards ($10.95) are also available for *Volume 2.*

Volume 3: World History Through Catholic Principles

by Sonya Romens

This volume covers the 11th through 17th centuries of world history, reserving United States history for the fourth volume. There are eight units that should take from three to four weeks each to complete. World history focuses more on western civilization, the source of our Christian culture. It takes "side trips" to other cultures primarily through stories of explorers and saints.

Core books for this volume for the beginner level are *Founders of Freedom, Once Upon a Time Saints* and *More Once Upon a Time Saints.* For the grammar level students use *The Old World's Gifts to the New* and *Heroes of God's Church.* Logic level students read *57 Stories of Saints* plus your choice of either *The Old World and America* or *Light to the Nations.* The rhetoric level uses *One Hundred Saints* plus your choice of either *The Catholic Church the First 2000 Years* or *The History of the Church: A Complete Course* (from the Didache series).

Summary

Each volume is likely to take most of a school year, depending upon how many of the suggestions you choose to use. Younger students will almost certainly spend less time than older on both reading and projects. Some of the activities require extensive research or are projects that will take a while to complete. For those unable to use all of the recommended resources, CWH has put together "Economy Packages" that include the most essential books.

CWH might require a significant amount of teacher preparation and presentation time, especially with younger students. However, the methodology is excellent if you have the time to implement it. The narrower you keep the study, the fewer resources you will need, and the less preparation time it will require. However, you are likely to best meet the needs of your children and their various learning styles by using some of the more time-consuming projects and assignments.

The publisher's website, www.rchistory.com, features articles, and sample pages from the program and ancillary items as well as all of the resources for *CWH*.

Purchasers of the program also gain free access to another website that has updates and additional resources that will enhance the program.

Volume 4 will cover both early and modern U.S. History.

. . . .

Five in a Row

by Jane Claire Lambert
Five in a Row Publishing
(Sold through Rainbow Resource Center)
888-841-3456
www.FiveInARow.com
www.RainbowResourceCenter.com
$24-$35 each

Five in a Row volumes have been written for preschool through eighth grade levels, although they are best known for use in the early grades since that was the target of the original *Five in a Row* volumes. These study guides are available for three levels, but level designations are very flexible.

This is a less intense approach to unit study than *KONOS*, *Tapestry of Grace*, and others that were designed to cover all grade levels and numerous subject areas.

Let's first look at the original *Five in a Row* volumes written for children ages four through eight. All four volumes available in this series follow the same format. For each volume, author Jane Claire Lambert has selected a number of outstanding books for children and built a "mini" unit study around each one. *Volume 1* has 19 units, *Volume 2* has 21 units, and *Volumes 3* and *4* each have 15.

Each study should take one week, with more or less time spent each day depending upon which lesson elements you choose to use. While there are no biblical references in the primary volumes, *Five in a Row* repeatedly teaches positive character qualities such as forgiveness, compassion, and honesty that tie easily to scripture. Likewise, the selected stories are not overtly Christian, but reflect Godly principles. For those who want more explicit Christian connections, a separate *Five in a Row Bible Supplement* ($35) contains 175 Bible lessons relating to the 55 studies in *Volumes 1* through *3*.

Examples of selected books are *The Story About Ping*, *Mike Mulligan and His Steam Shovel*, *Katy and the Big Snow*, *Wee Gillis*, *Make Way for Ducklings*, *All Those Secrets of the World*, *Harold and the Purple Crayon*, and *Gramma's Walk*. You will need to purchase or borrow the required storybooks for each volume. However, Rainbow Resource Center sells packages of these books if you prefer to buy them all at once.

Each story is to be read aloud every day for one week (five days). You select activities for social studies (the term loosely used to cover character qualities and relationships in addition to geography, history, and cultures), language arts, math, science, and art to build lessons derived from the story.

There are numerous hands-on activities and projects, although much of each detailed lesson plan is presented as "talk about this" type activities. An example of the activities is "story disks" in each volume, one per unit. These are to be cut out and laminated, then used by students to locate where stories take place on a world map. (These disks are also available as a ready-to-use set covering the first three volumes, printed in color and laminated - $20 for the set of 55.)

You can choose to select only one subject area per day or select a variety of activities from among the subject areas. Activities range from those appropriate for non-writers and non-readers to those for children who have mastered these skills. Thus, you can use the lessons to meet the academic needs of pre-schoolers up through about third grade level.

This is not intended to be a complete curriculum for math and language arts. It does not teach phonics, writing, or math in any sequential progression. In fact, you are encouraged to use stories in whatever order you please. (A calendar linking stories to calendar events suggests a possible progression you might follow.) For younger children, the material might be more than adequate to meet their learning needs. For six- and seven-year-olds, the instruction in social studies, science, and art is likely to be much better than that in traditional textbooks, so you might want to add only basic phonics and math, and possibly other language skill development for the oldest children.

An index lists what is covered under each subject area, sometimes broken down further under subheadings. This helps you if you have specific goals of your own. A reproducible planning sheet helps you with weekly lesson plans. Instructions for activities are quite detailed. Lambert includes valuable tips on questions to ask your children to prompt discussions. *Five in a Row* is very user-friendly, especially for the inexperienced homeschooler.

Other *Five in a Row* volumes are available for older and younger children. Those with preschoolers might want to use *Before Five in a Row*. This volume was developed for children ages two through four. Plenty of activities center around 23 books written for young children. The format is similar to that of the volumes described above.

Those with older children (approximately grades three through eight) should check out *Beyond Five in a Row, Volumes 1* through *3*. These three volumes were authored by Becky Jane Lambert, daughter of the original series author, Jane Lambert. These are excellent, one-semester courses. Four storybooks for each volume are the foundation for each unit study.

For example, *Volume 1* includes *The Boxcar Children, Thomas Edison: Young Inventor, Homer Price*, and *Betsy Ross: Designer of Our Flag*. Subject areas covered include literature, some language arts, history, composition, science, and fine arts.

Lessons are set up so that you read a chapter from the book, then work through your choice of the suggested activities. These vary greatly from day to day.

Quite a bit of historical and scientific information is included within each *Beyond Five in a Row* guide, but you need to use outside resources for additional research. Many such resources are suggested in the lessons. Lessons often include "Internet Connection" activities for students to do research at a particular site or sites on a topic related to the study.

About half of the lessons include an essay question; you will need to tailor requirements on these to suit the age of each student. Occasional "Career Paths" sections help students consider career possibilities and offer suggestions for further research or experience in the field. Timelines are recommended as a means of helping students understand chronological relationships between people and events. Numerous hands-on activities are included: art projects, cooking, science experiments, learning sign language, etc.

A list of all topics covered is located at the back of each book; this will help you for both planning and tracking your accomplishments.

· · · · · · · · ·

Heart of Dakota

Carrie Austin, M.Ed.
Heart of Dakota Publishing
1004 Westview Drive
Dell Rapids, SD 57022
605-428-4068
www.heartofdakota.com
See the publisher's website for package prices

The Heart of Dakota program is a comprehensive, Charlotte Mason oriented curriculum in nine volumes that might be used for preschool through eighth grade, possibly extending into high school. Titles and grade levels covered are:

- *Little Hands to Heaven*, ages 2-5
- *Little Hearts for His Glory*, ages 5-7
- *Beyond Little Hearts for His Glory*, ages 6-8
- *Bigger Hearts for His Glory*, ages 7-9 (extending to ages 10-11)
- *Preparing Hearts for His Glory*, ages 8-10 (extending to ages 11-12)
- *Hearts for Him Through Time: Creation to Christ*, ages 9-11 (extending to ages 12-13)
- *Hearts for Him Through Time: Resurrection to Reformation*, ages 10-12 (extending to ages 13-14)
- *Hearts for Him Through Time: Revival to Revolution*, ages 11-13 (extending to ages 13-14)
- *Hearts for Him Through Time: Missions to Modern Marvels*, will be for ages 12-14 (extending to ages 15-16)

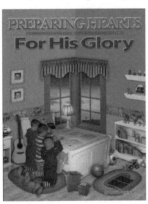

Four additional volumes are planned that will eventually cover high school. Each volume is a one-year curriculum, divided into 33 to 35 units, each of which will take one week to complete. The primary "tool" you work from is one large book that lays out daily lesson plans. It really covers everything! Subject areas and the amount of emphasis upon each vary from volume to volume.

Instructions for learning activities are written out in each manual. Some of the activities at lower levels for math and grammar direct you in the use of other resources, and most math and grammar is through other resources as you move into the upper level volumes. Read-aloud assignments also rely upon other books.

In every volume, each daily lesson plan is divided into two parts: "Learning the Basics" and "Learning through History." Each subject area is presented in a box with between nine and twelve boxes per daily lesson plan. This makes it very easy to see what needs to be done for each area. Lessons begin with history each day. The "Learning through History" parts of the lesson on the left-hand page are designed like a unit study. Daily assignments for history tell you which pages to read in the history book or Bible storybook (or your own Bible) and the key idea upon which to focus. That key idea is also incorporated in Bible, art, thinking skills, science, or some of the other lessons for that day. "Learning the Basics" activities on the right-hand page don't necessarily relate to the theme, but they cover language arts, math, and other needed subjects. For all subject areas, specific pages (tracks in the case of the CD) are assigned in each day's lesson plans for the other required resources. This is a huge time saver.

The four *Hearts for Him* volumes (upper levels) have required sets of student notebook pages. These are printed in full color and are not reproducible, so a set will be needed for each student.

Beginning with *Bigger Hearts*, extension resources and activities are listed so that you can accommodate older learners and teach more than one child the same subject matter at least part of the time. Reading schedules for these books are included in an appendix in each volume rather than within the lessons.

Author Carrie Austin says that completing all the activities should take about 90 minutes a day for *Little Hearts*, 120 to 150 minutes per day for *Beyond Little Hearts*, and about 3½ hours per day for *Bigger Hearts*. It becomes much more difficult to predict time requirements for upper level volumes since students are doing more independent work and you will be making a number of choices depending upon the needs of each student. Although the assumption is that you will complete all subject areas each day, you will find that skipping a subject now and then won't cause lasting harm, particularly in the first three volumes.

Science experiments and activities are included in all volumes, and you are referred to other books for additional reading at each level. Science notebooking assignments are added beginning with *Bigger Hearts*, while recording data and observations with lab work are added at upper levels. Science focuses on fewer topics each year than we typically find in textbooks, but science lessons do a much better job of covering those topics interestingly and in-depth with plenty of observation and experimentation.

For the younger levels, hands-on math activities are given in the manuals, then assignments are made from Singapore Math books at the appropriate level. Older levels drop the hands-on activities for math but continue to provide Singapore Math schedules. Math assignments are very specific with alternative page assignments at the back of the book for the different levels of Singapore Math books that you might be using. (You can substitute another math program if you prefer. For the lower levels, you can still use the suggested math activities along with another program.)

Little Hands to Heaven

Little Hands to Heaven serves as a preschool program teaching letters, sounds, numbers, pre-reading and pre-math skills, music, art, and Bible, all with lots of physical movement and hands-on activity.

Little Hearts for His Glory

In *Little Hearts for His Glory*, the subjects and skills covered are history, Bible, story time, science, phonics, math, art, dramatic play, music, thinking skills, and both fine and gross motor skills. Bible study in *Little Hearts* centers around *Devotions for the Children's Hour*. History readings come from the Christian Liberty Press (CLP) books *History for Little Pilgrims* and *History Stories for Children* as well

as a Bible storybook. (Note: in *Little Hearts*, the history book readings and themes give the study a decidedly Protestant slant with focus on Luther, Calvin, and Jonathan Edwards, but overall children learn a great deal of Bible history and U.S. history with brief introductions to a few other people and events.) Minimal instruction is given for phonics within *Little Hearts*. Instead, suggestions are made for the number of pages or lessons per day to complete in either *Reading Made Easy* or *The Reading Lesson*. You may also use another phonics program of your choice. Appendices in *Little Hearts* include a list of optional literature supplements for each of the 34 units and a "Rhymes in Motion" section with rhyming songs that incorporate large muscle movements. Math specifies assignments made from either *Early Bird Kindergarten Mathematics 2A & 2B* or *Primary Math 1A/1B* (Singapore). Other resources that you need are some storybooks, the Rod and Staff workbooks *Do It Carefully* and *Finding the Answers* OR McGraw-Hill's *Thinking Skills: Grade 1*, either *Italic Handwriting* OR *A Reason for Handwriting*, *The World God Made* OR CLP's *Our Father's World* OR CLP's *God's Wonderful Works* for science, and the musical CD *Hide 'Em in Your Heart Vol. I*.

Beyond Little Hearts

Beyond Little Hearts covers history, Bible, devotions, geography, timeline, art, science, poetry from classic poets, narration lessons, copywork, grammar lessons, spelling, daily literature study with read-alouds, math, and music. The level of difficulty and time required for each subject are greater than in *Little Hearts*. Bible study expands with the addition of Bible study questions used in conjunction with a devotional book. Required history resources include three CLP titles with an early American history theme; these cover American history in a selective but chronological fashion. "Poetry and Rhymes" appendices in both this and the *Bigger Hearts* volumes present one poem for each unit. Other suggested resources for this volume are *Morning Bells, God's Wonderful Works* (CLP science), *Primary Mathematics* (Singapore), and *Hide 'Em in Your Heart Vol. II. Beyond Little Hearts* offers reading plan options depending upon whether a child is a beginning, emerging, or independent reader. For beginners, either *Reading Made Easy* or *The Reading Lesson* is recommended. For emerging readers, there is a substantial appendix with a very detailed, annotated list of books that gradually increase in difficulty plus a schedule suggesting exactly which pages to read on which days. For independent readers, you are directed to use *Drawn into the Heart of Reading.* Spelling lists (two for each unit) are found at the back of the book along with an annotated bibliography of storytime read-aloud books that correlate with each unit. Copywork and beginning grammar are also included within language arts coverage.

Bigger Hearts for His Glory

Bigger Hearts for His Glory again advances in difficulty and skill levels as well as in time required for lessons. While each day's lesson is still presented on two pages, there are now ten boxes per day with a smaller font size used to fit more information. *Bigger Hearts* covers history, biblical character trait study, history notebooking, timeline, art, geography, math activities, hymns, English (with a Rod and Staff text), cursive, spelling and dictation, vocabulary, and classic poetry. It has literature study plans for read-alouds. For science, students learn from living books and experiments, responding with narrations and the creation of a science notebook.

The study of American history continues up through the 1970s using more of a biographical approach. Among the required books are *A First Book in American History, Stories of Great Americans, The Story of the Wright Brothers and Their Sister,* and *Journeys in Time: A New Atlas of American History.* A number of science resources are required for this volume. Among them are *One Small Square: Seashore, Science*

in Colonial America, and *John Audobon: Young Naturalist.*

You will need to choose your own cursive handwriting program. Both *Cheerful Cursive* (Mastery Publications) and *Italic D* (reviewed in this book) are scheduled in the daily plans. As with *Beyond Little Hearts,* there is a detailed schedule of reading for emerging readers that gradually increases in difficulty. For independent readers you are directed to use *Drawn into the Heart of Reading: Level 2/3.* Other resources are referenced, but they are not absolutely essential. Among them are *English 2* (Rod and Staff), *Primary Mathematics,* and *Hymns for a Kid's Heart: Vol. 1.* Dictation passages, spelling lists, and suggested read-aloud titles are also found in the appendices. The read alouds are much more than supplemental "bedtime" stories. These are carefully correlated with the rest of the program to cover different genres of literature and to teach story elements, character traits, and narration.

Preparing Hearts for His Glory

Preparing Hearts for His Glory continues with the same general format as earlier volumes while adding beginning research skills and guided written narrations. For Bible, students study and memorize the Psalms with the aid of musical selections from a CD. History and geography stretch from creation to the end of the twentieth century using *A Child's History of the World* along with other resources such as *Life in the Great Ice Age, Grandpa's Box: Retelling the Biblical Story of Redemption,* and *Hero Tales.* Science studies correspond loosely with history studies. For example, study of the stars correlates with reading about the Magi as well as with study of ancient civilizations where astronomy played an important role. For science, student read biographies of Columbus, da Vinci, and Einstein. Students are expected to do more independent study at this level than at younger levels. Reflecting increased emphasis on academics, *Preparing Hearts for His Glory* has weekly science experiments with notebooking, questions, and narration activities.

Hearts for Him Through Time: Creation to Christ

Hearts for Him Through Time: Creation to Christ follows the same layout, expanding student research skills and building independent reading and self-study into lessons for all students. Self-study assignments include reading, listening to CDs, written assignments, projects, timeline, copywork, map work, drawing, and more. Science continues with weekly experiments and notebooking while adding written lab sheets that help students comprehend the scientific process. *Creation to Christ* uses *Genesis: Finding Our Roots,* a study in both history and biblical worldview. Among other history resources for this level are *The Story of the Ancient World, Ancient Greece: Streams of History, Ancient Rome: Streams of History, What in the World?* CDs, and *A Child's Geography Vol. II.* Science addresses living things with *Exploring Creation with Zoology 3, Exploring the History of Medicine, Plant Life in Field and Garden, An Illustrated Adventure in Human Anatomy, Birds of the Air,* and *Galen and the Gateway to Medicine.*

Hearts for Him Through Time: Resurrection to Reformation

Hearts for Him Through Time: Resurrection to Reformation continues to move students toward more independent learning. This level also turns attention toward becoming a Godly young man or woman with a biblical Christian worldview. To that end, it leads students in a study of Philippians along with either *Boyhood and Beyond* or *Beautiful Girlhood.* History study uses a distinctly Christian approach with resources such as Diana Waring's *What in the World?* CDs, *Mystery of History Vol. III, Monks and Mystics,* and *Peril and Peace: Chronicles of the Ancient Church* combined with non-religious resources such as *Famous Men of the Middle Ages, The Story of the Middle Ages,* and *Draw and Write through History: Vikings, Middle*

Ages, Renaissance. Earth science is the theme for science studies with different options available depending upon which books have been used in previous years.

Hearts for Him Through Time: Revival to Revolution

Hearts for Him Through Time: Revival to Revolution begins with the mid-1700s and continues with history through the 1900s. While it covers some world history, U.S. and church history dominate. Both Bible and history resources include some that directly teach a biblical Christian worldview. Optional study of the 50 states is included. Science highlights inventors and physical science. An advanced option for science is included, but both options require the *Inventor Student Notebook.* Some of the key resources are *George Washington's World, The Story of the Great Republic, The Growth of the British Empire, Who Is God? And Can I Really Know Him?, What in the World? Vol. 3, The Story of Inventions,* and *Four American Inventors.*

Hearts for Him Through Time: Missions to Modern Marvels

Hearts for Him Through Time: Missions to Modern Marvels covers the 1890s through modern times. In this volume, U.S. history is interwoven with world history along with stories of Christian heroes and modern missions. A President Study and an optional Individual State Study are included. Science topics focus on an introduction to chemistry and creation versus evolution. Four additional volumes are planned for the high school years.

Summary

I like the way Carrie Austin has combined elements of unit study, living books, and textbooks in a format that makes it very easy for the parent or teacher to know exactly what to do each day. Art and math lessons might take a little more preparation time than other subjects, but other than that, lesson prep time is very minimal. The variety of learning methods should appeal to children of various learning styles. And you still have the freedom to use your own phonics program—a big issue for some parents since phonics is one of the most important subjects in the early years.

While courses follow a history chronology, you can begin at any level. For each course, you can purchase the main lesson plan book by itself as well as all of the recommended resources directly from Heart of Dakota Publishing. Or you might want to purchase one of the economy, basic, extension, or deluxe packages. The economy package includes all of the required items except those for which you need to choose from among selected options. The basic package consists of those additional items that are recommended and scheduled into the lesson plans but which are not absolutely essential. The deluxe package is available for *Beyond, Bigger,* or *Preparing Hearts* and consists of the storytime or additional student books recommended for each volume. The extension package adds the history and science books for older students.

• • • • • • • • •

History Links

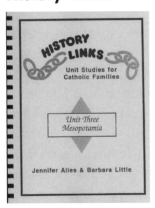

by Jennifer Alles, Barbara Little, Kim Staggenborg, and others
Full Spectrum Learning
170 East Guadalupe Rd. #108
Gilbert, AZ 85234
701-260-2599
email: catholichistorylinks@gmail.com
www.historylinks.info
$15-$20 each

History Links is a Catholic approach to unit studies that can be used to teach preschoolers through high school level. Thus far, there are ten units available, with others in development; they are *General Studies, Creation,* *Mesopotamia, Ancient Egypt, Ancient Israel, Ancient Greece, Ancient Rome: The Republic, Ancient Rome: Pax Romana, Ancient Rome: The Roman Empire,* and *Medieval Volume One: Early Medieval.* These units are in chronological sequence, although you need not use them in that order.

Most units should take from two to four months to complete, so you would complete approximately three units per school year. The first unit, *General Studies,* should take only one to two months. Apparently, some families using *The Well-Trained Mind* approach (see p. 16) are completing four or five units per year, albeit with more superficial coverage of each time period. *History Links* is designed such that you can go back through the entire series at least once more, using the more challenging learning activities suggested for upper grade levels.

This is truly a family-designed curriculum. Activities within each unit are presented for four levels: "P" for preschoolers, "1" for kindergarten and early elementary grades, "2" for intermediate through middle school levels, and "3" for advanced junior high through high school. In addition, ideas for keeping toddlers occupied are included at the bottom of many pages. For those enjoying new babies, there are suggestions for following the "baby track" that pares down the more time-consuming or messy activities. I expect that *History Links* should take about one to two hours per day, depending upon which activities you choose.

While *History Links* works well as a family curriculum, it might also be used in co-op settings for once or twice a month gatherings.

You will need reference resources: an encyclopedia, a Bible, a dictionary, either a globe or world map, and the *Catechism of the Catholic Church.* Much of the resource information might also be found on the internet. Some other books (e.g., *Usborne Book of World History, Usborne Book of the Ancient World, English from the Roots Up, National Geographic Magazines,*

The Antiquities of the Jews by Josephus) are recommended but are not essential. The authors purposely tried to keep the cost low by having just a few essential resources and recommending materials that you can usually get from the library or online.

The units also incorporate ideas borrowed from another one of my Top Picks, *Teaching Writing: Structure and Style* (Institute for Excellence in Writing), but the authors encourage you to purchase the seminar itself.

History Links provides complete coverage of history, with religion, science, language arts, music, math, critical thinking, research, fine arts, and crafts all taught within the context of history. Since only history is taught systematically, *History Links'* coverage of other subjects should be considered supplemental. On a side note, science units from Media Angels (reviewed in this book) should work well between or alongside *History Link* units.

Everyone needs to start with *Unit One: General Studies*. The first half of this book explains the methodology used throughout the series. The second half presents brief, introductory studies on the four key areas covered within all of the units: history, geography, archaeology, and theology.

The same format is used in these introductory studies and throughout all of the other units. Each unit begins with prayers and hymns to learn, vocabulary lists, punctuation and capitalization items to be learned, a Library List of recommended resources (books, videos, recordings, periodicals, websites, encyclicals, church documents, etc.). The bulk of each unit or book is presented under subtopics with brief introductory, background or explanatory information followed by activities coded by subject area and level of difficulty. Extensive appendices in most of the units include many of the source documents you might need. The more recently published units also include resource guides that help you select age-appropriate materials for your children.

Activities address all types of learning styles, but those for the upper two levels direct students toward independent research, reading, and writing much more than traditional curriculum and even more so than some other unit studies. For example, the two following activities from *Ancient Rome: The Roman Empire* present research questions for older students:

"Research Arianism. What belief did Arians promote? What role did Constantine play in this conflict? Who was the staunchest opponent of Arianism? What Church council was held to settle this dispute?" (p. 37).

"Do you think it is true to say the ancient philosophers lacked 'faith, humility, and chastity?' (Although we have already studied the works of Cicero, advanced students might want to do a research project and locate Cicero's and Ambrose's De Officiis to compare them.)" (p. 42).

While these activities might seem very challenging, I believe they provide the best type of education. In addition to developing academic skills, they help students think through and develop a thoroughly Catholic worldview. They draw on classical education in both content and methodology. They use primary sources, comparison of ideas, and investigation of important questions while covering content students need to learn.

Lest you think all the activities are overwhelming, here are two examples of activities for younger students:

"Divide an orange, cantaloupe, or other fruit. Draw a line around it, and then cut it on the line. Then discuss the concepts of hemisphere and symmetry. Did Diocletian actually divide his empire in 'half'? Did he divide the Empire along a line of symmetry?" (p. 31).

"Constantinople is now called Istanbul. Why? (The Ottoman Turks renamed it.) Locate Istanbul, Turkey on a map. Why was this such a desirable location for a city?" (p. 36). Note: children will have already learned something about Constantinople before tackling this activity.

Like other unit studies, *History Links* requires parental preparation and presentation time. You will probably need to work quite closely with young children, while older students will need only occasional assistance. Once students have developed their own research skills, they can work more independently. However, you will not have simple answer keys to consult to "check" their work.

Of course, hands-on activities like art projects and cooking will demand more of your time, but you can choose how many such activities to undertake. With younger students, you can research and read material together, then choose whether to have students do written work or discussion. Such choices should depend upon their abilities and your time.

One of the special benefits of *History Links* is that because it is presented in small units, it's a great way to try out unit study without making an expensive commitment.

· · · · · ● · · · ·

KONOS Character Curriculum

PO Box 250
Anna, TX 75409
972-924-2712
email:
info@konos.com
www.konos.com
*Volumes 1, 2, and 3 - $110 each,
timelines - $59.95 per volume,*
curriculum/timeline combos - $148.95 each, *Index - $20, KONOS In-A-Box - $225* each, *KONOS In-A-Bag - $99 each*

KONOS features Bible-based character traits as unit themes in their unit studies for children in grades K through 8.

Subjects included in *KONOS* are history (primarily American history), Bible, social studies, science, art, music, drama, practical living, health, critical thinking skills, and character training, as well as some language and math. The authors suggest you use other math and language programs as needed. If you use all three volumes of *KONOS*, you will cover material typically covered in history and science programs in elementary grades with the exception of world history. World history gets spotty coverage in the elementary grades but is covered extensively in their high school program.

Because the authors believe children learn best by "doing," this program is very hands-on—an ideal program for Wiggly Willys. The real strength of *KONOS* is in the number of activities from which you can choose. There are many more ideas than you can possibly use. Some people are overwhelmed at the choices, but the many alternatives allow you to choose how much time you spend, the number of hands-on activities, field trips, books, etc.—whatever fits your situation.

Lesson plans list materials and preparation needed, then recommend activities for younger, middle, and older children. The lesson plans are a tremendous help to those who are overwhelmed by too many choices and also to those who want just a little help in quickly sorting through all the ideas. *KONOS* lesson plans provide structure, yet they leave much room for individualizing. Parents who prefer a set structure and routine might have trouble using *KONOS*, while those who prefer variety will likely enjoy it.

While *Volume 1* should probably be the first volume used with children in grades K to 3, any volume, including the third, could be used at any level. Each volume of *KONOS* can be used for two years. *KONOS* provides detailed background information for some activities but not all. Library books and other sources will be needed to round out the lessons. Detailed lists of resources and activities are under each heading.

It is necessary to plan ahead to get books and

other resources that you will need. You might need to locate out-of-print books or arrange for inter-library loans. *KONOS* gives you so many titles to choose from that you should have no trouble finding appropriate resources if you are flexible about your choices.

Because *KONOS* covers history in a non-sequential fashion, you should use timelines to tie historical events together coherently. You can make your own, but KONOS sells beautiful, laminated timelines that include both biblical and historical figures; these timelines coordinate with each volume of the curriculum.

The *KONOS Index* ($20) is a separate book that shows which topics are covered where in each volume of *KONOS*. This is most valuable to those who have accumulated two or more *KONOS* volumes or want to use *KONOS* activities to jazz up their traditional curriculum. If you want to locate information on a particular topic the Index will help you find it quickly.

Those who like the methodology of *KONOS*

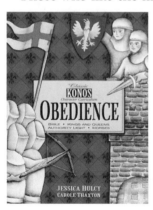

but feel overwhelmed with what it requires from the parent or teacher should love *KONOS In-A-Box*. There are three 18-week (semester) unit studies derived from the original *KONOS* volumes. While the original volumes contain many units, each revolving around a character trait theme, *KONOS In-A-Box* volumes each narrow down to a single character-trait theme. The titles are *Attentiveness, Obedience,* and *Orderliness.* The *Obedience* unit I reviewed contains the teacher's manual/curriculum (also sold separately), craft materials (e.g., copper foil, wire, brads, whistle, tapestry set, fake jewels), eight resource books, and timeline figures, all packaged in a sturdy cardboard case with carrying handle.

Each *KONOS In-A-Box* study is laid out with detailed, daily lessons and comes with just about everything you need. No more frantic trips to the library and the craft supply store. *KONOS In-A-Box* covers the same subject areas as the original *KONOS* but is more comprehensive than the original, particularly in the areas of language arts and literature where students are taught how to write and to analyze literature. Again, math and phonics are not covered.

With *KONOS In-A-Box* there are still some choices to be made. The studies can meet the needs of students in grades K to 8, but you must choose which activities to require of older and younger students. For example, when it says, "Write five simple sentences on index cards about what you learned yesterday about light," you might ask your third grader to write only three sentences, and spend time with your kindergartner on basic reading skills while older students write their sentences.

While some preparation time will still be necessary, it will be a fraction of that required for the original *KONOS*. If you've always wanted to try unit studies, but felt that it might be too overwhelming, this is a terrific way to try it out. Many families find that after using *KONOS In-A-Box* they can easily handle the regular *KONOS* volumes.

Similar in concept to *KONOS In-A-Box* is *KONOS In-A-Bag.* There are two units available in this format that *KONOS* calls its "New Culture Curriculum Series." The two "Bags," *Russia: The Land of Endurance* and *Africa: The Land of Stewardship,* couple country or continent themes with a character trait identified with each one. A detailed 200-page curriculum manual is included in the bag along with all the items needed for the study. For example the *Africa* tote bag includes the manual, a beautifully illustrated resource book, a map, and five craft kits with supplies for three children. The Culture series differs from the Box series in that the curriculum does not include the in-depth writing lessons or literary analysis.

Those with older students who would like to continue this style of teaching through high school might want to check out the four-volume *KONOS History of the World*, written for high school students.

KONOS Parent Helps

KONOS offers training resources that will help you learn how to implement the unit study method of teaching. All of their training resources are loaded with practical information and examples based on years of experience.

I recommend the book *KONOS Compass: An Orientation to Using KONOS* ($25) to anyone using KONOS at the elementary level. It gives an overview of all three volumes along with a comparison to typical state requirements so you can see if you are covering the necessary material. *KONOS Compass* also provides teaching information and sample lesson plans.

A visual option is *KONOS: Creating the Balance* ($125), a 6½ hour DVD presentation covering critical topics like the father's role, multilevel teaching, planning and scheduling, dealing with toddlers, discipline, and how to choose library books. In addition it features two hours of KONOS author Jessica Hulcy teaching her children, including hands-on activities, so you can really see what this looks like.

For those who want more help than what I've described thus far, HomeSchoolMentor.com offers subscription-based training via videos and interaction with a cohort group as you work through one of the KONOS volumes together with other homeschoolers. Check out www. HomeSchoolMentor.com for free video samples.

• • • • • • •

My Father's World

by Marie Hazell
My Father's World
PO Box 2140
Rolla, MO 65402
573-202-2000
email: info@mfwbooks.com
www.mfwbooks.com
basic packages range from $124 to $297, deluxe packages range from $206 to $385

My Father's World (MFW) offers complete or almost complete grade level programs for preschool through grade 12. MFW embodies methodologies from unit study, Charlotte Mason, and classical approaches with a strong biblical base (Protestant) and missionary emphasis throughout all levels. Each program centers around a single guide and uses a mixture of real books and hands on activities along with a few textbooks. Basic or deluxe packages are available for each level. Basic packages provide essential elements. Deluxe packages include additional resources for art, music, read aloud, etc. A Bible (not included) is required for every level.

MFW courses are clearly structured with easy-to-understand instructions. Lesson preparation time will be required primarily for gathering necessary materials, so planning ahead is essential.

MFW also sells many of the recommended books which might be helpful for those without easy access to a library. Interestingly, MFW has been able to keep some of the core resource books in print by working out agreements with the original publishers for MFW to publish their own editions. These often are edited regarding issues such as evolution to make them more appropriate for MFW's audience.

Samples for each level are available on the publisher's website. Because of space limitations, I have not reviewed the preschool program, and I include only a brief summary of the high school courses.

My Father's World from A to Z: A Complete Kindergarten Curriculum, second edition

Kindergarten level focuses on beginning reading, math, science, social studies, and Bible appropriate for children who are just ready to begin learning letters and sounds. (Expansion ideas are provided for kindergartners who are already reading.) Many activities in the book—especially those not targeting beginning number and letter skills—easily adapt for use with younger or older children.

Charlotte Mason's influence is strong with  the incorporation of real books and hands-on learning throughout the program. Susan Schaeffer Macaulay's book about Mason's methodology, *For the Children's Sake*, is referred to a number of times in *My Father's World* and is included in the deluxe package.

The introductory unit, which should take about ten days to complete, covers creation and introduces the names of the letters of the alphabet. The next 26 units (centered around themes such as the sun, leaves, or water) integrate lessons on sounds of the letters and beginning blending (short-vowel words only) with the unit themes. All learning is multisensory, combining worksheets, oral work, listening, movable alphabet, flashcards, and lots of hands-on activities. For example, Unit 11 teaches about insects, emphasizing the biblical concept of working hard (diligence). Ants, bees, and ladybugs are used as examples. Students learn the "A-a-Apple" song as they learn the /ĭ/ sound for insect. You are to read aloud about insects from any appropriate book—nine possible titles are suggested. Children either set up the ant farm from the deluxe kit or assist you in following the instructions for creating your own ant farm so they can watch insects at work.

Lessons should take 60 to 90 minutes per day, and there are sufficient lessons here for a full school year. Lessons for each unit are presented in a two-page grid so you can quickly get an overview of what you will be doing. Additional notes follow for each day, but there is not a lot of teacher manual information that you need to read before jumping into the lessons.

Simple science experiments, craft projects, and literature are built into the lessons. Reading lessons present a new letter sound in each unit, then use a wide variety of activities to teach the sound, letter formation (handwriting), recognition of sounds in spoken words and pictures, and—when children are ready—blending.

A variety of worksheets are provided in the large packet of Kindergarten Student Sheets. This packet includes worksheets—some for cut-and-paste activities, teaching charts, game cards, short-vowel song cards, monthly calendars, and patterns for badges. Many learning activities use textured letters (these come in the deluxe package), tactile activities (e.g., finger Jello cut into letter shapes, pancakes formed as letters), and verbal responses.

Day six in each unit features a "book time" for reading a real book and engaging in related activities plus an "outdoor time" activity. Math is often integrated in lessons; for example, sorting leaves by color and size or cutting an apple in half. Skills covered include shapes, comparing and sequencing, measuring, calendar, money, graphs, fractions, time, counting, writing numbers, and an introduction to addition and subtraction.

The basic program includes a beautiful full-color set of A to Z Alphabet Flashcards. These 5" x 8" flashcards feature illustrations from nature.

In addition to the textured letter set mentioned above, you need access to children's fiction and non-fiction books. Extensive, annotated lists of recommended books should make it easy to find suitable books at your local library.

To make things easier, My Father's World offers the deluxe package that includes the basic program (with alphabet cards and A-Z Textured Letters), Butterfly Garden, an ant farm, an inflatable globe, *Say Hello to Classical Music* CD, Cuisenaire Rods, *Cuisenaire Rods Alphabet Book,* and the books *What Really Happened to the Dinosaurs?* and *For the Children's Sake.* These items and a few others are also offered individually on the publisher's website. A separate, optional Kindergarten Literature Collection includes a set of classic picture books for "book time" reading.

Some inexpensive art supplies such as clay, watercolor paints, and paintbrushes will be required; a few more such as tempera paints and colored pencils will be optional. You will also need an extra set of Kindergarten Student Sheets for each additional student.

My Father's World First Grade

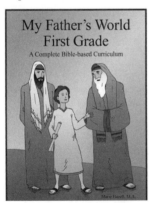

This first grade program very quickly reviews letters and sounds, then introduces short-vowel words. All basic phonics concepts are presented this year. Spelling and writing both receive much more emphasis this year than in kindergarten. Science in the first grade program relies heavily upon three Usborne books—*Things Outdoors, Science With Water,* and *Science With Plants*—in keeping with Marie Hazell's incorporation of Charlotte Mason's ideas for teaching science using real books and activities. A list of first grade math goals and ideas for informal math activities are included along with a daily math grid that uses hands-on math activities plus math resources from the First Grade deluxe package.

The First Grade basic package includes the teacher's manual, student workbook, student worksheets, *Bible Notebook,* timeline figures, *Bible Reader,* and three Usborne science books.

The *Bible Notebook* is a "blank" book with lines and spaces for children to create their own notebook from the lessons they study. The *Bible Reader* features simple retellings of Bible stories. Weekly memory verses from Proverbs reinforce key lesson ideas and are used for developing handwriting skills.

This program builds a very strong familiarity with the Bible since it uses lengthy readings in many lessons as well as the *Bible Reader.* Children also learn the names of the books of the Bible this year. Minimal lesson preparation is required. Daily lesson plans provide detailed instruction and are easy to follow. Some cut-and-paste activities are used from time to time, and there are a few projects you might use if you so choose (e.g., celebration of Purim).

Children are asked to draw in many of the lessons, and Hazell suggests using the book *Drawing with Children* for developing drawing skills. The First Grade deluxe package includes that book along with *Honey for a Child's Heart, Come Look with Me: Enjoying Art with Children, Come Look with Me: Enjoying Landscape Art with Children,* Pattern Blocks, *The Complete Book of Math* (300+ page book of math activities), *Pattern Animals: Puzzles for Pattern Blocks,* and *Introduction to the Orchestra* CD—in addition to all items in the basic package.

Adventures in My Father's World (2nd or 3rd Grade)

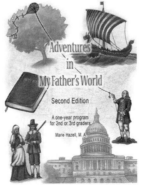

NOTE: This program is designed for a second or third grader who is an oldest child. Families with older siblings should instead purchase one of the 2nd-8th programs so that all students are working on the same topics.

Adventures in My Father's World provides complete curriculum for Bible, history, geography, science, art, and music, with United States history being the primary theme for the year. There is some language arts instruction, but it is not comprehensive. Math is not included. You need to add your own math and language arts resources. MFW recommends *Primary Language Lessons* by Emma Serl and *Spelling by Sound and Structure* (Rod and Staff). Study of a foreign language is recommended but not required.

Students will be doing increasing amounts of reading and writing at this level. Each student will need two three-ring binders—one for U.S. History and geography, the second for all other subjects.

Moderately detailed lesson plans are provided for each day. You need minimal prep work before teaching the program: gathering or buying general school supplies and art supplies for *I Can Do All Things*, gathering library books, and reading the first sections of the teacher's manual.

You may purchase either the basic or deluxe package. The basic package includes the teacher's manual, a map of the United States and of the world, student sheets (which also include state sheets/cards/stickers), *Patriotic Songs of the U.S.A.* CD, and the books *NIrV Discoverer's Bible for Young Readers*; *The Story of the U.S.*; *American Pioneers and Patriots*; *North American Indians*; *Red, White, and Blue*; *The Thanksgiving Story*; *The Fourth of July Story*; *First Encyclopedia of Science*; *Science in the Kitchen*; *Science with Air*; and *Birds, Nests, and Eggs*.

The deluxe package includes all of the above plus an art program, bird feeder, magnet kit, *Introduction to Tchaikovsky and the Nutcracker Suite* CD set, and seven additional read aloud books such as *The Courage of Sarah Noble*.

At the back of the teacher's manual are pages of still more book and video recommendations (annotated with short descriptions) that are arranged very helpfully week by week

so you can easily browse through possibilities for alternatives or additions to the curriculum.

Charlotte Mason methodology again dominates with the use of real books, hands-on activity, nature walks, narration, and other Mason techniques used throughout the program.

2nd - 8th Grade Multi-Age Curriculum

While the preceding programs all have narrower age or grade level designations, the next sequence in *MFW* consists of five volumes, any of which might be used for students in grades two through eight. Ideally, you would use them in sequence, no matter at what grade level you begin. You might complete all five volumes in grades two through six then repeat the first two volumes at a more advanced level for seventh and eighth grades.

The first year of the five-year cycle is dedicated to concentrated study of geography and cultures in *Exploring Countries and Cultures*. The next four volumes follow a chronological order:

- *Creation to the Greeks*
- *Rome to the Reformation*
- *Exploration to 1850* (U.S./World History)
- *1850 to Modern Times* (U.S./World History)

As with the other *MFW* volumes, these five levels use real books and lots of hands-on activities to cover Bible, social studies (history and geography), science, art, and music. You might consider this a unit study although study in all subjects is not as tightly linked to unit themes as in other unit studies. For example, music study might be about a composer from the time period studied in history, or students might study Greek and Latin word roots while working through the volumes that include study of the Greek and Roman empires. Textbooks and other resources are also incorporated to cover specific topics that might not fit with the main themes. For example, children learn the music of Bach, Vivaldi, and Handel during their study of *Creation to the Greeks*.

Language arts are covered separately,

although children will be working on some language arts activities within the curriculum itself. *MFW* suggests resources such as *Spelling Power, Writing Strands,* and *Intermediate Language Lessons* for language arts.

Math is not included in these volumes, although *Primary Mathematics* (Singapore Math) is recommended. *Rosetta Stone* is MFW's preferred resource for the study of a foreign language. Seventh and eighth graders also need to add an appropriate science course.

Teacher's manuals feature daily lesson plans with additional notes and explanations alongside each week's chart. Charts show specific pages and activities within the core resources. Some of the books included in the schedules are NOT included in the basic packages; generally these are read-aloud books that you might find at the library. However, all resources listed in the schedule charts ARE included in the deluxe packages.

Student sheets, included with each year's package, are pages for creating a timeline, plus many others for activities such as mapwork, crafts, and written work. As with *Adventures in My Father's World,* students will need to maintain two, three-ring binders for their work for each volume of this course.

Exploring Countries and Cultures

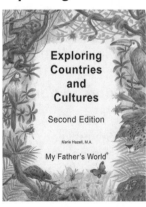

As the title suggests, this volume teaches about other countries and cultures. It is selective rather than comprehensive in coverage, an approach entirely suitable for a young audience. For example, while all continents are "visited," only a few representative countries are actually studied. Protestant missionary biographies, stories from *Hero Tales* (heroes of Protestantism), and information from *Window on the World* (missionary efforts

and status worldwide) are assigned for reading within the lesson plans, often coordinating with the country being studied that week. For example, the biography of Gladys Aylward, missionary to China, begins during the study of China, but continues through study of Japan.

Of course other resources are also used along with *Exploring Countries and Cultures.* The basic package includes the teacher's manual, Parent/ Teacher Supplement, student sheets, an imitation passport, *God Speaks Numanggang, Hero Tales, Window on the World, Illustrated World Atlas, Classroom Atlas,* a wall map of the world, *Maps and Globes, Geography from A to Z, A Trip around the World, Another Trip around the World, Exploring World Geography, Properties of Ecosystems, Living World Encyclopedia* (Usborne), *Global Art, Wee Sing Around the World* CD, and *Flags of the World Sticker Book.*

The deluxe package adds six missionary biographies, *Kingdom Tales* (read-aloud), a puzzle book, an inflatable globe, and *Fun with Easy Origami.*

Seventh and eighth graders have additional coursework scheduled in the lesson plans. You will need to purchase the *7th-8th Grade Supplement* if you are teaching older students.

Creation to the Greeks

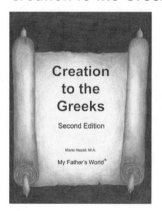

MFW strongly recommends that children complete *Exploring Countries and Cultures* before beginning this volume so that they have foundational knowledge of countries and geographic terms that will be used this year.

The outline for this study follows the Old Testament, beginning with Creation and continuing through the rebuilding of Jerusalem after the exile (book of Nehemiah). Following the biblical timeline, students also learn about ancient Mesopotamia; Egypt; the Babylonian kingdom; early North American cultures; other ancient cultures of the Middle East such as the Canaanites, Hittites and Philistines; Assyria; Greece (including some Greek mythology); India (including a brief study of Hinduism and Buddhism); early Russians; Phoenicians; and the Persian empire, culminating with Alexander the Great. *Celebrating Biblical Feasts* is used to incorporate study and celebration of the Old Testament biblical feasts.

Core books used with this volume seem to be significantly more challenging than those used for *Exploring Countries*. The basic package includes the teacher's manual, student sheets, *Journey through the Bible, Streams of Civilization Vol. 1, Ancient World, Ancient Egypt, Aesop's Fables for Children, The Trojan Horse: How the Greeks Won the War, The Children's Homer, Genesis for Kids, Dinosaurs of Eden, Pyramids, Archimedes and the Door of Science, English from the Roots Up,* and *Celebrating Biblical Feasts.*

The deluxe package adds *God and the History of Art* (art history for older students from a decidedly Protestant viewpoint); *Introduction to Vivaldi, Bach, and Handel* CD set; and three Patricia St. John books.

This volume also includes a list of recommended books to enrich topics addressed within each week's lesson as does *Exploring Countries*. If you are working with younger children, be sure to select and use resources that are age appropriate.

Rome to the Reformation

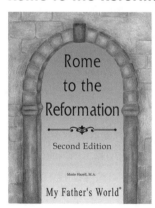

The layout and methodology for this volume is essentially the same as for *Creation to the Greeks*. This volume again includes many pages of optional book and video recommendations for each week of study. The

assumption is that you have just completed *Creation to the Greeks* and already have some of the resources used with that volume: *Journey Through the Bible, Streams of Civilization Vol. 1, English from the Roots Up,* and *Ancient World.* Other items included in the basic package are the teacher's manual, student sheets, *How the Bible Came to Us, The Roman Empire, Augustus Caesar's World, Galen and the Gateway to Medicine, The Story of the World Vol. 2, Medieval World* (Usborne), *Trial and Triumph: Stories from Church History, The Human Body for Every Kid, The Body Book, First Encyclopedia of the Human Body, The Wonderful Way Babies Are Made,* and *Exploring Creation with Astronomy.*

The deluxe package adds *Starting Chess; Make a Castle* kit; *Introduction to Haydn, Mozart and Beethoven* CD set; and four read-aloud books.

You might have noticed that the human body and astronomy are the primary science themes for this year. You might also have noticed that there is quite a lot of reading material included, some written at junior high level. However, the program is designed so the parent is reading the books aloud to the student, and pages to be read are listed under daily assignments. That means you will not be reading every page in every book, so it is not as overwhelming as it might seem.

It is important to note that history coverage is not restricted to Western Civilization but includes Japan, India, Australia, and other far flung places.

Exploration to 1850, second edition (U.S./World History)

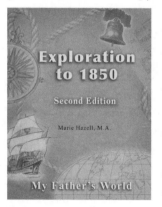

Exploration to 1850 is appropriate for students in grades four through eight. (You will need to add the *2nd-3rd Grade Supplement* if you are teaching younger student.) *Exploration* combines both world history and early U.S. history. It uses core resources such as *Story of the World, Volume 3* and *George Washington's World* that take a story-telling approach to history along with texts such as *Exploring American History* (CLP) and *Building a City on a Hill*. The last four to six weeks of the year are used for students to write a report on their own state while learning simultaneously how to write a research paper. Science this year is a study of plants and animals. Seventh and eighth graders should use either *Exploring Creation with General Science* or *Exploring Creation with Physical Science*. Resource recommendations for math and language arts vary by the student's grade level.

The basic package includes the teacher's manual; student sheets; the aforementioned history books; *Boy, Have I Got Problems!*; *U.S. Presidents Flashcards*; map of the U.S. and world (placemat size); *In God We Trust*; *The Last 500 Years*; *Writing a State Report*; U.S.A wall map; *The World of Animals* (Answers in Genesis); *The World of Animals* (MFW edition); and *Exploring Creation with Botany*.

The deluxe package adds *Then Sings My Soul*; *Introduction to Schubert, Mendelssohn, and Chopin*; a bird feeder; and six read aloud books.

1850 to Modern Times (U.S./World History)

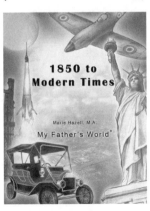

1850 to Modern Times continues to intermix U.S. and world history, covering events in chronological sequence. The target audience is grades four through eight. You will need the *2nd-3rd Grade Supplement* if you are teaching a younger student. It continues with a few books begun in *Exploration to 1850*. Science introduces students to physics and chemistry.

The basic package includes the teacher's manual; student sheets; *A Young Person's Guide to Knowing God*; *Tales of Persia*; *Witnesses to All the World*; *States & Capitals Songs*; *Jumbo U.S. Map Pad*; *The Story of the World, Vol. 4*; *The Story of the World, Activity Book 4*; *Timeline Book for 1850 to Modern Times*; *Children's Encyclopedia of American History*; *America's Favorite Patriotic Songs*; *The World of Science* (MFW edition); and *100 Science Experiments*.

The deluxe package adds: *The U.S. History Cookbook*, *The Stories of Foster & Sousa in Words and Music*, *The Best of George Gershwin*, *Sousa to Satchmo* DVD, *Wired!* kit, and *Fun with Magnets* kit, plus six read-aloud books that contribute to the underlying theme of heroic Christian virtue in response to God's call.

High School Level

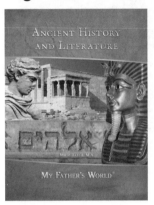

My Father's World also has a four-year program for high school level that covers history, literature, language arts, Bible, economics, and government. The Bible component is particularly strong as it includes serious Bible study, apologetics, worldview, comparative religions, prayer, and Christian living. In addition, over the course of the four years, students will read quite a few books such as *The Iliad*, *The Odyssey*, *Pilgrim's Progress*, *Silas Marner*, *Pride and Prejudice*, *The Great Gatsby*, *1984*, and *The Hiding Place*.

These courses are designed for independent study under parental guidance. Weekly parent-student meetings are required to discuss and review the week's work. Parents will almost certainly need to have additional discussions about some of the reading material in addition to the weekly meeting. Grading is based primarily upon parent evaluation of the student's written work, discussions, vocabulary quizzes, and essays with some use of traditional tests.

Science, math, foreign language, and other electives are not included.

Titles of the four courses are:
- *Ancient History and Literature*
- *World History and Literature*
- *U.S. History to 1877 with Government, American Literature, and Biblical Worldview*
- *U.S. History 1877 to the Present with Economics, English/Speech, and Bible*

See complete reviews of the high school level courses at www.cathyduffyreviews.com/unit-studies/My-Fathers-World-High-School.htm.

• • • • • • • • •

Sonlight

Sonlight Curriculum
8042 South Grant Way
Littleton, CO 80122-2705
(303) 730-6292
email: main@sonlight.com
www.sonlight.com

Sonlight was begun by a homeschooling family that wanted to provide the best materials at a reasonable cost that would work for families living overseas and working as missionaries. They wanted to base their programs on the educational philosophy of Dr. Ruth Beechick—structured, yet allowing for maximum real-life learning. Influenced by Charlotte Mason's ideas, they also wanted to include real books, but at the same time not create a program that required too much time and work from busy parents. These ideas actually reflected the needs of many homeschooling families, not just those in mission fields. As a result, Sonlight has grown to become one of the largest curriculum suppliers in the homeschool market.

Sonlight has designed comprehensive "grade/age level" programs with carefully selected resources and instructor's guides that outline lessons for each day using specific pages within the materials provided. While Sonlight offers no oversight or teaching assistance, on their website they have free how-to webinars, workshop videos, podcasts and one-on-one sessions with curriculum advisors.

But Sonlight is not for everyone. They actually have a page on their website titled, "27 Reasons NOT to Buy Sonlight." You should take time to read through this before ordering a program.

Sonlight offers a complete, eclectic, literature-based program integrated around historical themes for preschool through high school. They have arranged their program in an unusual fashion. There are 18 different Core Program Packages, each loosely designated for a range of from two to five grade levels (preschool through twelfth grade). This is possible because Core Packages primarily cover history, Bible, and language arts while also including many read-aloud books plus "readers" (real books rather than reading textbooks). History and Bible instruction are not especially dependent upon skill or maturity levels.

Most Core Packages focus on an area of history such as world history, U.S. history, or history of the eastern hemisphere. Core A is an introduction to world cultures. The two preschool Core themes are "Fiction, Fairy Tales, and Fun" and "Exploring God's World." At the upper end, Cores center around church history, British Literature, 20th Century World History, and Civics and American Government.

Read-aloud books for the Core programs are excellent choices that you would probably love to have in the family library even if you weren't using Sonlight. Bible instruction uses scripture and other resources, including biographies of missionaries and Christian heros. This is essentially a Protestant program, although the "History of God's Kingdom" Core presents a very even-handed study of church history and doctrinal issues comparing Protestant, Catholic, and Orthodox positions.

In the early years, you may choose the level of the Language Arts/Readers package that best matches each child's ability. In upper-elementary through high school, the language arts component is integrated into each Core level. Separate math and science packages are then combined with your choice of a Core Package to customize the curriculum. Math or science packages might be selected for the same grade level or various levels depending upon children's needs. Instructor's guides come with Core, language arts, and science packages. Language Arts Guides are included with the Core and refer to some of the books that come in the corresponding level Core Packages, so if a child needs a particular level of language arts, that might dictate which Core Package you choose. However, in the early Cores when reading and writing abilities vary widely, you may choose from several different language arts levels for each Core. Math and science function independent of the Core Package. Elective packages or resources are also available for critical thinking, foreign language, art, music, geography, Bible study, typing, creation/evolution, church history, driver's education, worldview, and physical education.

Language arts material in the Core guides incorporates all of the needed instruction for phonics, grammar, composition, and most other language skills. I am particularly impressed with the weekly writing assignments built into the curriculum as this area is lacking in many other programs. Additional books in the packages might be for handwriting or spelling, or they might be a dictionary or thesaurus. Sonlight has created some of their own phonetic readers for the early stages of reading, but after that they use real books from other sources.

Science packages include a guide, an assortment of books, and supplies for experiments and activities. The guides for both language arts and science all include lesson plans, calendars, instructions, student activity sheets, answer keys, and much more.

For math, Sonlight offers three or more choices for each level. Answer keys or solution manuals are part of each program, but there are no instructor's guides for math; they are not needed.

All Core Guides include week-by-week lesson plans with record-keeping calendars, and thorough instructions. In addition, they have geography and time line activities; study guides for all history, reader and read-aloud books; answer keys; and much more.

Sonlight emphasizes only those activities that have clear educational purposes; only recently have they started to add hands-on activities to some Core programs. Though parent-child interaction is required at certain times, little time is required for lesson preparation. What I hear from homeschooling parents is that the hardest thing is getting time to get through all of the read-aloud books.

While Sonlight Curriculum's hallmark is the use of real books—literature, historical fiction, and topical fiction rather than texts, they still occasionally use textbooks and workbooks. For example, they use *Saxon Math*, *Miquon Math*, *Teaching Textbooks*, *Primary Mathematics*, *All About Spelling*, Apologia science texts, and *Handwriting Without Tears*.

While Sonlight sells complete curriculum packages including each subject in preschool through fifth grade, and build-your-own packages for middle school and high school, they also permit you to purchase any individual items out of the complete packages or from their catalog for preschool through high school.

Sonlight offers a generous one-year money-back guarantee. You can read the details on their website. You can save by purchasing a multi-subject package for your complete curriculum. They will even help you customize your package. Returning Sonlight customers receive additional discounts. Prices for the Core or multi-subject packages might seem high (check the website or catalog for prices), but keep in mind that most of the books you receive are non-consumable and will be used either for more than one year or by another of your children. You save even more if you teach children from the same resources whenever practical even though they might be at different grade levels for math and language arts.

Sonlight has proven to be an excellent option for families who want something different from traditional curriculum but lack the experience to put it together on their own. I strongly recommend reading through Sonlight's information or chatting with one of their consultants before determining which program, levels, or resources to use.

• • • • • • • •

Tapestry of Grace

by Marcia Somerville
Lampstand Press
1135 North Eastman Road
Kingsport, TN 37664
800-705-7487

www.tapestryofgrace.com
digital edition (DE) - $170 per Year-Plan, print edition - $295 per Year-Plan, digital and print editions - $315 per Year-Plan, individual units are $45 each for DE and $80 each for print

Tapestry of Grace (TOG) is a unit study curriculum that covers most of the major subject areas for students in grades K through 12. Some features that make it especially appealing

are Christian worldview studies incorporated throughout the curriculum, a chronological approach to history as the basic organizing theme, and a classical education approach based on the grammar, dialectic, and rhetoric stages of learning that allow all of your children to learn the same subjects at the same time but at their own level.

Subject areas covered include history, writing, literature, fine arts, geography, church history including missions (more extensively covered than I recall seeing in most other curricula with the exception of My Father's World), and Bible. You will need to use other resources for phonics, English grammar, math, foreign languages, and science.

Like many other unit studies, while *TOG* uses many books, it also includes multi-sensory learning options to address different learning styles and interests. These range from reading, writing, and simple art projects through costumed reenactments.

TOG covers the same general topics for all students simultaneously, but instruction and activities are divided into four levels of learning reflecting the classical Trivium (with the Grammar stage divided into two sections). The divisions are: Lower Grammar (K-3), Upper Grammar (grades 3-6 with a purposeful overlap here to address the reality that young students at the same ages rarely progress at the same rate), Dialectic (grades 6-9), and Rhetoric (grades 9-12). If you are unfamiliar with these terms, you should read up on classical education in books such as *Designing Your Own Classical Curriculum* or *The Well-Trained Mind* or search for one of the many internet sites on the subject.

While the *TOG* volumes include actual World Book Encyclopedia information on many topics as background information for the teacher, for the most part students will read information from recommended books that you purchase or borrow for them. You will use some books frequently or over a long period of time, so you should purchase those, particularly history resources, literature anthologies, and some literary and reference books. Many others will be used for only a week or two and might be borrowed. While some titles are strongly recommended, in most cases there are a number of choices listed, which helps families with limited resources who need flexibility. If you don't have a big budget, having easy access to a library will be a real asset if you use *TOG*.

The lengthy resource lists in each level of *TOG* (referred to as Year-Plans) list all recommended books by category, with very informative annotations for most that will help you decide which will be most useful for your children. (Note: *TOG* has a sister store, Bookshelf Central, that sells all of the core books they recommend.)

There are four Year-Plans in *TOG*, and the idea is that you will progress through each Year-Plan at one level of difficulty for each child (lower grammar, upper grammar, etc.), then begin to go through each again in the fifth year, advancing children to the next level. You can see that the youngest children might go through each Year-Plan three times. A possible alternative is to take two years to cover a Year-Plan of *TOG* if you are starting with younger children. (The flexibility of this program is one of its major assets!)

Year One: The History of Redemption covers Creation through the fall of Rome. *Year Two* studies the medieval world through the signing of the U.S. Constitution. *Year Three: The 1800s* addresses both American and European history. *Year Four: The Twentieth Century* covers world history, although U.S. history is a major component.

TOG is available in either digital editions (DE) or print editions. Whichever edition they choose, customers may print or reproduce all the pages they wish for their family. Co-ops can reproduce pages if every family has purchased that Year-Plan of *TOG*. Classroom licenses are available for larger organizations. DEs can be updated for free. Lessons are presented in full color in both print and digital editions, but you might choose to print DE pages in black-and-white for practical reasons.

Each Year-Plan in the print edition comes three-hole-punched and ready to place in your own binder. Whether you purchase the digital or print edition, there is a hefty amount of material that might seem overwhelming. However, it is very logically organized, and there are free videos on the publisher's site that will help you understand the structure and organization.

Each Year-Plan of *TOG* consists of four units, with each unit covering nine weeks. Using tabbed separator pages for each week—available for $12.50 per set from Lampstand Press—will make it even easier to locate things. Overview charts actually work as general lesson plans. Reading assignment charts for each week provide all of the reading lesson plans. The overview charts are followed by student pages for each level that should be photocopied for each student. These pages include questions, activity instructions, charts to be completed, etc. Parents or teachers really need to familiarize themselves with the background material and discussion threads in advance for each week.

The Loom, which is accessed via a CD or online, is a crucial component of *TOG*. It has scheduling suggestions, sample lesson plans, planning charts, project instructions, grammar helps, high school planning information, course descriptions, a timeline template, and more in a section that is free for anyone to access online. Additional helps that are part of *The Loom* for each Year-Plan are accessible once you have purchased the program. These include book updates, supporting links, and corrections.

TOG also offers a few optional items that are very helpful.

Evaluations provide you with assessments and

tests for the program, year by year. This should be a great help to busy parents. *Evaluations* for each Year-Plan are available as either downloadable files or on CD-ROMs for $15 for each learning level or $50 for one Year-Plan's evaluations for all learning levels.

Pop Quiz is a supplement intended to help dads participate in the learning process in a practical fashion. Audio CDs, recorded by Scott Somerville, give dads an overview of each week's studies. They also include cards with questions for leading discussions. A set is available for each unit for $15 or sets for an entire Year-Plan are $50.

Another supplement, *Writing Aids*, is published as a book and CD-ROM combo product. The *Writing Aids* book serves as a teacher's guide with student pages and supplements to be printed from home computers. *Writing Aids* is also a writing handbook that interfaces with all *TOG* volumes. This will be a one-time purchase since it will cover all genres and assignments in all four *TOG* Year-Plans. Purchasing both book and supplements as digital products costs $40, with extra cost for print or CD versions.

Yet another valuable supplement, available on CD-ROM or as a digital download, is *Map Aids*. These are specially-designed maps and map activities for each year of the program. "Teacher's maps" that serve as your answer keys are included. *Map Aids* are $25 per Year-Plan.

Summary

A free, three-week *TOG* sample is available at the publisher's website so you can try it out before you buy anything—and with their digital delivery system, you can wait until you finish the first three weeks before you pay for and download the rest of your unit. The weekly topics covered by each Year-Plan and the resources used are listed on the *TOG* website along with other information about the curriculum.

Like most extensive unit study programs,

TOG requires a significant amount of parent or teacher preparation and presentation, and large blocks of time should be dedicated over the summer to plan and prepare for each school year. Keep in mind that most parents and teachers will be getting a great deal of education of their own as they work through *TOG*!

Overall, I think *TOG's* use of classical education methods combined with the chronological approach helps overcome one of the weaknesses of some unit studies—that children read good books and participate in fun activities but sometimes fail to make connections between topics studied and their chronological relationships. In addition, the worldview threads provide themes for discussions (ideally, directed by parents using Socratic methods) and activities that help children make important connections and understand the significance of what they are learning. *TOG* comes from a Reformed Protestant viewpoint, but it respectfully tries to include Orthodox and Catholic views as it explores Church history. Consequently, *TOG* should be easier for those of the latter religious persuasions to adapt than many other unit studies might be.

• • • • • • • •

Trail Guide to Learning

by Debbie Strayer and Linda Fowler
Geography Matters
P.O. Box 92
Nancy, KY 42544
606-636-4678

www.geomatters.com

Trail Guide to Learning is projected to be a complete program for students in grades K through 12, although only three years of the program are available thus far. The methodology is a combination of both Dr. Ruth Beechick's and Charlotte Mason's ideas, which overlap and complement each other very well. It uses a unit study approach built around geography in the context of historical events. Science, art, and language arts are also covered, with language arts receiving a great deal of attention in a manner somewhat like that used in *Learning Language Arts Through Literature*.

The first year, titled *Paths of Exploration*, targets grades three through five, although it can be easily adapted for use with second and sixth graders. The second year course, *Paths of Settlement*, aims for a slightly older audience in grades four through six. *Paths of Progress*, the third course, shifts up to grades five through seven. World History will be the focus of the next group of volumes that will target middle school. High school and kindergarten through second grade courses will follow after that. While the layout remains the same, the level of difficulty gradually increases as you move up through the courses.

Each course is divided into six units, with each unit focused on a single theme that reflects a tight integration of geography and history. This approach covers fewer topics but in greater depth than does the traditional textbooks approach. The six themes in *Paths of Exploration* are Columbus, Jamestown, Pilgrims, Daniel Boone, Lewis and Clark, and Trails West. In *Paths of Settlement*, the themes are Growing Pains, Freedom Decided, Nation Building, House Divided, Unity Restored, and Sea to Shining Sea. The six units in *Paths of Progress* are Great Leaps, Making Connections, Perseverance Pays Off, Cultivating Greatness, Success Takes Flight, and Reach for the Stars; these units cover from the Industrial Revolution into the beginning of the twentieth century.

You can discern the natural thread of the study of U.S. History reflected in these themes. *Paths of Settlement* includes study of the individual states as well as a "home state project" which should satisfy any requirement for state study you might have.

For each course, lessons are laid out in detail for each day in two large hard-cover volumes (sold as a set). Each volume should take a semester to complete. At the back of the first volume of each course is a Student Resources CD-ROM with PDF files—more than 2000 printable pages! These are primarily forms that students will use as they create their own notebooks, but they also include games and maps students use for assignments. Student worksheets often include check boxes at the bottom for students to check off as they complete other assignments for which there are no student notebook pages. This helps children take on personal responsibility for completing all assignments.

I first found it curious that at the beginning of each lesson there is a boxed list of "Steps for Thinking" where you would normally find the lesson objectives. The Steps for Thinking are more abstract and general than objectives. For example, for Lesson 3, Part 1 in *Paths of Exploration*, the Steps are "1. When you learn about people, it helps you learn about things. 2. Observation is a key skill needed for learning about things in our world. It is the basis for success in science. 3. The goal of reading is to gain understanding. Hopefully it is also a source of enjoyment." The book explains that these Steps are the main ideas in the topics presented in the lessons. Parents are to introduce these "big ideas" at the beginning of each lesson, then make connections to them as they work through the various lesson activities. The Steps for Thinking are revisited at the end of the lesson, at which point children should have a better understanding and ability to discuss what they mean.

The objectives one normally finds at the beginning are located in "Lesson at a Glance" in Appendix A at the back of the book. This is actually a record keeping chart where you can see and check off objectives as they are completed. Viewing all course objectives in one place and being able to keep track of it there certainly has its advantages, and I suspect it works better than simply having a list of objectives at the beginning of each lesson.

Copywork and dictation are important techniques used in this program. Some student pages with copywork models as well as lined space to do the copying are found on the CD-ROM, but most copywork is done from assigned literature. Parents should adjust the amount of copywork as needed for each child.

Worksheets are provided for word studies, dictation, drawing, writing assignments, word searches, map work, scientific observation, spelling, etc. The CD-ROM groups the pages by grade level so you can print out worksheets that are appropriate for each level.

Instructions in the main books are written to the student. For example, "Carefully read and then copy, or write as your teacher dictates...." This seems a little odd since a parent might be teaching more than one child from the same book, but it actually is quite useful as students become self-instructors. A parent or teacher can work directly from the book, telling children what to do, reading to them, and leading discussions—adapting the language as needed. As children become more independent, they can check on their next assignments and move ahead without requiring direction from parents except for those activities where it is necessary. A significant amount of course content is included within the main books.

Many assignments are marked with icons for third, fourth, or fifth grade level in the first volume, for fourth, fifth, and sixth grades in the second volume, and for fifth, sixth, and seventh grades in the third. Assign the appropriate level to each child or show them how to select those with their icon. You will need to provide more direction if you are including an older or younger student. For all courses there are optional Middle School Supplements (available either on CD-ROM or as downloadable files) with more challenging assignments on the same topics. These are terrific resources for keeping a broader span of children working in the same course.

Real books are used throughout the courses. A list of required resources is at the front of the first book, divided into lists for volume 1 and volume 2 so you can purchase what you a need a semester at a time. Examples of about half of the required resources for the first volume of *Paths of Exploration* are *Meet Christopher Columbus, Stories of the Pilgrims, Profiles from History Volume 1*, *Handbook of Nature Study, 1911 Boy Scout Handbook, North American Wildlife Guide, Eat Your Way Around the World*, and *Intermediate World Atlas*. Some of the resources used with *Paths of Settlement* are *DK Pockets: Weather Facts, Klutz Watercolor Book, Wee Sing America, The Courage of Sarah Noble, Matchlock Gun, Justin Morgan Had a Horse, Profiles from History Volume 2*, and *Abraham Lincoln*.

Students are assigned independent reading time each day and are encouraged to read something they enjoy. They keep track of their reading in a reading log in the student notebook. Biographies are prominent among the selected resources, and there is a strong emphasis on character building through study of exemplary characters. Narration—children retelling to you what they have read or heard in their own words—is another commonly used method used by *Trail Guides* that provides parents with feedback as to how well children comprehend their reading or books read aloud to them.

Language arts coverage is quite comprehensive including spelling, vocabulary, composition, grammar, public speaking, and reading comprehension. Some of these assignments focus on skill coverage, but as often as possible they tie to the lesson theme.

As mentioned at the beginning, geography is a critical part of each theme, so each lesson features map work and other geographical activities or learning that tie to the books and theme of that lesson. For example, those coming to Jamestown started from London. Thus, students locate London on a map, expand to tracing a map of the United Kingdom and identifying its countries, then expand further to neighboring countries across bodies of water.

Science takes a naturalist approach as children learn to observe and record nature through drawing and writing in *Paths of Exploration*. *The North American Wildlife Guide* and *Handbook of Nature Study* are the primary science resources for the first year.

Art lessons are often (but not always) connected to science as children sketch what they observe. Basic drawing lessons by Barry Stebbing and Sharon Jeffus are at the back of the first book. Additional art lessons are in *Lewis and Clark Hands On*, one of the required resources for the second half of this first course.

The second course, *Paths of Settlement*, teaches earth science. Two DK Pocket science books and a *Rock Study Kit* are used with the *Handbook of Nature Study* (also used with *Paths of Exploration*). Students do more reading, research, and discussion—more challenging work than for the first course. During the second course students learn watercolor techniques which are then applied as they paint features of regions or states they are studying.

Science in *Paths of Progress* teaches the scientific process and broadens out to both life and physical sciences, teaching about friction, machines, tools, and anatomy. Art activities connect with other topics studied in *Paths of Progress* as students learn sculpting and model creation. Under fine arts, children also learn about musicians and different types of music, orchestras, musical instruments, and listening along with learning to play a recorder.

In all courses, enrichment activities are included for students who complete their work very quickly or are more advanced. These might be a recommended book to read or a more elaborate project such as researching related topics or historical characters.

Hands-on learning methods are built into lessons as drawing assignments, games (e.g., Bingo, Newcomers Game, Mechanics Tool Kit Game), art projects, experiments, demonstrations, cooking, and organizing student-made cards. Frequent discussions are a required element of all lessons. Students create a notebook of their work that does double duty by providing a means of documenting what they have learned. In addition to creating their notebooks, students also do presentations that demonstrate what they have learned.

Optional lapbooks for all three courses are available in either print or CD-ROM versions. Lapbook activities might sometimes replace other activities. *Paths of Settlement* and *Progress* both show lapbook icons next to activities when this is the case. (Icons will be added to *Exploration* with the next printing.)

There is a good amount of reading and writing in the program, but parents are instructed to adjust the amount and methods to suit the child. Both reading and writing are often taught in relation to the lesson theme or a meaningful context to help children understand why they need those skills. Also, these assignments are interspersed with discussion, narration, and other interactive activities to keep children engaged.

Notes to the parent or teacher are in the margins of the books. These are frequently valuable tips or insights regarding teaching methods. The layout of the manuals actually makes them very easy to use. You work through each lesson, selecting your choice of activities for the appropriate levels. Some advance prep work is required to acquire books, print out student notebook pages, and obtain materials needed (shown on a list at the beginning of each week). Answer keys are provided at the end of each lesson for those questions where it is appropriate.

The *Trail Guide to Learning* series is not overtly Christian but is premised on a Christian worldview. Those who want to incorporate an overt Christian worldview should purchase the *Light for the Trail Bible Study Supplement* CD-ROM for each course. Lessons tie directly to the lesson themes of each course with suggestions for prayer and worship time, weekly memory verses, and ideas for making connections between faith and the topics being studied.

While the student notebook is the best way to document student accomplishments, you might need or prefer more traditional assessments. The optional Assessments CD-ROM for each course might prove very helpful in such situations.

The *Trail Guide* series looks like a promising solution for families seeking book-based unit study that takes the guess work out of the process and is easy to use.

Note: Geography Matters also sells pre-printed packages of student pages if you do not want to print them yourself from the CD. They also sell packages of all the required resources. Check their website for prices.

· · · · · · · · · ·

TRISMS

by Linda Thornhill
TRISMS

1203 S. Delaware Place
Tulsa, OK 74104-4129
918-585-2778
www.trisms.com
Discovering the Ancient World - $195, all other courses - $235 each except *Age of Revolution* - $235 per semester or $405.00 for both semesters

TRISMS (*Time Related Integrated Studies for Mastering Skills*) differs from most unit study programs because it is research-based rather than tied to a particular spine or core book, and it is designed for fifth grade through high school. The five TRISMS courses are:

• *History's Masterminds*
• *Discovering the Ancient World*
• *Expansion of Civilization*
• *Rise of Nations*
• *Age of Revolution*

History's Masterminds might be used for students as young as fifth grade level, but it should then be used as a two-year course. Its target audience is grades seven and eight. It covers the beginning of recorded history through 2011 A.D. *Discovering the Ancient World* is a one-year course for grade eight or nine. It goes back to the beginning, covering pre-history through 500 B.C. *Expansion of Civilization* and *Rise of Nations* are each one-year courses for high school level. The first covers 500 B.C. through A.D. 1500, while the second slightly overlaps, beginning at A.D. 1440 and continuing through 1860. *Age of Revolution* might be used as either a one- or two-year high school course. It covers 1850 through 2005. Those concerned about coverage of U.S. history will be pleased to note that *Age of Revolution* focuses primarily on the United States. However, U.S. history does not receive thorough coverage in TRISMS, so you might need to supplement or use another course simply to meet requirements.

In the TRISMS title, "Time Related" refers to the chronological approach of the study, which covers the history of the world from

Unit Studies, All-in-One Programs, & Online Courses

281

early civilizations to the present. I appreciate the chronological approach for upper levels, since most students still need to learn how events and ideas interact and influence each other in time.

"Integrated" refers to the integration of language arts, writing (with a *Teaching Writing: Structure and Style [TWSS]* component that you can use or not as you wish), history, science, geography, art, music, architecture, rhetoric, philosophy, economics, and culture-studies. High school students using the program earn full course credits for history/social studies and language arts. Science studies are historical in nature, and are adequate for junior high students if they complete all assignments at more than a superficial level. High school students might receive a credit for either a survey or general science course in all but the *Rise of Nations* and *Age of Revolution* volumes, but they will need to complete separate lab courses for other science credits.

Language arts assignments incorporate lessons and activities from *TWSS*. (See the *TWSS* review in chapter seven.) This makes *TRISMS* a great tool for applying lessons learned through *TWSS*, but literature and writing assignments can be completed without using it. *TWSS* does not normally come with *TRISMS* but is available from TRISMS as a stand-alone or in a discounted resource package.

Students might also earn partial or full credits for electives such as bible history, music or art history, critical thinking, philosophy, government, economics, or historical architecture. Any of the last four volumes might be supplemented to develop a credit for economics, but the last three volumes would likely be best for this purpose. (Suggestions for expanding the study of economics are included in each volume.) *TRISMS* provides detailed information on appropriate subject credits that might be given for each course.

As I mentioned, *TRISMS* is a research-based curriculum. For each time period or

region studied, students are given questionnaire forms, each with a standard list of questions (the same questions for each time period). Each time period or unit also includes a unique worksheet that addresses that particular civilization or time period. Students use reference works, biographies, historical fiction, and nonfiction books as their primary sources of learning rather than textbooks. Similar questionnaires are used for scientists, inventions, and explorers in *History's Masterminds* and for art history, music history, and architecture in the other volumes. *Age of Revolution* uniquely presents U.S. and world history side-by-side and includes questionnaires for Major Powers, Wars, Nobel Prize Winners, and U.S. Presidents. While the questionnaires focus on specific content, other student assignments require interviews, book reports, map work, drawing, research, and lengthy compositions. On top of these assignments, students will tackle one or more in-depth projects each year.

An overview of each unit is shown in chart form as a "Unit Plan." Charts show events in chronological order, then correlate (in other columns) topics or events in art, music, architecture, science, and literature. A Rhetoric column is added to *Expansion of Civilization* and *Age of Revolution*, and the Science column is dropped from *Rise of Nations* and *Age of Revolution*. Vocabulary words, map details, "Compare Questions" for writing assignments, and other related assignments for possible use for each unit are included in the unit plan charts. Expanded explanations of assignments follow under different subject area headings. While there might be space to write a date or other brief notation next to each assignment, there is not enough room on these charts to use them as your complete record of assignments.

TRISMS does not specify daily assignments, so some students might also benefit from a separate student assignment book that spells out what to do for each day. It should take about two weeks to complete each unit since there are 18 units per course.

Student work "output" is to be put into one or more "coursebook" binders. The student package pages that come with each course might be divided into their unit sections within the binder(s) to get set up. Other work such as drawings or compositions should also be inserted into the binder(s). Students will also be creating a timeline. You can make your own, purchase one from another publisher or purchase *TRISMS'* version, *It's About Time* ($10), a spiral-bound 28-page book of lined pages to be used for recording timeline information. Each page is sectioned into seven different areas with double lines. This is useful for written information, but the lines really preclude using it for illustrations.

The five *TRISMS* courses are ultimately similar in the way they work, but they are packaged differently. One consistent item for all courses is a large packet of student worksheets, activity pages, quizzes, and tests. Permission is given to reproduce these for family members but not for a co-op or other group class. Extra packets are sold separately for $30 each. Several of the volumes have the student pack available on CD-ROM or as a download. The downloadable student packs are $15 each and allow you to print forms for additional students in your family.

The other components for each course vary. *History's Masterminds* has three parts: a teacher's manual and answer key, student assignment book, and student pack/test packet. *Discovering the Ancient World, Expansion of Civilization,* and *Rise of Nations* each have a student manual that includes all of the literature selections plus a teacher key, a student pack (questionnaires, maps, and worksheets), and a test packet. *Age of Revolution* has four volumes: two teacher manuals, two student books, and two student packs that include tests. (You can purchase *Age of Revolution* one semester at a time if you wish.) *Map Keys* (with bonus maps and blank maps) are available in CD-ROM ($24.95) or downloadable ($15) formats for *History's Masterminds* and in downloadable form for *Expansion of Civilization* ($15).

Age of Revolution is about double the size of the other courses, including about twice as many work and activity sheets per unit. Each unit is also more extensive than in the other volumes. Some of this is because of the inclusion of more (and lengthier) literary works. Some space is taken up by studies of movies—at least one each of a historical movie and a literature-based movie per unit. Students also work on a 12 to 15 page research paper, producing it as a series of three research essays that they work on throughout the year. The paper's theme will be drawn from one of seven different types of "revolutions" that are studied: revolutions in economics, the arts, science, society, race, politics, and faith. This course, even more than the others, raises many philosophical and belief questions for students to consider, but it avoids promoting particular viewpoints.

Each *TRISMS* course except for *Age of Revolution* includes instructions for adaptation for a wider span of grade levels, including using the high school volumes with students as young as sixth grade level. *Age of Revolution* definitely targets a high school audience with a heavy emphasis on the humanities, rhetoric, and higher level thinking skills, so it would be more difficult than the other courses to adapt.

Biblical history plays a major role in *Discovering the Ancient World*, but biblical and religious history is also incorporated throughout the other volumes to a lesser extent. The other four volumes can easily be adapted by those who prefer a more secular approach since their Bible and religion coverage is not sufficient for a full course credit. Math is not included in any of the volumes, although some references are made to mathematical discoveries and accomplishments in history.

Language encompasses most language arts skills, but most especially composition, vocabulary, and literature. Grammar receives some attention in the first volume, but not in the others. You might use another resource if a student needs additional work on grammar.

TRISMS presents an interesting combination of both structured and discovery learning —especially through research. The questionnaires at first glance seem highly structured, but these are really recording and accountability devices for study that might be accomplished in a number of ways. *TRISMS* recommends resources but doesn't restrict users to those resources. Students need not do every assignment in *TRISMS*, but parents or teachers can select more or fewer structured learning activities depending upon the learning style and needs of each student.

As students move up through the levels, there is definitely a gradual shift in *TRISMS* that reflects a classical approach to education. The first level leans more toward informational learning (grammar stage) while other volumes shift toward more challenging thinking and philosophical ideas (dialectic and rhetoric stages).

Students at all levels read and respond to literature, especially as they develop composition skills through activities centered around the literature. Literature readings draw from writings of the civilizations or time periods studied. Many actual readings—especially poetry and excerpts from classical literature—are included in the curriculum, although you still need to borrow or buy other resource books. TRISMS offers resource packages at discounted prices that should appeal to those who would rather not search out their own resources.

In addition to the *TRISMS* components for each course there are a number of other essential resources: an atlas, globe, world map, encyclopedia, thesaurus, dictionary, one or more three-ring notebooks, colored pencils, and coil-bound index cards (for vocabulary words). Students also need library and internet access.

Catholic families might want to supplement any volume of *TRISMS* with *An Overview of Catholic History* by Katie Torrey (from TRISMS: $14.95 print, $7.50 download). This specialized guide adds questions, topics, timeline, and recommended resources for an expanded study of Catholic history.

Another TRISMS publication, *Reading through the Ages* ($18.95 print, $9.95 download), serves as a supplement alongside all the *TRISMS* volumes or can be used on its own. It contains lists of briefly-annotated recommended reading books which are arranged chronologically. A key is used to indicate reading level, page count, and whether the book is historical fiction or biography.

Parents or teachers need to put some effort into planning and overseeing student work, but *TRISMS* offers a stimulating alternative to traditional curriculum, especially for less-than-enthusiastic students. (Bear in mind that students with poor writing skills might have trouble with the many written assignments in the program.) *TRISMS* might be a comfortable form of unit study for parents shifting from traditional textbook and workbook type curricula to unit studies since it has the built-in structure and accountability tools that are lacking in many other unit studies. It might also appeal to parents who like unit studies but worry about accountability for high school students. College prep students should be well prepared with skills necessary for college level work, and they should have excellent documentation of their work in *TRISMS*. In addition, the curriculum is fully accredited by the North Atlantic Regional High School diploma program (www.narhs.org).

TRISMS offers a free *History's Masterminds* demo download on their website that gives an overview of the *TRISMS* curriculum (specifically *History's Masterminds*) and is useful in showing how the program actually functions.

• • • • • • • •

World Views of the Western World

by David Quine
Cornerstone Curriculum Project
2006 Flat Creek
Richardson, TX 75080
972-235-5149
www.cornerstonecurriculum.com
Starting Points - $45;
Starting Points package - $183
World Views of the Western World, Syllabus
for each of *Years I-III* - $125 per volume
for first student, $100 for each additional
student in the same family, packages
for *Years I-III* range from $533-$629

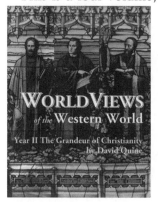

This is a four-volume, worldview, unit-study curriculum that draws heavily upon the works and ideas of Dr. Francis Schaeffer. *Starting Points*, the first volume, is followed by *Years I* through *III* of *World Views of the Western World*.

Each volume is published in an easy-to-handle, lay-flat-binding book. Each of these books serves as a course resource-teaching syllabus for students. It is designed so that students can work independently, although this would not preclude group discussion and interaction. In fact, the courses best lend themselves to a combination of independent and group work.

Following through the weekly lesson plans, students read from the research-teaching syllabus and answer questions and write essays directly in their books. They are also directed to view DVDs, listen to audio CDs, and read extensively from other sources. For each volume, you will need to purchase or borrow a number of other resources, most of which you will probably consider to be valuable additions to your library rather than resources to be used only for school. The list of resources seems daunting for a student to get through for all but *Starting Points*, but students will only use excerpts from a number of them.

Incorporating principles from classical education, this curriculum particularly suits the dialectic (logic) and rhetoric stages. Although it uses a mixture of Great Books and Good Books, it draws out of these books the important life questions. While Socratic dialogue is missing, Quine poses questions to students that direct them through the type of thinking that occurs in a Socratic discussion. In addition, students are challenged to logically defend their positions and conclusions in writing. Parents can also create a Socratic discussion themselves using the syllabus, although they would have to be familiar with the material to do. Even though students cover a huge amount of information, focus throughout is upon ideas and critical thinking rather than on memorization of information.

Starting Points: World View Primer can be used by junior high or high school students. This is an introductory course that most students should complete before tackling the other three volumes. However, it was developed after the original volumes, and it is possible for high school students to skip it and begin with *Year I*.

Starting Points lays a foundation for developing a biblical Christian worldview consistent with Schaeffer's Reformed Protestant perspective. Alongside this central theme is a subordinate theme advancing the concept of limited government.

The first part of the syllabus directs students through chapters of James Sire's *How to Read Slowly*, Paul Little's *Know What You Believe*, and David Quine's *Answers for Difficult Days*. This is a rather directive study that guides students into acceptance and support of a biblical worldview. It requires neither personal research nor a study of primary documents to evaluate all available options. Although it deals with contrary beliefs, it does so in a cursory fashion most of the time. This first section might be the most problematic for those who differ from David Quine in regard to what constitutes a biblical Christian worldview.

The second section deals with literature and movies, demonstrating how they present worldviews that are either consistent with or contrary to a biblical Christian worldview. Students learn what to look for and how to analyze what they read or view as they work through *The Chronicles of Narnia* (three books), *Frankenstein, Dr. Jekyll and Mr. Hyde, It's a Wonderful Life,* and *The Wizard of Oz.*

The third part of the syllabus guides students through C.S. Lewis's *Mere Christianity* and Christian Overman's *Assumptions* as they move into cultural applications of worldviews, both positive and negative. This section of *Starting Points,* as well as the next, both bring in philosophical background that helps students understand motivating ideas that shaped our country. The final section uses Gary Amos's *Never Before in History* as the foundation for a study of the founding of the United States, drawing upon information and ideas raised earlier in the study.

High school students can derive one credit each in Bible, literature, and U.S. History with this course. They will be required to do a significant amount of writing, including lengthy essays. As with the other volumes, assistance is provided within the syllabus for developing each essay.

The next three volumes, *World Views of the Western World,* follow a chronological timeline. *Year I, The Bible and Ancient Thought,* begins with an introduction to the course and covers the basics of defining worldviews. Thus, students could skip *Starting Points* and begin with this volume. From there it moves on to a comparison of a biblical Christian worldview and Greco-Roman worldviews roughly covering the time period 1200 BC - 1200 AD (Primary attention is given to Ancient Rome, Greece, and the Middle Ages.) In-depth studies of

the Book of Job, *The Iliad,* and *City of God* are representative of Quine's strategy of using significant pieces of literature as springboards for integrated study in each area. The second half of *Year I* shifts to the Middle Ages, examining changes in philosophical and theological ideas and their consequences through this era and beyond. Among other resources used with this volume are *The Aeneid, Affliction* (Edith Schaeffer), *How Should We Then Live?* (Francis Schaeffer), *The Republic, The Universe Next Door* (Sire), the *How Should We Then Live?* DVD series, Cornerstone's *Adventures in Art* and *Classical Composers and the Christian World View,* audio CDs by Francis Schaeffer, and audio CDs from the Knowledge Products series on figures such as Aristotle and Plato.

The second volume, *The Grandeur of Christianity and the Revolutionary Age,* covers 1200 to the 1800s addressing the Renaissance, the Reformation, the Revolutionary Age, political theory, early American history, and the rise of modern science. A primary focus is comparison and contrast of the Renaissance view of life with that of the Reformation. *Year II* uses such resources as *Calvin's Institutes of the Christian Religion, Reformation Overview* DVDs, *The Universe Next Door,* Machiavelli's *The Prince,* Knowledge Product's audio CD on John Locke and his *Two Treatises, The Shorter Catechism,* Luther's *95 Theses,* Bastiat's *The Law, The Communist Manifesto, Hamlet, A Tale of Two Cities,* and *Animal Farm* with extensive, in-depth study of *The Divine Comedy.* Development of Reformation theology is a major theme.

Year III: Christianity Answers the 21st Century, continues from the 1800s (the Age of Reason and the Age of Fragmentation) to the present, covering both world and U.S. history with a western civilization emphasis. *Year III* compares and contrasts the theistic ideas of the Bible with the naturalistic ideas of the 20th century. Examples of resources used with *Year III* are dramatized audio CDs on famous philosophers such as Hegel, Nietzsche, Marx, and Sartre; Hazlitt's *Economics in One Lesson, Darwin on Trial* (Johnson); *The Plague* (Camus); *The New Evidence that Demands a Verdict; Walden Two* (Skinner); C.S. Lewis' *That Hideous Strength*; three of the *Star Wars* movies as well as the movies *Gettysburg* and *Gone with the Wind; How Should We Then Live?* (both the book and the DVD series); and the *Of Pandas and People* science text. Quine's continual use of comparison and contrast effectively helps students understand both the underlying beliefs and the cultural outworking of different worldviews.

Since literature is a major part of these courses, Cornerstone Curriculum has been working to create The World View Library. This is a collection of significant literary works in readable translations to which they have added sidebars with definitions, occasional explanatory notes, and highlighted quotations. Fifteen books, including titles such *The Iliad, Frankenstein,* and *The Law,* are already available in the collection with others in the works. While you do not have to use these particular editions of the books, they will work especially well with these courses.

Rather than aiming for comprehensive coverage of history, these four Cornerstone courses instead focus upon key ideas that dominated each period. Following the lead of Francis Schaeffer in *How Should We Then Live?,* study centers primarily around the areas of philosophy, religion, literature, music, and the fine arts. It also ventures beyond Schaeffer into economics, law and government, and science. Extensive writing is required throughout all volumes, and basic paragraph and essay writing skills are taught for the lengthier assignments.

A chart at the beginning of *Year I* shows how many credits might be given for each subject area for the high school transcript; the entire three volumes are equivalent to 16 Carnegie units, so this is a major part of a student's high school course work. It includes enough units for basic requirements in English, history,

government, and fine arts, with the equivalent of 2 units of philosophy/theology, 1 unit of science history, and surplus units in government, political theory, and economics. The last two subjects look great on a transcript! You will need to add math, lab science, and foreign language classes (plus health, physical education, driver's ed, and other electives) to complete high school requirements.

While students can work through these volumes independently, there are no built-in mechanisms for accountability—no tests or quizzes. However, there are numerous essay questions and writing assignments. Parents should be looking over this work and discussing the course content with students. However, most parents are not familiar with the course content, which makes this rather difficult.

Ideally, parents should also participate in the study, at least reading through the material, watching DVDs, and listening to the CDs. If this is not possible, having a student narrate lesson content to the parent, summarizing what they have learned, might be adequate although less than ideal. Consider having a few students who are working through the study (simultaneously but independently) meet with a knowledgeable adult periodically to discuss course content.

If none of these ideas are practical, all is not lost. You might leave accountability at the student's doorstep: they get out of it what they put into it. When you consider how little students retain of what they supposedly learn under the most stringent accountability systems, there is something to be said for allowing them to absorb as much as they can without outside coercion. After all, this is most often how adults function when they want to learn something. The key here is student motivation. I have found in teaching worldviews that once most students grasp the idea of worldviews and how important it is, learning follows naturally. They easily understand that this is learning that matters!

Note that each volume is a consumable course and is intended for use by only one student. No photocopying or resale is allowed. Thus, you need to purchase a separate syllabus for each student, although additional books are purchased at discounted prices. Packages include the CDs, DVDs, and books needed for each level. However, you can also purchase selected items from any of the packages if you already have access to some of them.

Online Courses

Do you want to move your family to Asia for missionary work but wonder how on earth you can manage to continue homeschooling your teen? Did you flunk math all the way through high school and now desperately need someone else to teach your teenager algebra? Do you have an ambitious, bright student who is begging to go to a "regular" school so she can take Advanced Placement (AP) courses? Does your teen want a course on Greek philosophers with Socratic discussion, and you don't have the time, knowledge, or inclination to teach such a course yourself?

All these needs and more can be met with courses available to homeschoolers on the internet. Homeschoolers are at the cutting edge of online learning because of their openness to new ideas and the unusual needs many families have. For example, Fritz Hinrichs (www.gbt.org) began offering classical courses online back in the 1980s. He has continually developed his courses and delivery methods as new technology and software have developed.

Homeschoolers are not the only ones taking advantage of internet technology. Even government schools have jumped on board. A challenging dilemma has surfaced as a result. Courses offered by government schools are usually free or minimal cost to families, while those offered by private organizations can cost hundreds of dollars. But there is a significant nonfinancial cost when a homeschooling family uses courses funded by the government—loss of parental control.

While legal definitions vary from state to state, homeschoolers who enroll in government school courses are no longer considered to be homeschoolers. They are under the authority of the school's teachers rather than that of their parents, even if they are completing their coursework at home under parental supervision. Parents no longer have the final say over course content and requirements unless they pull a child out of the school.

While parents, theoretically, have the ability to oversee what their children are reading and doing, the reality is that in most situations, children will work independently, and parents won't know the actual course content. In most cases, they won't be able to determine in advance if their child's teacher will support or contradict their family beliefs and values. And for those interested in forming a Christian worldview in their children, government-school programs are usually counterproductive since they adhere to a secular, materialistic worldview.

In addition, there are political ramifications from homeschoolers enrolling in government programs that are damaging to the larger homeschool community, but those are beyond the scope of this book. The bottom line is that the "free" courses often come with a hidden price tag.

Content and viewpoint problems can also crop up in online courses offered by private organizations that hold different worldviews from that of your family. However, you are often able to ask questions about teachers and worldviews in these situations. I would urge you to carefully investigate any such program before enrolling your child.

There are many good programs that work well with homeschoolers and are up front about their religious beliefs and goals.

In addition to beliefs and goals, there are also choices regarding structure in online learning.

Some programs use the internet for automated course delivery. Students log on to a course, work through it answering questions as they go, and receive a grade based on their work. Some of these courses are mostly text—little different than reading a textbook, while others are heavily illustrated with computer graphics and animations. Some courses are largely discussion based—this is especially true of classical education courses. Some use bulletin-board posting as a part of course requirements. Some require separate written work such as essays that are emailed to instructors. Some use the internet sparingly, making assignments in traditional textbooks, relaying assignments and comments back and forth over the internet, with an occasional student chat room discussion. Anything that might be done is probably being done by some course provider somewhere.

Also, you need to think about your child's learning style when you choose online programs. Because most young children need more active learning and interaction, online education is rarely a good idea for the elementary grades. However, it becomes much more appropriate for junior and senior high students. Even so, an older child's learning style should still influence your choice of such programs. For example, a Sociable Sue will much prefer online discussions to courses where she primarily reads text material online with minimal interaction.

There are two terms you need to know in regard to online courses: synchronous and asynchronous. Synchronous courses mean there are times when students and teacher are online and interacting at the same time— synchronously. Asynchronous courses mean courses are prerecorded or there is written material that students may access at any time. There are no chats or sessions where students and teachers interact together simultaneously—unless they happen to do instant messaging. Referring back to my last example

of the sociable child, she is much more likely to succeed in synchronous courses because of the real-time interaction with others.

Below are some of the online options. These are only a sampling of the many options available. The grade levels served by the courses are noted in parentheses.

- Angelicum Academy - www.angelicum.net - Catholic, classical, mostly asynchronous but includes Socratic discussion groups (PreK-12)
- Apex Learning - www.apexlearning.com - secular, asynchronous; also AP, Honors, and exam prep courses (9-12)
- Calvert Virtual Academy - www.calvertschool.org - secular, asynchronous with occasional live, interactive sessions (6-8)
- CLASS.com - www.class.com - graphically-interesting courses equivalent to public high school courses, asynchronous, secular (9-12)
- Clonlara's Compuhigh - www.compuhigh.com - asynchronous, secular (9-12)
- Eagle Christian - www.eaglechristian.org - Christian program using textbooks with some on-line interaction (7-12)
- Escondido Tutorial Service - www.gbt.org - synchronous discussions, classical, Christian (9-12)
- K12 - www.k12.com - asynchronous; uses a mixture of online activity, real books, and textbooks; secular (K-12)
- The Compass Learning Odyssey - www.childu.com - secular, asynchronous, graphically interesting courses (K-12)
- NorthStar Academy - www.northstar-academy.org - Christian; asynchronous; students access prerecorded lessons presentations and use traditional textbooks; satisfies U.S., Canadian, or U.K. requirements (6-12)
- Oxford Tutorial Service - www.oxfordtutorials.com - classical, Christian,

synchronous discussions (9-12)
- The Potter's School - www.pottersschool. org - Christian, synchronous courses (6-12)
- Schola Classical Tutorials - www. scholatutorials.org - classical, Christian, synchronous discussions (ages 14 and up)
- Scholars' Online Academy - www. scholarsonline.org - classical, Christian, synchronous (7-12)
- Regina Coeli Academy (grades 9-12)/Agnus Dei Junior Program (grades 7-8) - www. reginacloeli.org - Catholic, synchronous, classical

Computer-Based Traditional Curriculum

I had to create a separate category to mention a few computer-based programs that offer fairly traditional courses entirely online. These are not the only such programs, but they are inexpensive and represent options for both Christian and secular homeschoolers.

Complete Curriculum

Complete Curriculum, LLC
PO Box 451
Flat Rock, MI 48134
888-675-8398
www.completecurriculum.com

Complete Curriculum has got to be one of the most inexpensive online curriculum providers available. They have digital-text courses for math, language arts, science, and social studies for kindergarten through twelfth grade, although a number of the high school courses are not yet available. For a $74.95 yearly membership fee, you have access to up to ten digital texts to use. While each text may be assigned to only one student at a time, you might have two or more students using the ten texts!

Course content is aligned with the national standards. The outlook is secular throughout all courses. Consequently, evolution and an

"old earth" perspective show up in science and history texts. While students learn vocabulary, concepts, and skills, courses stress critical thinking rather than rote learning.

Most courses have 180 lessons for the school year. (Some science and social studies courses have fewer.) The publisher says that lessons for each subject should take one to one and a half hours a day to complete, but many lessons I reviewed would not take that much time. The customer who alerted me to this curriculum told me that for kindergarten and first grade they usually completed all four subjects within about one and a half hours per day.

Lessons are laid out in a consistent fashion in the online teacher's manuals for each subject. For each lesson, the teacher's manual lists:
- the lesson objective
- key vocabulary words—might be used for spelling or vocabulary, or to help students comprehend what they will read
- materials needed
- literary selections when appropriate—some of which are presented within the online student manual
- an "engaging" question which the teacher uses to begin the lesson
- supplemental engagement activities for some lessons
- extensions included for some lessons—these might be used with accelerated or lagging students
- technology resources—for some lessons, suggestions are given for utilizing technology, especially websites that contribute to the lesson
- additional notes to the teacher—these outline or summarize the lesson
- advance preparation or homework required—gives the teacher a heads up when extra time will be required
- lesson Wrap-Ups—only in K-2 Math

For each course there are both a student manual and teacher's manual. These are accessed as PDF files from the publisher's website. You will certainly want to print out some or all of the student manual pages since many serve as worksheets. Lessons are presented in full color with plenty of illustrations. While a color printer makes using the pages much easier, you can work with a black-and-white printout if you have the computer file easily viewable. Some lessons or stories refer to colors in the illustrations that children will need to see. The teacher's manual for each course includes the student manual pages with answers placed either at the end of the teacher's manual portion or within all worksheets, exercises, and assessments.

Lessons are editable so you can add or subtract lessons from this or other texts in the series that you have added to your "shelf" (limit ten texts). You can also add attachments to a student lesson and then email a lesson to a student. The ability to email lessons might prove valuable as it allows students to work from one computer while the parent or teacher accesses the teacher's manual from another computer. For lessons that allow students to type directly on the computer, you can save the completed lessons as PDF files. (The program also offers you the option of subscribing to an Adobe service that will transform PDF files into Word documents which should be easier to edit if you should wish to do so.)

Some additional resources are needed from time to time. For example in the eighth grade language arts, there is a lesson on Thomas Nast, the famous cartoonist of the nineteenth century. Part of the lesson directs students to find and study present day political cartoons and comics. In another lesson, students need to access *Honi M'agel,* a Jewish folktale on the internet. Science lessons require resources for experiments and activities. Math might require pennies or other manipulatives in the early grades.

Sometimes, students can type directly onto worksheets on the computer, and those worksheets can be printed out. But this is not a computer-based curriculum like *Switched on Schoolhouse* where students type in all responses which are then graded by the computer. Students frequently complete work sheets that parents or teachers have printed out. Also, students create notebooks for some subjects such as spelling and writing as well as a Grammar Ring and a Vocabulary Ring where they collect rules and definitions they have written on index cards. High school students learn note taking skills, and apply them across the curriculum. Students learn to integrate knowledge and skills through projects such as creating brochures, PowerPoint presentations, and research reports.

Language Arts courses integrate all age-appropriate language arts skills—reading, literature, spelling, vocabulary, grammar, handwriting, vocabulary, and composition. It is expected that children have some familiarity with the alphabet prior to kindergarten; they should recognize at least some of the letters. Kindergarten teaches sounds and letters, beginning reading, writing, spelling, and printing along with other facets of language arts typically taught in kindergarten. Reading instruction is phonics based but includes the introduction of many sight words. For reading material, their own proprietary Progressive Readers are used in grades K through three, while classic literature is included within the student manuals in the upper grades. Language arts lessons often revolve around the literary selections. Students begin to create a journal in first grade. They continue to learn all forms of composition, applying those skills within language arts and across the curriculum.

Math follows a fairly standard scope and sequence, including coverage of a broad range of topics at each grade level. Simple manipulatives and visual illustrations are used to teach concepts in the early grades—e.g., lima beans are used in first grade to learn simple addition, and number cards and strips are used in second grade. Cumulative reviews help students retain skills learned in previous lessons. The sequence of high school math topics seems confused at the moment, but all high school level math texts are not yet complete. Algebra II and Geometry are both shown as complete courses for tenth grade level. Algebra I is studied in ninth grade and Pre-calculus in eleventh. Of course, you are free to select whichever course a student needs no matter the grade level indicated.

The science program is inquiry-based. Lessons begin by raising questions, observing, and/or experimenting. Students record and analyze data according to the scientific method even in kindergarten, albeit at a very simple level. However, the Biology course for tenth grade (which is not yet complete) seems to have a minimal amount of lab activity. Staff at www.CompleteCurriculum.com tell me that the "high school science texts will contain experiments within lessons and not call for a separate lab setting." This is an area you will need to watch to ensure that science lab courses meet requirements of the college a student wishes to attend. I did not find health included within the science curriculum, yet that is a requirement in most states that you will have to cover in some other fashion.

Social Studies courses cover history, geography, civics and government as well as economics, with emphasis varying from grade to grade. Kindergarten and first grade deal with community, citizenship, character, and very introductory geography and history. Second grade continues with these themes, adding state history as students create a brochure-style mini-book on their own state. Christian home educators might have issues with the fourth grade social studies that includes a number of lessons dealing with Native American myths presented with no contrasting Christian worldview (e.g., only Native American creation stories). Fifth grade presents a history of the U.S. while sixth grade broadens to history of the Americas. History of the Eastern Hemisphere is studied in seventh grade. Eighth graders study U.S. History again, this time from colonization through Reconstruction. Ninth grade continues through modern history. Separate civics/government and economics courses are slated for tenth grade level to meet those requirements. Then eleventh graders study world history and geography.

Throughout the social studies courses, and more so in junior and senior high, there are frequently challenging questions to consider, and students are often directed to read or research topics and present contrasting views. All of these texts reflect a typical secular outlook as you might find in other texts used in government schools. The quality of the writing in the social studies courses varies from text to text. Some texts seem to be collections of information while others have more of a story-telling feel—probably the result of different authors.

Complete Curriculum does not oversee student work or issue diplomas or report cards. However, for families looking for an inexpensive, secular curriculum, this is a real bargain.

· · · · · · · · ·

Switched-On Schoolhouse OR Monarch

Alpha Omega
804 N. 2nd Ave. E.
Rock Rapids, IA 51246-1759
800-622-3070
www.aophomeschooling.com
$95.95 per subject,
$439.99 for complete 5 subject set

Alpha Omega first developed their *LIFEPAC* curriculum, a self-instructional learning system using a number of worktext booklets for each subject. Alpha Omega responded to the proliferation of computers and improvements in technology by using their *LIFEPAC* curriculum as the foundation for their computer-based curriculum, *Switched-On Schoolhouse (SOS)*.

SOS is available for grades 3 through 12 in a completely computerized form that includes full-color graphics, videos, sound, a text-to-speech option, internet excursions, and many other features. Web excursions are not essential to the curriculum, so an internet connection is not absolutely necessary. However, the web links add extra interest and additional learning opportunities. Also, an internet connection allows for automatic updating of the curriculum.

Many parents love *SOS* because it really allows students to work independently. Parents only need to set up the initial program, customize lesson plans if necessary, check student progress which can be viewed in "teacher mode" on the computer, and review writing assignments. Parents can also build supplemental lessons within the *SOS* curriculum.

SOS runs only on Windows systems. Computer equipment should be fairly current for the program to run at a decent pace, for smooth viewing of video clips, and for the use of sound. Minimum systems requirements are Windows XP with Service Pack 3, Windows Vista with Service Pack 1, or Windows 7.

Bible, Math, Language Arts, Science, and History/Geography courses can be purchased individually or as complete grade level sets. The programs follow the same general format for each subject. A topic is introduced then students are given pertinent vocabulary words to learn. Activities and games help students to quickly master the vocabulary words. (Vocabulary words with definitions can also be printed for practice offline.) A number of games for reinforcing concepts and material are built into the lessons for math, geography, and vocabulary drill. Students may skip these games if they wish.

Students read through each section of instructional material on the screen, then click "Show problems" at the bottom of the screen to work through comprehension activities. Questions are presented mostly in multiple-choice, sorting, and matching formats. Incorrect answers are immediately identified, and students have an opportunity to correct them, but with a limited number of attempts available in each lesson.

These section questions in all subjects other than math allow students to scan the "text" material to figure out what the correct answer should be most of the time, but sometimes they must make inferences, read maps, or interpret data to arrive at correct answers. Math programs require students to solve problems. If students miss questions, those that were answered incorrectly are presented again. Sometimes hints are given such as pointing out that the error was in the spelling or indicating a map to which a student might refer to find the answer. However, such hints seem few and far between.

Once students have answered all questions correctly for a set number of lessons, they take a quiz. It is possible to set the program such that students cannot scan material when taking a quiz, so this is when you will really know whether or not they've learned anything. (The "open book" option allows students to exit and enter the quiz as many times as they wish, presumably allowing them to check the lesson for information they don't know.) Some written responses are required in the exercises and quizzes. Exercises, quizzes, and tests are scored by the computer although parent or teacher override is permitted if you choose to accept an answer as correct that the computer rejects as incorrect.

SOS is very professionally produced, and the publisher continually works at improving the courses. It allows parents control over which lessons are to be assigned in which order, how lenient or tough to be with spelling of answers, grade format, and access to the internet. In both *SOS* and *Monarch*, "At-a-Glance Assignment Indicators" highlight past-due lessons making them easy to spot, and a message center makes it easy for parents and students to send notes to each other. *SOS* truly allows students to work independently—a tremendous help for parents with little time to oversee schoolwork. Parents also set up a school calendar that allows the computer to schedule each student's rate of progress. The computer then alerts students if they get behind schedule.

The programs move at a fairly good pace for the most part so there's not a lot of wasted time as in software of the "edutainment" sort. While answers are each followed by a verbal affirmation (which can be turned off if students prefer), there are no "cute" graphics wasting time between answers and subsequent questions except in the games.

The content is non-denominationally Protestant throughout all subjects. Biblical concepts appear throughout all subjects, although less so in math than others.

The Bible program offers solid content, including some scripture memorization. You can choose either the KJB or NASB version for Bible content. Map identification is added to the typical questions and answers.

Language courses cover reading skills, grammar, composition, spelling, and vocabulary. Periodic writing projects stretch skills beyond the short answers students write within the lessons themselves. Book reports are included for grades 3 through 8.

History and geography are combined, with geography and map work intermixed throughout lessons. A historical timeline is available to students if they choose to click on "linked" data in their history studies. (The timeline also can be accessed from within other subjects besides history and geography.) Essays, reports, and special projects expand learning beyond the computer. Science programs also include a few experiments, essays, observations, and other non-computer activities.

SOS is a very sophisticated system, so it comes with a context-sensitive Help file, accessible by pressing F1. There are also links to specific tutorials from the locations where they are most likely to be needed (in the Teacher mode). In addition, free technical support is available for *SOS* users should they need help with either set up or use.

Once you've got one student and his or her courses set up, it is easy to add additional courses and students. There is so much customization available to users that most novices will stick with the basics until they get comfortable with the program. But once you've used it for a while, you should experiment with all of the fine-tuning features such as the ability to customize your calendar, create assignment options for students, change grade options, and even edit and create subjects. You should also take time to familiarize yourself and your student with the dictionary and calculator available through the "resource center" available at the click of a button. Optional placement tests are available for core subjects at www.aophomeschooling.com/diagnostic-tests. php.

SOS makes life easy for parents, but it's not perfect. As I have encountered in many other computerized programs, requested answers seemed highly debatable. Teacher overrides are helpful in dealing with such situations, but that requires more immediate oversight. I am continually surprised at questions curriculum authors come up with that have little value or might even be deemed incorrect by some children. For example, the science curriculum in one lesson focuses at least two questions on defining geraniums as plants that often grow in window boxes. Here in Southern California, geraniums are a common ground cover or bush and only rarely appear in window boxes since they grow too fast for such containers. And is not the focus on window boxes a distraction from more salient features of geraniums? To deal with this issue, *SOS* has added additional variations of possible answers to numerous questions in the attempt to reduce the number of computer-graded answers deemed unfair or unreasonable.

A problem cropped up in the math program immediately with the presentation of addition and subtraction problems with regrouping. Given 3-digit numbers, students will generally work from right to left to solve each problem, yet the cursor begins on the left, and it is a bother to get it to enter numbers in the logical order.

In the language program, students frequently work with reading selections, answering questions regarding content. Unfortunately, some of the questions are too nit-picky. For example, one question asked students how many trees were in the backyard (13) in a story about family members being friendly to birds and animals. The number of trees was irrelevant unless you really want children to memorize that sort of detail when reading.

With each new edition, *SOS* continues to improve. Graphics, games, and weblinks have been among the more visible improvements, while "behind-the-scenes" features such as the teacher search tool, customizable subject reports, the ability to zero out (reset) a lesson, and print capability for lessons, problems, assignments, and records provide parents and teachers with the tools they need. Another feature sure to be valuable to some students is "text-to-speech." Students highlight text they want to hear, choose from various electronic voices, and hear the passage read aloud. A couple of new features added for 2011-12 include attendance tracking and reporting as well as a template and report for creating transcripts. Note that you can add non-*SOS* courses to the transcript and otherwise customize it to create a complete transcript. New to *SOS* are other features such as a Bible lookup tool accessible from within any subject, a Past Due

Report form that lets parents know if any student assignments are late, and an enhanced assignment editor that allows you to include picture files, weblinks, and Flash videos within customized assignments.

Numerous *SOS* elective courses—some for elementary grades but most for high school level—can be added to an *SOS* core curriculum or used on their own. Among the electives are Spanish and French courses for elementary grades or for high school, plus consumer math, state history, *The Story of the Constitution*, *Physical Fitness*, *Personal Financial Literacy*, *Health*, and *College Planner*.

SOS is not a creative approach to learning since it must be very structured and controlled to be able to work within the computer format. Nevertheless, I expect that many parents will find *SOS* the tool that makes homeschooling possible for them.

Also from Alpha Omega, *Monarch* is a new twist on the popular *Switched-On Schoolhouse* curriculum. While *Switched-On Schoolhouse* is a CD-ROM-based, Christian homeschool curriculum, *Monarch* is web-based, accessible from any computer at any time. Like *SOS*, *Monarch* offers complete grade level programs for grades 3 through 12 plus electives for both elementary and high school levels.

While both programs share many features such as "text-to speech," automatic grading, customizable desktops, and one-click access to a historical timeline, *Monarch* adds some features. One of the most important differences is that *Monarch* will run on either Windows or Mac computers. Also, curriculum updates to *Monarch* are able to be released in real time all year round, rather than in an annual release like *SOS*. For instance, *Monarch* was updated to include Osama bin Laden's demise and the use of My Plate rather than the traditional food pyramid shortly after each event/change occurred. In addition, a virtual keyboard for foreign languages makes it easy for students to type the proper symbols and characters. And there's no worry about backing up data since it's stored at a secure location and is maintained for seven years after your subscription ends. Free placement tests for *Monarch* math and language arts are available at www.aophomeschooling.com/diagnostic-tests.php.

The other major difference between *Monarch* and *SOS* is the "ownership." Customers purchase *SOS* for up to five students on one installation at a given time. Their curriculum is reusable. On the other hand, *Monarch* is available on a subscription basis. One student may use the subscription curriculum for up to 18 months.

On the negative side, *Monarch* requires a reliable high speed internet connection for all student work which could be a problem for some families. Also, I understand that *Monarch* has fewer games than *SOS* at the moment, but more are being added.

Monarch and *SOS* are priced the same, so it seems to me that the number of potential students in your family who might use the curriculum, the computer platform, and your internet connection would be the biggest factors for determining which option best suits your needs.

Foreign Language

Choosing Top Picks for foreign language is problematic since I don't have room to pick a best product for every language, much less differentiate products for younger and older students in each language. So I've had to be very selective. I picked two top publishers that produce resources for many different languages that also address the needs of both older and younger learners. Then I follow with a fun resource for exploring Greek and a few of my favorites for learning Latin since Latin generally needs to be learned in a different fashion than other languages.

· · · · · · · ·

The Learnables—French, German, Spanish, Russian, Chinese, Japanese, Hebrew, or English (ESL)

International Linguistics Corporation
12220 Blue Ridge Blvd., Ste. G
Kansas City, MO 64030
800-237-1830
www.learnables.com
Level 1 either book and CD OR computer versions - $60-$65 each,
combination package with computer version of *Book 1* plus *Basic Structures* Book 1 and three audio CDs - $99,
Basic Structures with CDs for Level 1 - $60 each, *Basic Structures* for other levels range up to $150; ESL is priced differently; check the website for more pricing details

The *Learnables* approach to foreign language works well for homeschooling families for at least four reasons:

- flexibility for different age learners from elementary grades through high school (and even adults!)
- does not require the parent to know or teach the language
- multisensory format works for many different learning styles
- inductive, experiential methodology is a more natural learning method than traditional approaches to foreign language acquisition

The Learnables feature an immersion approach that uses illustrations and pictures with no text to build good listening skills that are essential in conversation. This type of learning happens prior to any reading in a foreign language. Lessons are presented either in books along with audio CDs or on CD-ROMs. This approach builds vocabulary and teaches sentence structure from extensive listening. The methodology aims to develop understanding and comprehension first then follow with reading, speaking, and writing skills in that order. This is similar to the way most of us learned English, except a child learns to speak before reading. *The Learnables* emphasis is on vocabulary and understanding and, most importantly, learning to think in the foreign language.

Books and CDs are gradually being replaced by versions that are completely computer-based. For some languages, only book and CD versions are available, for some only computer-based versions, and for some both versions are available. The cost is the same whichever version you select. (Computer versions have CDs specific to either Windows or Mac systems, so be certain to order the correct version.)

For the most part, the same picture books and computer illustrations are used with each language. However the sequence of sentences and some of the illustrations are specific to the language. All ages should start with *Level 1* (either the computer version or a book with

four CDs). Lessons begin with words and short phrases whose meaning is obvious from the pictures. Translation is not given. If the student is in doubt, repetition of a word in another picture will likely clear things up. Sentences gradually become more complex as do the pictures. Pronunciation is very clear. There are similar sets of books with CDs for three levels in French, and five or more levels in Spanish or German. English for ESL students has six levels. Fewer levels are available for Russian, Hebrew, Chinese, and Japanese.

This approach is more enjoyable than typical programs of either the textbook variety or the audio CDs that have you simply repeat the foreign language phrases after the speaker. The learner must think about what is happening in the pictures to understand the meaning. The illustrations used in *The Learnables* also add visual memory association to the words students hear, increasing vocabulary retention.

The computer versions work just like the book and CD versions, but they also feature some games, photographs, and movies that enhance the learning process.

It is sufficient for children in the early elementary grades to work through the picture books and CDs or computer programs. Older students need exposure to written forms of the language and its grammar. The *Basic Structures* and *Grammar Enhancement* programs from The Learnables add these elements.

Basic Structures programs are designed as companions for each level. Thus far, *Basic Structures* is available for four levels of Spanish, three levels of French and German, and one level of Russian and Hebrew. *Advanced* level (a fourth level) for French uses a different type of book that includes paragraphs with pictures. The number of CDs for each *Basic Structures* course varies depending upon the language.

Basic Structures books include pictures with phrases or sentences plus a very few reading and writing activities without pictures. The primary goal with *Basic Structures* is learning to read the language rather than learning to write it. Vocabulary in each *Basic Structures* program is very similar to that of the corresponding picture book program. Students listen to the CDs, read the phrases and sentences, and sometimes do matching, fill-in-the-blank, or similar written exercises. These can be done on separate paper so you are able to reuse the same book with more than one child. However, additional books are available without CDs if you need them. *Basic Structures* might be used with students from about fourth grade and up. Junior high and high school students definitely should use *Basic Structures* after completing each level of *The Learnables* picture books.

Grammar is not taught directly within either the picture books or *Basic Structures* programs, but students do acquire practical grammatical knowledge from actually using the language. At elementary levels this does not present a problem as it does for high school where students are expected to study the grammar of whatever foreign language they are learning. This is where *Grammar Enhancements* come in.

Grammar Enhancement programs are available for Spanish, French and German. Each *Grammar Enhancement* set includes a book and four CDs or a computer version for Spanish or French ($75 each for either version). These are designed to be used after completion of *Level 1* of a language, both the picture book program and *Basic Structures*. Thus, you could have young children work through only the picture book, intermediate children adding *Basic Structures*, and teens continuing through *Grammar Enhancement*. Alternatively, you could have students complete both *Levels 1* and *2* before tackling *Grammar Enhancement*.

The publisher sells a package of *Grammar Enhancement* with *Level 2* materials, suggesting it be used at the beginning of *Level 2*. However, if you are trying to create something comparable to a typical first year high school language course, *Grammar Enhancement* is essential alongside the *Level 1* resources. *Grammar*

Enhancement uses vocabulary from *Level 1* and adds a great deal more. For example, in the Spanish course, the preterit tense is introduced in *Grammar Enhancement* but not in the other *Level 1* books. Yet, the preterit tense is typically taught in a first year course. However, the order of teaching grammatical structures differs in immersion programs from grammar programs. In the end, students in an immersion program know not only the grammar, but how the grammar is used in sentences to enable them to talk automatically without reference to grammar, just as we speak English.

Grammatically, *Grammar Enhancement* focuses on prepositions, pronouns, plurals, and verbs. The second-year *Basic Structures* books continue teaching grammatical forms. Should a student wish to become fluent, there are advanced books in German and Spanish that cover all of the advanced grammar concepts in context with a sufficiently large vocabulary. The *Grammar Enhancement* book contains the words from the CDs as well as pictures, but no instruction is given in English and no grammar rules are provided. Instead, many examples are given so students learn the sometimes subtle distinctions as they look for patterns and listen to the correct usage. This method might be more effective for some students than traditional instruction about grammar rules.

None of the components requires any significant amount of writing, and there is no built-in requirement that students actually speak the language, although this is likely to happen naturally. If students really intend to learn to speak the language, there is really no substitute for immersion where the student listens to and converses with native language speakers.

The program is set up with four levels for most languages. Most of the time each level follows a similar plan. Spanish students have available to them many levels as well as specialized vocabulary books on verb usage that teach the modals and all the tenses in the context of interesting stories. There are also specialized books on eating, transportation, walking, and placement (use of Spanish words for place, put, lift, reach, etc.). German students also have many optional advanced books that teach in depth the important components of the German language.

It is impossible to correlate levels of this program directly with traditional language courses, although the combination of *Learnables 1*, *Basic Structures 1*, and *Grammar Enhancement* could be considered a first year course. The publisher claims that the four levels of Spanish are equivalent to four high school years, while four levels of German and French are equivalent to 3.5 high school years. High school students should aim to complete the four levels (and probably the fifth level of Spanish as well) using all basic components available for each level. The specialized vocabulary books would be optional elements.

The Learnables are continuing to update their courses by adding games, movies and advanced books and digital versions. Christians might want to use the supplemental *Bible Stories* in Spanish, French, or German (includes a book and CD for $25 each) after completion of *Level 2*. These incorporate all major biblical terms.

· · · · · · · · ·

Rosetta Stone Homeschool (CD-ROM computer programs)

Fairfield Language Technologies
135 W. Market St.
Harrisonburg, VA 22801
888-232-9245
email: homeschool@ rosettastone.com
www.rosettastone. com/homeschool

all individual levels - $159 each
set of Levels 1 & 2 - $279 per language
set of Levels 1, 2, & 3 - $379 each
set of Levels 1-5 - $479 each

Rosetta Stone is a series of foreign language programs that helps the student understand spoken words as well as written ones. These are also self-teaching programs, so parents need not know the language their child will study. *Rosetta Stone's* programs offer computer-based instruction that includes the student speaking and typing into the computer. While this is primarily a conversational approach, there is also some grammar instruction.

Rosetta Stone Homeschool Version 3 runs on Windows 2000, XP or Vista as well as Mac OS 10.4 or later. The speech recognition feature of the program requires use of the headset with a microphone that comes with each program.

Rosetta Stone uses essentially the same extremely interactive methodology for every language. For example in early lessons, first you look at four photos and listen to words by native speakers that are illustrated by the photos. Listen to the sequence over and over or choose a particular photo and hear the words as many times as you wish. Many lessons show the words on the screen as they are spoken. Later lessons frequently reuse the same photos, possibly asking the student to repeat a sentence describe a picture, make the correct response, or choose from a few options the correct word or response. The photos are multicultural to be appealing to various nationalities.

Parents can set up the program to follow a set lesson progression. There are eight choices ranging from the "Full Year" program for students working toward high school credits down to "Speaking & Listening Focus." Younger learners or those who don't need to read or write the language for some other reason might choose the latter. In between are choices that are more streamlined than the Full Year. One lesson path includes reading but no writing. Another path focuses on both reading and writing for the person already familiar with the spoken language. "Speaking" can be turned on or off, even in the Full Year lesson path.

Placement assistance is included for those who bring with them some prior familiarity with the language. Placement "tests" assess listening, reading, speaking, and writing skills.

Those who prefer can skip around the lessons as they please rather than follow a programmed lesson progression. This might be very helpful to those tackling an unfamiliar language who want much more repetition of a certain type exercise. Students can repeat a lesson as often as they like.

Rosetta Stone Homeschool Version 3 has an improved record-keeping and reporting system where parents can both manage and track each student's progress. The program can handle a large number of students, so it will certainly maintain records for your entire family. Tests at the end of each lesson show the number of answers correct and incorrect as well as a "percentage" score. Parents can access reports showing where the student is within a particular activity, which activities have been completed as well as when they were completed, length of time to complete each activity, scores for activities, plus an overall progress report. Reports are printable for those who need to maintain or turn in academic documentation.

The foreign languages available in *Homeschool Version 3* (with three levels each) are Arabic, Spanish (either Latin American or Castilian), French, Italian, German, Dutch, Russian, Portuguese, Polish, Japanese, Chinese (Mandarin), Hebrew, Hindi, Greek, Irish, Persian (Farsi), Swedish, Tagalog, Korean, Latin, Turkish, Vietnamese, and English (either U.S. or U.K.). French, German, Italian, Spanish (either Latin American or Castilian), and English (U.S.) also have levels 4 and 5.

Rosetta Stone packages also include a set of Audio Companion™ CDs for each level of the language. Audio Companions for the Spanish program I reviewed included four CDs for each level, with each CD presenting native language speakers pronouncing words and short phrases that the listener should practice repeating.

In addition, all *Rosetta Stone Homeschool Version 3* programs include a Supplemental Education Materials CD-ROM with PDF files you can view or print on your computer. This disc has the entire course content for the level purchased, including scripts for each lesson, plus an index to all the words taught.

The Latin American Spanish, English (both American and British), French (Levels 1-3), Latin, and German (Levels 1-3) programs have additional material on the Supplemental CD: a student workbook that includes a quiz for each lesson; unit tests; answer key for worksheets, quizzes, and tests; and instructions written in both the language and in English for the worksheets, quizzes, and tests. The Supplemental CD material certainly helps to make these courses sufficient for high school credit.

Because of the flexibility of the *Rosetta Stone* programs, the same program might be used with learners from about third grade through adult levels.

Rosetta Stone has on-line product tours so you can get a good idea of what it looks like before you buy. They also have a 6-month, money-back guarantee if you are not satisfied.

I had reviewed a *Version 2* program when I selected *Rosetta Stone* as one of my Top Picks in 2005, and *Version 3* has further solidified *Rosetta Stone's* position as one of the best foreign language options for homeschoolers.

· · · · · · · ·

Greek Alphabet Code Cracker

by Dr. Christopher Perrin
Classical Academic Press
3920 Market St.
Camp Hill, PA 17011
www.classicalacademic press.com
$16.95

If you've been considering teaching

Greek to your children or even learning it yourself, you might want to start with *Greek Alphabet Code Cracker*. Learning Greek begins with learning to recognize the Greek alphabet and the sounds of the letters. This 91-page book accomplishes that and a bit more, and it does so in an entertaining fashion that should appeal to learners of all ages.

Great graphic design combines with fun activities to make learning more like puzzle solving than real work. The book begins by introducing the case of the missing urn. The student's task is to decipher clues to determine the identity of the thief and recover the urn. This is accomplished by translating a few Greek words within each witness's statement that will provide the clues. In addition to solving the crime, students work on puzzles and worksheet type activities—word searches, matching columns, code-breaking puzzles, crossword puzzles, circling words, filling in blanks, and more. Students practice tracing then writing letters of the Greek alphabet and complete a number of more direct translation activities. Instruction is presented incrementally through the units. The eight units in this book should take about eight weeks to complete, but you can adjust the pace as you wish.

By the end of the book, students should be fairly proficient at translating Greek letters into their corresponding English letters, and they will also have learned something about breathing and accent marks. They will also have learned 25 NT/Koine words.

The publisher's website has a password-protected audio file of the "Greek Alphabet Song" you can listen to at no cost as well as three other songs that teach the names and sounds of the letters, consonant blends, and diphthongs. Also on the site are Greek alphabet writing-practice sheets, a reference chart, alphabet flash cards, and a code-cracker master sheet. Printing out the reference sheet and keeping it handy saves students having to flip pages in the book as they work. A few code-cracker activities are included in the book, but students might well like to do more with the master sheet.

Toward the back of the book are two pages to make a "Greek Alphabet Code Cracker Cypher Wheel" that might also serve as a handy reference tool. A complete answer key is included at the back.

Once students have completed this book, there's a good chance they will be eager to continue studying the Greek language. But even if they do not continue, what they will have learned here will be helpful as they encounter references to letters of the Greek alphabet in other contexts.

· · · · · · · · ·

Henle Latin courses

by Robert J. Henle, S. J.
Loyola Press
800-621-1008
www.loyolapress.com
available through Memoria Press
www.memoriapress.com
$15.95-$16.95 each, answer keys - $4.50-$5 each, teacher's manual - $2, *Grammar* - $9.50

The *Henle Latin* series, originally published in the 1940s, is a four-volume set that covers grammar in *First Year* and the traditional Latin literature sequence of Caesar, Cicero, and Vergil in *Second* through *Fourth Years*. *First Year* covers grammar, vocabulary, syntax, and translation so as to prepare students to read the first Latin author, Caesar, in *Second Year*. There is Christian content throughout the series, and although some is specifically Catholic, the educational value of the Christian content as a whole is a very positive addition to this series for all Christians.

The classical approach of this book fits perfectly with other elements of a classical education.

In the *First Year* book, grammar and vocabulary instruction take precedence as students work through numerous practice exercises. Some are labeled "essential" for students who master the material quickly and need not do all the exercises. It is not realistic to try to cover *First Year* in only one year. Middle school students might complete it over three years, while high school students might complete it in two years.

The *Second Year* book reviews the material taught in *First Year*. In the *Second, Third* and *Fourth Year* books, the first half or more of each text consists of readings to translate. In *Second Year*, notes and definitions are at the bottom of pages (footnote style), while *Third* and *Fourth Years* feature copious notes, background, and explanations on facing pages. Exercises are found in the second half of each of these three books, with accompanying instruction on new concepts. Reference helps and Latin-English and English-Latin vocabulary lists are at the back of each book.

The grammar forms and syntax rules are all gathered together in a separate reference manual called the *Henle's Latin Grammar* ($9.50). This grammar manual is a required reference book for all four Henle texts.

Companion answer keys for each book are inexpensive. You will definitely want to purchase these. There is also a small, 105-page *Teacher's Manual for Henle Latin Series First and Second Years* by Sister Mary Jeanne, S.N.D. that explains the philosophy of the course and teaching strategies. It was written in 1955 for classroom situations, but there are many helpful ideas that will be useful in homeschooling situations.

Memoria Press (www.MemoriaPress.com) has been selling the Henle series for years while also using it in their school and online academy, so they are very familiar with it. They frequently begin students as young as fifth grade in the first Henle text, taking three years to complete it. Consequently, they have developed three very helpful *Henle Latin Study Guide and Lesson Plan* books that cover the *First Year* book in sections. Even if you plan to complete the first book in two years, you might find these expanded teaching guides more helpful than the resources available from Loyola Press since they have helpful hints, lessons plans, syllabi, and check-off boxes for daily drill and recitation. These guides also include answer keys so you need not purchase answer keys separately. While each guide is organized into approximately 30 weeks of lessons, they can be completed at any pace that suits your situation. Memoria Press has also created Quizzes and Final Exams booklets ($9.95 each) corresponding to the three guides for *First Year*.

There are other good Latin programs available, but none are this reasonably priced for such a solidly academic Latin course.

· · · · · · · ·

Memoria Press Latin courses

Memoria Press
4603 Poplar Level Rd.
Louisville, KY 40213
877-862-1097
email: magister@memoriapress.com
www.memoriapress.com
Prima Latina - $32.95 for teacher manual, student book, and pronunciation CD
Latina Christiana I - $39.95 for eacher manual, student book, and pronunciation CD
Form Latin - $55 per level for teacher manual, student text, workbook, quizzes & tests, and pronunciation CD; this set plus DVDs and flashcards - $115 per level

Latina Christiana was among my Top Picks in 2005. *Prima Latina* for younger students was also mentioned in my earlier review. Memoria Press has since introduced *First Form Latin* and the follow-up books, *Second Form* and *Third Form Latin*. *Fourth Form* is still being written.

Cheryl Lowe of Memoria Press believes that

Latin is the ideal foundation for a classical education for children in the elementary grades. Ideally, Latin study replaces some English language study (particularly grammar and vocabulary) through these years. All of these courses teach grammar—both Latin and English. While conversational language is sometimes taught, these are not conversational programs that leave the grammar for high school. Memoria Press's Latin programs should appeal most to classical educators who want to capitalize on the younger child's ability to memorize and drill to build a strong grammar-level foundation.

Parents with no Latin background should find the Memoria Press courses very easy to use. Lesson preparation is minimal for the first two programs. These are not independent study workbooks. You really need to use the teacher manuals for lesson presentations.

Prima Latina offers a slower, gentler pace for learning Latin that might suit children in grades 2 through 4. *Latina Christiana I* might be the starting point for students in grades 3 to 5 while *First Form Latin* could be the first course for students in grades 5 and up. Parents unfamiliar with Latin themselves should probably choose the lower-level option when faced with two possibilities. Whichever courses you choose, by the end of eighth grade, students should be prepared for advanced Latin in high school, including reading Latin literature. They should also find the study of English and any of the Romance languages much easier.

All of these Memoria Press courses teach medieval or "church" Latin pronunciation rather than "classical." You should find the companion CDs very helpful for learning pronunciation. Words and phrases relating to Christianity are included; content should be appropriate for both Protestants and Catholics.

Memoria Press Latin courses were developed with small classes of homeschoolers, and that is the ideal setting for them. However, the courses also work fine with a single student and parent.

Optional DVDs with lesson presentations are available for all of these courses. The video presentations teach the content of the books, but you still need the course books for student exercises, practice, and review. Parents worried about their ability to teach Latin as well as those short on time should really appreciate this option.

Prima Latina

by Leigh Lowe

Unlike most resources for Latin for the early elementary grades, *Prima Latina* is a strong, grammatically-based program. It teaches both English grammar and beginning Latin. Students are introduced to the seven parts of speech and three verb tenses of English grammar. For Latin, students are introduced to the first two declensions of nouns and the first two verb conjugations while learning some basic vocabulary. While Memoria Press says it can be used by children in grades one through four, they qualify this by saying that it is "for students who are still becoming familiar with English grammar but are competent readers." I would add that students need to be fairly competent writers since there is quite a bit of writing in the course.

Children work directly in their worktext, but lessons need to be taught. Young children will need a great deal of teacher assistance.

Weekly lessons each begin with instruction on new material with examples. There is a vocabulary list with about five words per lesson. Children learn both the meaning and spelling of the vocabulary words through drills and exercises. Lessons also include lists of derivative words that help students begin to see how Latin roots are used to build English words. "Practical Latin" for each week introduces a word, phrase, or sentence such as "Vale" ("Goodbye" said to one person), that students can use immediately and frequently. Latin prayers are introduced one line at a time. Students respond both orally and in writing through the lessons. Review questions are built into the lessons, and there are five review lessons spaced throughout the course, each followed by a test. Review lessons incorporate translation work with Latin hymns. "Fun Practice" activities each week offer variety with something different just about every week—e.g., drawing, hunting for objects, finding "invisible" verbs (abstract verbs such as love) in a storybook, and writing a song or poem.

The teacher manual for *Prima Latina* has general teaching guidelines and reproducible vocabulary drill forms and tests. Other than that it has only overprinted answers on pages identical to those in the student text rather than expanded lesson plans. The companion CD helps with pronunciation and includes beautiful Latin hymns from another Memoria Press product, *Lingua Angelica*.

Prima Latina can be used prior to *Latina Christiana*. It covers some of the same vocabulary but more slowly and in a different format.

Latina Christiana

by Cheryl Lowe

Latina Christiana I might be used prior to *First Form Latin*, although it is not required. (Note: *Latina Christiana II* is being replaced by *First Form Latin*.)

Lessons need to be taught following instructions in the teacher manual. The teacher manual is very nicely designed both in appearance and functionality. Reduced student pages with overprinted answers are surrounded by lesson information.

Lessons are learned through repetition, memorization, and drill, but the teacher manual presents a number of ideas for making this interesting: vocabulary flash cards, games (e.g. Latin Pictionary), songs, and an audio CD.

Latina Christiana also serves as the focus for study of history and geography to a minor extent, correlating history questions based on *Famous Men of Rome* (another Memoria Press publication) with Latin lessons.

The student books are less intimidating than most other foreign language workbooks since they were written for young students. Students do oral work with new vocabulary, study words and phrases, learn a well-known Latin proverb or phrase, and complete exercises in their books. Students also listen to the CD that comes with each level and complete an exercise form that helps them review vocabulary, conjugations, and declensions. Most lessons include memorization of Latin prayers such as the "Pater Noster" (or "Our Father") or songs such as "Adeste Fideles."

Latina Christiana I covers first and second declension noun and adjective forms, first and second conjugations and three verb tenses, subject/verb agreement, personal pronouns, gender, and use of the nominative case. It includes lists of English words derived from Latin vocabulary words in each lesson.

First, Second, and Third Form Latin
by Cheryl Lowe

First Form Latin, *Second Form Latin*, and *Third Form Latin* are the first three of four levels in this projected series. The series may be used with students beginning in fifth grade and up. However, even if started at a younger level, completing *First Form Latin* is equivalent to a one-year high school Latin course by adding a little supplementation. Students who have completed *Latina Christiana* should be able to move into *First Form Latin* with ease in fifth grade. Sixth graders should probably skip *Latina Christiana* and begin with *First Form*. *First Form Latin* and the other three books in this series will comprise a gentler introduction to Latin than some of the more challenging programs such as *Henle Latin*.

First Form teaches students as if they are in the grammar stage of learning, which is actually true for beginning (or close to beginning) students in Latin no matter their actual grade level. That means students concentrate on learning vocabulary and grammatical forms through study, memorization, and drill. The translation work students complete is less than in some other programs. However, in keeping with the stress on grammar skills, students learn to diagram sentences in both English and Latin. A famous Latin saying along with some brief tidbits from Latin history and culture are incorporated into each lesson.

First Form Latin teaches the first two verb conjugations (six indicative active tenses), five noun declensions, and first and second declension adjectives while introducing 185 vocabulary words. *Second Form Latin* reviews everything covered in *First Form Latin*. By the end of *Second Form Latin* students will have added the indicative active of the third and fourth conjugations and the present system passive voice of all four conjugations, five noun declensions (including er-ir nouns of the second declension and i-stem nouns of the third declension), third declension adjectives of one termination, personal pronouns, and prepositions, while adding another 180 vocabulary words. *Third Form Latin* reviews

the content taught in the *First* and *Second Forms* then continues work with all four verb conjugations, including active and passive subjunctive. It moves on to fourth declension neuter nouns and more advanced work with adjectives. Irregular adjective and adverbs as well as advanced work with syntax are taught.

Fourth Form Latin will move a different direction. It will be keyed to the *First Year* of the *Henle Latin* series, using many of its readings. Students completing *Fourth Form* should be ready to advance into the *Second Year* of the Henle series.

There are a number of components for each course. You will need both the teacher manual and Teacher Manual Workbook & Test Key, two separate books sold as a set. Other core components are the student text, student workbook, and the Quizzes and Test book. Optional items are the pronunciation CD, DVDs, and flashcards.

The teacher manual explains how to teach the first course in the first twelve pages. Reading this section is essential for understanding how to work through the course components. The teacher manual presents each lesson with detailed instructions and reproduced pages from the student text. Extra information that is usually related to grammar is sometimes included for the teacher's benefit. The teacher might share some or all of this with students if it seems appropriate and helpful.

Lessons begin with oral recitation and review. The recitation aspect of this course is vital, so even if you use DVDs, someone needs to be present to supervise recitation and other activities. This is not an independent study course. The "Grammar – Chalk Talk" section of the lesson is for presenting the lesson content using direct instruction and a white board or chalk board. Teaching sessions are interactive. Much of this is scripted in the teacher manual. Students follow along in the student text. The student text includes charts and grammatical information in appendices.

Next, you shift to the student workbook where the parent or teacher will assist students as they work through the four to six pages of exercises. Student workbook pages are reproduced with answers in the Teacher Manual Workbook & Test Key. Grammar questions to be used for review at the beginning of lessons and Vocabulary Drill Sheets are included in the student workbook as well as in the key. Quiz and test answer keys are also in the key. This might sound a little confusing, but once you sort it out, it should be very easy to work through the lessons. Separating course content into the two separate books for students makes it easier for students to review from the text while also making the content seem very manageable.

Oral drill from the student text follows, with a quiz or test wrapping up the lesson. All of these steps should be spread out over a week for each lesson. The publisher suggests supplementing for students who are able to complete lessons very quickly with *Lingua Angelica* or *Famous Men of Rome*.

The comprehensive lessons with detailed plans enable parents or teachers without a Latin background to easily teach the courses. Nevertheless, teachers must prepare each lesson in advance. Those without Latin background should work through each entire lesson prior to teaching while those familiar with Latin might be able to prepare without completing all exercises in advance.

These are teacher-intensive courses, so if you are short on time, consider using the DVDs to help lighten the teaching load. Courses might be used with a single student but would work better with two or more students working together, especially for recitation and participation in the optional games.

There is some Christian content, but it is fairly minimal. One Latin sentence translates to "Christ gives faith." This was one of the rare examples I could find. Pages in the appendices have some prayers in Latin (e.g.,

"Pater Noster," "Sanctus and Benedictus," "Agnus Dei," "Ave Maria") and their translations which are optional.

While students as young as fifth grade might begin the *Form Latin* series, it might be best for junior high students who need a slower pace than most high school level programs yet are ready for more substantial content than is offered by most programs for the elementary grades. While it works as a high school program as well, you need to supplement with additional work or consider moving at a faster pace if students can handle it.

Supplements

To make the study of Latin a bit more fun or to add reinforcement, you might use Memoria Press's books of crossword, word search, and hangman puzzles, *Ludere Latine I* and *II* ($19.95 each), both written by Paul O'Brien. *Ludere Latine I* correlates with *Latina Christiana I*, and *Ludere Latine II* correlates fairly well with *First Form Latin*. The puzzles provide valuable practice on vocabulary, declensions, and conjugations. Answer keys for all the puzzles are at the back of each book.

Lingua Angelica is a supplemental study of Latin hymns. It consists of a single CD with 24 hymns, two levels of student workbooks with teacher manuals, and a songbook ($39.95 for first level, CD and song book). The same songbook and CD are used with both levels. While you can purchase the CD alone just for the beautiful music by a six-voice Gregorian chant choir, the workbooks do not function as a stand-alone course but must be used alongside a beginning Latin course.

. . . .

Lively Latin

by Catherine Drown
1250 Calle Colnett
San Marcos, CA 92069
760-509-5052
email: livelylatin@livelylatin.com
www.livelylatin.com

BigBook 1: print - $125, CDs - $79, downloadable files - $55
BigBook 2: print - $140, CDs - $89, downloadable files - $70

After years of teaching Latin to homeschooled students with existing curricula and doing a lot of adaptation, Catherine Drown decided it was time to create her own program for teaching Latin to students in the elementary grades.

There were a number of elements she decided were essential for her ideal program:

- study of English derivatives so students "could use their Latin knowledge to become more articulate and attentive to meaning in their own language"
- history of Rome incorporated into the course with related activities such as maps, timelines, internet links, and review
- use of traditional methods for learning Latin—recitation, chanting, parsing, and translating, but with a bit more fun and variety than in other programs
- an online component for students to play vocabulary games and connect with other students
- a program that is easy for both parents and students to use—requires minimal preparation and presentation time from the teacher and allows students to do a great deal of their work independently
- assumes no prior Latin study by the parent
- allows parents to choose either ecclesiastical or classical pronunciation

Drown was able to include all these features and sell it at an affordable price without requiring you to purchase extra components!

The BigBook of Lively Latin, Volumes *1* and *2* are available in three different formats. All formats provide students with access to additional online games and resources.

The online version includes access to the downloadable and printable PDF files for all the lessons, including answer keys (about 400 pages for *Volume 1* and 600 pages for *Volume 2*), and access to the audio files for learning pronunciation. Access never expires!

In the CD set option with two CDs per course, one CD has all pages from the *BigBook* in PDF format, including the answer key and notebook divider pages. The second CD has the audio pronunciation files.

The print version comes three-hole-punched with dividers and a binder—all ready to assemble. It includes the 2 CD-ROMs. The hardcopy version is printed in full-color throughout the book although the color printing is critical on only about 10% of the pages. Keep this in mind when considering printing it yourself. The answer key is on one of the CDs.

Keep in mind, that purchase of any of these versions allows you to reprint pages for all students in your immediate family. Even with the hardcopy version, you receive the CD with the printable files.

Online access that comes with any course purchase allows entry to the "Study with the Magistra" section of the website where you will find vocabulary games as well as extra teaching tips and resources. It also allows you to email the Magistra with questions.

The publisher describes *Lively Latin* as a program for the elementary grades, with a target audience of grades three through six. However, the content is more substantial than some other programs for this level. *BigBook 1* covers first and second declension nouns and adjectives. For nouns, students learn their cases and genders, but they learn the use of only nominative and ablative cases. They also learn first conjugation verbs (present, imperfect, and future tenses). *BigBook 2* adds the next three declensions of nouns and teaches the use of all of the cases. The second, third, and fourth verb conjugations are covered along with six tenses. The combined content of both volumes is approximately equal to that of a first-year high school Latin course! You might use this course with students beyond sixth grade level who need the slower pace of learning.

BigBook 1 begins with extensive background on the Latin language as well as its connection to other languages, especially to English. Even here, there are activities to reinforce the content: mapwork, timeline, fill-in-the-blanks, and internet links for further study.

Next, each student chooses a Latin name for him or herself then studies whichever form of pronunciation has been chosen—classical or ecclesiastical. Students use either the CD or online files to listen to correct pronunciation.

After the first few lessons, students begin each study session with a two- to three-minute warm-up session to review their vocabulary and chants. They do this out loud while using vocabulary cards they have created from either reproducible or preprinted pages.

New lesson material presented at the beginning of each lesson is written directly to students so they might work independently. Students continually encounter a variety of activities like underlining, circling, drawing, chanting, filling in blanks, and completing puzzles as they work through lessons.

Students construct a set of Mythology Playing Cards from pages in lesson three of *BigBook 1*. Even with the hardcopy version of the course, you might want to recopy these pages onto cardstock for easier handling and durability. Instructions are included for five different games, all of which might be played with as few as two players.

In addition to the Latin basics, *Lively Latin* uses stories from *The Famous Men of Rome* and *The Story of Rome* (public domain works), with activities, mapwork, and illustrations added to enhance the lessons. *BigBook 1* covers Roman history from the founding of the city (753 BC) to the end of the Punic Wars (146 BC). *BigBook 2* picks up from there and spans from the fall of the Republic to the end of the Empire (476 AD). Some full-color photos of famous artworks that relate to the history are included along with some comprehension and observation questions. Charlotte Mason methodology is evident here in these "Art Studies." Other artwork is sometimes incorporated into the Latin lessons themselves.

Although the author of this course is a Christian, the course is presented from a secular perspective. This includes learning about the gods and goddesses, their attributes, and their stories.

Students should work on their Latin lessons two to three days per week with sessions of 20 to 30 minutes each.

While much of the illustration (aside from the works of art) in *Lively Latin* is clipart, the entire product is very attractive in layout and design. Lesson material and exercises are presented with relatively brief portions of text interspersed with illustrations and activities to maintain student interest. The lengthiest blocks of reading material are in stories from *Famous Men* and *The Story of Rome*; these vary from one to three pages in length. You might want to read some of these aloud with children who are reluctant readers.

Included in each course is a glossary with all the vocabulary words plus a few pages of other useful reference material for students including declension and conjugation "chant sheets."

In my opinion, *Lively Latin* lives up to its name. Even though the methodology is quite traditional, the mix of multi-sensory learning methods and the use of stories, games, and art should be more appealing to most students than most other options trying to cover comparable material.

Selected Electives

After creating my initial list of my Top Picks for core subjects, I discovered I already had close to 100 items before even touching electives. I could not bring myself to totally eliminate any electives, since you might get the impression that they don't matter! So I have included just a few in this final chapter. Obviously this is a miniscule sampling of what's out there. I haven't touched many topics at all. Music, physical education, health, economics, government, keyboarding, home economics, driver's education, and many other topics are not represented here, and it's not because these subjects are not important or useful. Some of them are even required for high school graduation! You can check my website at www.CathyDuffyReviews.com for reviews of many more electives.

Critical Thinking and Logic

Logic beat out other electives for inclusion in this chapter because I am convinced that a grasp of logic—at a minimum, what is called "informal logic"—is essential to a good education. If you can't think straight and then express your ideas logically, if you can't spot the shysters and the propaganda and sort through it all to the truth, then your education is incomplete.

In addition, many logic books on the market are fun to use. My eldest son says that one of the best books we used in all of our homeschooling years was a small paperback titled *How to Lie with Statistics* (W.W. Norton and Company). This little gem has been reprinted numerous times since it was written in the 1950s. It will have you in stitches with some of its examples. It's a terrific way to inoculate your older teens against marketers, politicians, and media manipulation. The reason it is not in my Top Picks list is because it really serves as a supplement to logic studies rather than a primary resource and because it does require "parental editing"—read it yourself first before using it with your older teens since there are sections you will probably want to skip.

Even with the logic and critical thinking resources I selected, I cheated a little by including The Critical Thinking Co., a publisher with hundreds of items, most of which are supplementary. They are not the only publisher of critical thinking resources for younger children, but they have what I consider to be by far the broadest and best selection. Their line includes what some would call pre-logic books for young children, books relating to different subject areas that appeal to children of different learning styles, books for teens that address informal and formal logic, and software programs. These are great for challenging your children to stretch their thinking skills as well as helping them learn to function in other thinking/learning modes.

The Fallacy Detective and *The Art of Argument* are great resources for younger and older teens respectively to introduce them to informal logic—a required course for all students if it were up to me.

For more resources for teaching logic, check out reviews at my website or investigate the articles, reviews, and helps at www.fallacydetective.com/articles/, a site created by the authors of *The Fallacy Detective*.

• • • • • • • •

The Critical Thinking Co.™
PO Box 1610
Seaside, CA 93955
800-458-4849
www.criticalthinking.com

Building Thinking Skills series

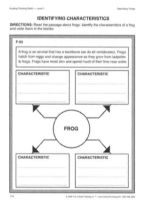

student books - $29.99-$32.99 each, *Primary* teacher's manual - $24.99

The *Building Thinking Skills* series is probably the most basic, comprehensive resource for thinking skills for younger students. Each reproducible student book, except for *Primary*, includes an answer key. While students will be able to complete some lessons independently, others will require interaction between teacher and student(s), more so with younger students. Each lesson should take about 10 to 20 minutes to complete and requires minimal preparation.

The first four books in the series are written for pre-K through grade 6. The first book, *Building Thinking Skills, Beginning* (224 pages) is suggested for ages 3 to 4. This colorful book helps children develop pre-reading and math skills, auditory processing, and logic and spatial concepts. Attribute blocks might be used along with some of the lessons, but they are not required.

In *Building Thinking Skills, Primary*, for grade K-1 (272 pages), children deal with similarities and differences, sequences, classifications, and analogies. Visual-figural skills get a workout in these lessons, too. Attribute blocks and interlocking cubes are required for some lessons—these are used both prior to and while students complete the worksheets. *Primary* is the only book in this series that has a teacher's manual which you need as an answer key and for instructional information.

Level 1 (376 pages), suggested for grades 2 and 3, works from visual-figural understanding such as was encountered in the *Primary* book to more abstract verbal work. For example, children work with figural analogies then with verbal analogies. Many of the lessons require children to analyze relationships between objects and words. Among other topics and skills addressed are deductive reasoning, classifying, describing, figural sequences, parts of a whole, spelling, vocabulary building, Venn diagrams, pattern folding, mental manipulation of two-dimensional objects, and sorting words into classes. This level is also available on CD-ROM.

Level 2 (416 pages), suggested for grades 4 through 6, does all of the above, expands to additional types of analogies, and adds map skills and directionality, branching diagrams, "if-then" statements, overlapping classes, and more. Some activities require students to write out their answers or explanations. Activities vary in difficulty, so select those that seem most appropriate for each child. This level is also available on CD-ROM. Note that these sizable books increase in length at each level.

Mind Benders and Crypto Mind Benders

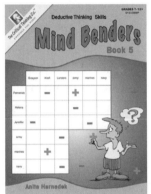

$9.99-$12.99 each

Mind Benders are a series of sets of 32- to 48-page books. Each book is self-contained with teaching suggestions and instructions in the front and detailed solutions in the back. Children organize clues (some direct and some indirect) in grids (except in the introductory *Warm Up* level) to derive logical conclusions. For example, in a very introductory lesson, students are told, "Edmund, Ida, Joanne, and Tony are two sets of twins. Tony is a month younger than Edmund. Joanne is a month older than Ida." Students must then answer two questions, "Which pair is the younger set of twins?" and "Which pair is the older set of twins?" These activities appeal to children, because they are like detective work as students try to match clues with identities. *Books 1* through 8 cover spans of grade levels from PreK through adults! For example, Book 1 is for PreK through K, and *Book 2* is for grades 1 and 2, and *Book 8* is for grade 7 through adult level. The first two levels are also available on CD-ROM for $25.99 for a family license allowing you to install it on one computer but use it for all family members. The CD-ROM version includes hints at the click of a mouse and reward games

after each puzzle.

Adding another dimension to the *Mind Bender* clues and grids, the new *Crypto Mind Benders* present clues and information as mathematical/logical statements such as this group of three: "$i > k > e$," "$m > k$," and "$m \neq 9$." Students have to determine which letters (e, i, k, and m) correspond on the grid to the numbers 1, 2, 9, and 10. After solving three grids, students can use the results to solve a cryptogram at the bottom of the page. Two *Crypto Mind Benders* are available in either print or ebook versions; cryptograms in one book are famous quotations and in the other are classic jokes.

James Madison Critical Thinking Course

student worktext - $42.99, instruction guide - $10.99

Students in high school and beyond—even adults—might want to tackle the *James Madison Critical Thinking Course*. This huge, 534-page worktext is more challenging than *The Fallacy Detective* but it seems more "approachable" than most other formal logic course. This is probably because most lessons are presented as cases being investigated by Detective Stephanie Wise of the Los Angeles Police Department. Other situations or subject matter are used, but almost everything is taught within a practical context. Instruction on each new topic is relatively brief and includes examples. The book begins with an introduction to critical thinking and continues with topics such as distinguishing between fact and opinion and hazards such as ambiguity or vagueness. Chapter four (of eight chapters in all) introduces symbols used to show the structure of an argument as it makes the distinction between inductive and deductive arguments.

From there it takes a plunge into propositional logic and categorical syllogisms, devoting about 250 pages to these two chapters. It wraps up with a briefer investigation of inductive arguments and informal fallacies. Students spend most of their time working through exercises which are mostly multiple-choice questions at first. These are not easy! In the fourth chapter, students begin to analyze and construct arguments and conclusions using letters to stand in the place of statements. In the next two chapters, students frame arguments and conclusions using symbols. Then the last two chapters shift back to multiple-choice questions. A quiz concludes each chapter. The instruction guide is vital since it has all the answers plus explanations which will help when both student and teacher are stumped.

And Others

The Critical Thinking Co. also publishes books that help develop thinking skills within various subject areas such as math, language arts, science, and history. (Reviews of *Developing Critical Thinking through Science*, *Sciencewise*, *Cranium Crackers*, and *Quick Thinks Math* can be found on my website at www.cathyduffyreviews.com.) Check out The Critical Thinking Co.'s website for more options. Sample pages are available for most books. (Note: this is a non-sectarian publisher, and you might find occasional, minor content problems.)

· · · · · · · · ·

The Fallacy Detective

by Nathaniel Bluedorn and Hans Bluedorn
Christian Logic
PO Box 46
Muscatine, Iowa 52761
309-537-3641
www.christianlogic.com
$22

The Bluedorn family, longtime promoters of Christian classical education, encountered content problems in most critical thinking and logic resources, so Nathaniel and Hans Bluedorn put their heads together and came up with this excellent introduction to practical logic from their conservative Christian home-schoolers' perspective. Subtitled *Thirty-Eight Lessons on How to Recognize Bad Reasoning*, it uses humor, historical references, and real life situations to help teens learn to think and express themselves clearly. Comic strips from *Calvin and Hobbes*, *Dilbert*, *Peanuts*, and *Nuna and Toodles* (the Bluedorn brothers' own creation) are a nice touch that was added to the second edition.

The authors' Christian homeschool perspective comes through in various ways. Verses from Proverbs are used to discuss knowledge and wisdom. One exercise statement reads, "I know everybody thinks Einstein's theory of relativity is correct, but I can't accept it. Einstein believed in evolution." Another on the same page relates this conversation: "Mrs. A: 'I'm going through a logic book with my kids. It's called *The Fallacy Detective*. I really like it.' Mrs. B.: 'Aw, the authors of that book are just a bunch of homeschoolers. What do they know about logic?'" (p.49).

The Fallacy Detective will likely appeal to many families for another reason: it doesn't need to be taught. Students can read and work through it independently. However, it might be enjoyable for both parent and student for the teen to read the lesson on his or her own, summarize the main idea to a parent, then go through the exercises out loud together. Some exercises require simple identification answers, but others might prompt some great discussion. The authors' answers are in the back of the book.

Instructions for a *Fallacy Detective Game* in which players make up their own fallacies are also at the back of the book. This would make great family fun for those with two or more teens.

You might also be interested in following *The Fallacy Detective* with *The Thinking Toolbox*, another excellent book by the same authors.

• • • • • • • • •

The Art of Argument

by Aaron Larsen and Joelle Hodge Classical Academic Press 3920 Market St. Camp Hill, PA 17011 866-730-0711 www.classical academicpress.com student book - $21.95, teacher's edition - $24.95, DVD set - $54.95, bundle of all three items - $88.95

The Art of Argument introduces students to informal fallacies, but at a slightly more challenging level than books like *The Fallacy Detective*. The content and style of delivery make this most suitable for high school level, although some students in junior high might be ready for it. The course seems to have been written for Christian students since it draws on examples familiar to and of interest to them. A non-Christian might find some topics provocative, but there's no "Christians are right and everyone else just isn't thinking clearly" attitude.

This course incorporates humor with examples drawn from current events, popular culture, advertising, religion, politics, and history. There are loads of photos and illustrations, many of them humorous. These include many phony print advertisements created by the authors that look authentic but which embody one or another of the fallacies. The authors sometimes create dialogues between two students, Nate and Tiffany, and the philosopher Socrates.

The text begins with an introduction to logic then divides the rest of the text into two units. The first unit deals with fallacies of relevance (e.g., ad hominem, snob appeal) and the second with fallacies of presumption (e.g., begging the question) and clarity (e.g., distinction without a difference).

Lessons don't follow a consistent format, which keeps things interesting. Review questions, review exercises, worksheets, and "dialectic exercises" show up unpredictably. Some writing is required and some review exercises direct students to do research such as "Look for examples of print advertisement that make use of the *argumentum ad verecundiam*" (p.86).

The text has a glossary at the end and a chart of the fallacies printed on the inside front and back covers. Two appendices are optional. One is a script for "Bill and Ted's Excellent Election," that can be read or acted out. The other is a dated but apropos short story, "Love is a Fallacy" by Max Shulman.

The course can easily be used for independent study, but it would be fun to have a group class meet about once a week for discussion.

The teacher's edition has the entire student text with answers overprinted. It also has quizzes, tests and their answer keys.

Busy parents might appreciate the new *Art of Argument* DVD set that includes five DVDs with 28 presentations—one for each fallacy that is taught. On the DVDs, the author joins with other logic teachers and a small group of students to model discussions for each lesson.

You might want to follow up with two other books from Classical Academic Press, *The Argument Builder* and *The Discovery of Deduction*.

Art

Art is a very broad area, but I have a selected only two Top Picks in this area. Both cover art skills, art appreciation, and projects. While *Artistic Pursuits* offers complete courses, each designed to be completed in one year, *Feed My Sheep* is a single volume that might be used over a number of years. *Feed My Sheep* also has a distinctly Christian outlook throughout while this doesn't appear in *Artistic Pursuits* until the upper levels.

• • • • • • • •

Artistic Pursuits

by Brenda Ellis
2626 E. 109th Avenue
Northglenn, CO 80233
303-467-0504
email: alltheanswers@artisticpursuits.com
www.artisticpursuits.com

$42.95 each

Artistic Pursuits is a series of art courses that cover art appreciation, art history, artists, and skills, with emphasis shifting from book to book. Even when studying works by the masters and learning art history, students work on their own projects, so this is a very hands-on approach. While there is an underlying Christian worldview, it isn't overtly presented until the junior and senior high level in articles about artists and the cultures of their times.

Written for students in kindergarten through twelfth grade, there are nine books in the series. Designed to work in either homeschools or classrooms, the books are labeled for a range of grade levels, so you might use one course for most of your children. You might stretch beyond the suggested grade levels, especially using a younger-level book with older students, since many skills and activities are challenging enough or offer scope for an older student to develop greater skill. For example, a lesson in the grades 4-6, *Book One* on "How to best show the subject" illustrates and discusses drawing animals at different angles. While a younger student might do a rough drawing with less detail, an older student might provide much more detail.

All books have a plastic comb-binding so they will lie flat. This is very helpful when you're trying to follow instructions while working on an art activity. Books are printed in full-color with illustrated instructions and samples of student artwork. Each book has a list of required art supplies both at the beginning of the book and within each lesson. Students work with a variety of art media, shifting to more difficult art techniques at upper levels.

Each book should take about one school year to complete with lessons two or three days a week. The books for grades K through 3 each have 32 projects which works out to about one project per week. Following is a list of the courses available, the grade levels they address, and a brief description of their content.

An Introduction to the Visual Arts, K-3 Book 1: This book has three sections: What Artists Do, What Artists See, and Where We Find Art. The first section deals with observation, imagination, composition, and subject matter. The second section gets into line, color, shapes, and other elements of art as students study some works by the masters and other illustrations. The third section emphasizes art appreciation and history as students study topics such as cave art, Greek pottery, Byzantine mosaics, and medieval illumination. (This volume might fit particularly well alongside study of ancient history, although it does touch on types of art up through the Middle Ages.)

Stories of Artists and Their Art, K-3 Book 2: This book continues the art appreciation and history emphasis of *Book 1*, picking up in the Middle Ages and continuing into the nineteenth century. Lessons each concentrate on a particular artist and one of his or her works of art.

Modern Painting and Sculpture, K-3 Book 3: Continuing to follow the historical timeline, this book moves from the nineteenth century to the present. Each lesson focuses on an artist or artistic movement, emphasizing positive and creative art. Children explore sculpture along with other art media.

Elements of Art and Composition, Grades 4-6 Book 1: Art elements and principles such as shadows, source of light, shading, texture, and balance are taught as students develop observation and application skills.

Color and Composition, Grades 4-6 Book 2: This book introduces students to color theory with an exploration of American art and artists. Students learn to work with colored pencils and watercolor pencils (with a brush), and they also learn to create collages from construction paper.

Elements of Art and Composition, Junior High Book 1: Although titled the same as *Book 1* for grades 4-6, this book definitely stretches students to a higher level as they work on elements and composition. For example, as they learn about balance, they also learn about asymmetry. There are some very challenging lessons such as one on how to "contain movement" within a picture and two entire units on depth. This course might be very challenging for students with little to no prior work with various media and art techniques.

Color and Composition, Junior High Book 2: Students explore color, working with hard pastels and oil pastels. Artists and their works are from around the world.

Elements of Art and Composition, Senior High, Book 1: The level jumps in difficulty as students apply the elements of art to learn about balance, rhythm, depth, perspective, and proportion. Most work in this course is done with drawing pencils and charcoal.

Color and Composition, Senior High Book 2: Students learn about topics such as hue, value, balance, rhythm, intensity, and emphasis as they learn to work with various art media and study principles related to color. Watercolors are the primary media.

The books really don't repeat themselves even though they sometimes treat the same topics. Each level approaches an element of art at a different level and with different examples and applications. There is a real synergy that builds from book to book, so it would be ideal if you could work through the entire series.

Students are exposed to many different art media over the years. While a greater variety of media are used in the K-3 books, the upper level books use fewer media each year but help students develop real expertise with those selected. I also appreciate that from grades 4-6 and up the author has students use "real" art supplies most of the time rather than tempera paints, crayons, and other media often used in schools. While K-3 students *do* use inexpensive water colors and tempera paints, they also learn to work with more sophisticated media.

Even though books are written to students, parents will need to work with students in the books for K-3, reading aloud, leading discussions, explaining the instructions, demonstrating techniques, and assisting as needed. For grades 4-6, students might be able to work more independently, especially sixth graders. Even if students are able to work independently, they are likely to benefit greatly from working alongside at least one other student, so they can inspire each other and share their work.

• • • • • • • •

Feed My Sheep

by Barry Stebbing
How Great
Thou ART
PO Box 48
McFarlan, NC
28102
800-982-3729
email: sales@
howgreatthouart.com
www.
howgreatthouart.com
$39.95, bundle pack - $59.95,

DVDs - $59.95

This is a combined art text and workbook for teaching drawing, color theory, art appreciation, perspective, portraiture, anatomy, lettering, painting, and more to students ages ten through adult. Older students and adults without art experience should find this a valuable course. It contains more than 250 lessons plus a packet of 17 paint cards. These are 8 1/2" x 11" in size and are a heavy, 110 lb. stock. For many of the lessons, students need only drawing pencils, a set of colored pencils, a kneaded eraser, a ruler, an extra-fine marker, sketchbook, and poster board. (Most of these items come in the bundle pack.) Later lessons on painting use pure pigment paints and brushes. A drawing board, triangle, and T-square are helpful in later lessons but are not essential.

Depending upon the age and ability of the student, this can be a three- to four-year curriculum using one lesson per week. One of the primary goals for the course is that students learn to draw realistic images. However, work with other media and skills, including cartooning, is also taught. You need to select lessons that are appropriate for each student. For example, you might save the painting lessons for older students.

If you want to tackle painting in the near future, purchase the bundle pack that includes the book plus a set of pure pigment paints, brushes, Prismacolor pencils, drawing pencils, and drawing pen. Otherwise, start with just the book and purchase paints later so they will be fresh when you want to use them.

Author Barry Stebbing's Christian perspective is evident throughout the course in Bible verses, lesson explanations, art appreciation lessons, and even the choices of examples. The book is written to the student so he or she can work independently. However, younger students will probably need some assistance. Instructions are fairly thorough so even parents with little art background should be able to help students through all of the lessons.

Art appreciation is incorporated into many of the lessons, and more focused lessons direct students to the library to locate and copy artists' works or examples from particular periods. Students also research answers to questions posed about art history, styles, artists, etc.

Overall, this is a very comprehensive course. For parents who wish to maintain academic accountability, there are occasional quizzes on art theory and appreciation with an answer key at the back of the book. This single volume offers a tremendous amount of art instruction at very low cost. Since students actually work in the book, it is best to purchase one for each student. However, for parents who would rather copy the lessons for multiple children, this is allowed for in-the-home use only.

Parents short on time or who prefer that someone else does the teaching might want to purchase the set of seven *Feed My Sheep* DVDs on which Stebbing walks through every lesson in the book. While he covers all of the instructional information in the book, he sometimes adds extra comments. He also shows examples of student artwork for some of the lessons. The DVDs makes it very easy to understand what is expected in each lesson. Students still need the book since they work directly in the book for all except the painting activities.

How Great Thou ART also publishes two less expensive volumes that cover content similar to some in *Feed My Sheep*. These are called the *Lamb's Book of ART, Books I* and *II*. For younger children, check out *I Can Do All things: A Beginning Book of Drawing and Painting*, and for older students, the company's flagship book titled *How Great Thou ART*.

- - - - - - - -

Endnotes

Chapter 2

1. Charlotte Mason, *Home Education: Training and Educating Children under Nine* (Wheaton, IL: Tyndale House, 1989), 281.

2. Ibid., 188.

3. Ibid., 177.

4. Ibid., 141.

5. Ibid., 232.

6. Ibid., 173.

7. Gene Edward Veith Jr. and Andrew Kern, *Classical Education: The Movement Sweeping America* (Washington, D.C.: Capital Research Center, 2001), p. x.

8. Ibid., 11.

9. Ibid., 11.

10. "The Logger's New Math," accessed March 22, 2003; available at http://www.geocities.com/geminilaz1/newmath.html.

Chapter 5

1. Common Core State Standards Initiative, "English Language Arts Standards/Reading Foundational Skills, Kindergarten," accessed May 23, 2012; available at http://www.corestandards.org/the-standards/english-language-arts-standards/reading-foundational-skills/kindergarten/.

2. Common Core State Standards Initiative, "Mathematics/Grade 4/Operations & Algebraic Thinking," accessed May 23, 2012; available at http://www.corestandards.org/the-standards/mathematics/grade-4/operations-and-algebraic-thinking/.

3. California State Board of Education, "Science Content Standards for California Public Schools, Kindergarten through Grade Twelve," accessed March 20, 2012; available at http://www.cde.ca.gov/be/st/ss/documents/sciencestnd.pdf.

4. California State Board of Education, "History-Social Science Content Standards for California Public Schools, Kindergarten through Grade Twelve," accessed March 20, 2012; available at http://www.cde.ca.gov/be/st/ss/documents/histsocscistnd.pdf.

5. California State Board of Education, "Science Content Standards for California Public Schools, Kindergarten through Grade Twelve," accessed March 20, 2012; available at http://www.cde.ca.gov/be/st/ss/documents/sciencestnd.pdf.

6. California State Board of Education, "Common Core State Standards for Mathematics," accessed May 23, 2012; available at http://www.scoe.net/castandards/agenda/2010/math_ccs_recommendations.pdf.

Index

Notes